SATELLITE REMOTE SENSING FOR ARCHAEOLOGY

This handbook is the first comprehensive overview of the field of satellite remote sensing for archaeology and of how it can be applied to ongoing archaelogical fieldwork projects across the globe. It provides a survey of the history and development of the field, connecting satellite remote sensing, archaeological method and theory, cultural resource management, and environmental studies. With a focus on the practical use of satellite remote sensing, Sarah H. Parcak evaluates satellite imagery types and remote sensing analysis techniques specific to the discovery, preservation, and management of archaeological sites.

Case studies from Asia, Central America, and the Middle East are explored, including Xi'an, China, Angkor Wat, Cambodia, and Egypt's floodplains. In-field surveying techniques particular to satellite remote sensing are emphasized, providing strategies for recording ancient features on the ground as observed from space. The book also discusses broader issues relating to archaeological remote sensing ethics, looting prevention, and archaeological site preservation. New sensing research is included and illustrated with the inclusion of over 160 satellite images of ancient sites.

With a companion website with further resources and colour images, *Satellite Remote Sensing for Archaeology* will provide anyone interested in scientific applications to uncovering past archaeological landscapes with a foundation for future research and study.

Sarah H. Parcak, PhD, is an Assistant Professor of Anthropology at the University of Alabama at Birmingham, USA and Director of the University's Laboratory of Global Health Observation. She directs the Middle Egypt Survey Project, and is co-Director of the Survey and Excavation Projects in Egypt.

SATELLITE REMOTE SENSING FOR ARCHAEOLOGY

Sarah H. Parcak

Routledge
Taylor & Francis Group

LONDON AND NEW YORK

First published 2009
by Routledge
2 Park Square, Milton Park, Abingdon, Oxon OX14 4RN

Simultaneously published in the USA and Canada
by Routledge
270 Madison Ave., New York, NY 10016

*Routledge is an imprint of the Taylor & Francis Group,
an informa business*

Typeset in Garamond by Keyword Group Ltd

British Library Cataloguing in Publication Data
A catalogue record for this book is available
from the British Library

Library of Congress Cataloging in Publication Data
Parcak, Sarah H.
Satellite remote sensing for archeaology/Sarah H. Parcak
p. cm.
1. Archaeology–Remote sensing. 2. Imaging systems in archaeology.
3. Remote-sensing images 4. Archaeology–Fieldwork. 5. Excavations
(Archaeology) 6. Historic sites–Conservation and restoration.
7. Antiquities–Collection and preservation. 8. Archaeology–Methodology.
9. Archaeology–Moral and ethical aspects. 10. Archaeologists–Professional
ethics. I. Title.
CC76.4.P37 2009
930.10285–dc22   2008040045

ISBN10: 0-415-44877-8 (hbk)
ISBN10: 0-415-44878-6 (pbk)
ISBN10: 0-203-88146-X (ebk)

ISBN13: 978-0-415-44877-2 (hbk)
ISBN13: 978-0-415-44878-9 (pbk)
ISBN13: 978-0-203-88146-0 (ebk)

FOR GRAMPY AND GREG
(WHO FINALLY MEET)

CONTENTS

ILLUSTRATIONS

Chapter 6

Chapter 7

TABLES

PREFACE

It is my sincere hope that students, professional archaeologists, archaeological researchers and all people fascinated by the potential for satellite remote sensing in archaeology will find this book useful. It is, more than anything else, a product of my thinking back to my graduate student days, and what I wish had existed then to help me get started with my work.

Before I proceed, it is important for me to explain why I have chosen to write this book in the first place. The use of satellite imagery in archaeology is a topic about which I am passionate, having spent eight years developing methods for archaeological site location in different regions of Egypt (Sinai, the Delta, and Nile Valley), teaching remote sensing courses, and (two years ago) starting a remote sensing laboratory. When I started doing research for a then undergraduate research paper in an introductory remote sensing course, I was struck by how little information could be found for general satellite remote sensing applications in archaeology. This became more apparent during my PhD years. Few papers existed that described how remote sensing could be applied to Egyptian archaeology, and no papers existed for the use of satellite remote sensing in the Nile Valley floodplain or Delta. I, quite literally, had to make it up as I went along, with all the expected pitfalls (significant trial and numerous errors) of doing something that had never been done before. Fortunately, my colleagues had written a number of excellent papers on satellite archaeology in other regions of the world, and I could rely on them for specific discussion points. Fieldwork proved to be something else entirely. Large-scale survey to locate previously unknown archaeological sites is not a significant part of Egyptian archaeology (Parcak 2008), and I had to develop a method for recording sites found during my remote sensing analysis.

As a result of that work and subsequent surveys, I had thought a great deal about initially editing a general methods book for satellite remote sensing for archaeology. Discussing the subject with my colleagues, many of whom I had approached about contributing to such a volume, I was encouraged to write the book, period. I stated that I would be more inclined to write the book at a future date, when I had many more surveys beneath my belt. After several lengthy discussions with the same colleagues, and many PhD students, I realized just how much of a gap existed between an ever-growing interest in the field of satellite archaeology and the materials available to those who wished to pursue it. Becoming the director of a remote sensing lab and teaching remote sensing courses (with many anthropology students) proved to be the impetus for moving the project ahead. Seeing first hand the remote sensing learning process allowed additional insights into how to present a methods book. Students and colleagues responded well to a more practical and hands-on approach, which is the general approach I have taken in this volume.

It should be noted that 99 percent of the satellite images in this book represent original remote sensing work and analysis by the author. Many imagery analysis techniques were based on archaeological studies from articles and books, but the images in this book are not specifically from those studies. This was done to provide specific examples of archaeological remote sensing subjects discussed in the book. It should also be noted that many of the images do not have scale bars, but instead have the scales indicated in the captions. This was done on purpose: although some of the images could have had scale pieces inserted, many of the images exist to illustrate a specific remote sensing point that requires all of the image to be clear. Given the book image sizing, inserting scale pieces would have detracted from the function of the images. This follows the example of the remote sensing textbook Remote Sensing and Image Interpretation (Lillesand *et al.* 2004). For additional information regarding obtaining satellite imagery and learning more about remote sensing, please visit this book's website, located at www.routledge.com

ACKNOWLEDGEMENTS

One cannot produce a book, especially one on such a focused topic, without the help of countless individuals. My initial thanks must go to Larry Bonneau of the Center for Earth Observation (CEO) at Yale University, whose patience with a Yale undergraduate helped her remote sensing career to start, as well as Ron Smith, director of the CEO, for his general support. When doing my initial remote sensing research at Cambridge University, I was lucky to have the help, support, and friendship of Janine Bourriau, Sally-Ann Ashton, Lucilla Burn, Ben Roberts, Chris Thornton, Hilary Soderland, Vicky Donnelly, Andrew Bednarski, Jenna Spellane, Fred and Jenny Hagen, Dirk Notz, Anne Chen, Shakira Christodoulou and family, Catherine French, Flora Spiegel, Ruth Adams, and James Williams, all of whom contributed to my academic as well as personal life.

There are far too many individuals who I have encountered at remote sensing, archaeology, and Egyptology conferences, and in the field to thank individually. I would like to list a few people whose support and encouragement at conferences and elsewhere have made the work I do far more enjoyable: Mirek Barta, Olaf Bubenzer, David Gill, Mauritzio Forte, Gao Huadong, Salima Ikram, Ellen Morris, Thomas Schneider, Janice Stargardt, and Kasia Szpakowska. For their amazing hospitality and support of my work when attending the International Conference on Remote Sensing Archaeology, I want to thank the Chinese Institute for Remote Sensing Archaeology, in particular Changlin Wang.

My escapes to Egypt for fieldwork have been made all the more pleasant by a wonderful group of people I am lucky enough to call my dig family: Zoe McQuinn, Kei Yamamoto, Debby Donnelly, Patrick Carstens, Rexine Hummel, Fran Cahill, and Larry Pavlish, whose untimely death in 2007 has left a big gap in my life. I can only imagine what his comments would be on this book. In Egypt my work is facilitated by the Supreme Council for Egyptian Antiquities, the Egyptian Antiquities Information Service, and the American Research Center in Egypt (with special thanks to Madame Amira Khattab and Mr Amir Hamid).

My academic influences are many, but I can certainly attribute my budding interest in Egyptology to William Kelly Simpson, under whom it was an honor to work and study at Yale. Colin Shell, my PhD advisor at Cambridge, challenged me to "think big" with remote sensing. My PhD supervisor, Barry Kemp, has been my academic mentor, and I will never be able to thank him properly for all his help, support and guidance. My remote sensing interest has been encouraged and supported by Ron Blom and Ray Williamson, whose encouragement via email and in person has been most welcomed. For their amazing support and *in loco parentis* in far-flung regions of the world, I owe a major debt to Payson and Fran Sheets. Payson has been a professional mentor to me, and I cannot express in words my gratitude for all he has done and continues to do.

Here at the University of Alabama at Birmingham, many people have supported my work, and the Laboratory for Global Health Observation (LGHO), which I started in 2007. Tennant McWilliams has been a constant supporter and mentor, and without him the LGHO would never have started. Max Michael, Jean Ann Linney, and members of the LGHO advisory board keep pushing me ahead in the broader remote sensing world. Dick Marchase saw (and continues to see) the big picture. I owe funding support to many sources, including UAB's NSF ADVANCE program (with special thanks to Claire Peel and Sherry Scott Pigford), the UAB Faculty Development Grant, the Department of Anthropology (with many thanks to Jannie Williamson and Kevin Johnson), and the School of Social and Behavioral Sciences. My friends and colleagues at UAB and in Birmingham, are too numerous the mention, but a few deserve special thanks for their support: Jim and Liz Reed, Dave and Yikun Schwebel and family, Sara Helms, Erik Angner and Elizabeth, Gypsy Abbott and George, Bob Novak, Michele Forman and Erik Lizee, and Rosie O'Beirne and family. Ami and Kenyon Ross and their family are wonderful, special people, and make being here a joy.

LGHO students have made me a better teacher and better researcher. Donna Burnett, LGHO Program Manager, has helped immeasurably. NASA's support – financial and otherwise – has been amazing. A major academic debt is due to NASA researcher, and now Professor, Tom Sever, who promoted, and in many ways started, the field of satellite remote sensing for archaeology (and, in a sense, this book celebrates the 25th anniversary of the field). For their help in editing chapters and other aspects, thanks are due to Donna Burnett, Scott Silver, Lauren Ristvet, Greg Mumford, Payson Sheets, Errin Weller, David Gill, Chris Thornton, Ben Roberts, Dave Cowley, Adam Pinson (bibliography), and David Gathings (images). Naturally, all errors are my own.

Routledge has been wonderful to work with on this project. They have always responded to my queries quickly, and have made the process of book writing much easier. I owe special thanks to Matthew Gibbons for his initial encouragement of this project, and to Lalle Pursglove for her help and support.

For their support and love, I need to thank my wonderful family: Mom, Dad, Aaron, Gram, Sue, Emily, Steve, Mike, Phil, Cindy, Harva, Kate, Barbara, Gordon, Ben, David, Jeanette, and Grammy. Thank you for always being there. Finally, this book is dedicated to the two people who have made the biggest difference in my life: My grandfather (now deceased), Harold Young, former world-renowned Forestry Professor at the University of Maine, and one of the pioneers of Aerial Photography in Forestry, who was a model human being and academic; and to my husband, Greg Mumford, who is amazing every day, and who has taught me more things than I could write in 100 books.

1

INTRODUCTION

Our Earth is ever changing. Continental plates shift, ocean levels rise and fall, mountains and shores erode, deserts and glaciers move, and natural disasters change the face of the globe. These are natural processes that have been shaping the surface of the Earth for billions of years. Over a much shorter period of time, formerly insignificant organisms known as homo sapiens began to shape natural environments to fit their needs. This is not unusual for organisms: Certainly, all plants and animals will transform natural surroundings to fit their needs. However, humans were different in that they not only sought actively to control their surroundings, but they managed to colonize every habitable surface ecosystem on the planet, from high mountains to low valleys, and from Arctic tundra to equatorial deserts. As the population of humans grew and their social structures became more complex, the effect of these creatures on the surface of the Earth became more noticeable. Indeed, as both social and cognizant creatures with a penchant for controlling the world around them, human beings developed a unique relationship with their surroundings. Understanding this special relationship between humans and their environment, which archaeologists, geographers, and other scholars often call "social landscapes," is one of the most pressing issues facing us in the 21st century.

How scholars and scientists detect these social landscapes has evolved with advances in technology, and stands to have an enormous impact on the fields of archaeology, history, geography, environmental sciences, and other related fields. How past places on Earth can be made visible (Gould 1987) is a topic that has received significant attention in the media and in classrooms. Although most archaeology relies on visual recognition of past remains, seen in Figure 1.1 (e.g. "the deposit of statues was found in a foundation trench," or "level 3B in square IV contains mainly broken faience amulets from the Middle Kingdom"), the majority of archaeological remains and features are hidden from view, whether buried underground by environmental processes (e.g. ancient river courses, old lakes, field boundaries), covered over by modern towns (e.g. Rome, seen in Figure 1.2, or in Greece), or by modern vegetation (e.g. forests covering settlements in Europe). The use of satellite remote sensing can not only reveal these hidden, or so-called "invisible," remains, but can place them in much larger contexts, showing past social landscapes in all their complexity.

What is satellite remote sensing, and how can it be applied to archaeological research? Satellite remote sensing is the specific application of satellite imagery (or images from space) to archaeological survey (Zubrow 2007), which entails searching for ancient sites

Figure 1.1 Digital elevation model of Chaco Canyon, New Mexico (scale 1:122 m), 2008 image courtesy of Google Earth™ Pro.

Figure 1.2 The Forum, Rome (scale 1:244 m), 2008 image courtesy of Google Earth™ Pro.

on a particular landscape at different scales (Wilkinson 2003). While aerial photography (Deuel 1973; Kenyon 1991; Wilson 2000), geophysics (Schmidt 2001; Witten 2005), laser scanning of monuments including Stonehenge, see Goskara et al. 2003), virtual reality (Broucke 1999; Barcelo *et al.* 2000), imagery analysis within geographic information systems (GIS) (Chapman 2006; Conolly and Lake 2006), and satellite imagery analysis are all forms of remote sensing—and all are invaluable for archaeological investigations—the application of satellite remote sensing in archaeology is the primary focus of this book.

All forms of remote sensing, including imagery analysis in a GIS, geophysics, satellite remote sensing, and aerial photography are concerned with the identification of "anthropogenic" features in such a landscape, whether they are detecting a structure, such as a building or a town, or a system of irrigation channels and roads. In fact, "remote sensing" is a term that refers to the remote viewing of our surrounding world, including all forms of photography, video and other forms of visualization. Satellite remote sensing has the added advantage of being able to see an entire landscape at different resolutions and scales on varying satellites imagery datasets, as well being able to record data beyond the visible part of electromagnetic spectrum. Remote sensors can analyze imagery so that distracting natural invisible or anthropogenic features on that landscape (such as forests or buildings) can be made, while ancient remains previously invisible to the naked eye appear with great clarity. In this way, satellite remote sensing can reconstruct how past landscapes may have looked, and thereby allows a better understanding of past human occupation of those landscapes.

How can people apply satellite remote sensing from space to archaeological investigations? As human beings, we can only see in the visible part of the electromagnetic spectrum. The electromagnetic spectrum extends far beyond the visible parts of the spectrum to the infrared, thermal, and microwave, all of which have been used by archaeologists to see through or beneath rainforests, deserts, and modern debris to locate past remains. Recent archaeological findings using the electromagnetic spectrum include the discovery of many ancient Mayan sites in Guatemala (Saturno *et al.* 2007), ancient water management strategies at Angkor Wat (Evans *et al.* 2007), and details of how Easter Island statues were transported (Hunt and Lipo 2005), to name a few. Satellites record reflected radiation from the surface of the Earth in different parts of the electromagnetic spectrum, with every satellite image type recording this information slightly differently. A more detailed discussion of the electromagnetic spectrum appears in Chapter 3. Ancient archaeological remains will affect their surrounding landscapes in different ways, whether through altering the surrounding soils, affecting vegetation, or absorbing moisture at a greater or lesser rate. On the ground, we cannot see these subtle landscape changes visually. Archaeologists are not necessarily "seeing" beneath the surface with multispectral satellite imagery when using remote sensing techniques; they are actually seeing the discrepancy between higher and lower moisture and heat contents of buried walls, which affect the overlying soils, sands, and vegetation. How individuals choose to manipulate satellite data to obtain these results will vary greatly depending on landscape type, satellite image type, and the overall research goals of the archaeological project.

The majority of satellite survey work in archaeology, however, has focused on visible archaeological site detection; enlarging satellite images to find sites or landscape features. There is much we can miss by being on the ground by not seeing things from an aerial perspective, as shown by Figure 1.3. Visual satellite datasets are a valuable tool

Figure 1.3 Babylon, Iraq (scale 1:1000 m), note modern reconstruction in the northern part of the site, 2008 image courtesy of Google Earth™ Pro.

for overall landscape visualization and site detection, as satellites give a far broader perspective on past landscapes. However, visual data represents only a tiny proportion of what satellites can offer the archaeologist in feature detection. Not making use of the full electromagnetic spectrum leaves countless archaeological features or sites undiscovered.

The development of this methodology has already contributed to the discovery of tens of thousands of new archaeological sites and features across the globe, with many of these studies discussed in detail here. If these case studies can serve as an example, there must be many hundreds of thousands (if not millions) of additional archaeological sites and features that remain currently undiscovered. This is particularly true, since in satellite remote sensing a specific methodology has not yet been developed to detect obscured ancient sites and features using the full range of satellite imagery analysis techniques. The ramifications of such new discoveries would be massive for historical and environmental research programs, and give tremendous insights into past social landscapes.

The second level of archaeological inference in satellite remote sensing is survey, or "ground truthing." Although finding potential archaeological sites or features on a computer screen is important, and relies on detailed scientific analysis, it is impossible to know more about an archaeological site without ground confirmation. Using a global positioning system (GPS), researchers can pinpoint areas on a computer screen for surface archaeological investigation (Arnold 1993). With the ever-increasing emphasis on reducing costs, satellite remote sensing allows archaeological teams to find sites and features that they would otherwise have had to locate randomly. This has certainly happened before in archaeology: Many tombs and deposits have been found accidentally, such as the catacombs of Alexandria, Egypt, which were found when the top of the tomb shaft was breeched by donkeys walking across it (Empereur 2000). This is hardly an ideal method for locating new sites.

In some cases, surface material culture may indicate the presence of an archaeological site, while in other cases the site will be revealed by growth patterns in vegetation, chemical alterations in the soil, or close proximity to a covered natural feature. On the ground during general archaeological survey, we can certainly observe differently colored soils (Van Andel 1998) and different aspects of material culture. Surveying an entire landscape through visual observation of these features and the collection of material culture allows archaeological teams to make observations about land occupation over time. Satellite remote sensing, in combination with ground survey, coring, and excavation, allows for a holistic landscape reconstruction, by enabling the detection and assessment of invisible sites and features. Both visible and invisible archaeological features combine to give a better understanding of anthropogenic effects on past landscapes.

The third level of inference in satellite remote sensing is targeted excavations, in which archaeologists open a limited number of trenches that are strategically placed to give the maximum amount of information about that site or that landscape. In a normal excavation in which satellite remote sensing is not involved, archaeologists often will use geophysics or ground survey to determine the best placement for their trenches. In instances where geophysics is not used, perhaps the archaeological team will decide to place their trenches at higher locations (where preservation is better), or where specific surface material culture indicates certain types of subsurface structures (e.g. large amounts of slag appearing on the surface of an archaeological site may indicate an industrial area beneath the ground—Figure 1.4).

When using satellite remote sensing for excavation, however, the archaeological team can use the electromagnetic spectrum and broader visual detection to reveal features not apparent on the ground. Satellite remote sensing, in a sense, acts as an aerial geophysical sensor, identifying potential buried features such as walls, streets, or houses. Once the archaeological team knows the exact location of any potential feature, they can target their excavation trenches accordingly. Satellites may be more cost-effective than other geophysical methods, as they can be used to analyze broader stretches of land, but everything will depend on the project aims of the archaeological team. The differences described here highlight how the research agenda of a traditional archaeologist differs from that of one informed by satellite remote sensing techniques.

While there is great interest in the use of satellite remote sensing, people are generally not aware of the full potential of satellite data for archaeological work. Satellite remote sensing studies are certainly becoming more popular, evidenced by increasing numbers of related articles in journals such as the *Journal of Field Archaeology*, *Antiquity*, and *Archaeological Prospection*, and an increasing presence of satellite remote sensing in popular media. Many general remote sensing handbooks exist (Jensen 1996; Lillesand *et al.* 2004), and form required readings in introductory remote sensing courses. These books, while excellent reference tools, can be too technical for people with a more general interest in satellite remote sensing. This book does not claim to be a general remote sensing introduction or even an environmental remote sensing book (Jensen 2000): It is a book aimed at describing and evaluating the numerous applications of satellite remote sensing to global archaeological landscape evaluation, and is written to be accessible to archaeologists, students, and others interested in applying this technology to their work or learning more about the subject of satellite archaeology. Hands-on coursework is required to learn specific remote sensing programs, much like any scientific specialization in archaeology, but few courses exist at present dedicated to the teaching of satellite remote sensing in archaeology.

The choice to use remote sensing as one's research is another topic. Does the existence of the technology alone merit developing an interest in the subject? Satellite remote sensing visualizes the confluence of human history and the environment, which archaeologists spend much of their time reconstructing. Anyone with an interest in comparing regional and national influences on a local level can benefit from having a better understanding of landscape changes and how they may have influenced site or feature placement. The very nature of archaeology is concerned with exposing hidden things, largely buried beneath the ground, to answer larger historical and anthropological questions. Satellite remote sensing in archaeology is virtually identical then to the larger scope archaeology, although the features it reveals are not necessarily buried in the same way. As in all scientific methods of analysis in archaeology, there is a right and a wrong way to conduct satellite remote sensing studies and related ground surveys.

This book will start with a detailed history of satellite remote sensing in archaeology (Chapter 2), which will emphasize the general development of satellite remote sensing versus ongoing developments in archaeology and remote sensing. Gaining an appreciation of how the field developed is important, because through understanding the history of satellite remote sensing, one can better appreciate where the field is headed.

Figure 1.4 Digital elevation model, Tell Tebilla, northeast Delta (scale 1:78 m). Note the checkerboard pattern from surface scraping during the 2003 excavation season, 2008 image courtesy of Google Earth™ Pro.

Archaeologists and other specialists have already written books on aerial photography (Deuel 1973; St. Joseph 1977; Riley 1982; Bourgeois and Marc 2003; Brophy and Cowley 2005), but it is necessary to provide an overview of basic concepts of remote sensing as they started in the early 1900s with the advent of aerial archaeology. It will also be important for archaeologists to understand the advantages and disadvantages of using satellite remote sensing in relationship to aerial photography. Used together, they present powerful past landscape visualization tools.

Chapter 3 discusses the various types of satellite imagery available to archaeologists, helping with the selection of most appropriate imagery, and provides information about ordering each image type. Access to satellite imagery is influencing how archaeologists conduct their fieldwork, while giving more individuals the ability to understand past landscapes. This access will only continue as free viewing programs, such as Google Earth™ or WorldWind, improve their resolution (Figure 1.5). Obtaining free satellite imagery is an important issue because adequate money for recent imagery may not be available. Chapter 3 also discusses the advantages and disadvantages of each satellite image type along with some of the various archaeological projects that have applied them.

Chapter 4 provides a developing archaeological remote sensing methodology, from basic remote sensing techniques to complex algorithms, which will allow cross applications of techniques across diverse regions of the globe. This chapter provides the most technical detail in the book. Satellite images are especially useful for mapmaking due to the paucity of high quality or recent maps in different regions and nations.

Figure 1.5 Digital elevation model, Hadrian's Wall, northern England (scale 1:50 m), 2008 image courtesy of Google Earth™ Pro.

How trustworthy are such maps for archaeological analysis? As Irwin Scollar (2002) points out, maps are not images, and landscapes tend to be altered according to the preferences of the maker, thus making the whole field of satellite map generation subjective. This question extends beyond mapping, however, as a wide range of techniques are required to model past sites and features. Good science promotes non-destructive archaeology, while appropriate training augments the optimum application of satellite remote sensing in archaeology. Describing how satellite remote sensing is different from geophysics and GIS is also important, as the three subjects often appear together in case study books and conference proceedings (Scollar *et al.* 1990; Zubrow *et al.* 1990; Behrens and Sever 1991; Bewley and Raczkowski 2002; Wang and Huadong 2004; Johnson 2006; Hamilton 2007; Peebles 2007; Wiseman and El-Baz 2007).

Satellite remote sensing in archaeology archaeological remote sensing is still a developing field, and much testing is required to advance it. Distinguishing an archaeological site from a similar, but non-related signature in satellite imagery requires knowledge of the advantages and disadvantages of using different remote sensing techniques. Even archaeologists who have accumulated many years of experience in satellite remote sensing can make incorrect assumptions about potential features revealed by satellite imagery. One never stops learning with remote sensing: Training, updating skills, and continuous and varying field experience enables those using remote sensing to stay on top of this dynamic discipline. At present, a broad range of satellite archaeology articles are accepted for publication, some of which are more archaeological, others of which are more remote sensing focused. However, this merely reflects that diverse specialists exist who bridge the gap between these two evolving fields. Chapter 4 covers some techniques for interpreting landscapes to assist with overall project work, and strategies for ground surveys, attempting to span both archaeological and remote sensing approaches.

Chapter 5 considers how and why archaeologists make particular choices regarding techniques and satellite images in their excavation and survey work, especially regarding major landscape site types. How individuals comprehend the development of ancient to modern landscapes is not a straightforward topic. Determining the geographical extent and time-span of a project is the first stage that should be addressed prior to archaeological analysis. Understanding how satellite remote sensing can contribute to a better understanding of macro- and micro-landscape studies is also crucial, especially when deciding on the types of imagery and the techniques of analysis required. At the macro-settlement scale, more broad-scale landscape issues are apparent, including overall environmental, economic, political, and social factors. Remote sensing assists with examining archaeological site placement, and has detected past river courses (James 1995), water sources (McHugh *et al.* 1988) or geological factors (Ostir and Nuninger 2006) that might have influenced site placement or abandonment. At the micro-settlement scale, such factors are apparent at a local level and are assessed via place-specific documentation or material culture remains. Satellite imagery may aid in determining where to excavate, or may render excavation unnecessary through specific feature detection. Satellite remote sensing may also encourage archaeologists to integrate either top-down and/or bottom-up models (Campana and Forte 2006). Remote sensing is, by necessity, a "top-down," approach, while the search for archaeological data to support "bottom-up" models takes into account broader factors.

Prior to discussing the implications of satellite remote sensing in archaeology, Chapter 5 reviews what satellite imagery can detect, covering a full range of

Figure 1.6 Medinet Habu, Luxor, Egypt (scale 1:159 m), extensive unexcavated archaeological remains surround the temple, 2008 image courtesy of Google Earth™ Pro.

archaeological site types that one might encounter during satellite remote sensing analysis. One key question is how can an archaeological site, or past landscape, be defined? There is no one correct definition of what constitutes an archaeological site, other than descriptions defining areas of varying sizes containing past remains. Geographical areas containing temples and tombs come to mind immediately but these are only a miniscule sample of the sites surviving from antiquity (Figure 1.6). Would a single sherd in a modern agricultural field be considered a true site (Bintliff and Snodgrass 1988)? Theoretically, one could associate material culture debris with a specific place, including a number of sherds scattered over a raised area of earth, which might reflect an ancient rest stop, campsite, or habitation area. A single sherd in a field can be indicative of numerous processes: Environmental agencies (e.g. flooding) might have moved the sherd from its original location, perhaps several kilometers away; the sherd might indicate an underlying site beneath, or might have been discarded by past or present peoples in transit. We cannot know for certain what it represents without further context and exploration. For instance, does it date to a period and transit route between known sites? Hence, any past remains should constitute a significant piece of archaeological data, whether it be a single sherd, a former village beneath a modern town, or a temple complex.

The previously mentioned topics lead to some further discussion concerning how archaeologists can evaluate remotely explored landscapes. Chapter 6 provides additional strategies for analyzing features from space, detailing six case studies covering remote sensing approaches to ancient landscapes ranging from rainforests to floodplains, and from deserts to grasslands. The chapter discusses Peten (Guatemala), Angkor Wat (Cambodia), Xi'an (China), Ubar (Oman), Homs (Syria), and the northeast Delta and region around Tell-el-Amarna (Egypt). The technical approaches and satellite imagery types chosen by each archaeological team are examined. The successes and failures of each approach are described, of particular note for other archaeologists who may wish to work in similar or related regions.

At present, various archaeologists are contributing to the development of satellite remote sensing in archaeology through much needed studies in methodology. Assessing ongoing and past landscape changes, however, should be one of the main goals for satellite archaeology, and how each project has approached this will be discussed. Topographical changes over time have influenced how people interacted with their local and regional resources, and how and why populations settled in various places initially. These changes are often partially or sometimes entirely obscured today, but it remains important to analyze how ancient sites developed in conjunction with their local landscapes. Landscapes are usually dynamic entities, changing over time according to environmental patterns at a local, regional, and global scales in tandem with global climate events as well as changes in the social landscape. Landscapes are not static and singular entities: They are palimpsests, with satellite imagery analysis helping to trace varying levels of change over time and space. How individual projects view these assorted layered landscapes via satellite data, survey work, and in some cases, excavation, will be evaluated, with further guidance suggested for similar future projects.

Chapter 7 introduces in-field considerations and ground survey. Ground survey is a crucial component in satellite remote sensing for archaeology. Only ground-truthing can currently determine data for newly discovered sites, while visualizing landscapes with layers of supplementary survey data can aid in reconstructing past landscapes. Beyond the scope of assessing past landscapes, archaeologists may face many fieldwork challenges. Locating archaeological sites using satellite remote sensing may signify little if there is not sufficient funding to verify preliminary results through ground survey. Understanding past human–environment interactions with satellite remote sensing is also much trickier without a good understanding of present day human–environment interactions, which aids in fieldwork, site preservation, and assessing ancient landscapes. Numerous satellite archaeology studies have focused on archaeological site location via computer analysis, but far fewer studies describe fully the techniques employed to locate sites on the ground, or how the discovered sites correlate with the original analysis and overall historical implications. Specialists using satellite remote sensing in archaeology need to move from an air-based viewpoint to a ground-based one in order to reveal broader, more meaningful archaeological landscapes.

Defining a "site" in the broader context of its archaeology and its social landscape is not a straightforward process during ground survey. Archaeologists can only begin to appreciate sites fully if their historical and geographic contexts are examined. Describing the physical nature of an area of archaeological interest is only the first step: Once archaeologists have examined the material culture remains, the site can be placed in its local, regional, continental, and even global contexts. Thus, individual site description is a process of evolution rather than a finite academic exercise. Initial observations play a crucial role in how future studies are conducted. Both past and present formation processes are equally important in how ancient sites obtain their present condition, and comprehending the nature of these processes assists in making preliminary assessments and asking the right questions in the field. Thus, it will be important to outline various approaches to recording these formation processes.

Other issues (Chapter 8) entail ethical considerations for the use of satellite imagery, and how remote sensing can be applied to efforts in conservation and heritage management. In some situations, a satellite study area may be inaccessible due to war, or other serious internal problems (e.g. natural disasters). Urban development, related population growth, and environmental changes (Akasheh 2002) can all be detected via remote sensing analysis, and stress the importance of locating archaeological sites to preserve and protect them. Unless broader collaborative efforts are encouraged between archaeologists and the host government agencies responsible for protecting sites, little can be done to preserve past remains. Archaeological landscapes are threatened everywhere (Figure 1.7), including ancient sites that are not visible from space. For example, deep-sea, drag-net trawling has destroyed many ancient and modern shipwrecks in the Mediterranean (Foley 2008). One can only extrapolate what affects deep-sea fishing and other activities have had on shipwrecks worldwide (Soreide 2000; Coleman *et al.* 2003; Ballard 2007; Mindell 2007). Timing is another issue: archaeologists may encounter too much material to complete ground surveys in the time available to them, thus stressing the importance of training local officials to assist in visiting and recording sites.

Chapter 8 explores these broader issues, focusing on what one can achieve with collected data. Certainly, looting is one of the main problems for archaeologists and heritage preservation today. Ironically, widespread data-sharing regarding newly discovered ancient sites threatens those same sites by alerting looters to their presence. A modified

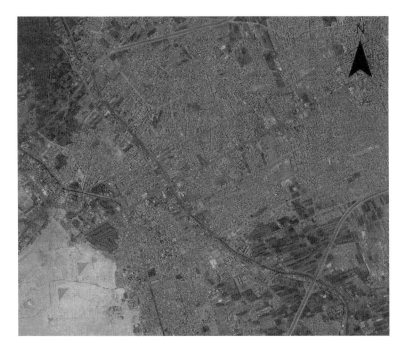

Figure 1.7 Giza Pyramids, Egypt (scale 1:1440 m). Modern buildings have come within 0.26 km of the Pyramids, 2008 image courtesy of Google Earth™ Pro.

archaeological remote sensing ethics statement is suggested to augment site protection in such circumstances. In addition, educating the public about satellite remote sensing use in archaeology, including both implications and responsible application of sensing, is emphasized, especially since scientific ignorance and pseudoarchaeology often go hand in hand. This author and many colleagues receive diverse communications from individuals making claims about finding "lost cities," "secret buried treasure," or "unlocking the secrets of the universe" using satellite imagery analysis or other techniques. This author has also received several invitations to find Atlantis from space. While often well-meaning and amusing, these proposals underscore the need for archaeologists, teachers, and the media to do a better job educating the public about new technologies and the need for good scientific practices in archaeology. The lack of an educational approach can muddy the waters of information dissemination, and allows the promotion of ideas that do not have a basis in scientific fact, even encouraging the nurturing of such ideas in even some serious entry level undergraduate students of archaeology (Cole *et al.* 1990).

The conclusion (Chapter 9) will discuss the future directions for satellite remote sensing in archaeology. Here, it is emphasized that limited time and resources require the maintenance of a careful balance between landscape analysis, topographical study, and excavation. Placing archaeological sites in their proper contexts requires all three methods. As satellite technology improves and becomes more widely available, archaeologists will be able to detect more subterranean sites, currently hidden from view. Shifting dunes in desert environments may reveal ancient fortifications, while desertification can obscure both well-known and undiscovered sites. This emphasizes the importance of satellite archaeology: Our ever-dynamic, ever-changing natural and human-engineered environments are causing more ancient sites to appear and disappear. The current global coverage by satellites represents the best technology already in place to reveal recorded and continuously refined levels of assessment for these ongoing, simultaneous changes in ancient and modern sites and landscapes. Archaeological satellite remote sensing bridges the gap between "dirt" archaeologists and remote sensing specialists by helping researchers to evaluate known archaeological sites in broader landscapes.

The importance and timeliness of such a work is emphasized by the partial or total destruction of archaeological sites by numerous man-made and natural factors. This book also addresses an inherent bias in archaeological remote sensing: How much information is missed beneath the ground that current (declassified) satellite technology cannot detect? This is a question for every archaeological project in the world. This inherent bias must be recognized, what satellite remote sensing can detect and what it cannot. Just as in excavation, remote sensing research must be well-planned and well-executed, using a comprehensive methodology. The remote senser's eyes become trowels, peeling away the layers of multispectral imagery, while different image types act as sieves to detect smaller features. For the moment, what lies beneath the ground can only be reached through ground-based coring, selected geophysical surveys, or deep trenching. Ultimately one deals with only a percentage of the overall surviving evidence and biased preservation. Nonetheless, archaeological remote sensing already has the ability to detect tens of thousands of "missing" sites across the globe from the past millennia of human activity, and future advances in satellite remote sensing in archaeology will detect many thousands more.

2

A HISTORY OF SATELLITE REMOTE
SENSING FOR ARCHAEOLOGY

Overview

"Remote sensing," in its most basic definition, has existed in archaeology for as long as practicing archaeologists have lived, as it can be defined as a means to observe the surrounding landscape. Many ancient cultures used mountain peaks or desert cliffs to survey their landscapes prior to choosing the most advantageous positions for their temples, tombs, settlements, or other building projects. These early architects, priests/priestesses, and leaders did what most satellite remote sensing specialists do: Using landscapes as computer screens, they focused on the natural relationship of landscape features to potential places for living, burial, or worship. Each landscape had its own intrinsic layered meaning to past peoples, as their "multispectral" approach involved seeing these palimpsests as a unified whole. The field of remote sensing, as more narrowly defined, has only existed for the past 100 years, with the field of satellite archaeology appearing in the early 1970s. While all landscapes of archaeological interest are imbued with these layers of interest, satellite and other remote sensing specialists see what the naked eye cannot, in the hopes that such analysis will allow a glimpse into the true hidden nature of past places. Memory and meaning in landscapes are intangible yet not unobtainable if one adopts a holistic approach to seeing otherwise invisible features.

Such holistic approaches require all above-ground remote sensing specialists to use all appropriate sources of data, including balloons, kites, aerial photographs, and satellite imagery in their work. Aerial photography, to which the field of satellite archaeology owes much, has merited a number of books devoted to its usage, as described in Chapter 1. These books, written by career aerial archaeology specialists, discuss the history of aerial archaeology, and general techniques for interpreting this imagery in a wide number of contexts, shown in Figure 2.1. This discussion will not be repeated in detail here, where the focus will be on the archaeological uses of satellites over the past 30 years. However, a general historical background of aerial archaeology allows for the evaluation of the full trajectory of satellite remote sensing and its uses in archaeology. This includes how the field developed in relationship to satellite endeavors in remote sensing, NASA's space program, anthropology, and geography. A generalized history of archaeology is also not appropriate: The field of remote sensing has developed independently of archaeology, while the usage of satellites in archaeology cannot outwardly be associated with any particular theoretical movement, although earlier technical developments seem to be connected to

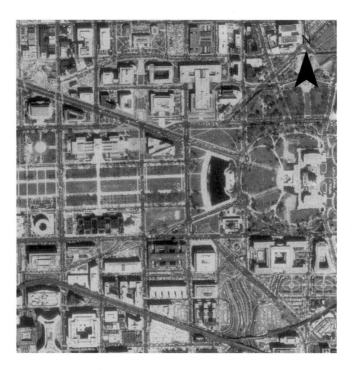

Figure 2.1 Orthophoto image of Washington, DC (scale 1:583 m), imagery courtesy of NASA World Wind.

the "New Archaeology" scientific movement of the late 1960s–early 1970s (Renfrew *et al.* 1966). Remote sensing in archaeology is more closely connected with generalized developments of the field of remote sensing rather than archaeological trends over the past 35 years.

1900s–1930s

A desire to view archaeological sites from the air, occurring just prior to and during World War I, essentially started the scientific field of remote sensing. Some of the earliest remote sensing in archaeology took place in the UK and Italy. The title of the "pioneer" of aerial archaeology belongs to UK army Lieutenant P.H. Sharpe, who took photographs of Salisbury Plain over Stonehenge in 1906, seen in Figure 2.2. Like many developments in archaeology, this was an accident: Winds had blown Lt. Sharpe off-course during an army exercise. The photographs, described by Colonel J.E. Clapper in *Archaeologia*, clearly show the stones in relationship to their surrounding earthworks (Capper 1907). Additional early aerial photos exist, taken from a balloon over the Tiber River, with images of Ostia Antiqua, and Venice from 1908, and of Pompeii in 1910 attributed to archaeologist Giacomo Boni (pers. comm., S. Campana and M. Forte, December 2006). Early photography taken for military purposes during World War I by Belgian pilots can even contribute to archaeology today (Stichelbaut 2006).

Figure 2.2 Stonehenge, UK (scale 1:43 m), 2008 image courtesy of Google Earth™ Pro.

Pilots flying over areas of natural and historical interest in the Middle East took a number of photographs with their personal cameras, and their superiors realized a significant military advantage when they viewed the photographs. Photos by taken by Obertendant Falk of the German Air Force in 1917 of Late Roman towns in the Negev were used by Theodore Wiegend in his book on Sinai (Wiegend 1920). The Bavarian State War archives in Munich have a number of archaeological photos of Israel and Jordan taken by Ottoman air force units who worked with German-Turkish *Denkmalschutzkommandos*. Under the Ottomans, there was a quick development of the use of aerial photographs. Royal Air Force flights assisted Alexander Kennedy's Petra work in 1923–4 (Kennedy 1925), Nelson Glueck's survey in Transjordan and Palestine in the late 1920s (Glueck 1965), Beazeley's early aerial photographs over different parts of Mesopotamia (Beazeley 1919, 1920), and O.G.S. Crawford's exploration of Iraq, Transjordan, and Palestine in 1928 (Crawford 1923a; Kennedy 2002), (See Figure 2.3). Crawford went on to found *Antiquity*, where he popularized the usage of aerial photography in archaeology as well as through more general publications such as the *Christian Science Monitor* (Crawford 1923b). Further uses of aerial photography occurred over the Transjordan (Rees 1929), various parts of the Middle East with famed aerial archaeologist Father Antoine Poidebard (Poidebard 1929, 1931, 1934), Sir Auriel Stein in Iraq and Transjordan during World War I and in 1938–9 (Stein 1919; Stein 1940), and in Egypt with Reginald Engelbach of the Royal Air Force (Engelbach 1929) and Gertrude Caton-Thompson in Kharga Oasis (who later did work with aerial photography in Zimbabwe) (Caton-Thompson 1929, 1931). Even Sir Mortimer Wheeler advocated the use of aerial

Figure 2.3 Jerusalem (Dome of the Rock), Israel, note the detail of the roofing and structure (scale 1:88 m), 2008 image courtesy of Google Earth™ Pro.

photography in India (Thakran 2000). Engelbach's work focused mainly on the pyramid fields and the archaeological sites of Luxor, but he lamented not being able to work elsewhere:

> For some reasons that will appear, I could have wished that flight has been over some of the Delta sites, but the experience was of interest since my department was anxious to ascertain whether any new surveys would be of value and whether, in certain of the old town-sites' tracks could be distinguished from the air which might reveal the situation of necropolis or other indications of interest far out in the desert.
>
> (Englebach, quoted in Rees 1929: 389–407)

This statement shows, at this early time, the recognition of the advantage height could give to new archaeological discoveries as well as the importance of crop marks that could indicate the location of sites buried beneath modern fields. For example, oblique aerial photos taken by the RAF in 1932 above the floodplain near Tell el-Amarna, Middle Egypt, reveal a number of crop marks suggestive of buried walls (as interpreted by the author). Quite surprisingly, crop marks have never played an influential role in the development of Egyptian archaeology (Parcak 2009). Cropmarks are not, however, a 20th-century idea. British antiquarian William Camden, in the 16th century, noted:

> But now has eras'd the very tracks and to teach us that cities dye as well as men, it is at this day a corn field, wherein the corn is grown up, one may observe the droughts of streets crossing one another, and such crossings they commonly call St. Augustine's cross.
>
> (Crawford and Keillor 1928: 37)

A reference to "they" shows that people nearly 500 years ago acknowledged crop marks with a special term. One wonders if earlier groups would have recognized them as well.

Aerial photography also played an important role in the archaeology of the Americas. Under the newly-appointed Director of the Carnegie Institution of Washington, Alfred Kidder, the Institution provided funding to support aerial reconnaissance missions by Charles Lindbergh and his wife in Central America to map known Mayan cities and record new features (Lindbergh 1929a, 1929b; see also Kidder 1929, 1930). Charles Lindberg and his wife photographed Chaco Canyon for Kidder, which aided in site visualization and comparison to the surrounding desert landscape. At other sites in the USA such as the Cahokia Mounds (Holley *et al.* 1993), shown in Figure 2.4, aerial photography played an important role in landscape interpretation (McKinley 1921). Sites difficult to reach in Peru proved much easier to visualize from space, thus setting the stage for broader aerial reconnaissance of the region (Johnson and Platt 1930). Archaeologists also used early aerial photography for archaeological site management

Figure 2.4 Cahokia Mounds, Illinois (scale 1:31 m), 2008 image courtesy of Google Earth™ Pro.

and protection, during World War II, while German (Crashaw 2001; Going 2002), American, and British armed forces photographed a majority of Europe for military reconnaissance purposes. Some of these photographs are stored in archives, such as in the Smithsonian Institution in Green Park, Maryland, the Aerial Reconnaissance Archives in Edinburgh, and the JARIC-National Image Exploitation Centre archives in Brampton, UK, and on numerous European websites which provide archaeologists today with valuable historical snapshots of landscapes as they were in the mid-20th century, before the dramatic changes wrought by urban sprawl and mechanization of agriculture in the second half of the 20th century.

1940s–1960s

During and following World War II, the number of aerial archaeology articles declined slightly, with a total of 73 publications between 1939–49, compared to 101 publications between 1928–38. This does not mean that World War II had a negative impact on the field of remote sensing: The very opposite is true. World War II had a large impact on archaeologists who learnt aerial photo interpretation skills working in intelligence during the War. In the early 1950s, more aerial archaeology scholarship was evident, with articles (not surprisingly) focusing on the parts of the world largely photographed during the aerial reconnaissance missions of World War II. This included Europe, the Americas, the Middle East, and the Far East (Goodchild 1950; Johnson 1950; Williams-Hunt 1950; Schaedel 1951), with a majority of publications focusing on the archaeology of the UK. These were as much based on new aerial photography, rather than using the older RAF photography. These publications started to address broader archaeological issues with the ongoing development of aerial archaeology methods. 1954 saw the first application of infrared (IR) photography in archaeology in Barbeau Creek Rock Shelter, Randolph County, North Carolina. Archaeologist J. Buettner-Januch compared the use of IR photography with normal film, and asserted that the photographed archaeological features appeared more clearly on the IR film. This was not without problems: The IR field needed variable exposure rates, so the general quality of the exposures could not be assessed prior to development. Buettner-Januch suggested that the IR field could be used for more aerial topographic surveys, but this would need to be done on a trial and error basis as scientists did not yet know the reflection and emission properties of ground objects (Buettner-Januch 1954). It was not until two years later that the first publication appeared that discussed the usage of IR film in aerial photography (Edeine 1956).

Usage of aerial photographs remained fairly consistent through the mid-1950s, with further developments in to the scale of study, extending to landscapes, and an emphasis on interpreting and finding meaning in the data (Bradford 1956; Green 1957). Advances in spatial remote sensing from the mid-1940s to the 1950s occurred with the V2 rocket-launching scheme in New Mexico, at the White Sands Proving Ground, seen in Figure 2.5. Although this and other concurrent programs did not produce high-quality photographs, they showed the value of imagery taken from space (Lillesand *et al.* 2004: 402). A decline in the usage of aerial photography in the USA occurred between 1958–60, which appears closely connected to the diversion of government funding to scientific and nuclear research following the Soviet Union's launch of Sputnik in 1957. Developing space and satellite technologies meant similar developments in space

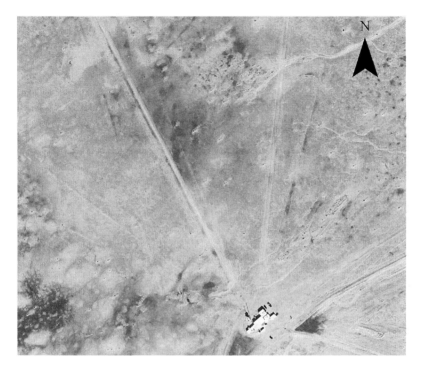

Figure 2.5 White Sands Proving Ground (scale 1:264 m), 2008 image courtesy of Google Earth™ Pro.

photography. The Television and Infrared Observation Satellite (TIROS), launched in 1960, showed meteorological patterns for the first time: Instead of just looking at clouds, scientists could now ponder the possibility of seeing through the Earth's atmosphere. Images from space taken by astronauts with handheld cameras also had applications to geological fields. The advent of the Cold War saw rapid development of the US space imaging program with the Corona, Argon, and Lanyard systems, with imagery taken from 1960–72. The Corona systems were termed KH-1, KH-2, KH-3, KH-4, KH-4A, and KH-4B, while the Argon system was designated KH-5 and the Lanyard system KH-6. The full impact of this program on archaeology would not be realized for another 25 years with the release of previously classified imagery, but the program contributed to the ongoing scientific programs involving global land coverage from space (Macdonald 1995).

Publications appearing in the mid-late 1960s more frequently focused on the multispectral capabilities of aerial photographs (Harp 1966; Agache 1968). With the first international colloquium on air archaeology in 1963 (Scollar 1963), aerial archaeology could be designated an "official" subfield in archaeology. While the Apollo 9 program made use of multispectral film (with black and white as well as color IR film) in 1969, archaeologists had started discussing its applications to landscapes impossible to visualize fully on normal film. Indeed, a review (Thompson 1967) of St. Joseph's (1966) *The Uses of Air Photography* demonstrated thinking some 15–20 years ahead of its time when the reviewer referred to electromagnetic remote sensing as "artificial satellites," and asked why scholars who had used it to study Earth resources had not considered electromagnetic remote sensing for archaeology. Thompson (1967) then suggested how the technology could be applied in rainforest research (Cantral 1975) with a ground resolution of between 1–200 feet. This was not put into practice until the work of Tom Sever and his NASA team in Central America nearly 30 years later (Sever 1995).

1970s

IR imagery and a move beyond the visual part of the electromagnetic spectrum proved to be the foci for new developments in aerial archaeology between 1969–73. In the Little Colorado River in North-Central Arizona, aerial IR scanner imagery located parallel linear features, which testing via soil and pollen studies showed to be prehistoric agricultural plots. Archaeologists could not recognize these features on the ground or from normal aerial photos (Gumerman and Schaber 1969). Studies on the spectral reflectance of soil (Condit 1970) would eventually assist archaeologists attempting to use optical filtering (Chevallier *et al.* 1970) and IR photography (Gillion 1970) in their work.

In 1971, George Gumerman and Theodore Lyons (1971) published the breakthrough article on IR aerial archaeology and the potential for multispectral remote sensing in archaeology under the title of "Archaeological Methodology and Remote Sensing." This article moved the field of aerial archaeology beyond basic interpretation and identification to more automated pattern recognition, on which the field of satellite archaeology is largely based. After providing a basic overview of remote sensing, the first time such an overview could be found in an archaeological publication, the article discussed site location in the Hohokam region, where archaeological sites in the Chaco Canyon region of New Mexico dating to between 500 BC–1500AD and prehistoric sites dating to 12,000–10,000 BC could be located. The area proved to be ideal for testing varying types of imagery, due to the relatively flat terrain and sparse ground cover. Infrared photography allowed for clearer viewing of terrace walls and roads at the Chetro Ketl ruin in Chaco Canyon (Pouls *et al.* 1976), seen in Figures 2.6a and 2.6b, when compared to regular black and white aerial photographs. A chart provided by the authors compared color and black and white photography with IR black and white photography, color IR film, as well as multispectral photography, radar imagery, and microwave imagery. Categories in which the archaeologists compared each image type included exploration and identification, component analysis, identification soils, rock types, soil moisture, vegetation, vegetation pattern analysis, plant vigor identification, geomorphology, and land use analysis. According to the team, only color IR film and multispectral photography allowed archaeologists to examine all of the categories (Gumerman and Lyons 1971).

This early article was not only valuable for providing an overview of the basic applications of IR imagery to archaeology, but also for discussing broader issues still relevant in satellite archaeology today. Already, cost proved to be a factor in the utilization of some imagery types, especially scanner imagery, which allowed for the identification of prehistoric soils from the Egyptian Delta via night readings. The article noted that buried cultural features absorb or emit radiation differently than the surrounding soil, with prehistoric garden plots appearing best in color IR film. Even at that time, the authors recognized the importance of ground-based survey as well as using as

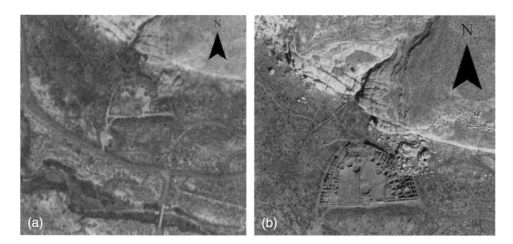

Figure 2.6 Chaco Canyon, New Mexico: (a) Orthophoto (scale 1:110 m); and (b) Quickbird imagery (scale 1:100 m), 2008 images courtesy of Google Earth™ Pro and NASA World Wind.

broad a range of imagery types from different seasons. They pointed out (and this remains true) that there is not one single type of remote sensing device on which archaeological prospecting should rely, since each archaeological site will have their own spectral properties. Radar imagery, mentioned for the first time with regards to its potential archaeological applications, was too poor in resolution to be used more widely.

Prior to the development of multispectral satellite imagery, archaeologists were already thinking of the advantages and disadvantages of aerial photography for broader archaeological survey (see Figure 2.7). With theoretical and general archaeological inference, archaeology was beginning to be thought of as a science (Watson 1976), which also aided the transition to the wider-spread application of multispectral imagery. Color IR film helped archaeologists to identify microenvironmental zones as well as alluvial valley centers and terraces in the Tehuacan Valley, Mexico (Gumerman and Neely 1972), showing the importance of considering different archaeological landscapes in the same imagery. Additional studies (Lyons *et al.* 1972; Tartaglia 1973; Harp 1975; Ebert 1976; Jorde and Bertram 1976) dealt with a wide range of archaeological issues (Ebert *et al.* 1979), moving aerial archaeology beyond mere site discovery to a problem-oriented field. The journal *Aerial Archaeology* first appeared in 1975, and attracted international attention while focusing mainly on studies from the UK (Edwards and Partridge 1977). In a review of the Impact of Natural Sciences on Archaeology, scientists presented the idea of using the electromagenetic spectrum for aerial research (Blank 1973). The idea of analyzing imagery for archaeology on a computer had not yet become a possibility. Producing "true-plan" mapping of archaeological features from oblique aerial photographs on a computer had been discussed (Palmer 1978), but the cost of computers was, at the time, beyond the means of most archaeologists. The launch of the Landsat program in

Figure 2.7 Celone Valley, Italy (scale 1:336 m), note cropmarks in the fields, 2008 image courtesy of Google Earth™ Pro.

1972 would soon change how archaeologists thought of applying imagery to their work (Hamlin 1977).

While the Apollo program was terminated in 1972, that year marked the beginning of the Landsat program, a image of which appears in Figure 2.8 (Wiseman and El-Baz 2007). The US Department of the Interior, in 1967, started the Earth Resources Technology satellites (ERTs), with the ultimate goal of gaining unsupervised and multispectral information about the Earth's surface. Launched in 1972 as ERTS-I with an orbit of 900 km, a resolution of 80 m and a revisit time of 18 days, the USA invited scientists from around the world to study the collected data, which was renamed the "Landsat" program in 1975. The USA has launched a total of six Landsat satellites (Landsat 6 failed at launch). Geology produced some of the earliest Landsat studies applicable to archaeology, with scientists using the imagery to study landscape geomorphology and to map large desert regions in Egypt (Moussa 1977; El-Etr *et al.* 1979; Khawaga 1979; El-Rakaiby *et al.* 1994). France started another multispectral satellite progect in 1978, called Systeme Pour l'Observation de Terre, or SPOT, which was launched in 1986. SPOT was the first satellite that could achieve stereoscopic imaging. Unlike the quick rise of interest in Landsat, SPOT did not prove popular with archaeologists carrying out remote sensing work until 10 years after its launch.

Archaeologists also considered the larger implications of archaeological remote sensing applications (Snow 1979). How archaeologists might consider remote sensing specialists as members of their team still remains a subject not well discussed (Rapp 1975). Why more archaeological applications of aerial photography could not be found in the USA also became as issue. Concentrated application of aerial photography to

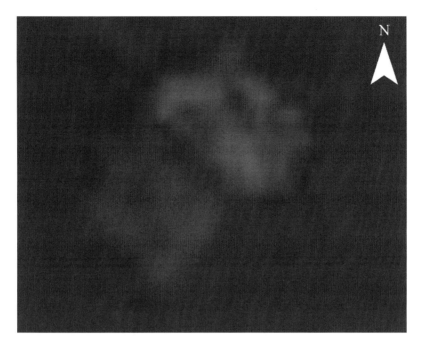

Figure 2.8 Ellis Island, New York City, New York, coarse resolution Landsat image (scale 1:180 m), note the pixel sizes and that the details of the imager are not possible to view, 1980 image courtesy of NASA.

the archaeology of the UK appeared to be expected. While UK archaeology could be seen as geological and historical in nature, the archaeology of the USA was viewed as more anthropological with a Native American focus. Issues involving bias and over-interpretation of remote sensing data were also important. Archaeologists placed an early emphasis on more methodical imagery analysis rather than focusing on surveying techniques (Ebert *et al.* 1979). Issues with archaeological sampling also contributed towards the development of archaeological remote sensing. In a prehistoric site study conducted in the Blue Ridge Mountains in Shenandoah National Park (Figure 2.9), archaeologists recognized the difficulties of searching for sites over an area covering 180,000 acres and the issue of sites not being evenly distributed across Earth's surface. They addressed the problem of getting a representative sample of sites by using geology and landscape geomorphology, and the extent to which IR photography could contribute to archaeological site location (Ebert and Gutierrez 1979).

1980s

The early 1980s saw some of the earliest application of multispectral Landsat satellites in archaeology with accompanying survey strategies (Campbell 1981; Drager 1983; Hardy 1983; Hoffman 1983; Parrington 1983). Although Landsat had an 80 m resolution and archaeologists saw the potential of applying Landsat satellite imagery for more economic site surveys, they recognized the need for much higher resolution satellite

Figure 2.9 Blue Ridge Mountains in Shenandoah National Park, the detail of the mountain terrain can be altered in Google Earth™ Pro (scale 1:757 m), 2008 image courtesy of Google Earth™ Pro.

imagery. An early study in Libya made use of the Landsat imagery (Figure 2.10) by dividing the survey area into facets with recognizable landforms, in order to compare past and present land usage, and analyze livestock and human carrying capacities. The team advocated that the imagery subdivided the landscape so they could have more effective sampling strategies. Terrain types included plateaus, uplands, colluvial slopes, aeolian sand and gravel deposits, fluvial sand and gravel deposits, upper colluvial slopes, and wadi deposits, with the land divided in three categories: Upland areas not suitable for farming or settlement, colluvial slopes suitable for settlement but not farming, and alluvial wadis suitable for farming but not settlement. The land facet maps showed that 54 percent of known archaeological sites could be found in alluvial wadis suitable for farming and not settlement, yet this landscape type only covered 23 percent of the total survey area (Allan and Richards 1983). This is, however, a cyclical argument, as it is based on a known distribution of sites, which is almost certainly biased.

Early applications of radar imagery in Belize and Guatemala allowed archaeologists to address questions relating to Mayan economic structure. With the Maya lowlands measuring more than 250,000 km^2 and being covered in dense vegetation, archaeologists needed a way to see beneath the thick canopy. The distribution of ancient sites was not well understood, and with 300 known Mayan centers, archaeologists assumed a number of ancient features remained to be discovered. Using airborne side-looking radar (initially developed as a method to map the surface of Venus) mounted on a CV-990 airplane, archaeologists took photos during 1977, 1978, and 1980. After examining the

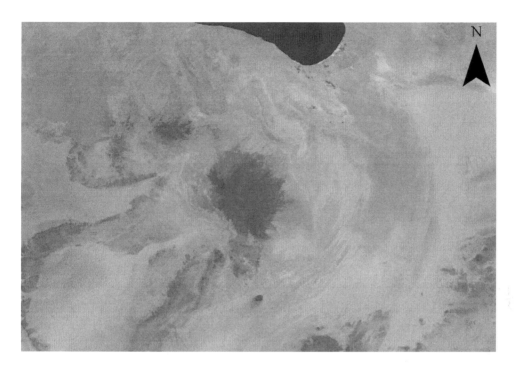

Figure 2.10 Landsat image of Libya (scale 1:1248 km), image courtesy of NASA World Wind.

data via light transparencies, the team noted grid patterns that were likely to represent Mayan canals. A number of non-archaeological features appeared as well, including modern roads and logging trails, so the team required detailed ground survey to confirm the features. With so many of the archaeological features observed during the ground survey being too small to show at the minimum radar resolution of 15 m, archaeologists recognized that future seasons would require higher resolution imagery. The minimum and maximum areas of late classic canal systems were estimated based on the total area of agricultural drainage. As a result, the team achieved a far better understanding of southern lowland classic Mayan uses of intensive agriculture and insights into Mayan economic structure (Adams *et al.* 1981; Adams and Wood 1982). Anthropological issues relating to the application of remote sensing also became apparent (Fedick and Ford 1990; Willey 1990; Folan *et al.* 1995; Fedick *et al.* 2000). Anthropologists could now utilize remote sensing to address cultural gaps across time and space through the examination of demographic changes, settlement patterns, and housing. Archaeologists also now advocated a move beyond the salvaging of sites to the evaluation of landscapes necessary to conceptualize past behavior (Posnansky 1982).

The early remote sensing work of Farouk El-Baz, now the Director of the Center for Remote Sensing at Boston University, contributed to the development of archaeological remote sensing. Expeditions to the Egyptian western desert verified patterns seen from Gemini and Apollo-Soyuz photographs, as well as Landsat imagery. Dune encroachment, now a major environmental and conservation problem, was noted at this early date (El-Baz 1980). The total area of reclaimed desert in Egypt between 1965 and 1975

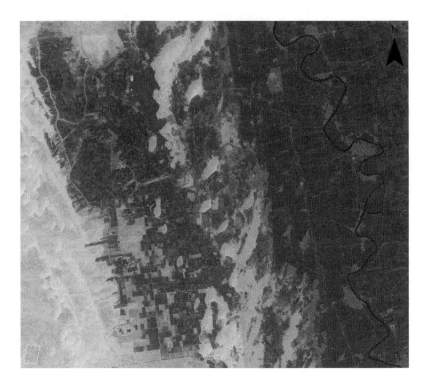

Figure 2.11 Land reclamation in Middle Egypt (scale 1:3413 m), note the areas being extended to the West for future development, 2008 image courtesy of Google Earth™ Pro.

could be calculated from space as being 1000 km^2, which is still increasing today (Figure 2.11) (El-Baz 1984). Human impact on the landscape was also examined by El-Baz with observed changes in water levels within Lake Nasser. Construction of the Aswan high dam aided the prevention of major damage from higher water levels recorded from 1973–84. From 1981–4, significant falls in the general water levels were noted in Lake Nasser (El-Baz 1989), perhaps indicating a drier period. El-Baz has spent the past 30 years advocating the use of satellites to map patterns of human behavior, in particular in relationship to changing environments.

Nothing had more of an effect on the direction of satellite archaeology in the mid-1980s than the first conference on Remote Sensing in Archaeology. Held in 1984, it was sponsored by NASA and organized by Tom Sever and James Wiseman; and called "Remote sensing and archaeology: Potential for the future." Taking place at Stennis Flight Center's National Space Technology Earth Resources Laboratory in Mississippi, 22 leading archaeologists attended several days of presentations and discussions on the applications of remote sensing to archaeology. The scientific implications of this conference cannot be understated, and support for the conference, with funding from NASA, NSF, and National Geographic, shows how much importance was attached to its implications for archaeological research. At the conference, NASA scientists and archaeologists presented the results of ongoing research at Poverty Point, Chaco Canyon, in addition to providing a comprehensive overview of remote sensing, various satellite types (including Landsat, SIR-A, TIMS, and LIDAR), and potential applications to archaeology. Archaeologists were invited by NASA's Jet Propulsion laboratory to examine the flight path of the SIR-B RADAR, to see if it coincided with their research area (Sever 1985; Sever and Wiseman 1985). This meeting resulted in several significant long-term archaeological partnerships: For example, NASA archaeologist Tom Sever joined Payson Sheets' research team in Costa Rica to examine the use of remote sensing in tropical environments. This would lead to the testing of thermal data from TIMS, 2-band SAR, and Landsat data in the Arenal region (Sheets and Sever 1988). In the report stemming from the NASA meeting, Tom Sever noted:

> New technologies to which they were introduced may represent the kind of scientific breakthrough for archaeology in the second half of the 20th century that radiocarbon dating was in the first half of the century ... advancements in these areas are occurring so fast that unless archaeologists apprise themselves of the technology now, they will be unable to keep pace with the technology in the near future. Moreover, they may find that developers and pot hunters have once again beaten them to the field.
>
> (Sever and Wiseman 1985: 2–11)

Some 25 years later, these words continue to ring true.

Ongoing work in Europe, the USA, and the Middle East continued to show the applications of satellites to archaeology. The First International Conference on Remote Sensing and Cartography in Archaeology was held 1983, where the establishment of a European remote sensing center in Strasbourg was announced (now known as the European Space Agency). Work in Morton Fen, Lincolnshire, UK (Figure 2.12) proved the feasibility of using Landsat imagery in wetland environments for site predictive modeling (Donoghue and Shennan 1987; Donoghue and Shennan 1988). Aerial thermography in Leksand, Dalecarlia, central Sweden showed buried walls and foundations during the mapping of the top layer of ground (Lunden 1985). In the USA, Landsat satellite imagery aided in predictive modeling in the Delaware Plains regions, with the team considering regional combinations of variables rather than exact site locations to great success (Custer et al. 1986). Even larger applications of satellite imagery were yet to be realized, as maps of Syria-Palestine (Cleave 1985) were created from seven Landsat images and aided in a UNESCO-funded survey project in Libya(Dorsett et al. 1984). The SIR-A Synthetic Aperture Radar Mission, flown in 1981 to support terrestrial geologic mapping over the Western Sahara desert, detected the so-called "radar rivers," or former riverbeds beneath the sand of the Sahara, viewed in Figure 2.13. A survey in a 6 × 15 km area along the edges of the river system found sites dating to the Middle-Late Neolithic, which archaeologists claimed to be temporary settlements. The team, led by Fred Wendorf, saw the "radar rivers" as bedrock basins dug out by wind, which would have collected soils and water during a more arid periods. Thus, they would have supported more seasonal occupations (Wendorf et al. 1987). Other scientists suggested these were rivers with long-term occupation, and that Wendorf did not survey in an appropriate area in relationship to the area exposed in the SIR-A imagery. Excavations revealed material from roughly 200,000 years ago, which the team suggests as the time the rivers dried up to smaller watering holes (McHugh et al. 1988, 1989). Satellite imagery played a critical role in the initial archaeological analysis, and allowed for the

Figure 2.12 Landsat image of Morton Fen, Linconshire, England (scale 1:609 m), image courtesy of NASA World Wind.

first major archaeological debate over the meaning of remote sensing results. Work with future satellite missions will help to shed light on the occupation sequences in Egypt's Western Desert.

1990s

In the late 1980s, major gaps in the utilization of GIS and remote sensing could be traced to a lack of funding and training, yet archaeologists recognized their potential (Fagan 1989; Myers 1989; Wiseman 1989). However, the early 1990s saw a change in this respect. The overall percentage of archaeological remote sensing articles would grow as well: 10 percent of articles cited in this volume date to the 1980s, while 30 percent date to the 1990s. In the first published overview of the use of satellites in archaeology (Limp 1989), the authors pointed out a nine-year gap in publications, due to a reluctance to embrace the new technology. While the book provided a detailed overview in three chapters of how multispectral satellite imagery analysis works, a chapter on ongoing remote sensing work in the Ozarks (a mountain range located in Missouri, USA), as well as a chapter on GIS and remote sensing integration, the book criticized a number of publications for doing only visual interpretation. Visual detection still continues to contribute immeasurably to the fields of aerial archaeology and satellite archaeology. The authors stressed usage of satellite technology for the detection of long-term sites, but stated the technology could not be used for locating short-term camps. The authors also emphasized locating transportation and communication networks in addition to the

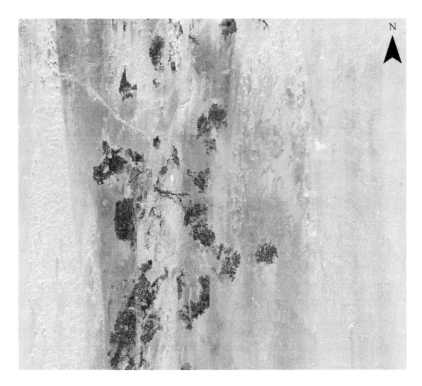

Figure 2.13 Kharga Oasis, Egypt (scale 1:6192 m), where the ancient river systems can be seen using Quickbird satellite imagery, 2008 image courtesy of Google Earth™ Pro.

environmental zones other projects had identified (Lorralde 1991). Other archaeologists recognized the importance of integrated usage of GIS and remote sensing (Madry and Crumley 1990), but training was still an issue.

A critical topic discussed by the authors was the lack of literature on predictive modeling. Flaws in the general idea of predictive site modeling were noted in a 1993 review of GIS in archaeology. Ultimately different models and techniques are needed to predict the location of sites in different environments (Davis 1993). As discussed by early remote sensers, a wide range of imagery types should be utilized in research. Additionally, there is no "one size fits all" approach to predictive site modeling: One would not necessarily run the same algorithms to detect sites in the desert as for sites in a rainforest. Was this the practice employed with early remote sensing in archaeology? As satellite archaeology evolved as a scientific practice, it has shown archaeological sites appear in locations that relate to landscape geomorphology, weather patterns, and historical changes. Remote sensers do not predict where archaeological sites will appear based solely on mathematical models: They also use historical data, much of it based/building on the pure visual analysis referenced above. Working in a mathematical vacuum has and always will be dangerous for satellite archaeologists, which underscores the need to use as much data as possible, evident from the very conception of the field.

Satellite archaeology started to attract the attention of the global media, with a 1992 article in the *New Scientist* discussing ongoing archaeological remote sensing projects.

These projects included NASA archaeologist Tom Sever's work in New Mexico and Costa Rica. Sever's work found that Landsat could be too coarse for most archaeological work, while Thematic Mapper simulators and the TIMS jet over Chaco Canyon, in NW New Mexico, revealed many previously unknown walls, roads, and other features, as well as footpaths in Costa Rica (Sheets and Sever 1991). This work showed applications of remote sensing in both humid and dry climates, and proved that the timing of imagery could be an issue. By 10 a.m., the roads in Chaco Canyon could not be distinguished from the surrounding terrain due to heat. Another project mentioned in the article was that of archaeologist Frederick Cooper, who found sites in the Western Peloponnesus of Greece (Figure 2.14). He used imagery that connected richer vegetation with scrub oak atop archaeological features (Joyce *et al.* 1992). Now archaeologists realized that satellites could not only be used to locate sites, but could be used to find vegetation that predicted site locations. Earlier concerns relating to larger climatic issues were also beginning to be explored. Reports appeared from other parts of the world: Comparing Landsat imagery to aerial photography in Thailand showed how well the satellites detected moated sites. Imagery only detected 75 percent of mounds and 23 percent canals (Parry 1992), but the satellite imagery could bridge the gap between predictive site modeling and archaeological site detection. Locating environmental features that could forecast archaeological site locations proved useful in Cumbria, UK, where Landsat imagery located areas of peat (Cox 1992). Landsat satellites also played a role in not only detecting archaeological sites, but also in examining overall prehistoric water management strategies (Kidder and Saucier 1991).

The application of satellite imagery to the archaeology of specific regions, focusing on more anthropological applications (Conant 1990), started in the mid-1990s (McGovern

Figure 2.14 Landsat image of Western Peloponnesus of Greece (scale 1:5300 m), image courtesy of NASA World Wind.

1995; Deo and Joglekar 1996). The book *Ancient road networks and settlement hierarchies in the New World* (Dubois 1996) had two studies focusing on applied remote sensing studies of ancient transportation and religious uses of the landscape (Sever and Wagner 1991; Sheets and Sever 1991). Additional reviews then appeared discussing applications of satellites to archaeology (Palmer 1993), with the first set of collected reports focusing on remote sensing appearing in the book *Applications of Space-age Technology in Archaeology* (Behrens and Sever 1991). Remote sensing was also making its way into general books on archaeological science (Tykot 1994), which, along with the *New Scientist* article, encouraged the more widespread usage of the technology.

Global media attention was also given to the discovery of the "lost" city of Ubar, located through a combination of SIR-A imagery, ground survey, and excavation (Fiennes 1991; Blom 1992). SPOT satellite imagery also started to play more of a role in archaeological site detection (Brewer *et al.* 1996; Guy 1993). Broader usage of satellite imagery also included using RADAR to map Angkor Wat (Anon. 1995), Landsat imagery to map prehistoric canal systems in Arizona (Showater 1993) as well as combining geological predictive modeling with archaeological feature location (Carr and Turner 1996). Satellite archaeology publications remained consistent throughout the 1990s, with an average of 10–14 publications per year appearing in peer-reviewed archaeology journals or reference volumes. The launch of 5 m resolution SPOT 4 in 1998, IRS-1C (India's remote sensing program) in 1995, Landsat 7 in 1999 with enhanced thematic mapper capabilities, and the 1 m resolution IKONOS satellite opened the door for even more applications in archaeology. At this time, some archaeologists lamented the overall lack of aerial archaeology, claiming that it was being largely neglected as a major survey tool (Palmer 1995). In the 1970s, aerial archaeology aided in the process of survey for site locations, and there was tremendous growth in the field of aerial archaeology from the mid 1980s to the present. This complimented the increase of satellite remote sensing in archaeology from the same time period. This does not take away from the importance of aerial photographs for archaeological work: They should be used in conjunction with satellites for the best overall results.

2000 onwards

From the late 1990s onwards, satellite archaeology has become even more prevalent in archaeological publications (Mahanta 1999), press coverage, conferences, grant applications, and courses, whether through individual classes or overall programs on landscape archaeology. Through the support of international organizations such as UNESCO, countries are being encouraged to consider the additional usage of satellite in preserving their cultural and natural heritage. UNESCO's remote sensing programs (directed by Mario Hernandez) support non-invasive techniques for heritage conservation. Via various space technologies, UNESCO conserves and monitors natural and cultural listed sites. UNESCO's remote sensing office has 24 international agencies and 16 universities or research institutes as partners, and also supports education and training in remote sensing to children and adults worldwide. In 2000, the project "Culture 2000—European Landscapes: Past, Present, and Future," sponsored by English Heritage, Belgium, Germany, Italy, and Hungary, started promoting archaeological field schools, the use of aerial and ground-based surveys for archaeological investigation, outreach, and additional fieldwork (Bewley and Musson 2006), thought the active use of satellite imagery was only a very minor component of this project, focusing as it did largely on "traditional" aerial archaeology. This was followed, in 2001, by the "Open initiative on the use of space technologies to monitor natural and cultural heritage of UNESCO sites," a cooperation framework to manage, monitor, and observe, formed of the International Working Group of Space Technologies for World Heritage, including UNESCO, NR-ITABC (Italy), GORS (Syria), the Chinese Academy of Sciences, NASA, ETH (Switzerland), and others.

Conferences in the 1990s and 2000s have featured additional panels or subsections devoted to the use of remote sensing in archaeology, with an increase in the number of outlets for research papers over the 10 years. Panels involving remote sensing have been a part of the Society for American Archaeology and American Institute of Archaeology conferences for over 10 years, while the Computing Applications in Archaeology (CAA) conference has long supported GIS and remote sensing papers. The American Schools for Oriental Research (ASOR) conference first supported papers in a panel on "Geographical Information Systems (GIS) and archaeology," which is now called "Geographic Information Systems (GIS), Remote Sensing, and Archaeology." The first international conference on remote sensing in archaeology, held at Boston University in 1998, was described in *Archaeology* magazine (Wiseman 1998). Now, papers on satellite archaeology are an accepted part of most archaeology conferences.

China organized the next major satellite archaeology conference in 2004, with the first International Conference for Remote Sensing Archaeology, attended by over 100 international scholars (Figure 2.15). China can claim the most comprehensive satellite archaeology program in the world (Banks 1995). Under the National Center for Remote Sensing, there are 10 Chinese regional centers for remote sensing in archaeology, supported by the Chinese Academy of Sciences and the National Remote Sensing Center of China (Jingjing 2006). China's developing space program has contributed to this support: China has launched 50 satellites from five spacecraft as part of the Chinese space program. The 2004 conference showed the international participants the cutting-edge research being done by a group of well-trained and motivated scholars. The overall purpose of remote sensing in China is to integrate the natural and humanistic sciences. The Center for Remote Sensing Archaeology, located in Beijing beside the 2008 Olympic complex, and founded in 2001, hosts a number of computers and state of the art 3D visualization systems. Students and professional Chinese archaeologists receive extensive training in the application of remote sensing for archaeological site detection, preservation, and protection (Liu *et al.* 2002).

In fact, the United Nations recently approved the National Center for Remote Sensing in China to be a major regional center on remote sensing and heritage, showing the global recognition of China's research on satellite archaeology. The first chinese general conference on remote sensing in archaeology was held in Beijing in 2002, with discussions of remote sensing on the Qinshihuang Mausoleum as well as other lesser, but no less valuable, archaeological sites throughout China, including cities along the Silk Road. The Joint Laboratory of Remote Sensing Archaeology did not apply aerial photographs to archaeology in China until the mid-1990s, but found that historical images could be invaluable for comparing past and present landscapes (Huadong and Changlin 2004). For example, aerial photographs from the 1960s around Sanmenxia Reservoir (Figure 2.16) showed how significant modern development has affected past remains (Tan *et al.* 2006). Chinese archaeologists have applied a wide range of remote sensing

Figure 2.15 Photograph of the International Conference on Remote Sensing Archaeology, image by Sarah Parcak.

to their research, including hyperspectral imagery, high-resolution data, and varying image types. Teams have focused on the Shangqui area, using old maps and black and white aerial photographs to locate old water transportation routes, canals, locks, and various relic landscapes (Li *et al.* 2004).

Remote sensing training schools held in Europe are teaching the next generation of landscape archaeology specialists through a comprehensive series on hands-on classes and fieldwork. Stemming from the Second International Conference on Remote Sensing in Archaeology, intensive field schools in Italy provide training in archaeological survey, GIS, remote sensing, and all issues relating to landscape archaeology analyses and landscape reconstruction (Campana and Forte 2006). The International Space University, active for over 20 years in Strasbourg, France, also encourages students to consider space-based archaeological applications. In the summer 2007 session, ISU students produced *START: Space Tools Supporting Archaeological Research and Task*, which had case studies from the Middle East, Central America, and South America discussing how satellite archaeology could be cost-beneficial to general archaeological survey and issues relating to landscape reconstruction.

In the past seven years, additional high resolution satellites, such as Quickbird, and hyperspectral satellites, such as the EO-Hyperion, have appeared on the market with significant implications for archaeological site detection. Nearly 300 publications have appeared since 2000 with satellite archaeology as their primary focus. Now, archaeologists are more likely to see remote sensing and GIS in university and cultural resource management (CRM) advertisements. As a result, many PhD students have taken an interest in the subject area. Although this chapter has provided an overview of the

Figure 2.16 Sanmenxia Reservoir, China (scale 1:2166 m) note significant urbanization, 2008 image courtesy of Google Earth™ Pro.

overall advances of remote sensing in archaeology in relationship to the field of aerial photography, their differences and similarities should be emphasized. Aerial photography still plays an important role in archaeology in countries where aerial photography is permitted (Lemmens *et al.* 1993; Fassbinder and Hetu 1997; Doneus 2001).

Many examples of its use can be found in the UK (Bewley 2001; Halkon 2006; Deegan and Foard 2008), France (Bezori *et al.* 2002), Italy (Campana *et al.* 2006; Bohemia (Godja 2004), El Salvador (Fowler *et al.* 2007), China (Zhang and Wu 2006), Syria (Weiss 1991), Israel (Riley 1992), Egypt (Zurawski 1963; Vercoutter 1976), Australia (Connah and Jones 1983), and Armenia (Hakobyan and Palmer 2002).

Jordan, in common with much of the Middle East, has extensive historic aerial photography, and more recently, with the support of the royal family, extensive aerial reconnaissance and oblique aerial photography has been taken of the country specifically for archaeological purposes (Kennedy and Bewley 2004). In other projects archaeologists have used aerial photography to examine water management strategies (Kennedy 1995) and discover early Roman period roads (Kennedy 1997). In the USA, aerial photography archives exist in each state, but are generally accessed through each state's forestry division. The AmericaView program (www.americaview.org) has connected the digital and photographic archives of each state, making it possible for archaeologists in the USA to have access to a broad range of free satellite imagery and

Figure 2.17 Boston, Massachusetts orthophoto (scale 1:3456 m), imagery courtesy of NASA World Wind.

aerial photographs. These images are also viewable on NASA's WorldWind program (Figure 2.17).

Examining how aerial photography and satellite archaeology can be used together is a topic not broached regularly by archaeologists, and belongs in a chapter on the history of satellite archaeology (and is also discussed in chapter 4). Without aerial photography, satellite archaeology would simply not exist. Each has advantages and disadvantages, which should be discussed, with the ultimate aim of using them together for archaeological analysis. Aerial photography has become a subspecialization within archaeology, just like satellite archaeology. Both require specialized training. Archaeologists, as a whole, still rely primarily on visible means to identify archaeological sites with aerial photographs and satellite images. This visible aspect of satellite images should not be overlooked, as it can allow the creation of maps in areas where they do not exist and make it possible to search for features over large tracts of land before any survey season. Satellite imagery can have a full range of the electromagnetic spectrum, thus making them valuable to use in tandem with aerial photographs. Both fall within the broader category of archaeological remote sensing, and are two halves of the same coin. It should be noted that LIDAR, TIMS, and other airplane-based imaging systems are not considered aerial photographs, although some of the issues affecting aerial photography quality can affect their imaging capabilities.

The similarities of the two landscape visualization techniques provide a good starting point. Both are in use by archaeologists today, and can contribute immeasurably towards the detection of previously unknown archaeological sites and features. Without prior training and ground experience, it becomes easy to misinterpret both sets of data, as well as "see" something that may or may not exist. Experienced remote sensers and aerial photography specialists will rely on previous studies and maps to determine potential features, especially if an anomaly occurs outside a known archaeological landscape. Cloud cover can inhibit each as well. Without good ground control points or maps, it is not possible to rectify or georeference imagery. Scale of data is important in each instance. Ground-truthing to locate major archaeological features (such as entire sites, large features such as barrows, etc.) may be different than ground-truthing for smaller features (such as walls) where excavation may be necessary. Everything depends on the presence or absence of material culture remains in the ground.

With aerial photography, the spectral resolution may be limited, yet the spatial resolution can be as good as 0.1 m (Quickbird high-resolution satellite imagery only has 0.6 m resolution). In aerial photographs, archaeologists can view aerial photographs in the visible and IR part of the electromagnetic spectrum, with the IR range of photographs in the 700–900 micron range of the spectrum, called near-infrared, or NIR). Satellite imagery provides data within more narrow parts of the IR, which may be useful in determining specific vegetation types. Importing aerial photographs into a GIS along with analyzed satellite imagery will allow archaeologists to have access to the highest resolution imagery as well as the non-visible part of the spectrum. Valuable comparisons can be made between features viewable on satellite imagery and on aerial photographs, seen in Figures 2.18a and 2.18b. Perhaps the features cannot be seen on visible Quickbird imagery, yet an unusual spectral signature appears, thus revealing the same ancient feature as a higher resolution aerial photograph.

Imagery quality is another topic archaeologists need to consider when using aerial photographs or satellite imagery. When any individual takes photos with film, they are in analog format, or providing a physical representation of an image. In order to view the imagery on a computer screen, the imagery needs to be converted to digital format. There are two ways to convert from analog to digital, either through scanning the print of the film, or the negative. Any time data is one step removed from its original format, quality is lost, so it is recommended that the scans be done from the negative. It is becoming increasingly rare for film processing labs to have the expertise to develop IR film. This has changed with the advent of digital cameras, which now have the ability to take photos in the IR range. These cameras will aid aerial archaeology immeasurably, especially as their spectral range increases.

Cost is another factor when using aerial photography and satellite imagery. While many satellite images are free online, costs can range up to many thousands of dollars. Going to an archive to copy aerial photographs can be relatively inexpensive, while many aerial photos can be found on free online archives. A good computer and remote sensing software are required to do satellite imagery analysis, in particular a computer with a high-end processor for dealing with larger satellite imagery datasets. Both aerial photographs and satellite images can also require significant storage space. Licenses for remote sensing software can cost thousands of dollars, although free programs are available online for downloading with more limited processing functions.

Getting the exact imagery needed for project work can also be a factor. With higher-resolution satellite imagery, if the funding is in place, one can specify the exact coordinates to be imaged. Aerial photography, using digital photos, can also image a specific area, but can have problems associated with weather. If the conditions are poor,

Figure 2.18 The Alamo, Texas: (a) Orthophoto (1:45 m); and (b) Quickbird imagery (scale 1:61 m), 2008 image courtesy of Google Earth™ Pro and NASA World Wind.

the plane cannot take off, or the pitch of the plane can be affected by winds that may not be evident on the ground. An archaeological team may need an image from an exact time of day to get the right lighting, which is easier to achieve with aerial photography. Satellite images are consistent in that each image of an area is taken at the same time of day. This aids with archaeological work using high-resolution Quickbird imagery, which is taken at 10.30 a.m. each morning. If the lighting is not correct, a team can control sunshade on imagery analysis programs. Varying factors affect imagery quality: Wind or camera issues can affect the quality of aerial photographs, while technical problems can affect the quality of satellite imagery. This happened in 2003 with Landsat imagery being striped, which can be seen in Figure 2.19. One relative advantage of aerial photography is its ability to test varying film types at different heights to compare results, as Gwil Owen (1993) has tested at Tell el-Amarna in Middle Egypt using a balloon. Other projects have used kites (Rossi and Ikram 2002), helicopters (Eisenbeiss *et al.* 2005, 2006; Eisenbeiss and Zhang 2006), or powered parachutes (Hailey 2005) with great success.

Every archaeological project will have different needs, yet there are few archaeological projects that could not benefit from using both satellite imagery and aerial photographs. Aerial photographs provide a historical landscape perspective, which the satellite imagery allows archaeologists to see additional features buried by soil, covered by vegetation, or partially to completely obscured by modern towns. Importing this data into a GIS with satellite data and maps will allow archaeologists the ability to analyze multiple levels of data. Archaeologists should recognize the benefits and weaknesses of

Figure 2.19 Southern California, 2004 striped Landsat image, image courtesy of NASA.

remotely sensed data as it is used, but should recognize it is through complimentary data sources that a more complete record of the past can be built. Having a holistic approach makes this possible.

Aerial photography is the closest thing archaeologists have, at present, to real-time imagery, making imagery taken from kites or balloons (Tartarton 2003) helpful during excavation. Given the restricted nature of aerial photographs in many areas of the world these methods have proven successful in obtaining similar results to air photography (Summers 1992; Knisely-Marpole 2001). Archaeologists also have additional control over balloons or blimps: One team used a blimp with a remotely controlled 35 mm camera with fixed base points for map creation (Summers 1992). Additional control may be provided through the use of a helikite, which allows (with no wind) for exact height control (Verhoven and Loenders 2006). If the quality of satellite imagery improves to a resolution of 10 cm or less, will the field of aerial archaeology merge with satellite archaeology? This is a likely outcome.

A note of the importance of individual scholars working in the field of satellite archaeology also belongs in a chapter on its history. From the beginning, NASA archaeologist Tom Sever has been a champion of the use of satellite archaeology, and has a worldwide reputation for his generosity regarding information sharing (whether providing satellite imagery or advice) and general support, in addition to his comprehensive scholarship. Without his encouragement, it is highly unlikely that many archaeologists would have even considered using satellites in their work in the early 1980s. Those archaeologists went on to encourage the present generation of young scholars writing many of the articles on satellite archaeology. Senior scholars in the field of satellite archaeology include James Wiseman, Payson Sheets, Elizabeth Stone, Ronald Blom, and Farouk el-Baz, who are also known for their willingness to help and support junior remote sensing scholars. This spirit of support can perhaps be connected to the general global nature of remote sensing, and is a notable feature at conference meetings. It is hoped that future generations of remote sensing scholars will carry on this torch: Only by having a global perspective on the past that we can begin to shed light on past changes to predict future outcomes.

3

SATELLITE IMAGE TYPES

Overview

Prior to conducting remote sensing research, an archaeological team must decide what imagery to use for their analyses. Where to start is not something previous authors have discussed in an in-depth fashion. This chapter will address many issues related to choosing appropriate satellite imagery for nearly any research area in the world. Before ordering a satellite image, information should be obtained about the cost, date, resolution, spectral coverage, spatial coverage, and availability of each imagery type under consideration. How will archaeologists know what imagery to consider for each landscape type? Teams may not be aware of the specific archaeological features they might encounter, or the most appropriate imagery to choose. Covering every type of known satellite imagery in this chapter would not help, as there are dozens of satellite image types. As with all technology, additional advances will make possible the use of an even wider variety of imagery types. For the purposes of this book, it is prudent to focus on the most common satellite imagery utilized by archaeologists, shown in Table 3.1. Important information will be provided for each imagery type, so archaeologists will have a good understanding of the spectral, spatial, and temporal properties of each, as well as the advantages or disadvantages for use in satellite archaeology.

Once archaeologists and remote sensing specialists have identified what imagery is most appropriate for their landscape type(s) and potential features, they can begin the process of ordering imagery. This chapter will walk potential users through the process ordering of satellite images from a variety of online sources, describing the general features of satellites one would need for ordering in a specific situation. Some imagery is easily obtained, while other types might require additional training or expertise. It is important to know how each satellite image type can be applied to archaeological work; however, until the imagery is acquired, it cannot be analyzed. This chapter allows for a discussion of how to obtain imagery. Viewing and analyzing archaeological features and landscape types with satellite imagery will be reviewed in great depth in Chapter 4 and 5.

The imagery types and imagery viewing online systems to be reviewed in this chapter include Google Earth™, NASA's World Wind, Corona High Resolution Space Photography, KH-7 and KH-9 imagery, Landsat, SPOT, ASTER, SRTM, IKONOS, Quickbird, SIR-A, SIR-B, SIR-C and X-SAR, as well as imaging systems flown on aircraft (LIDAR and SAR). Reference books on remote sensing cover additional types of imagery, and the images discussed in this chapter are by no means the only satellite images archaeologists may apply in their research. They are, however, the most versatile,

Table 3.1 Comparative satellite imagery and multiple imagery viewing programs table (prices are current as of January 1, 2009)

Satellite image	Cost	Spatial resolution	Spectral resolution
Google Earth™	Free–US$400	10cm–30 m	Visual
World Wind	Free	10 cm–30 m	Visual-pseudocolor
Corona/KH7/KH/9	$30	1–120 m	Visual
KVR-1000	US$1000–4000	2–3 m	0.49–0.59 μm
Landsat	Free–US$600	15–60 m	Visible (0.45–0.69 μm) IR (0.76–0.90 μm) Middle (1.55–1.75 μm) Thermal (10.4–12.5 μm) Mid-IR (2.08–2.35 μm)
SPOT	US$1200–11,750	0.8–20 m	Visible (0.43–0.47 μm; 0.50–0.59 μm; 0.61–0.68 μm) Near infrared (0.79–0.89 μm) Mid-infrared (1.58–1.75 μm)
ASTER	Free–US$80	15–90 m	VNIR (0.520–0.600 μm; 0.630–0.690 μm; 0.760–0.860 μm; 1.600–1.700 μm) SWIR (2.14–2.225 μm; 2.360–2.430 μm) TIR (8.125–8.825 μm; 8.925–9.275 μm; 10/120–11.650 μm)
SRTM	Free	0.3–90 m	N/A
Quickbird	US$10–28 per km²	0.6–2.4 m	Panchromatic (0.526–0.929 μm) Blue (0.445–0.516 μm) Green (0.506–0.595 μm) Red (0.632–0.698 μm) Near IR (0.757–0.853 μm)
IKONOS	US$7.70–13.20 km	1–3.2 m	Panchromatic (0.526–0.929 μm) Blue (0.445–0.516 μm) Green (0.506–0.595 μm) Red (0.632–0.608 μm) Near IR (0.757–0.853 μm)
SIR-A/B/C/X-SAR	US$40–50	15–45 m	HH, VV, L-Band, X-Band, C-Band

Note: IR = infrared, VNIR = Visible Near Infrared, SWIR = Shortwave Infrared, TIR = Thermal Infrared.

and largely, cost-effective, imagery types available; many are free, low-cost, or available for purchase.

Although the focus of this book is not specifically on satellite imagery analysis, some basic remote sensing terms and concepts are presented for the reader's convenience.

A discussion of the electromagnetic spectrum and what it represents is also crucial, given the overall importance of the electromagnetic spectrum in remote sensing. Satellites orbit the Earth collecting radiation reflected from its surface. These are what are known as "passive" satellites, collecting reflected radiation. "Active" satellites, such as RADAR, send pulses of energy to the Earth's surface, and reconstruct surfaces based on the amount of time it takes for the energy to return to the satellite. Passive satellites record data in different parts of the electromagnetic (EM) spectrum. Thus, what is the EM spectrum, and how is it related to satellite remote sensing? (see Figure 3.1) The EM spectrum is essentially a grouping of different types of radiation. It ranges from gamma rays and X-rays to radio and TV waves. The range recorded by satellite imagery ranges from the visible spectrum (which human beings can see) through the near, middle, far infrared (IR) and thermal portions, which humans cannot see. Fast moving particles such as the X-rays and gamma rays create higher energy radiation, while radio and TV waves have the lower energy radiation. We know that the Sun is a higher source of radiation, and falls under the "ultraviolet rays" category in the EM spectrum. EM radiation travels in wave-like patterns with different energy amounts. Satellites record this data in what are known as "bands." Each band within a satellite image corresponds to a specific range of the EM spectrum. Each satellite image has a varying number of bands composed of very different types of EM spectrum data, shown in Figure 3.2. "Hyperspectral" satellite images record data in multiple parts of the EM spectrum. For example, ASTER imagery records data in multiple bands, including the IR and thermal parts of the EM spectrum.

When viewing satellite data using remote sensing programs, the user specifies three bands to view simultaneously. By blending the data in varying combinations of bands, it is possible to make areas of interest appear more clearly. For instance, the thermal part of the EM spectrum shows reflected heat, while the IR part is useful for viewing different types of vegetation. A customary way to view satellite imagery is referred to as 3-2-1 RGB (red, green, blue) as shown in Figure 3.3. In other words, the third, second, and first bands of that particular satellite image are displayed in the red, green, and blue parts of the EM spectrum, respectively. In satellite imagery analysis, the term µm (micron) refers to wavelength, and is the measurement used to describe the electromagnetic spectrum (Jensen 1996: 40; Lillesand *et al.* 2004: 5–9). A measurement chart is provided in this chapter to show what parts of the EM spectrum each satellite image covers. As each satellite image type is described with reference to its archaeological applications, more specific remote sensing terms will be defined.

Google Earth™

Advantages: free; available 24 hours a day; global coverage; accessible from Mac or PC; easy to use; can upload photos or points; can view 3D landscapes

Disadvantages: non-global, high-resolution coverage, some areas have 30 m resolution coverage; limited 3D coverage of landscapes; difficult to see sites in dense canopy

Features: can view entire archaeological sites, buried walls, and architecture, can view old river courses in desert locations, etc.; users can upload photographs of sites and features

Resolution: .6m–.30m

Accessibility: http://earth.google.com/

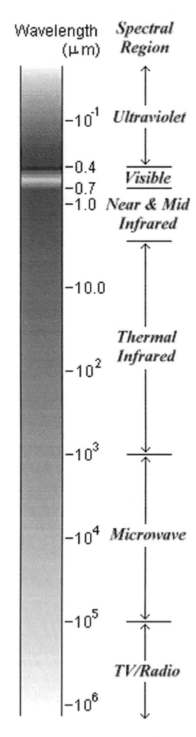

Figure 3.1 The electromagnetic spectrum, adapted from http://www.ghcc.msfc.nasa.gov/ archeology/images/remote_sensing/spectrum.gif, Image courtesy of NASA.

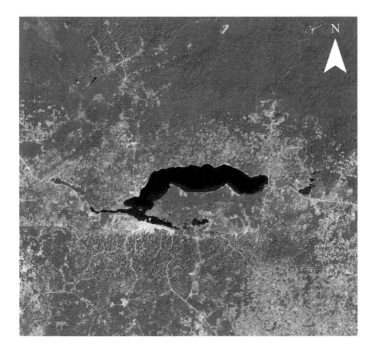

Figure 3.2 Lake Peten Itza, Guatemala, 4-3-2 RGB Landsat (scale 1:14400 m), the lighter pixels represent vegetation, 1988 image courtesy of NASA.

Cost: Google Earth, free; Google Earth™ Plus, US$20; Google Earth™ Pro, US$400 or free

Discussing Google Earth™ and its potential applications for satellite archaeology is a straightforward way to introduce archaeologists to the different types of satellite imagery available. Google Earth™ is a commonplace tool in everyday life; many people have zoomed in on their homes, universities, or favorite archaeological sites. For future archaeologists, Google Earth™ allows for a Victorian-style "grand-tour" every day. Young children, using Google Earth™, can visit Machu Picchu, The Great Wall of China, Stonehenge, and The Pyramids of Giza (Figure 3.4), all before bedtime. This will certainly have an enormous impact on the future of archaeological practice. University students no longer have to rely on black and white aerial photographs to see larger landscape views of archaeological sites discussed in class: Lecturers now use images from Google Earth™ in most archaeological lectures, bringing landscapes and past peoples to life. Such vivid imagery also allows for detailed discussions about the impact the modern world is making on past landscapes. Students can see for themselves how the cutting down of rainforests in Central America is affecting the illegal antiquities market, or how archaeological sites in Iraq have changed in appearance to look like "waffles" due to the extensive looting taking place there.

Google Earth™ is the most well-known public gateway to satellite imagery. Most people see Google Earth™ images on evening news broadcasts. Accessing Google Earth™ is straightforward: One goes to the Google Earth™ website, downloads one of three

Figure 3.3 Lake Peten Itza, Guatemala, 3-2-1 RGB Landsat (scale 1:14400 m), visual image, 1988 image courtesy of NASA.

versions (Standard, Plus, or Pro), and then zooms to any place in the world. Locations are accessed by name or by coordinates. Google Earth™ allows the user to turn on or turn off geographic content, roads, borders, labels, extensive global photo-gallery, terrain, and 3D buildings. Users have the ability to mark particular places of interest and polygons can be drawn over features, with varying colors, shapes, and lines. Users also may choose to have polygons appear at a certain altitude, or specific exact latitude and longitude. Paths can be drawn between one or more features, while users can produce their own imagery overlays, uploading their personal images or GIS data. All of these features have applications to archaeological work: Teams can upload features or photos from a season with a special "team only" user name and password, protecting information about locations of archaeological sites from looters.

Google Earth™ was started by Keyhole, Inc., and was formerly called Earth Viewer before Google acquired it in 2004. The name changed to Google Earth™ in 2006. Google Earth™ is essentially a virtual 3D globe with imagery and topographic data from multiple satellite image types, aerial photographs, and the Shuttle Radar Topography Mission (discussed later in this chapter). Google Earth™ can be run on a PC or Mac, but cannot currently be run on Linux. Resolution varies on Google Earth™: Some cities in the USA have aerial photography with a resolution of .1 m (Figure 3.5) while other parts of the world have resolutions ranging from 0.6 to 30 m. Being a publicly available resource has resulted in controversy, as both India and Thailand have asked Google Earth™ to remove higher resolution imagery revealing their military bases.

Figure 3.4 Giza Pyramids, Egypt (scale 1:351 m), 2008 image courtesy of Google Earth™ Pro.

Google Earth™ has refused to comply, underscoring the "democratization" of once highly classified information (Hafner and Rai 2005).

Google Earth™ Pro is required to download the highest resolution imagery, with a license fee of US$400, while the Google Earth™ Plus version is available for US$20. Using the free version of Google Earth™ provides only grainy imagery when zooming in on areas with otherwise higher resolutions. Academic researchers can obtain a free version of Google Earth™ Pro by writing to Google Earth™. This is a valuable resource, as Google Earth™ Pro allows its users to download TIFF image files at a resolution of 4800 dpi, compared with 1000 dpi for regular users, and allows users to import their GIS data, create movies, and have access to technical help.

Google Earth™'s applications in archaeology are being explored (Handwerk 2006), yet this form of remote sensing technology has disadvantages when used alone. While Google Earth™ is free and publicly available, there may be restricted access to this site in developing nations. Only some regions of the globe are covered by high-resolution satellite imagery and aerial photographs (Figure 3.6). Over large parts of Africa, the resolution of the satellite imagery can range from 30 m pixel resolution from Landsat imagery to 5–10 m resolution via SPOT satellite imagery. One can never predict the imagery quality in any given area, and imagery on Google Earth™ is constantly being updated. Most images are current to three years, while many are not stitched together correctly. Place names can also be incorrect. Lack of detailing in some mountainous regions can make some areas difficult to view, especially the shadow sides of tall features.

The advantages of using Google Earth™ for archaeological research outweigh the disadvantages, but the disadvantages must be acknowledged. Google Earth™ can provide

Figure 3.5 Timothy Dwight College (scale 1:58 m), Yale University, New Haven, CT, with the arrow pointing to a Ginko tree in the Timothy Dwight courtyard. Note the construction visible to the left in Silliman College, 2008 image courtesy of Google Earth™ Pro.

similar information to aerial photographs. The highest resolution satellite imagery in Google Earth™, Quickbird, has a standard 0.6 m resolution, while aerial photographs have widely varying resolutions, depending on the height of the airplane, type of film used, and general flying conditions, but can have a resolution as good as 10 cm. Sites that archaeologists know to exist, but do not appear in publications, can be examined in detail using Google Earth™. Being able to create wide-format maps for publication and in-field use are two additional valuable uses of Google Earth™. Potential applications of Google Earth™ and other imagery in the future of landscape archaeology are important for assessing ongoing issues relating to looting and urbanization. For example, one important contribution that Google Earth™ provides is determining which archaeological sites are being destroyed by urbanization or looting. Through comparison of current Google Earth™ imagery with past aerial photographs, or older satellite imagery, archaeologists might be able to see if looting has taken place at the sites. This is naturally limited by the single shot of Google Earth, which may not be recent enough to capture evidence of looting. Archaeological sites can be understood in their broader landscapes, especially in Google Earth™'s 3D mode.

Are we able to say one is truly "doing" remote sensing when using Google Earth™? Although the answer to this question is frequently "yes," in reality this action only deals with a small percentage of remote sensing possibilities. For example, most people can learn to zoom in on a target on a satellite image to find a mound or monument.

Figure 3.6 Aerial photograph of Trinity College (scale 1:61 m), Cambridge University, UK, the small dots in the courtyard are people, 2008 image courtesy of Google Earth™ Pro.

However, it is not curently possible to view multispectral imagery on Google Earth™, so no detailed remote sensing analysis is possible. Remote sensing offers a far greater range of applications. When utilizing satellite imagery, the bias, error rates and methods of analysis must be discussed in detail.

Even though Google Earth™ can be used to locate buried walls or structures using higher or lower levels of vegetation, or cropmarks, as seen in Figure 3.7, it is also possible to misinterpret what may exist beneath fields. In the fields surrounding the West Bank of Luxor, a number of possible crop marks appear that seem to be the paths of tractors. The image date is one of the most important features in satellite remote sensing: Seasonality influences crop types and weather patterns, which in turn influence how specific features such as archaeological sites can be viewed or revealed. In the Egyptian Delta, a majority of the Google Earth™ imagery currently online was taken in either late spring or fall, in the early part of the growing seasons, owing to the discernable height of the adjacent crops. A database for Delta sites thought to be "destroyed" assisted with locating specific areas in which to search for cropmarks (see www.ees.co.uk/deltasurvey). Due to the nature of the technology, the ability for archaeologists to rely upon cropmarks to indicate such well-defined subterranean features remains "hit and miss," as there are many variables which might affect possible cropmarks.

When Google Earth™ imagery is updated it aids ongoing excavation work. Visiting Google Earth™ on two different occasions provided the author with an "in progress" view of the 2002 and 2004 excavation seasons at the fortress of Tell Ras Budran, dating to ca. 2200 BC, located 160 km south of Suez along the West Coast of the Sinai Peninsula.

Figure 3.7 Cropmarks in the East Delta, Egypt (scale 1:201 m), near the well-known site of Tanis, the cropmarks are the lines in the vegetation at a 30-degree angle, 2008 image courtesy of Google Earth™ Pro.

The current image of the site was taken 3.5 years after the 2004 excavation season. Although the fort was not discovered via Google Earth™, one can explore the overall relationship between the fortress and other potentially undiscovered sites in the region (Figures 3.8a and 3.8b). Roughly 4 km to the south, within the compounds of several commercial and other installations that bound the coastline, several features appear on Google Earth™ with similar shapes to Tell Ras Budran. These circular "structures" appear to be roughly half the size of the northern fortress, and lie within a large wadi system that could have provided the expeditions with seasonal water. The forts appear to be within fire or smoke signaling distance, but lay beyond viewing distance of the northern fortress. Without Google Earth™, it would not have been possible to detect these sites, owing to their location within restricted areas. However, any remote sensing can only aid in selecting specific areas for survey, and cannot replace on-site ground assessments. Thus, while the first three circular features appear to be related to Tell Ras Budran based on their shape, size and location, it is hoped that permission will be granted for surface visits to confirm these assessments.

What does the future of Google Earth™ hold for archaeology? Many individuals have viewed Google Earth™ images of well-known archaeological sites along around the world (Beck 2006; Conroy *et al.* 2008; anonymous NASA report 2005). However, all archaeologists should consider the use of Google Earth for site survey in their areas of interest for the discovery of potential buried and unknown sites. This is not the work of one individual. Most governments have their own cultural heritage management bodies, and sharing new discoveries made with Google Earth™ could assist foreign governments with preserving and managing previously unknown sites. Archaeologists should keep in mind the limitations of Google Earth™, yet also should be aware of all that it can offer when used in combination with detailed ground survey work. The overview presented here is preliminary in that it summarizes what is and is not possible using Google Earth™. Much remains to be learned from publicly available satellite imagery, and Google Earth™ is one technological innovation that will continually be improved over time. Archaeologists can draw diverse conclusions from crop marks or apparent "sites" that appear on Google Earth™, but confirmation is needed through subsequent (and additional) remote sensing, ground survey, coring, excavation, and subsurface survey using magnetometer, resistivity, or ground penetrating radar.

NASA World Wind

Advantages: free; available 24 hours a day; global coverage; accessible from PC, Mac, or Linux; easy to use; can upload photos, points, or GIS data; can view 3D landscapes
Disadvantages: non-global, high-resolution coverage, some areas have 15–30 m resolution coverage; do not know exact time or date of imagery
Features: can view entire archaeological sites; can see buried walls or architecture and old river courses in desert locations; can see landscape changes over time, including vegetation changes
Resolution: 1–30 m
Accessibility: http://World Wind.arc.nasa.gov/
Cost: free

World Wind is an online global imagery viewing program, created and run by NASA, with many similarities to Google Earth™. The biggest difference is that the full version of World Wind is entirely free. Released in 2004, individuals can view not only the Earth, but can also view satellite imagery of the Moon, Mars, Venus, Jupiter, stars and galaxy. Viewers can use World Wind on PC, Macintosh and Linux systems. Over five million placenames exist in World Wind. Within the USA, aerial photographs have provides photographs with resolutions that range from 10 cm–1 m. Outside the USA, resolution can range from 15–30 m. Unlike Google Earth™, there are 13 possible views of the Earth, including NASA's "blue earth," composed of MODIS satellite imagery. Also unlike Google Earth™, users can compare Landsat imagery from 1990 with Landsat imagery from 2000 to track broad landscape changes. It is also possible to see the Earth using pseudocolor, or false-color imagery, and to see the Earth in NASA's scientific visualization system. This includes seeing satellite imagery that shows scenes of agriculture, the atmosphere, the biosphere, climate indicators, the cryosphere, human dimensions, oceans, the solid earth, spectral/engineering, and sun–earth interactions. These views include events such as the African fires in 2002, an aurora over the North Pole and changes before and after the El-Nino event.

While World Wind is not as user friend as Google Earth, it has more advantages from a remote sensing perspective. Google Earth™ is, essentially, a geographic viewing program. World Wind can be used for commercial and personal purposes by importing data through adding placemarks, paths, lines, polygons, ESRI shapefiles, 3D texture, Python or Direct X texts, layers for higher resolution imagery, and additional scripts.

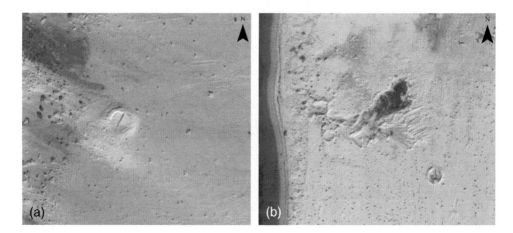

Figure 3.8 Tell el-Markha Fort, South Sinai, Egypt (scale 1:130 m) with: (a) the 2004 excavation visible from space; (b) the so-called southern "forts" (scale 1:81 m) need investigation, 2008 images courtesy of Google Earth™ Pro.

In this sense it is not as limited as Google Earth™. Users can also adjust sun shading and atmospheric scattering, two important remote sensing adjustments that affect how features appear within imagery. The Digital Elevation Model created in World Wind is generally more accurate than Google Earth™. Imagery used within World Wind include Landsat 4 and Landsat 5 imagery, visible bands of Landsat 7 imagery, and black and white and color aerial photos, mainly of the USA, but also of other cities in the world. It is possible to download and use images from World Wind, in remote sensing programs.

Viewing landscape changes through time is something that has become essential in archaeology: Only by understanding broad landscape changes can archaeologists make plans for preserving and protecting archaeological sites. One does not need intensive training to understand World Wind, although a scientific background helps with using the full range of tools available for use. By examining longer-term landscape changes and false-color imagery, shown in Figures 3.9a and 3.9b, archaeologists can get a better sense of what multispectral imagery can do for archaeology, and will aid in the remote sensing learning process. An online guide, "World Wind Central", can aid in importing user data, which makes World Wind a far more versatile tool than Google Earth™ for archaeologists.

Corona High Resolution Space Photography/KH-7/KH-9

Advantages: preserves views of many vanished landscapes; high resolution; inexpensive; fairly straightforward use; global coverage; viewable on any image viewing program
Disadvantages: imagery can be grainy; image distortion; need negatives for best resolution; non-multispectral; need to georeference; sometimes memory intensive
Features: can view entire archaeological sites, buried walls and architecture, vanished landscapes and associated environmental features
Resolution: .6–150 m

Accessibility: http://www.usgs.gov
Airphoto: http://www.uni-koeln.de/~al001/airphoto.html
Cost: US$30 per scanned negative

Corona high-resolution satellite photography is imagery that has become quite valuable to archaeologists, due to its high resolution, low cost, ease to obtain, and its value in recording landscapes now built over or destroyed, shown in Table 3.2. Declassified in 1995 by an executive order from President Bill Clinton, the US government released 860,000 images (taken between 1960 and 1972) to the public at the cost of reproduction only, now available through the United States Geological Service, EROS Data Center, near Sioux Falls, South Dakota. Initially, the military represented the body with primary access to this technology, with many advances taking place during the Cold War (Macdonald 1995). The declassified intelligence imagery was code-named Corona, Argon, and Lanyard, named after the satellites which took the imagery. The Corona satellite photographs represent the first global imagery dataset of the Earth, and can aid in filling in data gaps between aerial photographs from the 1940s–1950s and the earliest multispectral images from the 1970s. The CORONA systems included the names KH-1, KH-2, KH-3, KH-4, KH-4A, and KH-4B, while the ARGON system was designated KH-5 and the LANYARD system KH-6. The image resolution of each system varies greatly, from 1–2m for the KH-4B system to 460 feet for the KH-1 system (Fowler 1996b; Fowler 1997b). The imagery is inexpensive, costing US$30 for scanned negatives for negatives (which is generally recommended over prints, for each time the original information is copied the quality degrades). This imagery can be ordered through an electronic catalogue of the United States Geological Service Global Land Information System (GLIS), or through the Earth Observing System Data Gateway (EOS). It is important to view the actual image before purchasing, because more than 40 percent of the imagery contains cloud cover. Imagery comes digitally in "strips" measuring 2.8 × 29.8 inches (Figure 3.10).

KH-7 and KH-9 space photography represent 50,000 images taken between 1963 and 1980 by the KH-7 Surveillance System and the KH-9 Mapping System. These images were the second set of imagery declassified by the National Imagery and Mapping Agency's "Historical Imagery Declassification Conference: 'America's Eyes: What we were seeing.' " The KH-7 satellite took images of Soviet and Chinese nuclear installations as part of the Cold War and flew from July 1963 to June 1967. KH-7 imagery covers an area 22 km wide and between 9 km and 740 km in length with as good as a 0.6–1.2 m pixel resolution. The KH-9 satellite mission, flown from 1973 to 1980, was dedicated to mapping. Each KH-9 image comes in either black and white or color satellite photos, covers an area of 130 × 260 km at a scale of 1:500,000 and has a pixel resolution of 8–10 m (Fowler 2004). The world is generally well-covered by the KH-7 and KH-9 missions (black and white), while KH-9 color images only cover select parts of the globe. When used as part of the author's research in Egypt's Delta regions, it was found that the KH-7 imagery did not have as high a resolution as the scanned KH-4B Corona imagery.

Corona imagery is one of the most widely-used datasets for archaeological research (Fowler 1997a, 1997b; Mathys 1997; Fowler and Fowler 2005), especially in the Middle East. This is due largely to the 1111 mission of the KH-4B system, one of the primary missions mapping the cease-fire between Egypt and Israel. In some cases, the ground

Table 3.2 Corona and KH-9 imagery adapted from http://edc.usgs.gov/products/satellite/declass1.html

Image type	Film size	Micron size	File size	Cost (US$)	Resolution
KH-1; KH-2; KH-3; KH-4; KH-4A KH-4B (Corona)	2.8 mm × 29.8 inches	Ranges: 21 μm (1200 dpi); 14 μm (1800 dpi); 7 μm (3600 dpi)	36 MB × 4 files 80 MB × 4 files 319 MB × 4 files	30	1–8m, varies
KH-5 (Argon)	5 × in	Ranges: 21 μm (1200 dpi); 14 μm (1800 dpi); 7 μm (3600 dpi)	40 MB 80 MB 325 MB	30	varies
KH-6 (Lanyard)	5 × 25 in	Ranges: 21 μm (1200 dpi); 14 μm (1800 dpi); 7 μm (3600 dpi)	40 MB 80 MB 325 MB	30	varies
KH-7	9 in × variable	Ranges: 21 μm (1200 dpi); 14 μm (1800 dpi); 7 μm (3600 dpi)	Ranges: 95 MB × 4 files 214 MB × 4 files 854 MB × 4 files	30	0.6–1.2 m
KH-9	9 in 18 inch	Ranges: 21 μm (1200 dpi); 14 μm (1800 dpi); 7 μm (3600 dpi)	Ranges: 117 MB × 2 files 262 MB × 2 files 1.3 GB × 2 files	30	8–10 m

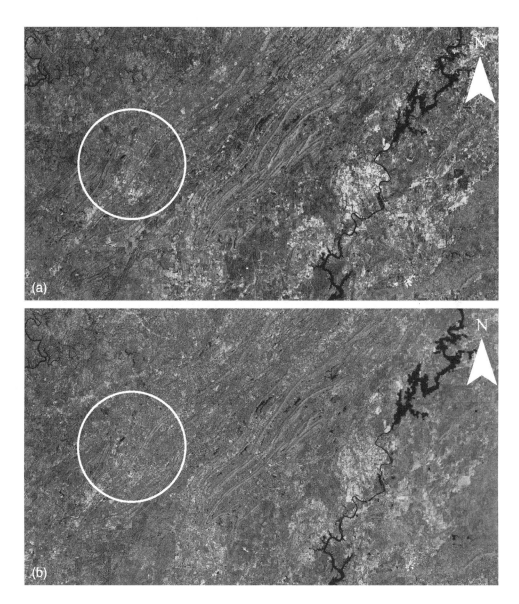

Figure 3.9 Landsat images of Alabama in: (a) 1990 (scale 1:25792 m); and (b) 2000 (scale 1:25792 m), the growth is represented by the slightly lighter pixel colors, images courtesy of NASA World Wind.

resolution of this mission can reach 1 m. Corona imagery has helped to reveal locations of "hollow ways," or tracks between settlements of Syria (Ur 2003), and has assisted with confirming the location of previously unknown settlement sites in Egypt (Parcak 2007a, 2007b). Population increases and urbanization have greatly altered landscapes over the past 40 years, and Corona imagery can help detect features long-since buried, destroyed, or altered by modern farming techniques (Donoghue *et al.* 2002). Sites now gone due to dam construction or additional building can be mapped, and in same cases, relocated, using Corona imagery (Donoghue *et al.* 1998; Kennedy 2002). Corona images also allowed an intensive landscape assessment to be made in South Siberia's Altai Mountains. A cold climate had preserved many of the burial mounds built by nomads. Archaeologists studied the relationship of burial mounds to cemeteries in a survey of more than 3000 sites (Goossens *et al.* 2006).

Corona imagery has a number of disadvantages compared to other forms of satellite imagery. It is essentially high resolution black and white space photography, and does not contain any color or multispectral data. Imagery from the Corona satellites cannot be used alone to create maps due to significant s-shaped distortion: Different resolutions appear on different parts of the imagery, with a smaller scale appearing the further one gets from the main axis of the imagery. Issues exist with the pitch and yaw (or movement) of the satellites. Stereoscopy, or viewing imagery in 3D, is possible with forward and backwards-looking imagery taken from the same locations, but imagery displacement and distortion can cause issues with height differences. Additionally, both images, though taken from the same point, can have different viewing angles and contrast. Good ground control points are needed to correct these problems, which can be an issue with landscape changes over time. Multiple imagery datasets can also correct parallax, or displacement of an image when viewed from multiple locations. Different GPS tools can be used to help correct the view depending on the level of accuracy needed for ground control points (Goossens *et al.* 2006).

Corona imagery's many advantages make them attractive to archaeologists everywhere. Prior to 2005, archaeologists needed to scan their own Corona imagery. Now, the USGS website sends digitally scanned negatives at 23, 14 or 7 µm. Although this saves time, archaeologists have determined that the best results occur from Corona imagery when it is scanned at a minimum of 5 µm. Experimentation by the author comparing 10 µm and 5 µm scanned Corona imagery produced noticeable results. At 5 µm, the imagery's details proved to be sharper, with small lines defined more clearly, shown in Figure 3.11a when compared to Figure 3.11b. In order to georeference the Corona data, either imagery maps of study sites or unchanged ground control points are needed for plotting points. The latter can be difficult to obtain, especially in areas not yet surveyed. Google Earth™ can help in determining if an area is unchanged if maps are not available, but only in cases where higher resolution data exists. Computer programs such as ArcView or Airphoto allow for georeferencing. Airphoto, available for a small cost on the "Bonn Archaeology Software Package" homepage, is a program developed by renowned aerial archaeology specialist Irwin Scollar. The program was developed especially for any types of aerial imagery with significant amounts of distortion, and requires a small amount of user input other than selected ground control points. Airphoto also creates Digital Elevation Models (DEMS), or 3D digital landscape reconstructions.

Imagery quality will vary, but the KH-4A, KH-4B and KH-6 systems have the best resolution and quality for archaeological work. Earlier images may be useful for documenting site change. The KH-4B system solved problems, including satellite vibrations and static electricity, and had a far better film quality than previous systems with 160 line pairs per nanometer. Even though the 1970 KH-4B mission has an approximate 1 m resolution, atmospheric conditions affected additional imagery (Donoghue *et al.* 2002). Corona imagery can provide forward and back views on the

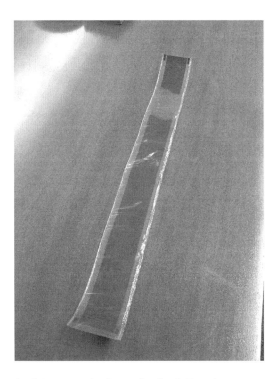

Figure 3.10 Photograph of Corona strip, image by Sarah Parcak.

same areas, and can be used as orthophotos to create basemaps for archaeological projects (Goossens *et al.* 2005; Kennedy 1998). While cropmarks may be difficult to view on Corona imagery, the imagery can detect buried features on archaeological sites. Corona imagery of Tell Tebilla, a ca. 600 BC site in the eastern Egyptian Delta, led to the discovery and subsequent excavation of a temple enclosure wall (Mumford 2002, 2003).

Studying a region in depth in Corona imagery prior to georeferencing can give a "feel" for the landscape. In some instances, a landscape will be little altered in over 40 years, thus facilitating archaeological analysis. These cases are rare: Most archaeologists comment on how landscapes have changed over a 40-year period. Viewing Corona imagery is similar to viewing black and white aerial photography. Choosing easily recognizable ground control points such as large rocky outcroppings, unchanged buildings, or other significant landmarks aid in the georeferencing process. Once georeferencing is complete, archaeologists should spend time describing a known archaeological site, which can assist in picking out features not noticed previously. Perhaps the site changed little in 40 years, or perhaps farming has destroyed a large portion of it. Features such as hollow ways may not be apparent in modern-day imagery. Noting any unusual features in the landscape or on top of archaeological sites will assist with additional imagery analysis. Importing Corona imagery into a GIS allows comparison with multispectral remote sensing data, as turning the Corona layer on or off may show archaeologists how much landscapes have changed.

KVR-1000

Advantages: preserves high resolution views of vanished landscapes; fairly straightforward use

Disadvantages: expensive; some image distortion; non-multispectral, non-global coverage

Features: can view entire archaeological sites, buried walls or architecture, and large parts of sites now removed due to urbanization over the past 20 years

Resolution: 2–3 m

Accessibility: http://www.npagroup.com/imagery/satimagery/russian.htm

Cost: US$1000–$4000

KVR-1000 imagery, from Russian COSMOS satellites released in 1987 (Fowler 1995a; Donoghue and Galiastagos 2002), is high-resolution black and white space photography, with a resolution of 2 m. Resolution ranges between 2–4 m, with each image covering an area of 40×40 km or 40×160 km at a scale of 1:220,000. Images come in scanned strips measuring 18×18 cm. Through private companies, each user can request imaging for specific areas if they are not available online. Currently, all parts of the world are available for order except Russia. Images come as either "raw" (meaning there are no geometric or radiometric corrections) or "orthorectified", meaning that these corrections have been applied with a $+/-20$ m accuracy without ground control points. The high costs of KVR-1000 imagery make it prohibitively expensive for archaeologists, compared with Quickbird high resolution satellite imagery; typically costs range from US$1000 for 16 km, US$2500 for 1000 km; US$1600 for 160 km; and US$4000 for 1600 km. Spectral data is restricted to the visual part of the spectrum, from 510–760 nm. Archaeologists have not used KVR-1000 photography as widely as other types of satellite imagery. The first tested use of KVR-1000 detected Stonehenge from space (Fowler and Curtis 1995). It has also helped to detect previously unknown Roman roads and Turkish walls (Comfort 1997a, 1997b, 1998, 1999). Until the cost of KVR-1000 imagery comes down, it is unlikely it will play a major role in future archaeological remote sensing research.

Landsat

Advantages: global coverage from 1972–present; multispectral; can analyze a wide range of landscape types

Disadvantages: non-high-resolution banding on imagery from 2003–present; requires knowledge of remote sensing analysis; need remote sensing programs for multispectral use

Features: mutispectral data highlights vegetation, soil and geological features associated with past remains; shows how remains can be viewed in seven bands of the EM spectrum

Resolution: 15–80 m

Accessibility: http://www.landsat.org (click on "search for imagery" to access free data) http://glcfapp.umiacs.umd.edu:8080/esdi/index.jsp

Cost: free–US$600

Landsat imagery, first recorded in 1972, has had the broadest usage in archaeology of all the types of satellite imagery. This is due to its low cost, worldwide coverage, and the numerous techniques one can apply with it. Landsat imagery of a majority of the globe can be freely obtained on several websites (listed above). With resolutions ranging from 15—80 m, Landsat imagery's versatility makes it useful to archaeological projects with budgets that make higher-resolution data such as IKONOS and Quickbird prohibitive. Landsat imagery is most versatile in diverse landscape conditions because of varying band lengths in the electromagnetic spectrum (Figure 3.12). The band lengths can be combined in various ways in remote sensing programs, or can have algorithms or computer programs applied to group together like pixel types (Table 3.3). Each band of Landsat data is useful for viewing different aspects of the spectrum, and can be combined in three-band patterns to make distinct certain parts of the landscape. The Landsat satellite image band combination most used by archaeologists in their analytical work is a 4-3-2 RGB (IR, red, green). These bands (2, 3, and 4) are useful for investigating the reflectance (green) of healthy vegetation, soil-boundary, and geological boundary analyses, as well as vegetation discrimination and vegetation biomass, respectively (Jensen 1996: 40; Lillesand *et al.* 2004: 5–9). Vegetation detection from space is closely connected to archaeological discovery: Different types of vegetation, compared to "typical" vegetation types for the region, can group on top of or next to archaeological sites. Archaeological features are also affected by water sources, making band 5 another useful band for archaeological remote sensing analysis.

The "orthophoto" section of http://www.landsat.org provides archaeologists Landsat imagery from the 1970s, 1980s, 1990s, and 2000s. Some imagery on the commercial http://www.landsat.org site costs US$50, which is discounted from the standard price of either US$450 or US$600. Landsat images cover a 185 × 185 km area and are sun synchronous, meaning that they follow the path of the sun on a 16-day cycle around the Earth. Landsat imagery appears in a path and row format: Satellites follow a consistent orbit around the earth, recording imagery data over set paths and rows. The path and row numbers of a Landsat image are available on the Landsat website by clicking on any part of the globe. To download free imagery, one needs to choose the year of interest and then the path folder of interest. In each path folder, additional folders with row numbers are visible. After opening the appropriate row folder, the imagery is downloaded in a

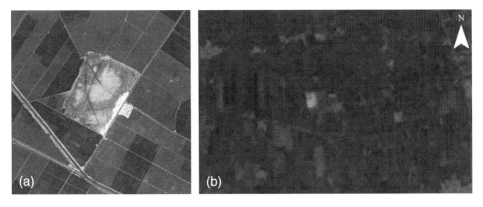

Figure 3.11 Corona image of Tell Tebilla, Egypt (scale 1:585 m): (a) 1972 image courtesy of US Geological Service; and (b) Landsat image of Tell Tebilla (scale 1:1600 m), note the lack of detail in the Landsat image, image courtesy of NASA World Wind.

Table 3.3 Chart of Landsat band values, adapted from http://geo.arc.nasa.gov/sge/landsat/17.html

Band	Spectrum type	Part of spectrum (μm)	Analytical capabilities
1	Visible (blue)	0.45–0.52	Soil, land-use and vegetation characteristics
2	Visible (green)	0.52–0.60	Reflectance (green) of healthy vegetation
3	Visible (red)	0.63–0.69	Soil-boundary and geological boundary analysis, as well as vegetation discrimination
4	Infrared	0.76–0.90	Vegetation biomass
5	Middle infrared	1.55–1.75	Can assess the amount of water in plants and assists in hydraulic research
6	Thermal infrared	10.4–12.5	Geothermal activity and vegetation classification
7	Mid-infrared	2.08–2.35	Geological rock formations

zipped format. Typically, each band is downloaded separately into the same folder, after which the bands are combined into a multilayered image using one of a number of remote sensing software packages.

How can users chose the correct version of Landsat imagery for their archaeological work? Landsat 1 imagery, with a spatial resolution of 80 m, is generally too coarse to view anything but the largest monumental archaeological features, but can aid in examining longer-term environmental trends. Landsat 2 and 3 satellites, with 80 and 30 m pixel resolutions, respectively, followed in 1975 and 1978. With the 1982 and 1984 launch of the Landsat 4 and 5 satellites, which contained 30 and 120 m pixel (with the 120m resolution) in the thermal band (or the band most useful for detecting surface temperatures), researchers now have access to seven bands of information from the electromagnetic spectrum. With the earlier Landsat satellites, researchers could only utilize five bands of information. The Landsat 4 and 5 bands match the banding of Landsat 7 data, save the thermal pixel size. Landsat 6 failed in its launch, but the successfully launched Landsat 7 ETM+ ("Enhanced Thematic Mapper," with a 30 m pixel resolution for every band except thermal, which has a 60 m pixel resolution) provides the most current images of the earth of the Landsat satellite group. Landsat 7 ETM+ imagery also has 15 m panchromatic imagery. Through various computer programs, the user can merge the 15 m data with the multispectral 30 m data to create 15 m multispectral data. In 2003, a technical malfunction caused the Landsat 7 ETM+ imagery to have a series of horizontal stripes. This is corrected through destriping the imagery with sections of earlier imagery from the same month. Most archaeological projects use both the Landsat 4 or 5 imagery and the Landsat 7 ETM+ imagery.

Over the past 30 years, archaeologists around the world have conducted many studies using Landsat satellite images (Stargardt 2004). With free imagery, cost is not necessarily a prohibitive factor, although the area covered by the free imagery is sometimes limited. Features 15 m or greater in size appear quite well on Landsat 7 ETM+ imagery, although features smaller than a few meters in size can appear in Landsat images if they contrast sharply with their surroundings (Lillesand *et al.* 2004: 377–414). For example, roads

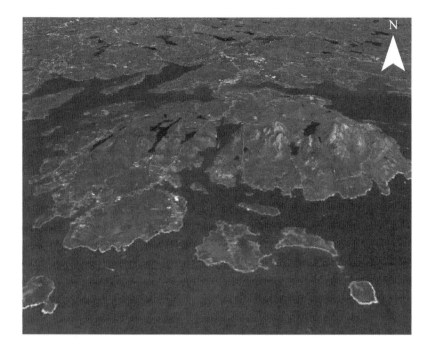

Figure 3.12 Mt. Desert Island, Maine, Landsat image (scale 1:2245 m), draped over SRTM data, image courtesy of NASA World Wind.

or paths only 5 m wide in the desert show up on Landsat imagery due to major color differences in the pixels (Figure 3.13).

Landsat imagery has a number of advantages and disadvantages for archaeological research, with the main advantage being its multispectral data. The various analytical methods employed to analyze such multispectral data will be discussed in greater detail in Chapter 4, while this section will deal with the broad archaeological questions one can approach using Landsat data. With a broad range of multispectral data, Landsat satellites can detect not only archaeological sites and features, but environmental factors associated with past sites. The first archaeological study using Landsat imagery helped to map Angkor Wat through mainly visual site detection (Limp 1992a). By using one of Landsat's bands in an image viewing program (whether through Irfanview, Adobe® Photoshop®, or ArcGIS®), general visual assessments can be made of an archaeological area of interest by individuals without remote sensing training. One does not generally have to identify the exact location of an archaeological site with Landsat imagery. Without satellite imagery, where would one begin to look for features of interest (see Chapter 7)? Coarser resolution imagery can help archaeologists to zoom in on potential environmental indicators. One study used Landsat imagery to locate potential peat bogs in the UK to suggest areas for archaeological reconnaissance (Cox 1992).

An overview of the methodologies in studies using Landsat imagery has implications for archaeological remote sensing, especially considering the diverse types of techniques applied in studies across the globe. One archaeologist used a Landsat 5 image in the southeast region of Mallorca, Spain, to investigate Roman field division systems. Multispectral

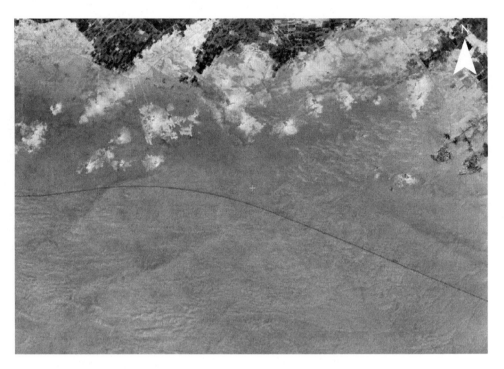

Figure 3.13 Sahara Desert (scale 1:7712 m), note that the road running E–W is visible from space on 30 m Landsat data, even though it is only 5 m wide, image courtesy of NASA World Wind.

analysis did not play a significant role in identifying the ancient field systems; instead, the study looked at rural patterns by correcting the images' geographical points and applying basic image enhancement techniques. Although ground-truthing did not play a role, the study observed suggestive patterns (Montufo 1997). Use of Landsat's infrared bands helped to detect various architectural features surrounding Stonehenge (Fowler 1994a, 1995a), although this can be hard to view, as seen in Figure 3.14. The IR bands have assisted in identifying many features on sites invisible through the use of conventional aerial photography. In some cases Landsat analyses are combined with airborne remote sensing data to great success. One study used airborne remote sensing data and Landsat data to identify sites for future investigation in Scotland (Winterbottom and Dawson 2003)

Not all uses of Landsat images are intended to detect specific archaeological sites; past environmental indicators can be just as valuable. Along the west coast of Sinai, Landsat satellite imagery detected water sources connected with past mining expedition campsites dating to between ca. 2500–1800 BC (Mumford and Parcak 2002, 2003). In northeast Thailand, Landsat imagery's IR bands detected an area covered with ancient settlements and canals, archaeological mounds, and smaller dams. There was an 80 percent success rate reported for detecting known mounds, with implications for detecting previously unknown ancient sites (Parry 1992; Palmer 1993). Changes in water sources also affect how populations move and change. Landsat imagery has

Figure 3.14 Stonehenge, UK (scale 1:142 m), located just below the cross-hatch mark, image
courtesy of NASA World Wind.

allowed a study on changing river courses and their affects on human groups in the
Mississippi region (Showater 1993; Parssinen *et al.* 1996), as well as Andean lowland
and the migration of Indians caused by sudden river relocation. Landsat data aided in
discovering faults near the site of Sagalassens, southwest Turkey, which appeared to have
caused the abandonment of the site in the mid-7th century AD (Sintubin *et al.* 2003).

Archaeologists have enumerated that Landsat imagery resolution is too coarse to
allow intersite or intrasite remote sensing (Wynn 1990). Although Landsat imagery
cannot detect small structures, it can detect walls thinner than 15 m or stone features if
they contrast spectrally with the structures surrounding them. For example, at the site of
Mendes in the northeast Egyptian Delta, one can see the granite naos (a large, ceremonial
stone structure built to house images of deities), which measures 3 × 3.5m, in the central
part of the site, shown in Figures 3.15a and 3.15b. The granite stone of the naos contrasts
spectrally with the limestone platform beneath it (Soghor 1967). Archaeologists should
evaluate Landsat's abilities on a case-by-base basis. Vegetation, in particular in rainforest
areas, can obscure archaeological features beneath the forest canopy, causing temporal
issues to become important in imagery acquisition. Certain features may or may not
appear depending on the time of year; therefore, archaeologists need to obtain Landsat
imagery accordingly. Landsat imagery is best used for grouping together similar pixel
groups through imagery analysis, or for running additional algorithms to clarify spectral
data. At the very least, Landsat images can be used to create basemaps and to assess broad
landscape changes over time.

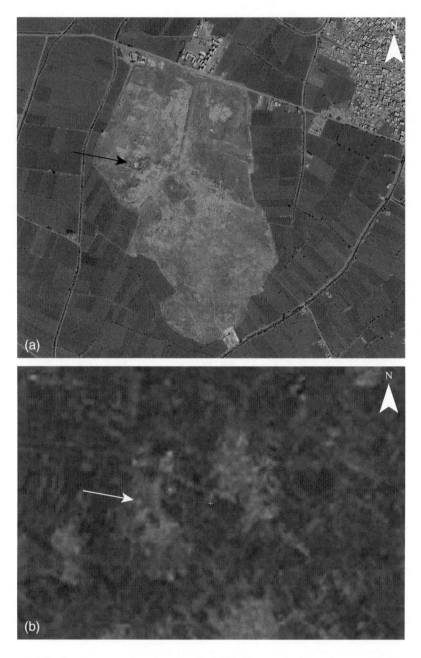

Figure 3.15 Mendes, Egypt, comparing: (a) a Quickbird image (scale 1:548 m); with (b) a Landsat image (scale 1:981 m) note that the arrows point to the granite naos in each image, 2008 image courtesy of Google Earth™ Pro and Landsat image courtesy of NASA World Wind.

SPOT

Advantages: global coverage from 1978–present; multispectral; can analyze wide range of landscape types

Disadvantages: requires knowledge of remote sensing analysis; need remote sensing programs for multispectral use

Features: suitable for detecting vegetation changes associated with archaeological sites; panchromatic data can detect smaller architectural features

Resolution: 0.8 m (panchromatic), 5–20 m (multispectral)

Accessibility: http://www.spot.com/web/SICORP/425-sicorp-price-list.php; http://www.americaview.org/

Cost: US$1200 (normal scene, 5 m panchromatic, 20 × 20 km, or 1/8th scene); US$11,750 (orthorectified 2.5 m color merge, 60 × 60 km, full scene), see pricing list on the website above; 35–85 percent discount for academic researchers through the AmericaView program.

SPOT, or System Pour L'Observation de Terre, launched in 1978 by the French government, is utilized in all areas of scientific research, and is especially well suited for mapping and producing digital elevation models through stereo pairs. SPOT 1, 2, 3, and 4 launched in 1986, 1990, 1993, and 1998, respectively, have a 10–20 m pixel resolution (Lillesand *et al.* 2004: 439–53). SPOT 5, active since 2001, has multiple pixel resolutions in both color and black and white, ranging from 0.8 m to 20 m. SPOT 5 contains five bands, comprised of the visible (RGB), near IR and mid-IR bands, shown in Table 3.4. The two bands in the IR make SPOT a useful satellite image for archaeological investigations that involve vegetation (Guy 1993; Hijazi and Qudah 1997), shown in Figure 3.16. One can order imagery from SPOT's website through a global server. SPOT provides educational discounts, but the user must request this service by completing additional forms. Imagery costs depend on the size of the overall scene, the type of scene ordered, image resolution, and additional services. Generally, the cost for SPOT imagery ranges in thousands of dollars.

It is necessary to preview each image before purchase, due to possible cloud cover. SPOT images can be ordered at a number of levels, depending on the needs of the user. Level 1A is not geometrically corrected (i.e. corrected to a known geometric correction with removal of geographic distortion) while Level 1B contains corrections but only for systemic effects. Unlike Level 1B, Level 2A has geometric corrections matching standard map projections such as UTM WGS 84. Level 2B uses known ground control points, with a locational error of less than 30 m. Level 3 (ortho) uses a digital elevation model (DEM)

Table 3.4 SPOT-4 values, adapted from http://www.spotimage.fr/web/en/172-spot-images.php

Band	Spectrum type	Part of spectrum (μm)
1	Visible (blue)	0.43–0.47
2	Visible (green)	0.50–0.59
3	Visible (red)	0.61–0.68
4	Near infrared	0.79–0.89
5	Mid Infrared	1.58–1.75

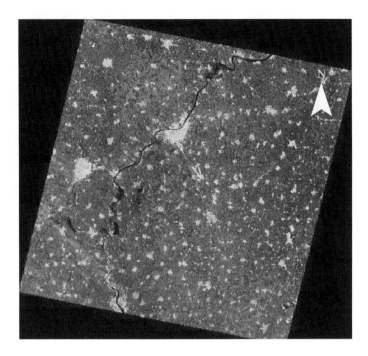

Figure 3.16 East Delta, Egypt SPOT image (scale 1:14100 m), 2002 image courtesy of SPOT.

to correct errors, with a location error of less than 15 m per pixel (http://www.spot.com). Future satellites are being developed with radar and sub-meter capabilities.

A number of archaeological projects have applied SPOT imagery in their work (Aldenderfer 2003). Visually, SPOT imagery was tested for archaeological research, and located a variety of archaeological landscapes in Danebury, UK (Fowler 1993, 1994d). With better resolution than Landsat imagery, and concentrated bands in the visible and IR, the imagery was valuable for detecting archaeological features through a technique called classification (grouping similar pixels within an image). One study classified data in order to identify faults and ancient road networks in the Arroux river valley in Burgundy, France. A SPOT image aided the team in mapping their results, which were then fieldwalked (Madry and Crumley 1990). One team did not think that remote sensing would be of use due to dense vegetation cover in Greece. The SPOT imagery, in fact, was useful in classifying landscapes (Wiseman and Zachos 2003). The classification of landscapes also assisted with archaeological site discovery in the Arkansas River Valley (Farley *et al.* 1990). SPOT imagery, along with Landsat and SAR data, helped archaeologists analyze alluvial deposits from Yellow River plain in China (Blom *et al.* 2000). SPOT data also aided archaeologists in examining long-term landscape changes relating to settlement patterns in Madagascar (Clark *et al.* 1998).

SPOT has similar advantages and disadvantages as Landsat imagery. The coarser resolution imagery makes it difficult to identify smaller archaeological features. Users, however, can merge the multispectral data with the 0.8 m resolution panchromatic (single band) data, to get 0.8 m IR data. A major disadvantage of this approach is the overall cost of SPOT imagery. Images start between US$1500–2000, with some imagery costing as much as US$4500 per scene. Through the "AmericaView" program (see website above), academic researchers can pay a US$2500 fee, which is credited towards any imagery. With sufficient subscribers to this program, researchers can receive up to an 85 percent discount on SPOT imagery, which makes SPOT imagery much more affordable to archaeological researchers.

ASTER

Advantages: most of the globe is covered; hyperspectral; can analyze a wide range of landscape types
Disadvantages: requires knowledge of remote sensing analysis; need remote sensing programs for multispectral interpretation
Features: hyperspectral data allows more detailed mutispectral analysis
Resolution: 15–90 m
Accessibility: http://glovis.usgs.gov/
Cost: US$80 per scene, free if a NASA partner

Advanced Spaceborne Thermal Emission and Reflection Radiometer (ASTER), costs US$80 per scene, including free digital elevation models, with scanners in the visible, near-mid and thermal IR portions of the electromagnetic spectrum. It is known as hyperspectral imagery, which refers to the multiple bands (15) that compose ASTER, seen in Table 3.5. Each ASTER image represents a 60 × 60 km area. Three subsystems make up ASTER: (1) the visible and near IR (VNIR), with a 15 m resolution and three spectral bands, seen in Figure 3.16; (2) the short wave IR (SWIR), with a 30 m pixel resolution and six spectral bands; and (3) the thermal IR (TIR), with a 90 m pixel resolution and five spectral bands. This system is particularly useful for digital elevation models, which the original data can be draped over to create 3D imagery. This aids in

Table 3.5 ASTER spectral values, adapted from http://lpdaac.usgs.gov/aster/ast_llb.asp

Band type	Number	Spectral range (μm)	Resolution (m)
VNIR	1	0.520–0.600	15
VNIR	2	0.630–0.690	15
VNIR	3N/B	0.780–0.860	15
VNIR	4	1.600–1.700	30
SWIR	5	2.145–2.185	30
SWIR	6	2.185–2.225	30
SWIR	7	2.235–2.285	30
SWIR	8	2.295–2.365	30
SWIR	9	2.360–2.430	30
TIR	10	8.125–8.475	90
TIR	11	8.475–8.825	90
TIR	12	8.925–9.275	90
TIR	13	10.250–10.950	90
TIR	14	10.950–11.650	90

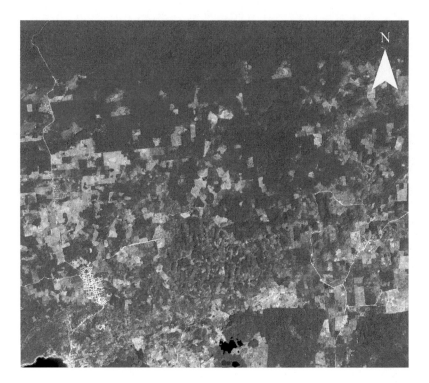

Figure 3.17 Lake Peten Itza, Guatemala, 3-2-1 ASTER image (scale 1:6400 m), 2001 image courtesy of NASA.

studying regional vegetation and geology. Like in all remote sensing datasets, the users can view only three bands of ASTER data at once, seen in Figure 3.17. It is recommended that the user stay within the same resolution groupings when applying algorithms for ease of analysis.

Fewer case studies exist for ASTER use in archaeology. This is surprising given that ASTER is fairly inexpensive and has much to offer for multispectral analysis. In fact, if an institution or individual has a connection with NASA or a funded NASA-partner, it is possible to download ASTER imagery for free. The ASTER imagery website is set up in a global search mode. The user can specify path and row numbers (similar to Landsat), or can zoom in on a particular part of the globe. Imagery appears in tiles: Some areas have multiple images from different times (months and years), while others do not have any imagery. Many ASTER images have cloud cover, especially in regions of the world with denser ground cover or in rainforest areas. This cloud cover can be the biggest obstacle to using ASTER imagery. Even if an image has cloud cover, it may contain a small section useful to the researcher.

ASTER's hyperspectral data, coupled with 15 m resolution, allow for the detection of broader archaeological features, especially using the thermal band of the spectrum with features larger than 90 m in size. One study modeled past lakeshores using ASTER imagery to create digital elevation models (DEMs) in Egypt's Western Desert (Bubenzer and Bolten 2003). The TIR ASTER imagery is too coarse to detect smaller archaeological

Figure 3.18 Lake Peten Itza, entire ASTER image, image measures 60 × 60 km, note the small percentage of cloud cover in the center upper portion of the image, 2001 image courtesy of NASA.

sites, while the VNIR imagery is useful for detecting different vegetation types but is not for differentiating between different soil types (Lillesand *et al.* 2004: 481–3). Looking at ground surface vegetation may help detect buried features that affect growth patterns. It is likely that sites would be detectable beneath the soil with the application of the SWIR ASTER composite image. This band range can differentiate soil types when there are large enough openings in the vegetation, and can detect denser concentrations of vegetation where moisture content might be greater. This assisted in site detection in the Agredos Valley, Italy, where a combination of ASTER and IKONOS imagery imported into a GIS was used to find Roman boundaries of old fields (Marcolongo *et al.* 2006). Using combinations of different bands of ASTER and algorithms also detected multi-period settlement sites in Iraq (Altaweel 2005).

ASTER imagery's applications to archaeological site and feature detection have not yet been fully explored by archaeologists. Use of low cost, medium resolution, visible and IR data, combined with coarser resolution thermal data, may lead to discoveries of additional features buried beneath modern landscapes. How archaeological sites affect the vegetation covering them is an area not fully catalogued by archaeologists using satellite remote sensing. Past cultures built varying walls, temples, tombs, and other structures out of numerous materials. These materials all decomposed (and are decomposing) in different ways, with chemicals leeching into the soil and absorbed by local vegetation. Some materials may cause the plants to grow more leaves, absorb additional moisture, or reflect absorbed light in a slightly different part of the spectrum, thus appearing as a different color on multispectral satellite imagery. The soil itself may appear differently with chemicals or moisture (Figure 3.18). Hyperspectral satellites such as ASTER and the recently released EO-I Hyperion satellite (with 220 bands in the electromagnetic spectrum ranging from 0.4–2.5 μm with a 30 m spatial resolution, see http://eo1.gsfc.nasa.gov/Technology/Hyperion.html) are the best tools archaeologists have to detect these subtle changes.

SRTM

Advantages: free; available 24 hours a day; global coverage; accessible from Mac or PC; easy to use; can download in multiple formats

Disadvantages: limited, high-resolution coverage; some areas have 30 m resolution coverage, some imagery is more detailed than others

Features: can view landscapes in 3D; can drape other satellite imagery on top of SRTM

Resolution: 1–90 m

Accessibility: http://www.jpl.nasa.gov/srtm/cbanddataproducts.html; http://edc.usgs.gov/products/elevation.html; http://seamless.usgs.gov/; http://glcf.umiacs.umd.edu/data/srtm/index.shtml; http://srtm.csi.cgiar.org/

Cost: free

The SRTM (Shuttle Radar Topography Mission) provides 3D global elevation data without charge to any user. Flown on the Space Shuttle *Endeavor* during an 11-day mission in February of 2000, NASA collected the data through a specialized radar system onboard the shuttle. The mission represented a joint project between NASA, the National Geospatial-Intelligence Agency, and the German and Italian Space Agencies. The mission was flown as part of the X-SAR/SIR-C mission. There is global 30 and 90 m pixel resolution elevation data, with 1–10 m elevation data for the USA. SRTM data is employed in many archaeological projects due to its cost and applications to a wide range of archaeological questions. Archaeologists can import the data into either a remote sensing program or a GIS, and then layer additional satellite data on top of it (Figure 3.19).

Having a good understanding of the Earth's topography is important to the geosciences, especially geology and hydrology, and is an essential part of cartography. Good digital elevation models (DEMs) also have numerous military and civilian applications, in addition to archaeological applications, as they all rely greatly on landscape reconstruction and visualization. Prior to the launch of the SRTM system, no consistent, global topographic map existed. Taking aerial photographs of the Earth did not prove feasible due to issues of cost, time, and country-specific military regulations. Previous aerial images of the world varied in quality and resolution, if such imagery existed at all, so could not be used to create a global database. Cloud cover provided another major problem, thus necessitating a scientific technique that would image the Earth's surface in 3D. Data for the SRTM was collected through the Shuttle Interferometric SAR, or InSAR, acquired by dual antennas with a small base-to-height ratio. As the radar signals are returned to the satellite, the measurements are recorded according to a consistent reference coordinate system. Where there is dense surface vegetation, the SRTM data

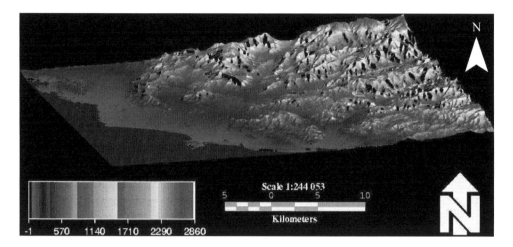

Figure 3.19 SRTM image of Lima, Peru, (scale 1:244053 m) processed to reflect height differences, image courtesy of NASA.

will reflect its surface and not the ground cover. Rough water, rocky ground, and scattered areas of vegetation are the ground types best recorded with the SRTM data; flat sand or still water can be incorrectly recorded.

SRTM data offers archaeologists many advantages. Ordering high resolution Quickbird data and draping it on top of the SRTM data allows for a near-complete landscape reconstruction. One can navigate through a landscape, comparing discovered features and sites to natural resources and terrain. Elevation may be an important factor for site or feature detection, and people using satellite imagery may note correlations between discovered features and their elevations. Global data now exists through a measurement of 1 arc second by 1 arc second (30 × 30 m), with a relative height position error of 6 m, and a ground position error of 20 m. This error is within mapping standards, and allows for good correlation with additional satellite datasets.

SRTM data is available through a number of websites. On the USGS SRTM website, it is advisable that all potential users complete the tutorial, as the website can be difficult to navigate. Some basic points to follow include checking the box for "STRM finished arc 1 sec shaded relief" and "SRTM finished 3 arc sec shaded relief" under "elevation" (on the right-hand menu). This will allow the search engine to look for the SRTM 10 and 30 m data. Once the user has selected an area, the next step is to check "SRTM 3 arc sec," or whatever other dataset they wish to download. The user can specify in which format to download the SRTM data: It is recommended to choose "GeoTIFF" for ease of use in remote sensing and GIS programs. Data size will range from 2–15 MB. With more terrain detail chosen for display within a remote sensing program, this may exponentially increase the size of the imagery, especially if the satellite dataset on which the SRTM data is draped is of a large size (such as Quickbird imagery).

Archaeological teams have used SRTM data to model past landscapes (Golchale and Bapat 2006; Evans and Farr 2007), especially in past paleo-hydrological studies (Timor 2004). Some scholars have suggested using SRTM data to locate or scan for multi-period archaeological sites in the Middle East, showing small mounds appearing on the SRTM imagery to be past occupation sites (Sherratt 2004; Menze *et al.* 2006). This is problematic in that many of these sites, called "tells," have modern occupations overlying them. One cannot show from SRTM data whether a site that is raised is free from modern occupation or if it is a raised area with no archaeological material. Combined with multispectral imagery, this would be a powerful tool to locate such tell sites (Parcak 2007b). Any past landscape reconstruction studies would benefit from SRTM data, considering the cost of the imagery and the terrain detail it can provide.

High resolution imagery: Quickbird and IKONOS

Advantages: global coverage; multispectral
Disadvantages: high cost; need remote sensing programs for multispectral use
Features: both images can detect buried walls, archaeological sites, and aid in detailed mapmaking; locate vegetation associated with archaeological sites and features
Resolution: 0.6–3.2 m (Quickbird 0.6–2.4 m and 0.82–3.2 m IKONOS)
Accessibility: http://www.digitalglobe.com; http://www.satimagingcorp.com/; http://www.geoeye.com/CorpSite/
Cost: Quickbird costs US$10–28 per km^2 with additional costs if imagery is express ordered; IKONOS costs US$7.70 per km^2, or orthorectified at US$13.20 per km^2

Launched in 2001 by Digital Globe, Quickbird satellite imagery is the highest resolution multispectral data available for commercial use in archaeological research. Quickbird imagery can be ordered in panchromatic (black and white), multispectral, natural color, color IR, or in 4-band pan sharpened. With collected points for georeferencing, Quickbird imagery can be accurate to within 2.6 m at a scale of 1:5000 (if Digital Globe georeferences the data), or to within 15.4 m at a scale of 1:50,000. This makes it the highest resolution data for cartographic usage. Quickbird records data in strips measuring 16.5 × 16.5 km, or 16.5 × 165 km. There can be 2048 levels of grey scale (with 11-bit digitization), and non-overlapping spectral bands, so pixels can be more easily distinguished from one another, especially during processing. One advantage to Quickbird imagery is that there is a revisit time between 1–3.5 days, so multiple images can be obtained. Quickbird orbits at a height of 450 km.

Prices vary for Quickbird imagery. Ordering directly from Digital Globe, archived natural color imagery costs US$10 per km^2, with a discount of 20 percent applied to academic research projects. If researchers on a project need multispectral or pan sharpened data (a process that transforms lower resolution multispectral imagery to higher resolution color data via georegistering pixels), the imagery becomes more expensive, ranging from US$14–28 per km^2. There is a minimum order area of 25 km^2 for library imagery, and 64 km^2 for new imagery. If imagery needs to be specially obtained because it is not available from the image library, or if the imagery there is not sufficient, then costs rise. Prices vary depending on the total area to be taken and the type of imagery needed. Rush orders can double the price of imagery, but orders are not always able to be rushed if there are a number of orders already "in line." If imagery needs to be specially georeferenced at a scale of 1:5000, with Digital Globe responsible for taking points, costs can escalate to tens of thousands of dollars (see http://www.digitalglobe.com). Many of the additional processes (pan sharpening, mosaicing, color balancing, and tiling) can be done through remote sensing programs, and archaeological teams can save money by performing these additional processes on their own.

IKONOS imagery is similar to Quickbird. IKONOS imagery was launched by Space Imaging (now GeoEye) in 1999, and has a resolution of 0.8 m for color imagery and 3.2 m for the near IR band. IKONOS imagery is used in many of the geosciences. With a swatch width of 11.3×11.3 km, IKONOS imagery can be ordered at 50 km^2 for US\$7.70, or orthorectified at US\$13.20 km^2. Specifying areas to be imaged adds additional costs. While there is not an academic discount per se, researchers can negotiate with GeoEye for discounts. IKONOS orbits at 681 km, and records data at 10.30 a.m. each morning with a three-day revisit time. Like Quickbird, it records data at 11 bits.

Many archaeological projects have used IKONOS and Quickbird imagery (Fowler 1999; Hoffman 2001). Both datasets can be used to view architecture with a greater than 0.6 m resolution (or less if the architecture is spectrally distinct from the landscape surrounding it). If specific crop types are growing on top on the architecture, the near-IR band should allow researchers to detect them. Both imagery types are useful for detecting buried walls which have absorbed significant amounts of moisture or are made of materials (stones, mudbrick) that can be detected from space (Figure 3.20a and 3.20b).

One team used both datasets to interpret a landscape in Norway, and then checked the data with geo-chemistry and excavation (Gron *et al.* 2006). Another team utilized IKONOS imagery to define damaged areas from the Vietnam War in the Plain of Jars, Laos (Box 2002). Archaeologists have not yet applied a full range of remote sensing techniques to IKONOS and Quickbird imagery, thus, future studies will undoubtedly have much greater success using them in their archaeological projects.

IKONOS and Quickbird imagery have distinctly more advantages than disadvantages. With high-resolution data, they can be used in mapping exposed architecture on many archaeological site types. This data can be tied into any existing grid systems, with the imagery corrected accordingly. High-resolution data can be draped over SRTM data to obtain virtual reconstructions of landscapes. Many remote sensing techniques, discussed in Chapter 4, have yet to be attempted on Quickbird and IKONOS data. Like all remote sensing analysis, there is no one way or automated procedure to use to detect ancient features, even with high resolution data. Each landscape will present its own challenges, with geology and archaeological features specific to a time and place in history. Thus, archaeologists must adopt different approaches. Cost can be a major prohibitive factor, but with educational discounts, Quickbird and IKONOS data represent the best value high-resolution imagery currently available.

RADAR (SIR-A, SIR-B, SIR-C, X-SAR)

Advantages: near global coverage; can see beneath sand and rainforest canopy
Disadvantages: need remote sensing programs for multispectral use; difficult to open
Features: buried features (roads, rivers) can have associated archaeological remains alongside or near them
Resolution: 15–45 m
Accessibility: http://www.jpl.nasa.gov/radar/sircxsar/; ; http://www.dlr.de/caf/en/desktop-default.aspx
Cost: SIR-C US\$50 (three scenes); X-SAR US\$40 per scene

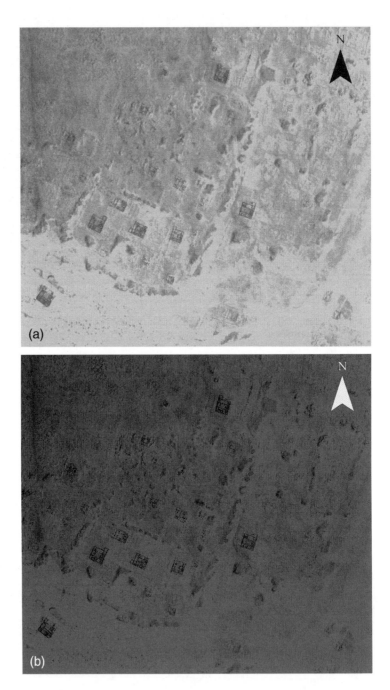

Figure 3.20 Quickbird images of Tell el-Amarna (scale 1:184 m): (a) showing housing in the central city; (b) using filtering to make subsurface architecture appear more clearly, 2005 imagery courtesy of Google Earth™ Pro.

SIR-A, or Shuttle Imaging Radar-A, was carried aboard the Space Shuttle *Columbia* in 1981, carried a singly-polarized (HH: horizontal send and receive) L-band (23.5 cm wavelength), which included a synthetic aperture radar. SIR-B, launched on the 1984 Challenger mission, had an L-Band and was HH polarized like SIR-A. The Sir-C/X-SAR missions were conducted aboard the US Space Shuttle *Endeavor* in April and September of 1994, covering 230 test sites around the world. The missions represent a cooperative effort between NASA/JPL (Jet Propulsion Laboratory), DARA (Deutsche Agentur für Raumfahrtangelegenheiten, German Space Agency) and ASI (Agenzia Spaziale Italiana, Italian Space Agency). Advances in the SIR-C/X-SAR included an L-band and C-band (5.6 cm) radar and a X-band (3.1 cm) single polarization (VV: vertical send and receive) radar. SIR-C data can be ordered through the USGS data gateway server, while the X-SAR data can be ordered through the DLR-DFD in Germany on their webpage (Blumberg 1998; Blumberg *et al.* 2002) at a cost of US$40–50. With a ground resolution of 15–45 m, each SIR-C/X-SAR scene covers an area between 15–90 km (listed above). Additional commercial radar systems include ERS 1, ERS-2, JERS-1, RADARSAT, and ENVISAT, which have varying resolutions and band data.

Radar imagery has many advantages and disadvantages for archaeological use (Elachi 1982; Fowler and Darling 1988; Holcomb 1992). Radar imagery is used to detect a wide range of sites and features ranging from natural to human-made, including trails, roads, and canals. For a low cost, archaeologists can obtain high-quality imagery, but the limited coverage of radar imagery is an issue. Commercial radar data can cost many thousands of dollars (beyond the budget of most archaeologists), while SIR-C/X-SAR requires specialized training for interpretation. Radar imagery can have significant relief distortion, and there can be issues with feature interpretation. Wet surfaces (including soil and vegetation) will cause pixel scattering. Resolution ranges from 13 to 25 m, and like other imagery, can have sub-pixel feature detection. Many errors appear in radar imagery, including speckle noise (making features difficult to view), and the imagery must be georeferenced. Sun angle and shaded relief are more important to radar imagery, and altering them on remote sensing programs can cause additional features to appear.

SIR-A (Figure 3.21) and SIR-B's best-known application in archaeological work was the discovery of the so-called "radar rivers" in Egypt's western desert (McCauley *et al.* 1982; McHugh *et al.* 1988; Holcomb and Shingiray 2007). Unlike conventional satellite or aerial photographs, radar images are not affected by atmospheric or sunlight conditions and can see through clouds and smoke. Using three bands of data (the SIR-C instrument contains the C and L-band radars, while the X-SAR contains the X-band radar), it is possible to gain information on a wide range of geophysical phenomena. While soil can limit penetration of the ground to a few centimeters, using the L-band in dry (desert) conditions makes it useful to see up to several meters below the earth's surface. This method is particularly useful to archaeological missions looking at ancient water courses, roads and sand-covered architecture. Longer wavelengths mean a deeper penetration of the ground to detect subsurface features. The best combinations include using the L-band and C-HH. SIR-C imagery aided in identifying alluvial fans in the Gobi desert of Mongolia, thus showing where archaeologists could look to locate additional archaeological sites (Holcomb 2002). SIR-C imagery cannot be used globally due to issues of coverage. X-SAR imagery also helped researchers to detect previous Nile River channels around the area of the great Nile Bend near Luxor (Stern and Salam 1996). Only certain sections of Egypt had SIR-C/X-SAR mission coverage, including areas of

Figure 3.21 SIR-A image of Egypt, 1981 image courtesy of NASA.

the eastern Delta, Sinai and Nile Valley, thus restricting where archaeologists could apply radar imagery. Radar imagery is excellent for regional survey, but archaeologists need access to digital imaging processing software to open the imagery. Additionally, researchers must be aware of the types of error potentially encountered and the techniques (such as georeferencing, smoothing, speckle reduction) that should be applied in order to obtain the best results.

LIDAR

Advantages: can view subtle landscape changes; high-resolution feature detection
Disadvantages: high cost; not possible to fly everywhere in the world
Features: can detect field patterns, architecture and other archaeological features not visible on aerial photographs; very high resolution data can detect features not visible on other satellite images
Resolution: 3 cm
Accessibility: http://www.geoeye.com/CorpSite/products/products/mjharden/lidar.aspx (US projects); http://www.lidar.co.uk/ or http://www.geomatics-group.co.uk/lidar.html?lang=_e (UK/European projects)
Cost: depends on project

LIDAR (for LIght Detection And Ranging) provides high resolution detail on features beneath the ground. The detail provided by such images is unparalleled and will open up many new avenues for archaeological research, perhaps allowing for detailed mapping that, until this point, has been limited to aerial photographs, ground penetrating radar, magnetometry, and resistivity surveys. LIDAR data is recorded from a device on an airplane, but can be flown on smaller airborne devices such as ultralights (small, lightweight, single, or double-person aircraft). The LIDAR system measures distances to the ground through a pulse of light, taking 20–100,000 points per second. Points are calculated using a GPS system, with heights displayed with color coding. With the ability to operate at a rate of 35 scans per second, LIDAR records strips 450 m wide. Each flight path has a lateral overlap to make sure an entire area is covered. Landscapes can be simultaneously recorded with a vertical survey camera or airborne digital sensor, making LIDAR a companion to aerial photography when singular shots are required.

The cost of LIDAR depends entirely on the length of time a system is needed, or if a team has to rent a plane and a pilot. Cost also depends on the total area being mapped, and the country where the project is taking place. It is possible to purchase flight times from commercial companies, but again, this can be expensive. Many countries in the world will not allow LIDAR to be flown due to military restrictions, so this must be taken into consideration when planning projects. The cost is generally in the range of thousands of dollars, but each commercial company will have varying rates.

LIDAR imagery has helped archaeologists in many ways, most specifically in allowing them to map with high accuracy in a time efficient manner. In a 2001 study on Stonehenge (one of the most well-mapped archaeological landscapes in the world), LIDAR data helped archaeologists to make locational corrections to known sites (with an accuracy of 15 cm), detect new sites, including field systems, cross banks and slight earthworks, digitally eliminate surface features (trees and buildings) to create digital terrain models, and examine topographic relationships (Holden *et al.* 2002; Shell 2002; Bewley *et al.* 2005) In the Vale of Pickering, UK, the team found that an absence of crop marks did not equal an absence of archaeological features, with many additional features found using LIDAR (Powesland 2006, 2007). In the Loughcrew region of Ireland, LIDAR aided archaeologists in identifying previously unknown archaeological features (Shell and Roughley 2004). In Brittany, France, LIDAR has allowed archaeologists to visualize the landscape surrounding the well-known site of Carnac (Roughley 2001, 2002, 2004; Roughley *et al.* 2002). Each archaeological site requires testing the LIDAR at different heights based on the landscape types.

Using LIDAR, archaeologists can create either a digital terrain model or a 3D visualization of landscapes. Archaeologists can also pre-program the LIDAR system to collect data with reference to any global grid or coordinate system. One test of LIDAR data occurred in the River Trent regions in the English Midlands for the Rivers Ouse, and Foss in the Vale of York, North Yorkshire and River Witham in Lincolnshire. The archaeological team wanted to test the utility of LIDAR data in an alluviated landscape to examine geomorphological developments and to model past flooding. Combining the LIDAR data with aerial photographs allowed for comparative data analysis. The LIDAR system was connected to a differential GPS system, allowing for ease of data reconstruction. LIDAR data allowed the team to examine how humans had modified the overall landscape. Terraces appeared clearly, along with past creek ridges. The team also found that peat deposits had once covered the entire landscape, and that palaeochannels had higher soil moisture and additional organic debris. Future applications with LIDAR might take place in landscapes where features are only marginally different than surrounding landscape, or in areas where aggregate extraction, housing, and development affect landscapes (Challis 2006; Challis and Howard 2006; Challis *et al.* 2006)

Other airborne sensors: RADARSAT, airborne thermal radiometry

Advantages: can see beneath cloud cover and vegetation
Disadvantages: high cost, limited global data
Features: possible to identify roads, pathways, and entire sites in rainforest areas
Resolution: 3 m (RADARSAT-2), 8–30 m (RADARSAT-1); 2.4–13.7 m (SAR)
Accessibility: http://www.space.gc.ca/asc/eng/satellites/radarsat1/; http://gs.mdacorpo ration.com/products/sensor/radarsat/rs1_price_ca.asp
Cost: RADARSAT-1 Archived imagery US$1500; other imagery US$3600–4500; RADARSAT-2 depends on scene size, higher cost for additional processing and rush orders; ATR depends on scene size, must be worked out with NASA

RADARSAT and AIRSAR are SAR (Synthetic Aperture Radar) satellites, both with similar capabilities. RADARSAT is a commercial satellite controlled by the Canadian Space Agency, while AIRSAR belongs to NASA. RADARSAT 1 provides horizontal-transmit and horizontal-receive (HH) data, while RADARSAT-2, launched in 2008, provides VV polarization, cross-polarization (HV or VH), dual-polarization (HH+HV or VV+VH) and quad-polarization (HH+VV+HV+VH). This makes RADARSAT an incredibly versatile imagery type. RADARSAT collects data in swaths of between 10 and 30 km, with a resolution of 3 m. Pricing for RADARSAT 1 ranges from US$1500 for an archived scene (prior to 2001) to US$4500 for an 8 m resolution scene. RADARSAR-2 costs vary depending on the overall image size, while the cost for flying an AISAR mission must be worked out with NASA pending details required and the size of the area to be imaged.

First flown in 1988, and flown since once per year, AIRSAR (for Airborne Synthetic Aperture Radar) is a NASA all-weather imaging tool. Like SIR-C data, AIRSAR can see beneath clouds and obtain night data. The data also is useful in dry snow, thin sand, and in areas with dense forest canopies. Flown on the NASA DC-8 sub-orbital platform, the AIRSAR has an accompanying lab and crew. The AIRSAR mission has been flown primarily over Central and South America and Antarctica, where it mapped large forested areas, oceans, hydrological patterns, and a number of natural hazards. AIRSAR utilized polarimetric SAR instrumentation, first demonstrated on the SIR-C mission. AIRSAR will achieve 1.5 m resolution in future missions. The C and X bands of SAR are sensitive to surface microtopography, and the P and L bands can penetrate both soils and vegetation (adapted from http://earthobservatory.nasa.gov/Newsroom/Campaigns/ AIRSAR_Mission.html).

SAR datasets, with the ability to record data beneath the Earth's surface, have been applied to a number of archaeological investigations. In the Central Iberian Peninsula of Spain, SAR data (with a 2.4–13.7 m resolution) found potentially buried architecture (Ayuga *et al.* 2006). SAR data has also been used to detect archaeological sites not discovered during foot survey. In examining structural patterns at Petra, Jordan, SAR detected previously unknown linear features. The data also showed ancient pathways, open subterranean chambers, and natural landforms related to known archaeological sites. This study continued at Beidha, Jordan though a cultural site analysis initiative, which identified the general landscape condition of the area (Comer 1999). On San Clemente Island, in California, AIRSAR Data (with resolutions of C-band 5.7 m, L-band 23 cm, and P-band 67 cm), aided in surveying Department of Defense (DoD) land. Eighty percent of DoD land remains unsurveyed. With newly located sites imported in the DoD GIS database, land management agencies can be better informed and Cultural Resource Management (CRM) guidelines can be changed (Comer and Blom 2002). AIRSAR has also been used extensively at Angkor Wat to understand more complicated human–environment interactions (Evans *et al.* 2007).

Airborne thermal radiometry involves the use of a thermal sensor to detect buried objects via significant heat flux, or absorbed heat from the sun. Non-heated objects can be more difficult to locate. Features are visible based on their depth, vegetation cover, the time of year, and the environment in which they are located. The thermal radiometer can be placed on either a helicopter or an airplane, with the video detectors sensitive to the visual, near IR, and thermal IR parts of the spectrum. Work done at an early Bronze Age site in Israel, Leviah Enclosure (not seen on the ground or in aerial photographs), was detected with ATR and later confirmed with excavation (Ben-Dor *et al.* 1999, 2001). Archaeologists have found ATR helpful for locating ancient road networks in Costa Rica due to the thermal properties of the roads (Sheets and Sever 1991). As with all remote sensing, timing is everything when using ATR. Teams must decide what the most advantageous time might be for recording differences in heat beneath the soil. This is generally in the early mornings when the upper soils are cool and the lower soils are warm, thus creating a maximum thermal gradient (Ben-Dor *et al.* 1999).

Data quality

When preparing for a remote sensing project, and during the process of remote sensing analysis, each team must assess overall data quality versus budgetary restraints. A great deal can be accomplished with free or low-cost imagery, yet what are the tradeoffs? Quickbird imagery represents the highest resolution data, and ordering a small area from the archives of each imagery type only costs around US$250. If one has even a limited budget (less than US$1000) for purchasing imagery data, this is well within budgetary restraints; combined with free data sources, this can allow for a detailed remote sensing analysis. Data at a 30 cm resolution will soon be available, with higher resolution satellites on the horizon for the next three to five years.

With high-resolution data available at a generally low cost, why should archaeologists use Landsat data? Should they be required to learn about other satellite imagery types aside from high resolution data? Future archaeological analysis will require detailed assessments of landscape changes. If one does not know how to assess imagery from the 1970s and 1980s, one cannot evaluate landscape changes. Archaeologists rely a great deal on archived data, whether through historical sources or old maps. Assessing historical information often requires specialized training; this is true also for Landsat and other older multispectral satellite data essential for any remote sensing studies. Learning how to assess the advantages and disadvantages of each imagery type was the focus of this chapter, but additional advantages and disadvantages may become apparent as the field becomes more developed. How archaeologists use and integrate multiple satellite image types as possible into their research is also an important factor.

Advances in data quality will affect how archaeologists approach remote sensing analysis (Failmezger 2001). One pixel of MODIS satellite imagery (at a resolution of 1 × 1 km) is represented by 27,778,889 Landsat pixels, while one pixel of Landsat imagery (30 × 30 m) is represented by 2500 Quickbird pixels. The scale of the data is something to think about during the process of imagery analysis. One wonders if archaeologists in 100 years will be using Landsat data, or if future satellites will be able to detect all landscape changes through time. Regardless of advances, archaeologists will need to learn basic remote sensing skills in order to analyze data for their research. Google Earth™, World Wind and other online imagery viewing programs will keep advancing, and it is difficult to predict how much automated remote sensing "analysis" one will be able to do in 5, 10 or even 20 years. Ultimately, everything depends on individual projects, landscape types, and the remote sensing techniques researchers hope to apply in their research projects.

4

PROCESSING TECHNIQUES AND IMAGERY ANALYSIS

Overview

Once archaeologists have obtained suitable satellite imagery, the next logical step is imagery analysis. Without taking an introductory remote sensing or GIS course (through a university or an online course, see http://rst.gsfc.nasa.gov/), and without access to commercial or free remote sensing and GIS programs, it will not be possible to use many of the techniques to be discussed in this chapter. However, visual identification techniques will be discussed, as well as what can be seen with basic imagery enhancement. A project may already have a remote sensing specialist. If so, then this chapter will help the remote sensing specialist choose appropriate techniques of analysis and will assist archaeological teams in understanding how different remote sensing methods work on ancient sites and features, seen in Table 4.1. Students may find that the discussion of techniques can aid in their project work. As so much of the world remains to be analyzed from the perspective of satellite archaeology, trying as many analytical techniques as possible (within a feasibile timeframe) may be a good choice. One will not know the techniques that will work best, given the variables affecting imagery interpretation. This includes weather, anthropomorphic factors, as well as image spectral, spatial, and temporal factors (Figures 4.1a and 4.1b).

Prior to discussing processing applications for satellite imagery, it is necessary to differentiate satellite imagery from another from of remote sensing which is no less important, which is geophysics. Satellite remote sensing covers large areas of the Earth, while geophysical instruments are run along the Earth's surface and look below the ground surface in concentrated areas. Unlike most satellite satellite remote sensing, geophysical investigations can go deeper beneath the Earth's surface. Wide-scale satellite remote sensing survey, magnetometry, and ground-penetrating radar (GPR) (Conyers 2007; Goodman *et al.* 2007) may be similar in purpose (i.e. locating archaeological materials hidden to the naked eye), but differ in their scale and the ways in which the results can be obtained. Understanding these differences is important when designing field and survey seasons, and determining which technology is most appropriate to apply. The four main geophysical instruments include resistivity, magnetometry, electromagnetic induction, and GPR (Wynn 1986; Meats and Tite 1995; Meats 1996; Marcolongo and Bonacossi 1997; Sarris *et al.* 1998; Sarris and Jones 2000; Leucci 2002; Lorenzo *et al.* 2002; Conyers 2004; Sarris 2005; Kvamme 2007; Roosevelt 2007; Sarris *et al.* 2007; Williams *et al.* 2007; Ernenwein and Kvamme 2008). They are tools archaeologists have used to see subsurface ancient structures (Becker and Fassbinder 2001; Herbich 2003), including

Table 4.1 Techniques for imagery analysis per main imagery type used in archaeology

	Aerial photography	Corona	Landsat	SPOT	ASTER	Quickbird/ IKONOS	SIR-C/ X-SAR	SRTM
Visual interpretation	X	X	X	X	X	X	X	X
Contrast enhancement	X	X	X	X	X	X		
Georeferencing	X	X	X	X	X	X	X	
NDVI			X	X	X	X		
Classification			X	X	X	X		
Thresholding			X	X	X	X		
Principal Components Analysis			X	X	X	X		
Land use land cover change	X	X	X	X	X	X		
DEM creation		X		X	X			X
Hyperspectral analysis					X			
Filtering			X	X	X	X	X	
RADAR analysis							X	

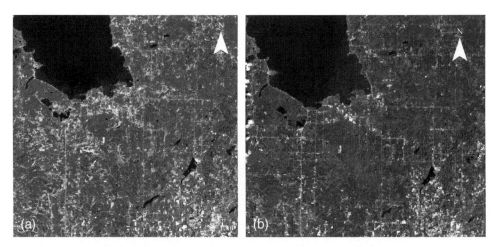

Figure 4.1 Mille Lacs Lake, National Wildlife Refuge, Minnesota, Landsat images from: (a) May 2001; and (b) July 2001 (scale 1:10432 m) note the difference in vegetation cover between May and July, images courtesy of NASA.

temple enclosure walls (Pavlish 2004), houses, tombs, and palaces (Pavlish *et al.* 2004), and have even helped to map entire cities (Becker and Fassbinder 1999). They are crucial tools within archaeology and should not be overlooked when dealing with the wide range of available tools for surveys and archaeological excavations (Dolphin *et al.* 1977; Giddy and Jeffreys 1992; Becker 2001; Rizzo *et al.* 2003; Kvamme 2008).

Resistivity, magnetometry, and GPR surveys can detect subsurface features with a reasonable degree of accuracy and have a spatial resolution matched only by the most expensive satellite images (Quickbird and Spin-2). These tools are best applied to small areas and would require prohibitive labor costs and time for a large-scale survey. Furthermore, specially trained scientists and archaeologists are required to conduct magnetometry, resistivity, and GPR surveys, to operate equipment, and address technical problems. Inexpert handling of the equipment and diverse situations can introduce irreparable error into crucial data. The overall cost of purchasing such equipment, and the need to upgrade every few years, can also be a deterrent. For instance, fluxgate gradiometers cost many thousands of dollars. Hence, projects can borrow geophysicists from universities, along with their equipment. Other projects rent equipment and bring out specialists from surveying companies, which may still be expensive depending on daily rental and stipend rates. Depending on individual projects, surveying can be more time consuming than expected, especially with equipment failures.

Satellite remote sensing techniques can provide the exact location of surface sites prior to more detailed magnetometry, GPR, and coring surveys. Magnetometry, resistivity, and GPR surveys are best used once archaeologists have found archaeological sites and want to gain detail about subsurface structures before excavation or in place of excavation. Is it more crucial to locate as many archaeological sites and features as possible before they disappear from plain view, in order to facilitate future ground-based surveying? The best answer is to increase the scope of work to cover both approaches, or, failing funds and personnel, try to record as much as possible before things vanish completely. If archaeologists know the locations of new sites found using satellite remote sensing, they can return to do additional subsurface geophysical ground surveying in future seasons. Attempting a limited number of algorithms over a 12-month or seasonal set of the same free or inexpensive satellite images allows for comparison, especially if an individual or team has not visited the region in question. One method may work particularly well in drier seasons, while other methods may work well in wet seasons. Landscape types will also influence what techniques to use. Prior to ordering more expensive high-resolution or SAR imagery, an individual or team should know from what time of year to order imagery. With budgets for archaeological work becoming even more restricted, with limited funding available for undergraduate or graduate projects, students and professional archaeologists need to have as focused an approach as possible. Papers that evaluate a limited number of methods will be valuable for other projects in the same geographic region. Field survey work may allow the team to identify additional methods to apply, or to refine already applied methods even further.

Some surface features identifiable from space may appear seasonally, monthly, or over an even shorter period of time. This is why understanding local landscapes and their seasonal variance is critical to the success of remote sensing analysis. Cropmarks appear during the initial growth of crops or vegetation, when their growth period is fastest. This will vary as per crop type. Frost may act like cropmarks and make certain features or sites appear due to heat absorption or, in a reverse situation, water may melt snow or ice faster or slower atop archaeological remains (Myers 1989). For example, during survey, a team may discover that a specific type of shrub grows on top of ancient walls during March to May of each year. This shrub may have its own distinct spectral signature that can be identified using high-resolution Quickbird imagery. Coarser resolution ASTER or Landsat imagery may or may not detect this shrub type. Even though initial analysis might not have detected the shrub, future analysis with higher resolution imagery from a specific time of year should detect it and contribute to future seasons.

Remote sensing experts can never predict which analytical methods will work best for project-specific analysis of satellite imagery. Even if a particular technique worked on a SPOT satellite image from the spring of 1995 to identify a buried river channel in a floodplain, the same technique might not work on a SPOT image from the spring of 2005. Atmospheric conditions change, weather patterns are variable, and a great deal can affect a landscape over the course of 10 years. Perhaps farmers reclaimed a large portion of the floodplain, or the government decided to start a massive relocation project to construct a new city in the floodplain area. One might attribute the location of the river channel in 1995 to heavy snowfall during the winter that left the floodplain wetter than usual, with extra soils clogging the channel and absorbing the additional ground moisture. SPOT imagery may exist from the spring of 2005, but with significant cloud cover, rendering it useless for project work. All ancient remains leave distinct spectral signatures on the landscape, yet each satellite image is a scan of the landscape taken at a particular time with various spectral and spatial resolutions that may detect the remains in a different way. Additionally, current satellite imagery may not be able to detect each type of buried or partially exposed ancient sites and features.

Each remote sensing specialist approaches imagery analysis from their own perspective and will "see" ancient remains in a different way. Should we trust imagery interpretation more from an archaeologist with limited remote sensing experience and 30 years of survey and excavation experience, or is a remote sensing specialist with 30 years of imagery processing experience and a limited archaeological background more reliable? Each expert will have different ideas for how to approach the imagery. Archaeologists are likely to view landscapes in their totality, combining ancient and modern landscape perceptions and searching for greater meaning in the findings. Remote sensing specialists often concern themselves more with meaning on the level of the pixel, asking why specific pixels appear in a certain way. Both approaches are invaluable, and show why remote sensing specialists and archaeologists should collaborate as much as possible.

Imagery processing programs

There are a number of remote sensing and GIS programs that allow archaeologists to conduct remote sensing analyses. They are similar in that they allow the user to open and use a wide variety of satellite imagery as well as apply different algorithms. Their cost will vary depending on the use: Commercial licenses are far more expensive than educational licenses and both depend on the number of licenses ordered. If an institution already holds licenses for remote sensing or GIS programs, it may be possible for students to obtain a student license for a nominal fee. ER Mapper (Earth Mapper), PCI Geomatica, ERDAS Imagine®, and ENVI are the most common remote sensing programs, with the majority of introductory remote sensing classes using ER Mapper, ERDAS Imagine®, or ENVI. Most GIS courses will use ArcGIS®. Some remote sensing programs are more conducive to advanced remote sensing processes than others. Prior to purchasing imagery software, one should consult with the dealer to see if the program will work with lab or personal computers, and will be able to process the required imagery. All of the remote sensing programs mentioned have a free 30-day trial period.

Free downloadable remote sensing programs are available, but they do not have the total processing capacity of the aforementioned programs, or the ability to run as many algorithms, although they can be run on both Macintosh and PC computers. Using commercial remote sensing programs, archaeologists and remote sensing specialists have the ability to patch together and compress large satellite datasets, program their own algorithms, save and export imagery in a wide range of formats, process RADAR imagery, and analyze data at the pixel level. Multispec© (see http://cobweb.ecn.purdue.edu/~biehl/MultiSpec/), a program available from Purdue University, is compatible with either Macintosh or Windows operating systems. The programs can read .lan and .hdf image extensions (which are the formats for most free Landsat and ASTER data), and have the ability to run different image classifications as well as contrast enhancement. GRASS (see http://grass.osgeo.org/), a combined GIS and remote sensing program designed initially by the US Army Construction Engineering Research Labs, is a much more versatile program than Multispec. It has many GIS and remote sensing capabilities, offers many remote sensing analysis tools described in this chapter, and can open a wide range of file types for Landsat, SPOT, ASTER, and SAR images. Both Multispec and GRASS have online user manuals and discussion boards, making them good options for archaeologists who do not have the funding to purchase the previously mentioned commercial remote sensing programs.

If archaeologists wish to make maps, or just open satellite imagery for visual inspection, a number of free imagery viewing programs exist online (with websites current as of Jan. 1, 2009). They include:

- MrSID GeoExpress View (http://www.lizardtech.com/)
- ER Viewer (http://www.ermapper.com/productview.aspx?t=160)
- Geomatica Freview (http://www.pcigeomatics.com/services/support_center/down loads/downloads_main.php)
- ERDAS Viewer (requires registration): (http://gi.leicageosystems.com/LGISub2x 44x0.aspx)
- ENVI Freelook (http://rsinc.com/download/download.asp?searchstring=Free Look& ProductVersion=All+Products)

Each program allows the user to view satellite imagery in restricted formats, zoom in and out, create maps, adjust contrast, and combine different bands of spectral data. It is advisable to archaeologists and students without previous remote sensing experience to open free satellite imagery in any of the aforementioned programs. This will allow some basic imagery processing to take place. As many archaeological features have seen during the process of visual examination (see below), one never knows what might appear.

Integrating satellite images and aerial photographs, and visual interpretation

Aerial photographs can certainly contribute to remote sensing projects. What happens when remote sensing datasets are treated as either high resolution or multispectral photographs? There are many analytical techniques archaeologists and remote sensing specialists can use on imagery, but the initial visual inspection of the imagery is critical. Archaeologists gain a "lay of the land," and assess imagery for further analysis.

Much can be gleaned from a pure visual inspection of satellite imagery, which is possible on any free image viewing program. Irfanview (see http://www.irfanview.com/_) is one of the most versatile image viewing programs available, and allows users to enhance imagery in a variety of ways. Archaeologists have discovered many ancient features treating satellite images as high resolution aerial photographs. When this happens, archaeologists need to address their advantages and disadvantages, much as one would do with aerial photographs (as described in Chapter 2). As in all imagery interpretation, much remains in the eye of the beholder (Rapp 1975; Ebert and Lyons 1980a, 1980b).

One of the most straightforward ways to enhance an image for visual inspection is to apply a contrast stretch through histogram equalization. This will highlight certain features in the image. Each pixel in a satellite image can range in value from 0–255 (digital numbers, or DNs). This 256-number range refers to 8-bit imagery, or 2^8 power. 11-bit imagery will have a value of 0–2047, or 2^{11} power. The contrast stretching expands the brightness values over a bigger range so that certain aspects of the image appear in greater contrast to one another (Lillesand *et al.* 2004: 492–9). Histogram equalization is an important step in the preparation of satellite images for analysis. Not only must they be georeferenced, but also they must be prepared in a way that optimizes recognition of important features. Allowing for contrast enhancement makes this possible, shown in Figures 4.2a and 4.2b.

Enhancement of Corona high-resolution satellite photography has allowed archaeologists to discover past road systems and old canals with visual detection in landscapes now largely vanished in Syria and Egypt. Landsat, SPOT, and ASTER imagery have resolutions too coarse to detect many small ground features, while Corona imagery, especially the KH-4B series, reveals features as small as 1–2 m thick. Largely invisible due to landscape changes, Corona imagery has allowed the detection of Sennacherib's northern Asyrian canals (Ur 2005), and a number of ancient road systems (called "hollow ways")

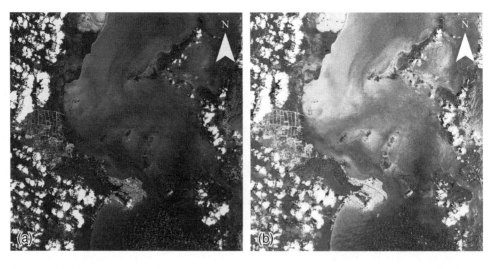

Figure 4.2 Belize coast, Landsat images: (a) with; and (b) without contrast stretch (scale 1:11200 m), images courtesy of NASA.

Figure 4.3 East Delta, Egypt, Corona image, image courtesy of US Geological Service.

between settlement sites in northeast Syria. Some hollow ways are visible today on high-resolution satellite imagery (Emberling 1996), but moisture in the soil of these ancient roadways allowed them to be distinguished on the Corona imagery (Ur 2003, 2006). In Egypt, visual inspection of KH-4B Corona imagery, seen in Figure 4.3, confirmed the location of previously unknown ancient sites in Middle Egypt and the Delta, and tracked the destruction rates of nearly 200 known settlement sites (Parcak 2004b, 2007a).

Analyzing satellite imagery through visual inspection has advantages and disadvantages. Control points for older imagery can be hard to obtain, especially where modernization has greatly altered landscapes. A lack of good documentation can also hinder research. This is what makes georeferencing, or putting the imagery in a known mapping reference system, so important. One study at the Roman town of Corinthia, located in the southern part of Austria, combined aerial photography with Corona high-resolution space photography over a 23,000 m^2 area. The team used the Corona imagery to create a DEM, and revealed a dense settlement area that was connected with excavated samples (Doneus 2001). Draping aerial photographs over Corona imagery to create DEMs is one low-cost way to reconstruct older landscapes (Dengfeng and Dengrong 2004). Another study compared aerial photography with airborne thematic mapper imagery (which has 11 bands ranging from the visible to the NIR). The study examined seasonality of imagery with ground moisture and ground temperature, and found that timing was one of the most important factors for all the examined imagery. Linear anomalies were observed in June, while old field boundaries appeared in August but not in March. Thermal inertia, or the ability of buried features or cropmarks to reflect heat differently, proved to be another major factor (McManus at al. 2002).

Figure 4.4 North Sinai Lagoon system, Egypt (scale 1:4560 m), arrow points to paleo-lagoon in western part of the image, 2008 image courtesy of Google Earth™ Pro.

The timing of imagery also affects how archaeologists can visually interpret Corona and high-resolution imagery such as IKONOS and Quickbird. Visual inspection of past imagery datasets can aid in reconstructing entire landscapes, and allows for insights into key historical periods of time. In Egypt's New Kingdom (ca. 1550–1070 BC), a series of fortresses dotted the "Ways of Horus," or the North Sinai road between Egypt and their eastern frontier. One team used Corona high-resolution space photography to reveal the location of a fort along the edge of an ancient lagoon system (seen in Figure 4.4), which helped in reconstructing New Kingdom military routes (Moshier and El-Kalani 2008).

Georeferencing

Most satellite images, when ordered or downloaded from the Internet, are georeferenced, or mapped to a specific projection system (Figures 4.5a and 4.5b). Corona imagery, aerial photographs, and some high-resolution datasets may not be georeferenced, necessitating the selection of ground control points for correcting the imagery. This process has a number of names: Georeferencing, georectification, image rectification, or image correction. Ground control points can be obtained from good maps of an area, or another satellite image that has already undergone georeferencing. Thanks to Google Earth™, World Wind, and Landsat imagery on MrSid GeoViewer, remote sensers have access to global ground control points of varying resolutions. Error rates (called "root square mean error", or RSME), or point offset, will vary depending on the type of imagery. This refers to the distance than any pixel will be "off" the actual

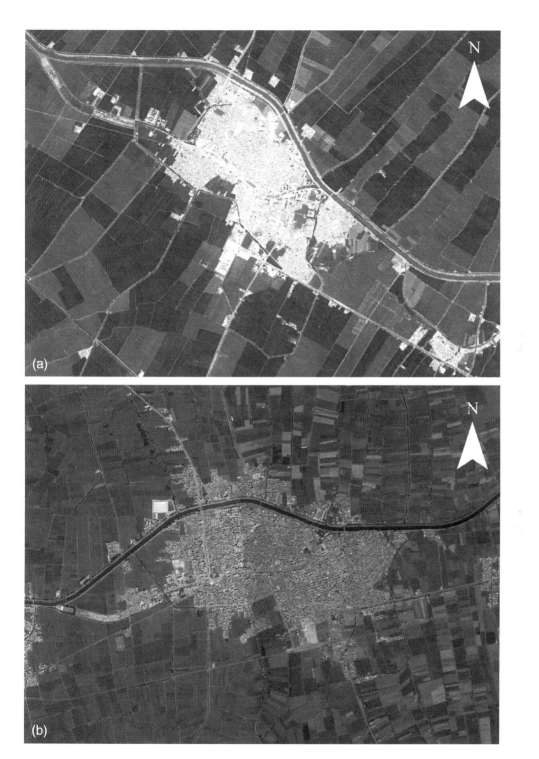

Figure 4.5 Georeferencing, compare: (a) non-georeferenced 1972 Corona image of Dikirnis, East Delta Egypt; with (b) 2008 Quickbird image of the same town, note the distortion in the non-georeferenced Corona imagery, images courtesy of US Geological Service and Google Earth™ Pro.

ground location. During survey, if one is within 30 m of any site with RSME, the site or feature is likely to be located. During the 2002–5 survey seasons, the author found that georeferenced Landsat imagery proved highly accurate, and was more reliable than recent government maps made from georeferenced aerial photographs.

How does georeferencing work? Normally a map displays geographical locations in latitude and longitude. This system, which originated in ancient Greece, is not without complications. Any map projection of the Earth is distorted in terms of distance, size, shape or direction, since one is attempting to place a curved, round surface onto a flat, 2D surface. Most satellite images are received as "raw" data without any coordinate system applied to them. Thus, any remote sensing analysis must choose which coordinate systems to use in a Cartesian, or an X–Y coordinate system, called a map projection (Bugayevskiy and Snyder 1995: 1–17). Most remote sensing research expresses locations through eastings and northings, which are obtained by using a Universal Transverse Mercator (UTM) projection. Sixty UTM zones cover the Earth. The projection is essentially a flat grid square applied against an elliptical point running along the surface of the Earth. The numbered part of the UTM refers to the local ellipsoid against which the projection is applied. Using a UTM system, the central point in the projection is accurate but the distortion grows as distances increase (Johnson 2005).

This distortion is corrected in remote sensing programs through the selection of ground control points within a known reference system. Eastings and northings are figures used to obtain the exact location of a particular point. Eastings represent lines running from East–West and northings represent lines running from South–North. They are used instead of latitude and longitude when precision is required, something which is particularly useful in archaeological survey (Lillesand *et al.* 2004: 47–9). Six or more ground control points are generally needed to have a low root square mean error rate. Georeferencing can be done with any commercial remote sensing program, Airphoto, and Multispec©. After selecting ground control points, the user then connects the points to the same points in the non-corrected image. The computer program then corrects the original image through a process known as "rubber sheeting," or stretching certain portions of the non-corrected image to orient them within the same coordinate system. If coordinate points need to be changed, the site http://www.jeeep.com allows points to be exchanged within coordinate systems.

Many archaeological projects use georeferencing to correct their Corona imagery or other non-georeferenced imagery as a standard first processing step. Not as many projects exist which have it as their only processing step, but georeferencing did aid historians in reconstructing the path of the Lewis and Clark expedition across the USA. During the expedition, Lewis used chain poles and other mapping and plotting tools to map their route, which had 600 campsites. Lewis estimated a total trip of 4162 miles. Georeferencing allowed scholars to correct old maps of the expedition with Landsat data, and showed that Lewis and Clark's map was only 40 miles off-route (Landis 2004). Georeferencing Landsat 5 data also helped to reconstruct past land use patterns in Mallorca (Montufo 1997). Old maps may exist for regions that identify now "lost" archaeological sites, and georeferencing will help archaeologists to relocate those sites. Combining georeferencing with the examination of long-term landscape changes will aid in relocating former branches of river courses or lakeshores. Georeferencing is a valuable remote sensing method, yet in general is only the first step of many taken in a remote sensing study.

Band combinations

All multispectral satellite images have multiple bands of data, which remote sensers can use to make certain features stand out. Each satellite image type will have various numbers of bands and each band will show a different range of the electromagnetic spectrum. ASTER imagery has 15 bands, Landsat 7 has seven bands, SPOT imagery has four bands, while the EO-1 Hyperion has 220 bands. No more than three bands can be viewed at once on any satellite image program. By blending the different types of information visible on satellite images, it is possible to make vegetation and geological features not viewable in the visible part of the electromagnetic spectrum appear more clearly. Each band of data can be correlated with specific ground features, and this will vary on each image. This was described briefly in Chapter 3, but many other studies detail the full range of detectable features in every band of satellite imagery.

The way most satellite images are viewed is as visible images, or a 3-2-1 RGB (red, green, and blue, referring to each of the three viewing bands in remote sensing programs compare Figure 4.6a to Figure 4.6b). Landsat satellite images can commonly be viewed as a 4-3-2 RGB, or IR-R-G (infrared, red, and green, each band viewed in the red, green, and blue bands). In this image type, vegetation appears as red because vegetation reflects more strongly as red in the infrared part of the electromagnetic spectrum (Jensen 1996: 40; Lillesand *et al.*, 2004: 5–9). There are a total of 343 possible combinations for viewing Landsat satellite imagery (7 bands × 7 bands × 7 bands), so attempting limited band combinations can be useful for archaeological projects. A 4-3-2 RGB also represents the band combination most commonly used for satellite imagery processing in archaeological analyses. This is because vegetation is so often connected to archaeological features. Other bands helpful for archaeological work are bands 4, 5, and 6. In one survey, band 4 helped to pick out dark tones on the image that equated to round barrows in Turkey. These were visually confirmed though a KVR-1000 photograph. Combining these bands also helped to isolate canals, and clarified areas of vegetation in each region of study (Fowler 1996a; Comfort 1997b, 1997c).

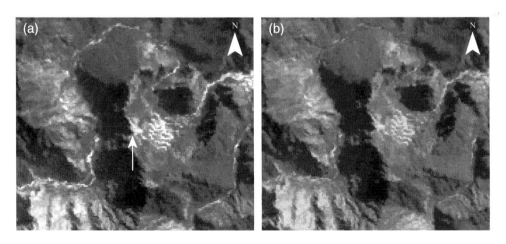

Figure 4.6 Macchu Piccu, Peru: (a) is a Landsat 3-2-1 RGB; and (b) is a Landsat 4-3-2, note that Maccu Piccu, the white area indicated by the arrow, appears more clearly in image (a), images courtesy of NASA.

Even a 3-2-1 RGB visible image may pick out features from space not noticeable on the ground, and allow for general geographic details to be noted. The image will be "false color" which means that the pixel values will not be an exact representation of a true color aerial photograph. SPOT satellite images have 125 total possible band combinations ($5 \times 5 \times 5$ bands). Although the bands are in slightly different spectral ranges than Landsat imagery, combining them in multiple ways did not make any archaeological sites appear as distinct in a study in the northeast Delta of Egypt. In a number of cases, features such as crops became highlighted, but, much like in the Landsat imagery, the analysis did not make ancient sites stand out as distinct unless one knew exactly where to look (Parcak 2007b).

How band combinations can best be used in archaeological projects is an area that needs much work. One archaeological study compared Landsat TM and SPOT satellite images in the Lasithi district of Greece and the ancient site of Zhouyuan in China. The researcher used both image types, with different band combinations to identify the spectral signatures of archaeological sites in Greece, identifying many Minoan period sites. Ground survey detected well preserved and poorly preserved sites, as well as a number of sites not visible. This contributed to the creation of a regional risk map. In Zhouyuan, Landsat TM imagery was used in combination with aerial photographs. A 4-7-5 Landsat TM image aided in identifying rammed earth used for building tombs and other structures (Sarris *et al.* 2002). Using band combinations other than a 4-3-2 RGB for running algorithms may aid future archaeological remote sensing projects. Experimentation is the only way remote sensers will learn which band combinations work, and which do not.

Normalized Difference Vegetation Index

Normalized Difference Vegetation Index (NDVI) is a method for measuring vegetation vigor in satellite imagery. This analytical technique compares the IR and red bands from multispectral satellite imagery (the red band and the near-IR band) in the following formula: B4 − B3/B4 + B3, or NDVI = NIR − Red / NIR + Red. The closer the value of the formula is to 1, the higher the overall vegetation value, while the closer the value is to zero, the closer the landscape will be to barren. Other comparative techniques include ARVI and SAVI (Atmospheric Value Index and Shade Area Value Index, respectively), but do not generally apply as well to archaeological site and feature detection. The vegetation vigor may be associated with better general plant health, or may be associated with buried archaeological features affecting the health of the vegetation atop it. Vegetation values over broad landscapes fluctuate depending on dry or wet seasons (Schmidt and Karnieli 2002) and should be considered when using NDVI as a part of archaeological projects. Semi-arid or arid regions will have different vegetation signatures, with vegetation decomposing at varying rates (Hurcom and Harrison 1998). Rainfall and seasonality remain two of the most important factors for all remote sensing techniques.

Archaeological features affect vegetation in a variety of ways. In some cases, completely different vegetation types may grow atop archaeological sites, while in other cases the general vegetation signatures will be stronger (Saturno *et al.* 2007). Buried walls or decomposing organic matter may retain higher amounts of moisture and increase vegetation density in these areas. Using NDVI to examine broader human–environment interactions may aid in reconstructing past agricultural practices. Using low-resolution AVHRR satellite imagery (with a resolution of 1 km) over the course of a year, one study showed high NDVI values with the maturation of winter crops. The project revealed a range of complicated agricultural and irrigation practices, and compared the results to the location of known archaeological sites (Kouchoukos 2001). Studying overall capacity of landscapes with satellite based biomass production estimates may help some archaeological projects with estimating past land use issues (Tieszen *et al.* 1997; Ganzin and Mulama 2002).

NDVI can be used to study more modern issues that may have affected past archaeological sites. In an exploration of ancient sites in Western China, one team used Landsat TM, SPOT, Quickbird, and IKONOS imagery to study the abandonment of the town of Tongwangcheng, a major Hun city. The town used to be located on the Wuding River, but as the river dried up, sands covered the city. NDVI helped the team in understanding patterns of desertification (Changlin and Ning 2004) (Figures 4.7a and 4.7b). On the other side of the world, NDVI assisted in studying the spectral response of archaeological sites in the Calakmul Biosphere reserve along the base of the Yucatán Peninsula in Mexico. The study compared known archaeological sites with random points using bands 4 and 5 on SPOT and Landsat imagery (Ostir *et al.* 2006).

Italy has the largest number of archaeological studies examined using NDVI. The number of archaeological sites containing buried walls makes Italy an ideal region in which to test NDVI. Using MVIS imagery with 102 bands (ranging from visible to thermal IR) one team studied the site of Arpi in central Italy. Vegetation indices revealed the outline of the city, its moat, and many linear anomalies (Merola *et al.* 2006). At two test sites in southern Italy, one team used Quickbird imagery to locate several buried walls via cropmarks in areas with ground vegetation. The team compared images with dry vegetation and NDVI at Monte Issi and Iure Vetere, both medieval sites in regions with Greek and Roman colonization. Overall resolution was noted to be lower than

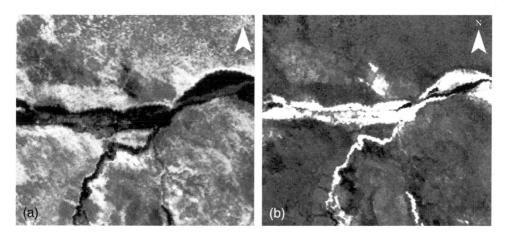

Figure 4.7 Western China, Tongwangcheng: (a) 3-2-1 RGB Landsat images; (b) NDVI (scale 1:2100 m), note the vegetation is brighter in image (b) and the archaeological site appears as white, images courtesy of NASA.

aerial photography. Results were confirmed using geophysical prospection (Lasaponara and Masini 2006a, 2006b, 2007; Masini and Lasaponara 2006a, 2006b, 2007).

Classification

Imagery classification is the most applied technique in archaeological remote sensing analysis through either supervised or unsupervised techniques (Forte 1993). The purpose of classification is to place each pixel in a satellite image in a specific land cover or information class through the use of the spectral pattern of the pixel (i.e. only within the same image would trees and desert each have a different spectral pattern). At a very basic level, it is a way of organizing the satellite image into specific clusters of similar pixel groups. The classification does not have to be based solely on the spectral pattern. It could include spatial or temporal patterns in combination with the spectral pattern, or it could simply stand on its own. Only ground-truthing can reveal which classes have been classified correctly, since classification is only as good as the information one has about the region (Jensen 1996: 247).

In a supervised classification (Figure 4.8) one can identify the subsets of information classes composing the entire image. One can first determine the spectral signature of each information class (e.g. lake, forest, wetland, and desert) in what is called the "training stage." Training stage sites have a specific value due to the homogeneity of the area from which they were selected, and by selecting training regions, classes of data can be separated from one another (Jensen 1996: 205). The person running the classification creates polygons that enclose whatever specific areas they wish assessed (e.g. lake, forest, wetland, or desert areas). Once the user has outlined a number of such regions (the number of regions, placed in polygons, is determined by the user),

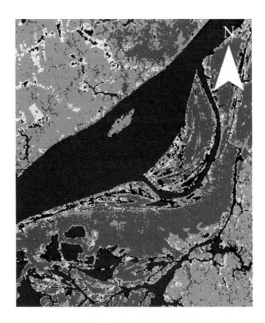

Figure 4.8 Manuas, Brazil, X-SAR, supervised classification, image courtesy of NASA.

the spectral properties of each pixel in the entire image are compared to the spectral signature of each information class. Every pixel from the image is then assigned to an information class based on the closest matches. Within the image data, one has to outline the areas of homogeneous cover and ignore the relative variance in specific signature classes (i.e. all high vegetation cover would be classified under "trees").

If training data is selected from specific bands, then the formulae >10 n pixels of training data must be selected, where n equals number of bands. For example, in the selection of three bands in a Landsat image, more than 30 (or 10 × 3 bands(n)) pixels must be contained within a polygon of any landcover class. If this number of pixels is not obtainable due to insufficient area coverage, the classification will not work (pers. comm., Gregoire 2001). Many classification results may be ambiguous due to this reason (Wilkinson 2003). A GPS instrument can be used to increase the accuracy of using pixels less than 30 × 30 m, but only after ground-truthing has been conducted. This may not be feasible in the initial stages of an archaeological project.

Unsupervised classification is different from supervised classification in that the computer automatically defines each region, while the user either specifies only the number of classes to display, or allows the computer to run pre-programmed "passes" through the data and decides when to stop (e.g. at 5 or 10 classes). The computer groups pixels according to statistically determined criteria, seen in Figure 4.9. When using this method, one needs reference data and field knowledge, without which the information classes can be confusing (Jensen 1996: 197–200). The computer does not know what it is classifying and could group classes together that may seem similar from a spectral

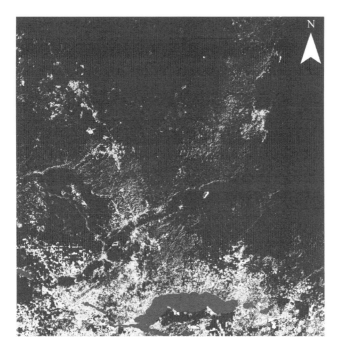

Figure 4.9 Lake Peten Itza, Guatemala, 4-3-2 Landsat unsupervised classification (scale 1:19400 m), image courtesy of NASA.

perspective but in reality may not belong together (for example, different types of crops). Someone conducting a classification will have a better idea about how to group pixel classes together and will be able to make informed choices based on maps or previous experience visiting the area in question.

Classification remains the primary tool of analysis for most archaeological projects using remote sensing, as the ultimate goal of most remote sensing projects is to identify the specific spectral signature of ancient archaeological sites and features, and to distinguish them from the rest of the satellite image. Examples of projects using classification include work in England applying a Landsat MSS in the Stonehenge region (Fowler 1994c) and in Greece, where a Landsat TM image and classification methods showed the extension of fans and faults, not otherwise seen on maps (Barasino and Helly 1985; Helly et al. 1992). In the USA, one project used electromagnetic induction, surveying, aerial photography, and a Landsat image in creating a spectral class signature, and then applied the information in creating a supervised classification. This showed undocumented quarry areas, with a 20 percent success rate for finding new sites in comparison to a 0.001 percent success rate for randomly achieving results (Carr and Turner 1996).

Since classification is a method that groups regions sharing spectral characteristics, it can help to locate areas with similar characteristics, including environmental settings for site placement. One project used a supervised classification along the Delaware coastal plain in order to relate their findings to environmental variables (Custer et al. 1986) such as soil or vegetation types. Classification in the Arroux River Valley region of Burgundy, France, aided in the creation of land cover use maps, incorporated into a GIS for the Celtic Iron Age (Madry and Crumley 1990). Detection of specific soil types can aid in archaeological site detection, or can detect pollutants in the soil that may affect archaeological sites (Goossens and Van Ranst 1998). Image classification has helped archaeologists to understand broad landscapes in Central America (Sever and Wagner 1991; Sheets and Sever 1991), the Middle East (Donoghue et al. 2002), and Europe (Cooper et al. 1991; Fowler 1994b, 1995b; Montufu 1997; Bailey et al. 1998). In Egypt, running a supervised classification to detect previously unknown ancient sites in the Delta region did not work in differentiating modern sites from ancient settlement, while it did work in Middle Egypt (Parcak 2007b). This proves that the same remote sensing techniques may work or not work in different regions of the same country.

Classification will allow for the identification of spectral signatures of either entire archaeological sites or vegetation types associated with ancient sites. If anomalies appear during satellite imagery analysis of an archaeological landscape, one cannot immediately assume that they represent ancient remains. One of the training areas, if possible, should be a known archaeological site or a large feature (if dealing with coarser resolution imagery). Once classified, a spectral signature can be associated with that feature or site. One might assume that other parts of the classified satellite image that have the same spectral signature (shown by the same color in the classification) would be the same site or feature. If in a poorly surveyed area, this could only be confirmed through ground-truthing. The classification would help the team to zoom in on specific areas to visit. Not all classified data with the same spectral signature of the ancient remains will turn out to be sites or features. Using data collected during ground survey will help refine the remote sensing analyses, as other types of classification may need to be attempted.

Figure 4.10 The Great Wall of China, showing reconstructed and unreconstructed sections (scale 1:70 m) the arrow points to an unreconstructed section, 2008 image courtesy of Google Earth™ Pro.

Thresholding

Image thresholding is a form of classification, whereby the user can specify what parts of image values are to remain visible, and what parts to obscure. For example, if something has a certain NDVI value, the user can tell the computer that they only want vegetation within a certain NDVI range to remain visible. One archaeological team used this technique to identify vegetation patches associated with ancient wells and subterranean streams along the West coast of Sinai, Egypt. Pharaonic expeditions would go to Sinai to obtain copper and turquoise, and would need these water sources for their seasonal camps (Mumford and Parcak 2002). Using the "Beijing No. 1" satellite, launched in 2001 with a 32 m resolution, archaeologists used thresholding to locate largely non-collapsed sections of the Great Wall of China (Yuqing *et al.* 2004) (Figure 4.10).

Principal Components Analysis

Principal Components Analysis (PCA) is another form of imagery classification. PCA reduces the amount of spectral redundancy in remotely sensed data. With seven bands of information being recorded in Landsat imagery, there can often be inter-band correlation and information from the digital data gets repeated (Lillesand *et al.* 2004: 518–19).

Since this repetition can obscure data, running a PCA can help to clarify classifications or band combinations (Figures 4.11a and 4.11b). In calculating the principal components, there will be much greater variance with first principal component compared with the second, third, and others. All of the information is compressed into "x" new

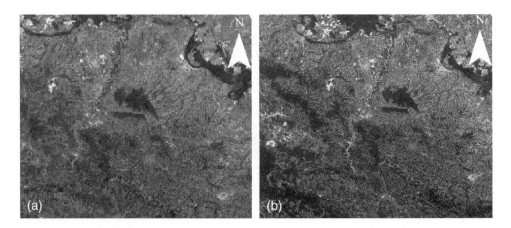

Figure 4.11 North Croatia: (a) Landsat band 1 PCA; (b) Landsat bands 1-4-7 PCA (scale 1:40000 m), images courtesy of NASA.

bands, known as the components. It essentially is another method of classification through which variables can be classified. With PCA, the first principal component (PC1) contains the greatest variance with the satellite image. Each subsequent principal component has less and less of the image variance (Lillesand *et al.* 2004: 536–42). There is a maximum of six components, each representing a band in a Landsat image (minus the thermal band). Other satellite images with more or less bands (such as ASTER or Quickbird) will have more or less components depending on band numbers.

PCA is an advanced remote sensing analytical tool, and one that several archaeological projects have used to make otherwise invisible features and sites appear. The region of the Western Karakum Desert in Central Asia, around the Amu Darya River, once formed part of the Achaemenid Empire, from the 7th–5th centuries BC. This river changed its course often, thus making locating ancient sites difficult. Predictive modeling was attempted using Landsat 5 imagery and PCA. The second principal component detected an eastward migration of the river, thus aiding future site detection (Gore 2004). PCA has also helped teams to detect archaeological sites in the Mississippi River Valley and buried walls in Russia (Stafford *et al.* 1992; Garbuzow 2003a; Garbuzow 2003b). In Tuscany, PCA located many archaeological anomalies on IKONOS imagery first noted in aerial photographs (Campana 2002).

One of the most detailed uses of PCA took place during a remote survey of the area surrounding the sites of Ninevah and Ashur in northern Iraq. This study combined negatives from Corona imagery georeferenced to SPOT data and corrected L2 ASTER data. The data aided the study in identifying both human and naturally created paths, yet the Corona imagery did not do as well identifying the "hollow ways" as the other imagery. As ASTER is sensitive to many different types of moisture and IR, the study used a PCA on bands 1–3. These bands are particularly sensitive to plants and soils. It was necessary for the study to examine the reflectance curves of different types of minerals and materials (material culture remains such as pottery and other items with high organic content). After variance was identified in the imagery, the SWIR (30 m) data was merged with the VNIR. PCA identified many different types of soils, vegetation, and minerals. In another study area west of Mosul, PCA was applied to bands 2–4 and identified hollow ways and ancient canals. Due to the dark brown moist clays in an arid soil area, PCA identified an Islamic period canal. Overall, the study emphasized matching the wavelength of reflectance data of unknown features with known data (Altaweel 2005).

With advanced remote sensing techniques, a number of factors become important. The resolution of ASTER data is not ideal, yet there is much more spectral data when compared to Quickbird imagery. Even though archaeologists could attempt to merge Quickbird and ASTER data, the 15 m resolution is still too broad (625 Quickbird pixels fit into one ASTER pixel). Corona imagery may identify older landscape features now lost, but there is no way to make Corona imagery multispectral. Archaeologists need to consider the best possible combinations of imagery data when planning to run PCAs. Some image band combinations may be better than others; the only way to know is to test different combinations on a variety of images. Buried features will appear depending on the season and the vegetation surrounding them. Archaeologists already know that past sites tend to have higher concentration of phosphorus, which is another chemical to search for using PCA. NASA's Jet Propulsion Laboratory has a library of reflectance data that can be used to compare pixel values in satellite imagery (see http:// asterweb.jpl.nasa.gov/instrument/character.htm). This library is by no means complete, and there may be confusion arising from pixels containing mixed data. Archaeologists should also have a good understanding of the soils and geology of the regions in which they are working. PCA is an excellent method to attempt when using multispectral imagery with a number of bands, and where spectral mixing is likely.

Land Use Land Cover Changes

Comparing Land Use Land Cover Changes (LULC) over time is a remote sensing technique with much to offer archaeologists (Figures 4.12a and 4.12b). After running classifications on satellite data from two or three periods, archaeologists can begin to assess overall landscape changes. This is a technique that works best with a smaller number of landscape classes. Once the spectral signatures of archaeological sites have been identified, perhaps the study can reclassify the data into groups such as "archaeological site," "urban," "vegetation," and "soils." Using remote sensing programs, the user can specify colors for pixels that change between each dataset and pixels that do not change. For example, pixels may show "vegetation to urban," "archaeological site to vegetation," or "vegetation (unchanged)." This technique can show how much landscapes have changed over time, or can show how much of an archaeological site remains after destruction from natural or anthropomorphic factors. In a rich archaeological landscape in the Crimea, where there are 140 known Greek and Roman archaeological sites, Landsat imagery from 1972–2000, IKONOS imagery, and Corona high-resolution space photography showed that urban encroachment was affecting archaeological sites (Trelogan and Carter 2002). Comparing 2002 Landsat imagery with 1972 Corona images in Middle Egypt showed a 200 percent increase in urbanization, which affected the preservation of many multi-period sites (Parcak 2003, 2004c, 2007a). Assessing how LULC might affect conservation issues (discussed in Chapter 8) is a good approach.

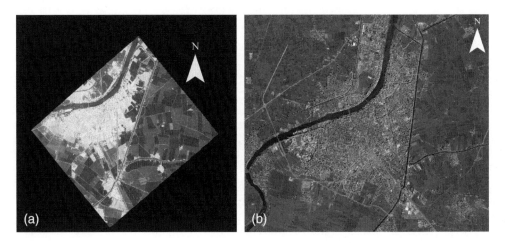

Figure 4.12 Mansourah, Egypt, Land use land cover change showing urbanization, compare:
(a) 1972 Corona image; with (b) 2008 Google Earth™ Pro image (scale 1:4130 m),
especially the extensive southern growth, images courtesy of US Geological Service
and Google Earth™ Pro.

DEM techniques

SRTM data, discussed in Chapter 3, allows archaeologists to model landscapes in 3D
(Forte 2000; Hagerman and Bennett 2000) (Figure 4.13). Techniques for turning flat
data into 3D vary per remote sensing or GIS program. The coarser the satellite data, the
easier it will be to drape it over SRTM data to create a DEM. DEM data can be extracted
from either SRTM data, stereo-pair SPOT data, ASTER data, or from stereo Corona
images. Archaeological projects have used SRTM data to create 3D landscape models in
India (Golchale and Bapat 2006), Ecuador (Yugsi *et al.* 2006), and Mongolia (Kumatsu
et al. 2006). Broader uses include creating DEMs for paleohydrology (Piovan *et al.* 2006)
to detect river changes over time in Italy (Ferrarese *et al.* 2006). In Languedoc, France,
SPOT, Landsat, ASTER, and SAR data allowed the reconstruction of a Bronze Age
landscape with 350 sites. The edge of the sea and previous river channels were detected
and the DEM allowed the team to compare the locations and dates of the known sites
with the old coastline (Ostir and Nuninger 2006). In a study of the Wari Empire of
Peru, archaeologists used DEMs to show relationships between 20 administrative centers
found in 12 valleys across modern Peru as well as the general landscape topography.
They used this data to predict correctly additional ancient site placement (Jennings and
Craig 2003).

Landscapes change in different ways across the globe. DEMs show change at varying
scales if archaeologists use the topography as a form of proto-architecture. DEMs can be
combined with satellite imagery to create detailed basemaps, which can then be imported
into a GIS. Viewshed analyses show the locations of river courses and other water sources,
which archaeologists can use to predict archaeological site locations. Landscape models
can show migration or diffusion paths, and locate the most likely places for settlement
(Evans and Farr 2007). On a generally flat terrain, past peoples were more likely to
settle on a raised area to give them a defensive position in times of conflict. Each culture

Figure 4.13 DEM of Machu Picchu, Peru, SRTM, (Scale 1:202 m)2008 image courtesy of Google Earth™ Pro.

will have varying relationships with their landscapes. Understanding how past peoples interacted with their topographies allows better archaeological analyses to take place.

Hyperspectral studies

Hyperspectral satellites, with large numbers of bands, allows for more targeted analyses. If the investigator knows the spectral signatures of the features in question, especially if they are built from a specific type of stone, or have a certain type of vegetation growing atop them, then they can do specialized classifications, PCAs or other analytical techniques. One study detected shell mounds in the Jiangsu province of China using 128 bands of data from an Optical Monitor Imaging Spectrometer (OMIS) sensor with a resolution of 6.6 m. Shells are composed of calcium carbonite and have a strong spectral absorption between 2000–2550 nm. The analysis detected the XiXi shell mound (see Figure 4.14) measuring 15 × 100 m, with associate material culture remains of jade, stone, pottery, and bronze. Results were tested in the field with a spectrometer, which found that the shell had a higher spectral response than the surrounding soils (Qingjiu and Jianqiu 2004). Another study using an OMIS sensor noted that values can vary, and that resampling is needed to correct the images. Atmospheric interference can affect the imagery readings (Xiaohu 2004).

If the groundcover is mixed, results from hyperspectral analyses can be problematic. When vegetation cover is less than 30 percent an AVIRIS senser (Airborne Visible/Infrared Imaging Spectrometer) will not be reliable. With low spectral contrasts, vegetation types cannot be modeled correctly even where there is high density

Figure 4.14 Shell Mound, Cagayun River, Philippines (scale 1:80 m), used as a comparative shell mound image from space, the shell mounds are numerous and dot the entire image, 2008 image courtesy of Google Earth™ Pro.

vegetation cover (Okin *et al.* 2001). This shows how important it is for archaeologists to have a holistic approach to landscapes. Using a MIVIS (Multispectral IR and Visible Imaging Spectrometer) sensor with 102 bands at the archaeological site of Aquila, Italy, archaeologists revealed how problems could result from hyperspectral remote sensing. Anomalies were often improperly detected (Traviglia 2006). Just because linear features appear in an image does not mean that archaeologists should equate them with archaeological features. Caution remains the best approach with satellite archaeology, even when using the most advanced sensors and most advanced remote sensing techniques.

Filtering

Spatial filtering is a common remote sensing method used to highlight differences in tonal image variations, and has many applications for archaeological contexts. Subtle variations between neighboring pixels can be emphasized or de-emphasized depending on the filters applied (Figure 4.15). This is done via the image process of convolution, where kernels or coefficients can be applied to weight the digital numbers. For example, in a 5 × 5 kernel with coefficients equal to 1/25th, all of the kernel's original digital numbers would be multiplied by 1/25th, added together, and divided by 25 to get a central pixel value. Filtering can remove image noise, or can stress differences in edge

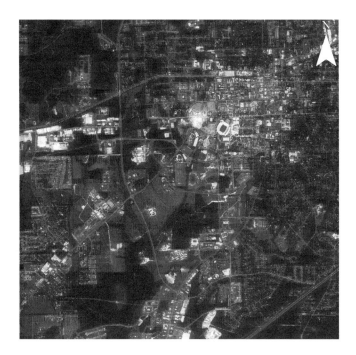

Figure 4.15 Auburn University, Alabama, Quickbird low pass filter (scale 1:100 m), 2008 image courtesy of Google Earth™ Pro.

values in either low or high frequency change areas (i.e. desert dunes versus a large city) (Lillesand *et al.* 2004: 517–31). Different remote sensing programs will offer varying filtering options, which may include curvature, digital elevation models, Gaussian, high pass, low pass, standard, sun angle, or user code, under the algorithm load filter. Each listed filter may then have a subset of many additional filter types. Filters can be applied before or after specific remote sensing formulae, or the user can apply more than one filter for advanced applications or code in C.

Edge detection will generally be the most useful filter archaeologists can apply in their work, yet testing the full range of filter types is important. Like all remote sensing techniques, the filters that may work best depend on local conditions and satellite image types. Not all studies using high-resolution data will apply filters (Richetti 2004), yet each study is case-specific. One example from the Peten in Central America used Landsat TM, IKONOS, and SAR data to examine relationships between landform types, vegetation and settlements using a 3 × 3 filter (Estrada-Belli and Koch 2007). Using CASI and LIDAR data in Greece at the archaeological site of Itanos, one team found a garrison wall and additional stone walls with edge detection (Rowlands *et al.* 2006). Another study at the site of Hieropolis, Turkey, used a combination of high-resolution SPOT imagery and edge detection to identify faults affecting the site (Leucci *et al.* 2002). The archaeological site of Xucutaco-Hueitapalan in Mexico was mapped using ERS-2 and SAR data over an area measuring 3 × 3.5 km. Archaeologists compared filtered versus unfiltered data, and found the filtered data revealed a previously unknown complex of structures (Yakam-Simen *et al.* 1997).

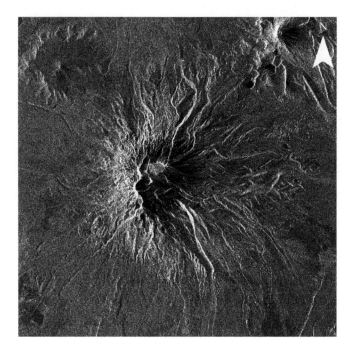

Figure 4.16 Mt. Ruapehu volcano, New Zealand (scale 1:531 m), image courtesy of NASA.

RADAR/LIDAR analysis techniques

SAR and LIDAR data can be difficult to process, and the techniques one can apply depend on the quality of the imagery. SAR imagery cannot be seen the same way as multispectral imagery due to imagery distortions, oblique viewing geometry, and the way the microwave sensors work. Although SAR imagery is an "all weather" imaging system, there can be problems associated with mapping landscapes with varying types of relief. Additional landscape distortions may appear with regions that have higher reliefs, such as mountainous landscapes (Gatsis *et al.* 2001). When landscapes have homogenous and fine-grained surfaces, RADAR data can help with identifying subsurface features (Figure 4.16). In the Sahara, where it rains once every 20–50 years, a scientific team examined how wind shifted sand over time in Egypt's western desert using SIR-C and RADARSAT data. With less than 1 percent surface moisture content, this area proved to be an ideal testing area for RADAR imagery: Surface moisture can increase image backscatter. The team identified two major river courses as well as inland basins (El-Baz *et al.* 2007). Combining SAR data with multispectral data is generally the best way to approach archaeological site discovery. One archaeological team used a combination of SAR, SPOT, Landsat, and SIR-C data to aid in identifying three missing pyramids in a survey south of Cairo, Egypt from Abu Rawash to Dashur. SPOT and Landsat data allowed the team to search for artificial shapes, and they then found four sites in the area of Dashur North. Polarizing the L-band from the SAR data SIR-C DATA made it possible for the team to locate two previously unknown sites. With excavation, these proved to be two tomb shafts (Etaya *et al.* 2000).

One of the most focused studies using SAR data took place on San Clemente Island, California. The team used SAR data to develop protocols for archaeological inventory surveying Department of Defense (DoD) land and assessed both archaeological and environmental factors. SAR data collects physical rather than chemical aspects of landscapes, so prior site knowledge is important. Surveying DoD and Federal lands for archaeological materials consumes US$19 million a year, and if protocols can be developed using satellite imagery (being a non-destructive and non-invasive technology), up to 30% of project costs can be saved. The SAR data was flown on a DC-8 jet with three bands (P, L, and C, with resolutions ranging from 1.8–7.5 m). The L and C bands worked best for archaeological site identification. Overall, the SAR data identified 701 sites. Sites were associated with slope and aspect, soil drainage patterns, and water collection areas. Of identified sites 95 percent faced west, towards the wind, in the northernmost survey area. This was likely the most advantageous area for food and a defensive lookout position (Comer and Blom 2007). Site positions in landscapes can reveal a great deal about landscape meaning, while thinking about advantageous site positioning can aid archaeologists when using slope, aspect, and other landscape-specific techniques to assess SAR data.

Similar issues need to be considered when using LIDAR data (Figure 4.17). Backscattering from the target area depends on its overall size distance from the aircraft, overall reflectivity, and the direction of the scattering. In a study using LIDAR for archaeological detection in Leitha, Austria, a number of techniques were attempted to locate features in dense forests. The project stressed the importance of testing a number of methods,

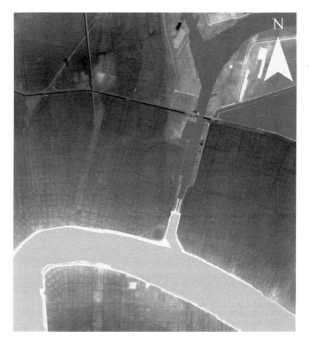

Figure 4.17 New Orleans, LIDAR imagery (scale 1:827 m), note how LIDAR makes the roads and canals much clearer, image courtesy of NASA.

as previous studies had distinguished trees from the ground but not vegetation from the ground. Vegetation comes in different heights, and is distributed unevenly across the terrain. LIDAR laser sensors can read between two and four echoes, with individual point scatters being distinguished. As a result, location scattering properties of single targets can be read and given coordinates. Each type of forest canopy will require the user to choose optimal sensor characteristics, and will require special tuning so archaeological features will not be missed. Thresholding assisted the team with eliminating points off the terrain from the analysis. Overall, the project identified ramparts and a graveyard with 50 barrows (not visible in aerial photographs). The study represents one of the first times LIDAR was used to detect archaeological remains in forested and vegetated areas, which required a far more accurate landscape analysis (Doneus and Briese 2006a, 2006b). A similar study in the Midlands and in York, UK used LIDAR data to examine different returns from the lasers. The study determined that a fall-off in light intensity can equate with river paleochannels. The first pulse return showed forest canopy, the second return showed bushes, and the third return showed features on the ground (Challis 2006).

GIS and remote sensing

GIS and satellite remote sensing are outwardly even more closely related than subsurface surveying techniques and satellite remote sensing They are often confused, but together can be used to bridge the gap between remote sensing specialists and archaeologists (Castleford 1992). Both offer ways of visualizing and organizing remote sensing and additional data for archaeological discovery and predictive modeling, and do so in different yet related ways (Stine and Decker 1990; Johnson 1996; Forte 1998; Limp 2000; Forte 2002; Rabeil *et al.* 2002; Som 2002; Gupta *et al.* 2004; Rajamanickam *et al.* 2004; Belvedere *et al.* 2006). How GIS and remote sensing can be combined to further archaeological analysis is discussed here. A GIS is a detailed data visualization system, and allows the input of multiple layers of data to view spatially view and organize statistical information. Within a GIS, layers can be created, turned on, or turned off, for comparative and analytical purposes. Shapefiles can be created to highlight specific data, and data can be added to specific points or shapefiles. Users have the ability to observe patterns between the layers of data (Figure 4.18). Statistical data can also be compared in a GIS, which may aid in archaeological predictive models (Symanzik *et al.* 2000).

Ultimately, a GIS is only as good as imputed or imported data. While a GIS allows viewing of satellite imagery, it cannot run the same processing algorithms as a specific remote sensing program. Satellite remote sensing programs allow GIS layers to be added as well as the creation of shapefiles that can then be exported to a GIS. With satellite remote sensing, the analysis is only as good as the understanding of the processes behind the imagery analysis. The remote sensing user needs to be able to make choices regarding type of imagery and processing techniques. Both GIS and satellite remote sensing work require previous training, and an understanding of the pitfalls of each method of analysis. Many courses, in fact, combine training in satellite remote sensing and GIS. Satellite remote sensing is, at its core, how radiation reflected off the Earth's surface is captured and interpreted, while GIS is about evaluating, analyzing, comparing, and contrasting layers of imported data. Together, satellite remote sensing and GIS are effective tools for

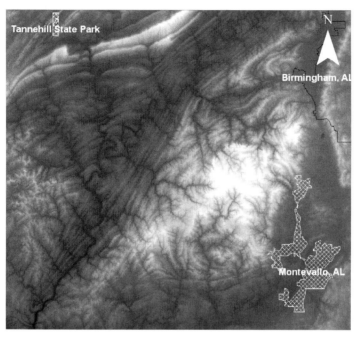

Figure 4.18 Tannehill, Alabama, GIS map showing digital elevation model (scale 1:3200 m), image courtesy of NASA.

archaeological analysis, and discussing the best ways they can be combined will allow archaeological projects to make the best of each tool.

Correlating known and unknown data is another useful feature of integrating GIS and remotely sensed data. There may be additional patterns that remote sensers cannot see on the satellite imagery alone. This includes examining regional archaeological site orientation (if the satellite imagery used is too coarse when identifying "new" features) and looking at site-specific data. If 80 percent of known archaeological sites in an area have a hilltop temple nearby, then any sites found in a regional survey will likely have an 80 percent chance of having this similar feature. Examining known site distribution and associated features in a GIS will aid in regional surveys. Perhaps the remote sensing analysis only had a 50 percent success rate for identifying known archaeological sites in an area. A GIS may help remote sensers understand why the other 50 percent of sites were not seen. In a GIS, data can be entered on a site's date, features, soil types, and any other features the user may deem important. Turning on and off layers that display those features in relationship to the remotely identified known sites may aid archaeologists in attempting additional methods of analysis.

Once cultural resource managers have examined multiple phases of data in a GIS, they can spot varying trends, and create site management plans. In a study of the flooding surrounding the Usumacinta River in Mexico and Guatemala, the project used Landsat and SRTM imagery to locate 18 previously unknown ancient sites. This data was imported into a GIS to show the flooding risk to known Mayan sites as well as the recently identified archaeological remains (Beredes, as cited in Stubbs and McKees 2007).

In Khirbet Iskander, Jordan, archaeologists produced a DEM to show an archaeological site drainage plan at varying levels of elevation across the site. Placing this data in a GIS aided cultural resource managers in identifying flood impact zones (Peterman 1992). Urbanization, a cultural resource problem surrounding many archaeological sites, can also be addressed through using a GIS. One project looked at old maps and modern high-resolution satellite imagery in Cairo to map the change from rural to urban areas through time (Stewart 2001). Using a combination of old maps, aerial photographs, and satellite images will give the widest range for comparative purposes.

Archaeological sites can never be thought of in a mere "there or not there" context when combining satellite imagery and GIS. Sites need to be considered from the perspective of their accessibility, visibility, and defensibility. In a modeling project in the region of Pinchango Alto, Peru, archaeologists carried out spatial modeling using orthophotos, terrestrial laser scanning, and 270 million differential GPS points, and put everything together in a GIS to understand structure and site placement through time (Lambers *et al.* 2007). Through a GIS, archaeological projects can also combine space- and ground-based remote sensing tools. One project in Metaponto, Italy, placed digital imagery and magnetic data in a GIS for comparative purposes (Riccetti 2001). Spatial organization of specific sites is another factor which can be assessed using satellite data in a GIS: Newly located features on a site can be compared with excavated or ground-sensed data (Williams *et al.* 2007).

A GIS can allow layering of information to assess landscape changes and the plotting of archaeological site placement through time, especially in relationship to needed natural resources. This can be helpful in riverine regions where ancient sites change location based on access to water (Timor 2004). In Russia, one study examined forestry resources and subsistence practices during the Bronze Age. After establishing palynological sequences, the study compared pollen analyses to vegetation zone mapping using Landsat TM, ASTER imagery, and NDVI. All the data was imported into a GIS to assess overall changes, and both scale and general patterns were deemed difficult to see (Vicent *et al.* 2006). One can also use a GIS to compare analyzed satellite imagery with soils that may have similar geophysical characteristics. A study examining data from Ureturituri Pa and Fort Resolution, New Zealand used a GIS to characterize remotely sensed data and identify previously unknown archaeological remains (Ladefoged *et al.* 1995).

Integrating remote sensing and GIS allows for a full range of archaeological assessment activities, especially protecting past sites. Ancient sites do not move by themselves, and a combination of past and future data is needed to protect cultural resources. One study claims that few papers have gone beyond using GIS for data collection. The authors advocate four main uses for GIS in archaeological research: Studying the spatial structure of modern agricultural landscape, assessing ground visibility of archaeological remains, defining and characterizing sites, and, looking at decision making behind archaeological site location (Bevan and Conolly 2002). Finding spectral signatures in a landscape is only the first step: How should archaeologists work with government organizations to protect cultural landscapes? Many major sites are tourist destinations, but their hinterlands should be protected as well. Governments do not always realize the impact of modern building on preserving the past. For example, roads in northern Thailand were built through temple complexes (Stubbs and McKees 2007), yet this and other similar situations may be more closely connected to issues of corruption. Managing past sites requires a full understanding of past and present landscape processes, and this can be best understood through satellite remote sensing analysis, which can detect most forms of encroachment, whether through urbanization or deforestation.

What are the advantages and disadvantages for using remote sensing in combination with a GIS? Remote sensing programs do not cope well with large imported databases, which are always necessary when carrying out ground survey. ArcGIS® has imagery extension programs that allow users to import a number of image types. Archaeologists can take analyzed imagery and link specific sites in a GIS with data they collect during their ground survey seasons. Broader landscape changes can be quantified, especially when a land use land cover change study is conducted. Regional dynamics can be better understood in a GIS, as archaeologists can layer dozens of different data types. Predictive modeling is another area now beginning to be explored with satellite archaeology. Data in a GIS can help narrow down possible archaeological site locations even further, as old maps may show previous landscape features that the remote sensing analysis did not detect. Importing archaeological satellite data into a GIS will give the broadest range of results to a remote sensing project (Limp 2000).

Combined techniques

Most archaeological remote sensing projects attempt more than one analytical approach. How teams or individuals choose to combine approaches gives insights into how people should model their own remote sensing projects for archaeological exploration. Each region will present specific problems or issues that only multiple algorithms can assess. No archaeological project will be able to predict which techniques will work best in feature identification. How to approach specific landscape and site types and design remote sensing analyses accordingly is discussed in great detail in Chapter 5. Here, select projects will be discussed for the overall remote sensing problems they faced, and how they addressed specific challenges with multiple types of inquiries.

In regions where no remote sensing for archaeological work has been conducted, teams may need to adopt a more geological approach. This was the case in many early remote sensing studies in archaeology. In Libya, a team used Landsat MSS imagery to discriminate landscape types using maximum likelihood classification, principal components analysis, and smoothing with a 3×3 filter. The landscape classification revealed limestone plateaus, basalt formations, alluvial basins, and different types of cultivation. This analysis aided in a paleoenvironmental survey (Dorsett *et al.* 1984).

Finding archaeological sites in areas with alluvial deposits presents a great challenge to archaeologists. One does not know if the alluvial deposits will have covered over ancient remains fully or partially, and if the area still has a great deal of moisture in the soil, it may affect the techniques that remote sensers can apply. In a project detecting sites in the Yellow River region of China, dating to the early Shang Dynasty, archaeologists used Landsat 5, Landsat 7, SPOT, Corona, and SAR data. Seasonal moisture changes affected the methods archaeologists could use to detect buried rectilinear features, detected largely from the SAR data (Blom *et al.* 2000). Landsat TM imagery also contributed to a study mapping prehistoric Hohokam culture features (ca. 300 BC–AD 1450) along the Salt River in Arizona. The culture used canal irrigation to grow corn, cotton, squash, and beans. As known canals measured between 200–600 km long and 26 km wide, it was assumed that remote sensing analysis would detect additional canals. The study used contrast stretching, spatial filtering, and band combinations, as well as a subsequent ground check, to detect a potential canal fragment, which proved problematic given that the imagery used was taken in July. Future work using imagery from a wetter time of year would likely reveal additional canals. A number of faint linear features appeared, but they were likely to be modern (Showater 1993).

Using ASTER 1B imagery, SPOT 5, IKONOS 2, and Corona imagery, one project at the site of Hisar in Turkey compared how imagery affected the general visibility of archaeological remains. The project noted that Landsat ETM+ imagery did not have the resolution to detect smaller features, with IKONOS, Quickbird, Corona imagery, aerial hyperspectral imagery, and aerial photography having the highest resolution available. Numerous studies, however, have made use of far coarser resolution imagery to detect sites. Maximum likelihood classification, segmentation, nearest neighborhood classification, and filtering were the methods chosen by the team for the remote sensing analysis. Archaeological features did not appear in the classes in which the team expected them to appear, and the filtering did not detect exposed walls. Perhaps the imagery did not date to the appropriate time of year, or atmospheric conditions strongly affected the imagery (De Laet *et al.* 2007).

Towards automated archaeological site detection?

Automated archaeological site detection would be an ideal outcome for archaeologists. Using known algorithms, archaeologists could enter their imagery data in remote sensing programs, and click "locate feature X." The computer program would run through a list of algorithms based on the imagery being analyzed, and would ask questions regarding archaeological site types in the area, ground conditions, and any other pertinent information. Unfortunately, this is not possible, based on the very tenets of archaeology. Archaeologists excavate sites following strict scientific methods, while local conditions, rules, and general support will influence the methods chosen to excavate those sites. Perhaps a team is more interested in excavating graves to study paleopathological issues, or is interested in comparing industrial production techniques across a region. Satellite archaeology is the same: Every project will be different, with each project director determining the direction the work will take. A team may be more interested in environmental issues, locating past river courses, or may be interested in locating features on sites to excavate. Each project drives the remote sensing techniques that can be applied, and ultimately, the survey design.

Computers simply do not have the same ability as human eyes have to pick out subtleties in remotely sensed images. Only the viewer will know what he or she is looking for, based on their background and understanding of the archaeological situation. One cannot input the thousands of minor variables into computers that influence archaeologists when making choices about archaeological data. How will a computer be able to assess similar broad issues for ground surveying? As archaeologists, we can make choices regarding what information we want displayed on satellite imagery, and how we use that information to plan survey seasons. Computers cannot tell if a site or feature is present or not; they just facilitate the display of pixels. It is up to us to determine what those pixels mean.

Thus, there is no "one size fits all" for remote sensing techniques in archaeology, and there can never be any "automatic" feature extraction in archaeological remote sensing.

Archaeologists must assess project needs on local and regional levels, and attempt to find, specific remote sensing algorithms that best fit project goals. The importance of knowing the archaeology and related architecture of a region cannot be understated: Depending on the type and size of structures in question, archaeologists can apply alternate analytical methods to different imagery. Why does there even need to be an automated process for satellite archaeology? One would not want the process of archaeological discovery to be automated on the ground, and the same would apply for locating sites and features from space. Certainly, more mathematical models are needed for satellite archaeology (Li *et al.* 2004), yet all projects will be affected by data quality. Ultimately, the question should not be if there is any "automatic" way to locate sites, but how archaeologists can approach individual remote sensing projects in a scientific way, with a good understanding of what remote sensing analytical methods can offer their work, and what they cannot.

5

LANDSCAPE APPROACHES AND
PROJECT DESIGN

Overview

How we interpret the visual world is a combination of perception and comprehension. Perception may differ from person to person, yet the scientific laws by which the Earth is observed are immutable. It is the crossroads of perception and comprehension where we can place the field of remote sensing. While the science behind remote sensing is fairly well understood, how researchers can interpret the meaning behind what they see is not. Everyone's eyes remotely sense through their own unique "lens" that provides each person with a completely different perception of the world surrounding them. Transforming alternative perceptions into a common archaeological approach would at the outset seem unlikely. What one archaeologist sees as a stable, another would see as a storehouse (Holladay 1986). There are countless additional examples of similar archaeological debates. If archaeologists cannot agree on defining the meaning of basic structures, can they adopt similar approaches for characterizing entire past landscapes for feature location from space? Every landscape is different, depending on weather, climatic conditions, population density, seasonality, and innumerable additional environmental and anthropogenic factors. Similar things affect satellite imagery (Hirata *et al.* 2001).

Approaching landscapes systematically from space mean any remote senser should have a broad archaeological understanding of landscapes. This chapter will provide strategies for overcoming these landscape-based problems from the perspective of completed and ongoing satellite archaeology projects, and provide alternative suggestions for additional approaches archaeologists might have taken. This is not meant as a critique of the projects, as the discussion will be based on project successes and will aid other teams working in similar places or on related feature detection. When thinking about implementing a remote sensing project, archaeologists need a starting point. Even if no maps or aerial photography exist of the regions archaeologists will be exploring from space, and if they have not visited the area before, at the very least they will need to have an idea about the landscape types they will encounter, seen in Tables 5.1 and 5.2. Once an archaeologist has a starting point, it is appropriate to begin to consider the satellites and remote sensing techniques needed for various landscape types. Satellite remote sensing techniques will be discussed in this chapter for the following categories of landscapes: Rainforest, urban (modern), rural, mixed (urban/rural), desert, scrub/grassland, mountainous/hilly, mixed landscape, coastal, waterlogged/wetland (including swamps), alluvial plain, tundra, frozen/glaciated areas. Although these categories are not exhaustive, they represent the majority of landscape types archaeologists will encounter in their work.

Table 5.1 Landscape types and the most applicable satellite images for archaeological projects

	Aerial photography	Corona	Landsat	SPOT	ASTER	Quickbird/ IKONOS	SIR-C/ X-SAR	SRTM
Rainforest			X	X	X	X	X	X
Urban	X	X	X	X	X	X		X
Mixed	X	X	X	X	X	X		X
Rural	X	X	X	X	X	X		X
Desert	X	X	X	X	X	X	X	X
Grassland	X	X	X	X	X	X		X
Mountainous	X	X	X	X	X	X		X
Hilly	X	X	X	X	X	X		X
Mixed	X	X	X	X	X	X		X
Coastal	X	X	X	X	X	X		X
Waterlogged		X	X	X	X	X		
Alluvial Plain	X	X	X	X	X	X	X	X
Tundra	X	X	X	X	X	X		
Frozen			X	X	X	X		X

Table 5.2 Archaeological site types and the most applicable satellite images for archaeological projects

	Aerial photography	Corona	Landsat	SPOT	ASTER	Quickbird/ IKONOS	SIR-C/ X-SAR	SRTM
Settlements	X	X	X	X	X	X		X
Linking	X	X	X	X	X	X	X	X
Temporary	X	X	X	X	X	X		X
Installation	X	X	X	X	X	X		X
Agriculture	X	X	X	X	X	X	X	
Mortuary	X	X	X	X	X	X		X
Religion	X	X	X	X	X	X		X
Ceremonial	X	X	X	X	X	X		X

How much of a role virtual landscapes should play in the analysis of these real world landscapes remains a topic of debate in archaeology. Archeologists deal with past landscapes undergoing real-time alterations, whose changing features have been illuminated by the use of satellite remote sensing. All multispectral satellites, at the level of the pixel, display reflected data on computer through digital numbers in false color. This is not "true" data in the sense that our human eyes cannot view anything beyond the visible part of the electromagnetic spectrum. As such, archaeologists using multispectral data create virtual worlds through digital landscapes. This includes draping aerial photographs over SRTM or LIDAR data which, even with the 3 cm resolution of LIDAR, creates small errors and distortion even with georeferenced aerial photographs.

Some archaeologists emphasize integrating remote sensing with "traditional" techniques by creating managed layers of data using virtual reality. Virtual reality does have an important place in archaeology, as it allows potential reconstructions of past

Figure 5.1 The Acropolis, Athens (scale 1:96 m), note the partial distortion in the image, 2008 image courtesy of Google Earth™ Pro.

landscapes according to what each individual archaeologist wishes to emphasize. This can lead to an overemphasis on things such as 3D imagery, seen in Figure 5.1. Just because it is seen as highly technical should not make something correct or scientifically valid (Campana and Forte 2006). Digital landscapes, however, remain in the eye of the beholder. Past landscapes have been so altered by innumerable processes and events that, with the science currently available, archaeologists cannot make perfect reconstructions of them. This must be recognized even as archaeologists use all the science available to them to create the best possible imagined ancient landscapes. How this data is communicated to allow multiple interpretations is crucial, as all remote sensing will be subjective based on each user's experience. Instead of a "virtual reality," which assumes some type of imagination to reconstruct what is not there, why not a "digital reality?" Archaeologists see their own interpretations of multispectral imagery based on their backgrounds and biases, yet imagery interpretation is quite different than using a computer program to reconstruct a largely destroyed temple. It is unlikely that rigorous excavation will reveal all a temple's missing pieces, while detailed ground survey allows archaeological teams to test their remote sensing hypotheses on ground features initially seen on computer screens.

A full catalogue of site typologies in archaeology would be invaluable for archaeological survey and remote sensing analysis. Differing site types require the use of appropriate satellite remote sensing techniques, and a full range of archaeological sites (ranging from sherd scatters to massive urban complex) can be encountered during each ground survey season. The process of site recognition from space and during survey should not be undervalued: As in excavation, it becomes easy to miss important features by not being completely aware of one's surroundings or what is directly underfoot. Just as mud brick wall debris may subtly give way to a well-defined wall, gentle sloping of the land might obscure an ancient mound mostly covered over by a modern settlement.

This chapter categorizes archaeological site types into 10 broad categories, and describes remote sensing techniques and satellite types that archaeologists can use to identify those sites and features. It draws upon many examples, and discusses pitfalls to avoid for each category. These landscape categories are by no means comprehensive, nor do they suggest that each feature within the landscape type belongs to that category alone. Indeed, nearly every feature type can fit into two or more categories. The categories are merely meant to aid remote sensing researchers in devising strategies for their remote sensing projects. These categories include: Settlements, linking features, water management systems, features temporary and border, installations, agricultural features, mortuary features, religious structures, and ceremonial installations.

Defining an archaeological site is thus not as straightforward as one might assume, and begs the question: Is it an archaeological site or feature if it is not visible to human eyes or satellite imagery interpretation? What is located 6 or 12 m below the ground under a well-defined archaeological site is still considered a part of the site, even though it can only be reached through coring or deep trenching. Vertical remains are not questioned in terms of whether or not they are part of sites. What about the horizontal remains? Just as today, at all points in the past, settlements would have been surrounded by some combination of field systems, canals, vegetation, waterways, or roads. These are excavated and evaluated in the same manner as archaeological sites. Given the density of human settlement and the importance of agricultural land and waterways in the ancient world, defining a true "site" is closely connected to ancient landscapes and how the individual site remains are interacting with ongoing modern processes. Having a holistic view of archaeological landscapes versus specific site locations supports how sites can be explored from space, and will guide the suggestions made for their interpretation with satellite image types and specific analytical techniques from space. This chapter is also not meant as the final word on what will and will not work in each landscape context. It should be viewed more as a general guide and starting point, as all landscapes and archaeological features will vary in size, shape, and spectral signature.

Finding meaning in archaeological landscapes will ultimately depend on the background and experience of the person responsible for the analysis. All people will view a landscape differently, whether one is an artist, geographer, biologist, remote sensing specialist, or an archaeologist (Knapp 2000). Each person will bring the tools of their craft to the table, along with their biases. As an example, this author would not dare to attempt a painting of a scene overlooking the Nile. My artistic skills are limited to drawing pottery, sections, and detailed plans with the aid of rulers. Does this mean I am any less capable of "seeing" a landscape, or deriving meaning from it, when it is viewed from space? Just as an artist will spend hours looking at every detail of a tree or branch so they can draw it correctly, I spend hours examining pixels of important features in satellite imagery so it can be analyzed correctly. No two archaeologists will see a satellite image in the same way, which is why it is important to outline specific landscape and features types as a starting point.

Landscape types

Each landscape type will have various associated features depending on where they are located in the world. Deserts will have higher or lower rainfall levels, rainforests will have different types of vegetation, and urban areas will contrast in their form and function. It is the shared attributes of each landscape type that complicate archaeological site and feature detection from space. Through discussing each remote sensing technique and why they worked or will work well for a particular region, archaeologists will be able to apply those same techniques on imagery in their own landscape-specific work. Some techniques might not apply in a particular region, as discussed in Chapter 4, but problems archaeologists might encounter during remote landscape analysis will be reviewed. The types of information teams or individuals might need to take into the field from the satellite imagery is covered more in Chapter 7, but is discussed here briefly with regards to what might be seen during fieldwork.

Ultimately, from space, archaeologists are searching for landscape relationships, whether through the sense of multispectral data to see how landscapes have changed in relationship to other factors, or how past peoples may have related to landscape types and features within them. How past peoples may have reacted to global climate events is not something that can be addressed alone through remote sensing. However, archaeologists always need to take into account the environmental factors that may have affected site and feature placement. These past events (including natural disasters) may have caused ancient sites and features to be hidden from plain view, yet infrared and thermal satellite bands may reveal them on screen. Finding potential water and food sources, especially in non-resource-rich environments, would have been primary concerns of past peoples. These sources, too, may not be visible unless seen with multispectral data, shown in Tables 5.3 and 5.4. Many case studies have shown that identifying resources used by past peoples from space will generally lead to archaeological site discovery. Archaeologists must look at landscapes from space from a backwards-viewing lens. Thinking about how populations survived in these landscapes can aid in formulating research strategies and in posing broader questions rather than merely finding additional sites.

Rainforest

Rainforests present many challenges to archaeologists who wish to use remote sensing for archaeological site and feature detection (Hixson 2005) (Figure 5.2). Vegetation density makes searching for sites on foot alone virtually impossible. Transportation issues abound, as there may be few paths for trucks to follow. Through pinpointing exact places to survey, archaeologists can plan surveying strategies to maximize their resources. Archaeologists should first examine Landsat ETM+ imagery (with merged 15 m multispectral data) and ASTER imagery, depending on seasonal constraints. Wet season multispectral imagery may not work in detecting vegetation color changes, one of the most likely indicators of hidden archaeological sites. Quickbird and IKONOS imagery, with a much higher resolution, may aid in detecting more specific areas once initial coarser resolution analysis is completed (Saturno *et al.* 2007). Putting the sites into a GIS will aid in areas where little is known, especially for suggesting potential routes or trails between major sites (Herrera *et al.* 2002).

Table 5.3 Landscape types and the most applicable analytical techniques for archaeological work

	Visual	Contrast enhancement	NDVI	Classification	Thresholding	PCA	LULC	DEM	Filtering
Rainforest		X	X	X	X	X	X	X	X
Urban	X	X		X	X	X	X		X
Mixed	X	X	X	X	X	X	X	X	X
Rural	X	X	X	X	X	X	X	X	X
Desert	X	X	X	X	X	X	X	X	X
Grassland	X	X	X	X	X	X	X	X	X
Mountainous	X	X	X	X	X	X	X	X	X
Mixed	X	X		X	X	X	X	X	X
Coastal	X	X		X	X	X	X	X	X
Waterlogged		X	X	X	X	X	X		X
Alluvial Plain	X	X	X	X	X	X	X	X	X
Tundra	X	X	X	X	X		X		X
Frozen	X	X					X		X

Table 5.4 Archaeological site types and the most applicable analytical techniques for archaeological work

	Visual	Contrast enhancement	NDVI	Classification	Thresholding	PCA	DEM	Filtering
Settlements	X	X	X	X	X	X	X	X
Linking	X	X	X	X	X	X	X	X
Temporary	X	X	X	X	X	X	X	X
Installation	X	X		X	X	X		X
Agriculture	X	X	X	X	X	X	X	X
Mortuary	X	X	X	X	X	X	X	X
Religion	X	X	X	X	X	X	X	X
Ceremonial	X	X	X	X	X	X	X	X

Monumental remains of ancient sites, whether in the rainforests of Central America, Asia, or Africa, will most likely consist of stone. This material affects vegetation through chemical leeching into the soils, which is absorbed by the surrounding vegetation. Archaeologists do not have the ability to detect vegetation changes with pure visual detection, as the chemicals cause the leaves to reflect differently in the electromagnetic spectrum. This changed reflection might be detectable using classification (supervised and unsupervised), principal components analysis (PCA), and varying band combinations, which should first be tested on the known ancient sites in the region being explored. If the vegetation atop archaeological features is healthier or less healthy, the surrounding vegetation then NDVI will detect it. A focus should be made on the infrared (IR) part of the spectrum as vegetation will be the most likely indicator of ancient remains. These remains may include: Structures (Willey 1990), extensions of previously known sites, lakes, water reserves, and swampy areas associated with settlements. Broader issues of site abandonment can also be considered. In the Amazon Basin,

Figure 5.2 Rainforest in Brazil (scale 1:11328 m), showing extensive illegal logging and deforestation, which has destroyed many archaeological sites around the world, 2008 image
courtesy of Google Earth™ Pro.

Landsat imagery revealed an abandoned floodplain, now covered with forests and lakes.
It would have been difficult to assess the overall landscape changes without the help
of missionary writings. Combining this information with the satellite data helped the
team understand past patterns of warfare (Parssinen *et al.* 1996).

RADAR imagery, including SAR and SIR-C, may work to detect potential canals
and other linear features. Archaeologists should exercise caution when examining this
data, as linear patterns may be larger than actual features and the overall resolution of
sensors may be too poor to detect anything. As with all archaeological site detection
from space, features must be detected on the ground before any claims can be made
(Pope *et al.* 1993). There can be significant noise from RADAR imagery, which can
confuse even experienced remote sensing eyes. The L-band on SIR-C may aid in feature
detection, but its low resolution may not detect smaller features. In rainforest areas, it
may be of value for archaeologists to invest in high-resolution RADAR data, especially
in areas where canals are well known, such as northern Belize and the Candelaria area in
Campeche, Mexico (Pope and Dahlin 1989). LIDAR imagery will have much to offer the
archaeology of rainforest regions, especially with its ability to see beneath dense canopy
at high resolutions. LIDAR will probably contribute the most to the archaeology of
rainforest regions over the next five years because it can detect archaeological features
that would otherwise be unrecognizable due to vegetation cover.

Figure 5.3 Colosseum, Rome, Italy (scale 1:82 m), 2008 image courtesy of Google Earth™ Pro.

Urban (modern)

Urban areas covering archaeological sites present a great challenge to archaeologists who wish to use satellite imagery. Human beings generally have great continuity of occupation, with many of the world's great cities (Rome, Athens, Cairo, etc.) covering layers of ancient debris (Figure 5.3). The ancient remains of a town may be deeply buried beneath modern buildings, with layers of concrete, piping, and wires obscuring site detection. Even on the ground, methods such as ground penetrating radar may not be able to detect the buried remains. Urban expansion is a global issue, which both helps and hinders the process of archaeological site discovery. Any time construction takes place in an old city, it is likely that ancient remains will appear. In the USA and parts of Europe, strict regulations govern the process of construction. Archaeological cultural resource management firms need to excavate the area in question to map and record any remains prior to construction. In other parts of the world, however, the same rules and regulations are not in force, and much has certainly been lost over the past 50 years.

Diverse remote sensing strategies must be employed when attempting to detect archaeological sites from space in urban settings. If a city or large town is suspected of being atop an ancient site, Landsat, SPOT, and ASTER imagery can detect land cover land use changes, which can be used to determine general rates of urbanization and its effects on archaeological sites. Religious structures can often be centrally located in a town, and may be in the oldest part. That knowledge can help with knowing where to look for ancient sites. Classification techniques may aid in differentiating between an older part of town and a newer part, with the assumption that a newer part of town will have different building materials. From space, it is not possible to see beneath modern structures. One can assess the general topography and search for the parts of a town site with higher elevation by draping satellite imagery over SRTM data. Using high-resolution data in parks, exposed lots, or playgrounds may show crop-marks in the infrared range, which may be further revealed through frost or heavy rains. For example, on soccer fields in Cambridge, UK, the author noted that crop-marks of circular structures appeared more strongly following a period of rain. Edge detection on Quickbird imagery may also help. If a known archaeological site is partially covered by a settlement, then archaeologists can determine the spectral signature and use classification to discern other exposed parts of sites (Parcak 2007b).

Rural or forested

The term "rural" does not refer to a uniform landform type. In general, rural areas can be defined as areas that are: without dense occupation, forested areas, grasslands, or partial deserts. The latter two categories are discussed further in this chapter. Even more modern dwellings in rural regions will aid in archaeological site location, as they may be strategically placed near long-used resources. These may include water sources, forests, or other natural resources. Using ASTER, SPOT, and Landsat to examine land cover change through time will help see any general landscape trends. Like in rainforest areas, vegetation vigor may vary on top of dense ancient remains. Smaller ancient sites, such as shell middens, will not be detectable from space if obscured by dense vegetation. Rural occupations might be near specific geological formations, such as mountainous terrain, good for feeding sheep or goats. Human beings affect landscapes in so many subtle ways, with terracing, housing abandonment, and their associated waste products, that sometimes only LIDAR has the ability to see beneath the dense vegetation. Structures deteriorate and decay over time, while their appearance from above is stabilized by vegetation, and can be detected with relief variations. Filtering a digital terrain model created with LIDAR in a forested area can show solid ground versus vegetation cover, slopes, and other ancient remains not visible from aerial photographs alone. The key is slower moving platforms to allow more of the pulses to reach the ground (Doneus and Briesse 2006b). Quickbird and IKONOS data may aid the detection of cropmarks and other buried features once a team has chosen a specific area with known archaeological generally remains. Starting with the known and working towards the unknown in large rural areas is the best way to proceed.

Mixed (urban/rural)

Transition zones may exist between urban and rural areas, as many cities can be a mix of both rural and urban zones. Using a combination of approaches is the best way to detect sites in mixed environments. When sites are located in urban areas, archaeologists should use urban detection techniques, and vise versa for rural areas.

Desert

Deserts present a unique set of challenges to archaeologists. They are, by nature, arid places, yet many past groups lived in regions now classified as desert. Some of these

Figure 5.4 Merv, Turkmenistan (scale 1:109 m), showing the great and small Kyz Kala, 2008 image courtesy of Google Earth™ Pro.

current deserts used to be wetter grassland areas, while others have been deserts for some time. People traveled extensively in desert areas following trading routes such as the Silk Road, or along paths in Egypt's Western Desert used as military access routes (Darnell 2002). People could travel along desert roads as part of caravans, to access trading depots, military outposts, camps, or processional routes. Around the archaeological site of Merv in the Kara Kum Desert (Figure 5.4) archaeologists used varying satellite images to map cities along the Silk Road (Sykes 1997). These past peoples would have settled along the Silk Road permanently, while other cultures had varied relationships with desert landscapes. For people like the ancient Egyptians, the desert was "deshret," or the red land, the opposite of the fertile Nile Valley, and a place to be feared and worshipped.

In desert areas, people would have needed ready access to water and food, if the distances traveled made it difficult to transport these items themselves. Water could be found by digging deep wells, or by having access to oases, seasonal lakes, streams, or more semi-annual bodies of water that may have flowed more strongly in the winter and spring seasons. If past groups stayed longer term in a desert area, then they would have needed some type of permanent shelter. Trails or paths are additional features archaeologists can search for in desert areas. If groups permanently resided in a place removed from food sources, they may have had to support their own agriculture. SIR-C and SAR data have a history of being used to detect buried water sources, especially the so-called "radar rivers" in Egypt's Western Desert, which used to be savannah land in the late Pleistocene Period (ca. 130,000–10,000 B.C.) (McHugh *et al.* 1988).

Overall landscape modeling should be done with SRTM data, as depressions can lead to the discovery of former water sources, including wells. Using NDVI on ASTER, Landsat, or SPOT data may help locate seasonal vegetation bursts (Karnieli *et al.* 2002) or modern vegetation watered from old wells and water sources (Parker *et al.* 2006). High-resolution imagery may even detect modern wells associated with now defunct riverbeds. In one study conducted to produce a record of Holocene surface water extension in a desert region of Mali, spectral data detected Holocene paleolakes fed by annual runoff between 7000–2000 BC (+/−500 years). Classification allowed a minimum area of the lake to be reconstructed (Lambin *et al.* 1995). Using Landsat, RADARSAT, and SIR-C imagery, a team of geologists mapped the Kharga depression in Egypt's Western Desert, showing that it was a main area for ground water accumulation (Robinson 2002).

When searching over a broad area for past remains in a desert, a range of imagery will be needed. SRTM data can be draped over ASTER imagery for general landscape modeling to find the edges of past water sources (Bubenzer and Bolten 2003). Old traces of fields may appear in Corona imagery, or aerial photographs, or through edge detection with Quickbird imagery. This may be seasonal, with some vegetation growing atop field boundaries in winter months (Okin *et al.* 2001). Modern groups may be seasonal in terms of where they live and herd their animals, so studying these groups may give clues to past subsistence patterns and what might be able to be detected from space. Too much sand may be covering past remains, and the size of the past building will vary. Spectral signatures of known sites in the area being explored should be obtained for comparative purposes, whether the material used included stone, mudbrick, straw, or other materials. The size of the past structures and features will determine what satellites are most appropriate to use.

Detecting past trails from space may be harder, especially as so many ancient trails are reused in modern contexts. Landsat, SPOT, and ASTER may reveal larger desert trails with classification, PCA, and band combinations. Edge detection with IKONOS and Quickbird may aid in picking out smaller trails. If ancient peoples lined their paths with stones or other material, they will have a distinct spectral signature, and if compact enough or filled with enough past debris, the roads may retain water for longer periods. This can be detected with NDVI during winter and spring months as vegetation may concentrate along these paths. For overall landscape visualization and recreating ancient routes, SRTM data can be used in a form of techno-ethnoarchaeology: Archaeologists can determine strategies past peoples devised to travel along desert paths, and recreate ancient routes based on any known, historic texts that may exist. In Egypt's Western Desert (Figure 5.5) one team studied routes between the oases using ASTER and Landsat data. These routes, important during the late Roman Period (ca. 400–800 AD), traversed landscapes where the precipitation was less than 5 mm per year with a few wells lining the caravan routes. The team recognized that additional routes had yet to be located, mapped, and surveyed (Eichhorn *et al.* 2005).

Grassland

Grassland regions may be the locations of former forests or other types of landscapes. Cultures living in grassland areas would have practiced either grazing or hunting animals such as buffalo. Past peoples in grasslands would have had seasonal campsites, but the

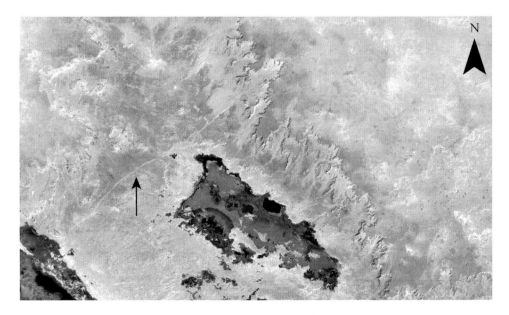

Figure 5.5 Western Desert, Egypt Landsat (scale 1:40000 m), note ancient desert paths are visible from space, image courtesy of NASA World Wind.

relationship of these occupations to natural resources needs to be well understood when using satellite imagery. From space, archaeologists might find ancient migration routes of animals or cropmarks showing evidence of seasonal settlements. This would be difficult if the structures did not require any foundations or did not disturb the soil in any way. Historic-period houses may lend themselves more to this type of detection. It may be that past groups living in grassland areas did not alter the landscape enough for it to be detected from space thousands of years later (Roberts 1990). Certainly, ancient groups would have followed water resources, so crop marks or specific spectral signatures may reveal now-silted up river sources or other bodies of water. These may be seasonally detected after periods of heavy rain or in periods of heavy vegetation growth. Landsat and ASTER imagery can classify landscape types, as ancient remains might be detectable in specific classes of land. Old roads may be visible on Quickbird or IKONOS satellite imagery with edge detection, while ancient migration routes may be buried deeply beneath the soil.

In general, archaeologists will likely be carrying out broad landscape analysis, so they will need large landscape coverage with coarser resolution satellite imagery. Large communities in countries such as Mongolia may have occupied specific areas for long periods of time, altering the soil enough to change its spectral signature, thus making it detectable with multispectral satellite imagery. In a more modern study in Mongolia, a team used Landsat imagery, NDVI variation, and DEMs to study spatial grazing patterns. The team found that pastoralists concentrated around permanent settlements. Political changes in Mongolia in the 1990s from socialism to capitalism caused a collapse in grazing pressure (Okayasu *et al.* 2007). This study shows the importance of how centrally located and peripheral groups might have functioned in the past.

Mountainous/hilly

Past peoples would have occupied hilly and mountainous regions for many reasons, including: defensive purposes, mining, general settlements, or settlements in association with religious structures or cults. Uneven terrain makes it difficult to search for remains, as they may be partially obscured by overhanging rocks. Obtaining SRTM data and draping Landsat imagery over it is the first step in analyzing archaeological material in elevated areas. The elevations of known archaeological sites and features can be compared to other suggestive signatures. Settlements and features may appear at approximately the same elevation, or there may be linear relationships between site locations. ASTER, SPOT, and Landsat imagery can classify mountainous landscapes to see if actual sites have definite spectral signatures, or if known sites appear connected with discreet geological formations. Paths to and from sites may be located with higher resolution imagery; everything depends on the purpose and function of the structures being examined. Ancient and modern mountain paths may be impossible to distinguish from one another (especially in association with mining regions still being used today), while reuse will only be determined by collecting material culture on the ground.

Google Earth™ Pro may aid in viewing sites and features in 3D with high-resolution data (Figure 5.6). Hyperspectral data may be the most effective tool when working in a mining region, as features may be found in association with specific minerals. Overall landscape visualization in 3D will help archaeologists assess why cultures built in mountainous regions in the first place. Even creating maps of mountainous regions can aid teams in creating base maps for their topographic surveys (Romano and Schoenbruan 1993). Religious structures in hilly areas will vary in purpose and function: Whether to

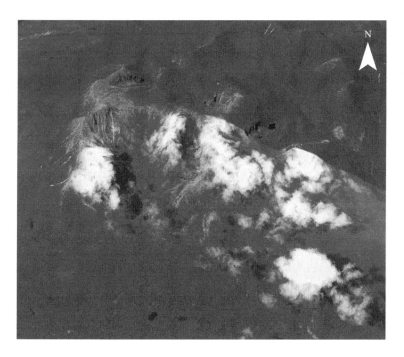

Figure 5.6 Mt. Katahdin, Maine (scale 1:3000 m), 2008 image courtesy of Google Earth™ Pro.

be seen, such as the Bamiyan Buddhas; or to remain hidden, such as cave dwellings for ascetics. "Hilly" includes wadi or valley regions, such as Petra, which are even harder to map, as satellite imagery can be taken at an angle, which may prevent archaeologists from seeing the base of wadis. Additional problems in detecting mountainous features include surface topography, erosion, faults, and sites covered over by avalanches, mudslides, or earthquakes (Toprak 2002).

Archaeologists have noted that working in mountainous terrain can be problematic, which is why a range of image types should be employed. Vegetation can mask soil types covering ancient remains, again making the case for hyperspectral data. In the Itanos area of Eastern Crete, a team used Airborne Thematic Mapper (ATM), Compact Airborne Spectrographic Images (CASI), and LIDAR data to map the harbor region. This area was important for trade between Crete and the Eastern Mediterranean during the Greek through Byzantine Periods. Rains were found to be at higher levels between one to three meters below the surface. Stones used for the ancient buildings were noted to be the same as the stones lying on the ground surface. Early morning was the time the archaeologists took the imagery, when heat differences with buried features and the ground were the greatest. After correcting the data, the team used NDVI and classification. The CATA and ATM data showed some anomalies, and the LIDAR data revealed one wall. The remote sensing showed abandoned terraces as well as a threshing floor. The authors commented on the problems of using remote sensing to detect subsurface remains with many mixed pixels. One wonders why they did not use Quickbird imagery. In the areas the team was investigating, it would not have been too costly and would have provided them with high resolution for subsurface feature detection, and could have been combined with the LIDAR data. (Rowlands and Sarris 2007).

Mixed landscapes

Most remote sensing will include mixed landscapes, which will require archaeologists to have differentiated approaches (Urwin and Ireland 1992). This is why broad multispectral datasets (such as ASTER, SPOT, Landsat, and Corona) are needed. Archaeological sites will appear differently in each landscape site, so approaches need to be adapted accordingly. Similar features in different landscape types may have identical spectral signatures. Major landscape projects surveying across different landscape types will use satellite imagery types they determine to be most appropriate (Palmer 2002a; Campana *et al.* 2006; Powlesland *et al.* 2006).

Coastal

Coastal settlements may be either permanent or seasonal, but their overall purpose and function will vary (Franco 1996). Such settlements may be trading towns, simple coastal fishing villages, or located within fortresses, which may have some type of docking system, harbor, or shipbuilding areas. Structures will also be built of varied materials. How these can be detected from space depend on this material, as well as the waste products left behind by past groups. These would most likely include fish bones and shell middens. Actual places of settlement may not be visible from space if they are obscured by dense coastal vegetation. Many coastal towns have remained important

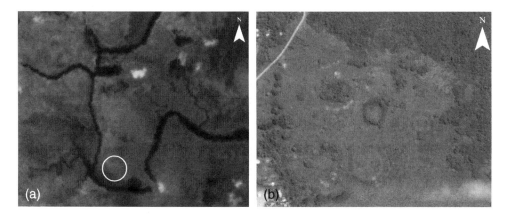

Figure 5.7 Vanua Levu, Fiji: (a) 3-2-1 Landsat image showing region with dense cropmarks one of
which can be seen in the circle; (b) Quickbird satellite image showing fort structures,
images courtesy of NASA and Google Earth™ Pro.

through time, so ancient parts of towns may be covered over partially or entirely by
modern structures.

Multispectral or hyperspectral imagery will work best in detecting the spectral signatures of past settlements or, through NDVI, PCA, and classifications, will detect
vegetation atop ancient remains. In Fiji, on the island on Vanua Levu (Figures 5.7a
and 5.7b) Landsat ETM+ data revealed the spectral signatures of fortress-like structures
that appeared more clearly on Quickbird data (as observed by the author). These inland
sites were likely built with an increased need for more defensive positions. Clusters of
over 100 structures were seen. This was unusual on the Landsat data, as the walls of
the structure were not more than a few meters thick, showing how smaller features can
appear on coarser data if the spectral signature is distinct enough from the surrounding
landscape.

Ocean and sea edges change constantly, with many ancient sites being partially or
entirely washed into the sea. This can clearly be seen along the coast in Ireland, or at the
edges of sites in the Mediterranean, where many earthquakes have sunk cities such as
Alexandria. Low tides may reveal partially washed away sites, which makes knowing the
timing of tides important when ordering high resolution imagery: One would wish to
place an order for imagery when the tide is low in the morning. Can waterlogged features
be seen from space? The author observed remnants of what appears to be old docking
systems in Brittany, France, using World Wind. Satellites cannot see underwater due
to the reflective properties of water. Settlements along the coast may have their own
spectral signatures, which may or may not be affected by tides. SRTM data can model
coastal sites, and predict the elevations where similar sites may appear.

Waterlogged/wetland (including swamps)

This is an area that has received virtually no attention from archaeologists using satellite
imagery. Waterlogged ancient sites may or may not be detectable from space, depending
on how much of the ancient site remains exposed today. Features could be too deeply

buried beneath debris to be located. If people lived in waterlogged areas, then they would have needed to live on elevated areas in structures built above watercourses. High humidity may cause such elevated platforms to disintegrate over time. Broad landscape classification with SPOT, Landsat, and ASTER will help define wetland or swampy areas in broader landscapes, where archaeologists will search for features. For example, in past swampy areas in England, ancient groups threw in what were likely sacrificial victims, known today as "bog bodies." An archaeologist identified peat deposit Landsat and classification data, which represent past swampy regions where additional bog bodies might be located (Cox 1992).

Former swampy or waterlogged regions may now be filled in with earth, and therefore detectable. If not, there may be some elevated areas where ancient remains might be found. SRTM data will detect general landscape topography, and may help archaeologists zoom in on potential areas to examine. In swampy regions, issues of access might be a problem, for how might one search for sites in an almost entirely waterlogged area? Vegetation remains may appear with different colors when examined with multispectral imagery. Even if exact coordinates are known for potential sites, an archaeologist can canoe or kayak to reach the sites, the GPS units may malfunction with dense foliage as described above. PCA, classification, and hyperspectral data combinations may detect vegetation differences above ancient sites, but if an area is still too waterlogged, those remains will probably not appear from space.

Alluvial plain

Alluvial plains differ in size and shape across the globe. How much the rivers in the plains would have flooded in the past, or how much the rivers continue to flood in the present, depended on (or depends on) climactic conditions and annual rainfall patterns. Some alluvial plains have many ancient remains visible today, while others have partially silted over sites, totally silted over sites, or a mix of all three. Alluvial plains were ideal areas of settlement for past peoples, given the large amounts of nutrients in the soils for agricultural purposes. Alluvial regions were also ideal for transportation, livestock feeding, and trading, as past settlements would have concentrated along rivers in alluvial plains that connected much larger bodies of water. These settlements would have varied in size, with a central area of settlement (either a regional or local capital) surrounded by a hinterland of smaller sites. These sites may follow canals or rivers long since silted over, so identifying past water sources is the central goal when working in alluvial regions.

Alluvial plans can first be mapped with Landsat imagery draped over SRTM data to gain a general sense of topography. Slightly higher areas of elevation may indicate former places of settlement. Landsat, SPOT, ASTER, and other hyperspectral data may reveal spectral signatures of ancient sites, which is why it helps to have known sites in the region for testing techniques such as classification, PCA, band combinations, and others. Corona imagery is important to use for landscapes now largely altered by modernization. Many landscape changes have occurred in the past 30 years, so Corona imagery or aerial photography, dating prior to 1975, may show features now destroyed by increasing agricultural practices in alluvial regions. It may be difficult to differentiate archaeological site material from the silt surrounding it, but extensive past human occupation debris should alter a site's spectral signature sufficiently for it to be detected from space.

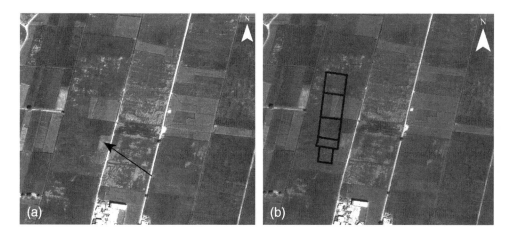

Figure 5.8 Tell Sariri, Delta (scale 1:86 m): (a) showing cropmarks; and (b) cultic structure, 2008 image courtesy of Google Earth™ Pro.

These sites will range from tiny settlements to massive cities, or may appear to be a small city based on surface remains, yet magnetometer survey will reveal a major site long since silted over. This is where crop marks may aid in determining a site's former extent.

Once archaeologists have identified potential sites, they can purchase higher resolution imagery to view crop marks, which may be viewable on Google Earth™ or World Wind. For example, an archaeological site declared as "destroyed" in Egypt's East Delta, Tell Sariri, had clear crop marks that showed the potential foundations of a cultic structure (Parcak 2009) (Figures 5.8a and 5.8b). This was a site archaeologists said was destroyed over 100 years ago, and shows the power satellite imagery can have in reconstructing supposedly "lost" landscapes.

Assessing changes in alluvial plains is made difficult by exponentially increasing changes (Brivio *et al.* 2000), which is why land use land cover change analyses are so important in alluvial areas. SIR-C and RADAR imagery may aid in detecting past alluvial courses, and will help archaeologists reconstruct rates of change. Dams will affect silt discharge, which, in turn, will affect how much river courses shift. If rivers rise because of dams, then large alluvial areas may disappear, and satellite imagery may be the only record of areas under water. It will not be possible to ground truth those sites, but at least identifying features will contribute to a better archaeological understanding of a region.

Rivers would have had specific periods of maximum discharge, yet the overall amount of discharge would have varied through time. This discharge, through time, would have affected ancient site placement, for if a river started to cut into a settlement, it would have moved partially or entirely. Modern floodplains have levees, active channels, crevasse splays, and abandoned channels, and some of these factors, such as levees, may be mistaken from space as being ancient occupation areas. Levee height will vary in each floodplain, and may represent ancient levees worn away through time. In Lower Mesopotamia, which was irrigated mainly by the Euphrates (the Tigris was more violent and less predictable), SPOT imagery and aerial photographs identified ancient river courses, abandoned channels, and crevasse splays associated with early agriculture. Early groups of people could change channels to support irrigation, thus aiding the growth of early city states. These splays show a sedimentation rate of 1–1.8 mm per year between 6400–1000 BC (Morozova 2005), similar rates to the Nile Delta (Butzer 1976) but lower than Middle Egypt, which seemed to have rates of 5 mm per year (Parcak 2007a).

With Landsat, SPOT, ASTER, RADARSAT, and Corona imagery, a team of archaeologists studied landscape change in the region surrounding the region of Nippur and Lake Dalmaj in Iraq (Southern Mesopotamia). This region consists of floodplains, abandoned floodplains, and some dune areas, with no survey done since the 1990s. Artificial coloring of grayscale Corona imagery aided the team in landscape assessment. With significant modern land use changes, the team used a number of remote sensing techniques to make past sites appear. Histogram equalization and linear stretching revealed additional canals, while the RADAR imagery revealed canals, dunes, levees, and agricultural systems. Even with speckle reduction, the RADAR imagery needed to be used with the SPOT and Landsat imagery. These images were classified into 25 categories to examine past versus present drainage patterns, then integrated into a GIS. Corona imagery showed that land changes through time revealed more levees as dunes shifted. 33 previously unknown features that seemed likely to be ancient appeared, but ground truthing was impossible with the ongoing Iraq conflict (Richardson and Hritz 2007).

Tundra

Tundra may be challenging for remote sensing work, depending on how much of the year it remains frozen. As there are short growing seasons, archaeologists can take advantage of the window when vegetation is starting to emerge (Figure 5.9) or when frost is starting to appear. Using high-resolution imagery, either crop marks or frostmarks may appear. Densely settled seasonal encampments may have their own spectral signatures, detectable during warmer months. It is worth classifying Landsat, ASTER, or SPOT imagery prior to purchasing higher-resolution imagery to see if any specific landscape class types show potential archaeological remains. This depends on the overall survey size. It may help comparing the spectral signatures of modern groups with potential areas for past remains. When examining areas with indigenous groups, the remains these groups may leave behind before shifting camps may show how past peoples affected the landscapes. Also, archaeologists can examine where these groups live in relationship to food, water, and transportation routes. If teams know that settlements have not altered greatly in hundreds of years, it might help them think about groups of people even further back in time. Global warming is also affecting settlements in tundra regions. With warming temperatures, frostmarks may not be around for as long, and remains preserved by the frost may have deteriorated. ASTER imagery, with three thermal bands, can determine how much warming may have affected past remains. Hyperspectral imagery can also assess known remains in the thermal band, and see how warmer temperatures may have affected potentially "new" sites as well.

Frozen/glaciated areas

Frozen areas will likely completely obscure past remains, especially areas covered with glaciers that would have covered over traces of human remains from the last interglacial period. There may be evidence of seasonal encampments, but if covered over by ice, it

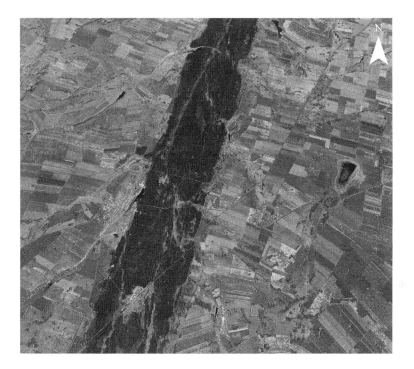

Figure 5.9 Siberia (scale 1:4688 m), 2008 image courtesy of Google Earth™ Pro.

will not be possible to see them from space at present. Archaeological remains from frozen areas, like that of Utzi, or "The Iceman", can be discovered randomly. There may be many other frozen people or past remains in glaciers, but the chances of high-resolution imagery detecting them are small (Utzi would have been measured by one by two Quickbird pixels). Certainly, archaeologists can scan frozen areas to check for anomalies, and with global warming, larger areas hidden by glaciers appear each year. These areas can be detected through land use land cover change on coarser resolution imagery, and then searched more carefully with high-resolution imagery, but only if one has a good idea of what features might appear. These will vary depending on what part of the world the work is taking place.

Feature types

Settlements

Cities, villages, towns, seasonal campsites (varying landscape types), walls/architecture, industrial installations (inside and outside of settlements, crossing zones)

All villages, towns, and cities will vary in size. What may be considered a major city in one archaeological region may be a village in another. Scale of construction will depend on local, regional, and national factors, while landscapes will continue to play a considerable role. Resources of cultures will vary through time, and growth or collapse of civilizations or empires will present challenges for finding archaeological sites with satellite imagery as site placement changes. Through locating important natural resources, satellites will aid archaeologists in determining how and why settlements and features have changed location through time.

No matter the size, all occupied areas will contain some form of architecture, though it will vary in size, shape, and material. Identifying what material past peoples used for their occupations will aid in determining what remote sensing methods will work for feature detection. Each material may have its own individual spectral signature, or will alter how vegetation and surrounding soils reflect light. Most occupation sites have mixed architecture, depending on the function of the structures. A temple will likely be built out of better (and longer-lasting) material than a poor family home. Material durability also needs to be considered in comparison to the overall surrounding environment. A mudbrick structure preserved in an ancient layered settlement in Egypt above the floodplain will be easier to detect from space than the same type of structure in a still-active, low-lying floodplain area. Having extensive knowledge of known sites and architecture types will determine what similar features might appear at other sites, and what their spectral signatures might be.

Architecture of varying size has appeared on many types of satellite imagery. If walls are sufficiently thick, or are easily discernable from the surrounding soils with a distinct spectral signature (Ben-Dor 1999), then coarser resolution Landsat or SPOT imagery will be able to detect them. Thick features covered by agriculture will be viewable on Google Earth™ or World Wind with crop marks. If imagery is taken at the right time of year, then a number of subsurface features will appear. Knowing the correct time of year to purchase imagery will help to map subsurface features with Quickbird imagery. At Tell el-Amarna, Egypt's most well-preserved ancient city, Quickbird satellite imagery detected a number of subsurface architectural remains. Most of the mudbrick walls for houses at Amarna in the central city are less than 1 m in thickness, with a large part of the size covered in debris from past excavations. Using edge detection revealed several unexcavated structures (Parcak 2005).

Town layout may be a factor in satellite mapping. Many urban centers, especially if connected to state governments, were planned, or could be laid out according to cosmic patterns or diagrams. Some streets may be straight (Thakker 2002) (Figure 5.10), while others may meander in a seemingly random pattern. Street directions may vary depending on where in the town they are located. A number of ancient cities would have had central main streets or an axis. These features, even if filled in today, would likely be large enough to be detected from space on several satellite image types (if not already mapped). If archaeologists have planned well-known archaeological sites, the remote sensing may reveal a small to major part of the site covered by a modern town or agricultural fields. Knowing the orientation of structures and building types will aid in mapping the newly discovered features.

Detecting "cities" from space should not be an outward goal of archaeological remote sensing projects. First, one can never know what one has found until ground-truthing and excavation are performed, unless a great deal is already known about archaeological sites in the region. Settlements can be obscured by shifting sands, rainforest growth,

Figure 5.10 Mohenjodaro, Pakistan (scale 1:250 m), note detailed street plans, 2008 image courtesy of Google Earth™ Pro.

oceans, forests, and deposits from rivers. How archaeologists decide to detect the occupation areas is more a function of landscape type than settlement type. Coarser resolution imagery is best if one is working in a broad area, while Corona imagery and aerial photographs will give a good sense of what the landscape was like prior to major urbanization (if it occurred post-1970s). Higher-resolution data should be purchased once a team has decided to focus on a specific site or sites detected from coarser data, or archaeologists want to attempt subsurface feature detection on known sites.

Ancient settlements were affected by landscape processes occurring at different rates through time (Kamei and Nakagoshi 2002), but would have been most affected by changes to water and food sources. In Mumbai and Calcutta, maps at varying scales in addition to SPOT and IKONOS imagery detected water catchment areas attractive for settlement (Som 2002). Water sources may have dried up quickly or over hundreds of years, changing settlements from permanent to seasonal to nonexistent. By mapping areas where water once flowed, archaeologists can follow the paths of these water sources, or perhaps locate vegetation signatures that mark past water sources still used today (Mumford and Parcak 2002; Parcak 2004a). In China, RADARSAT and Landsat 4-3-2 imagery detected a canal silted over in Jin Dynasty (ca. AD 1115–1234), along which major cities prospered during the Song Dynasties (ca. AD 605–1279) due to trade (Xin-Yuan *et al.* 2004).

Seasonal campsites present more of a challenge for satellite archaeology. Many seasonal encampments would have had temporary buildings (i.e. tents or yurts), yet if an area were occupied over enough seasons, enough waste debris would accumulate to alter the landscape enough to be detected from space. A number of permanent yet seasonally occupied structures exist at archaeological sites around the world. For example, a military garrison may only need to occupy a stone-built fortress during a certain time of year. These structures would be much easier to locate, especially if located in more rural or removed areas such as deserts where their spectral signatures would stand out.

Archaeologists need to focus on past and present factors affecting ancient settlements. Using a combination of IRS, SPOT, and Landsat imagery, archaeologists mapped two fort sites in Hyderabad (Golconda Fort and Purana Qila). Satellites aided the team in specific site location, spatial distribution of archaeological sites, and the general extent of the monuments. Golconda Fort covers an area of 317 hectares, and was important as a medieval fort as well as laying the foundations for Hyderabad city. Purana Qila was also a medieval city. Archaeologists had serious concerns regarding urbanization in both sites, with urbanization increasing 82 percent in 15 years at Golconda Fort and 667 percent in 15 years at Purana Qila (Balaji et al. 1996).

Industrial areas within settlements or cities will have distinct spectral signatures if they are large enough and their waste products occur in large quantities. How these sites may be detected from space depends on the type of fuel past peoples used and what byproducts might have been produced. Slag may litter the surface of an archaeological site enough to be detected through space, either through a distinct spectral signature, or through color differences in visual imagery. In southeast Norway, archaeologists used LIDAR to detect forested sites dating to AD 650–1350 (late Viking–Middle Ages). The team created a digital terrain model to detect concave and convex anomalies, which included 17 possible iron extraction heaps. Fieldwork showed that five of the 17 sites were indeed iron extraction heaps, with the others being natural structures or errors. The ability of the imagery to detect iron sites depended on the overall size of the remains, the density of the ground iron, and the time of the survey season (in either autumn or spring, when no leaf ground cover obscures features) (Risbol et al. 2006).

Linking

Footpaths, roads, trails, former river courses (as a linking entity), canals

Paths, roads, and trails all differ in meaning and function. Some exist as a main transportation route between major settlements, while others may be a processional route or a way for past peoples to access types of natural resources. Most past linking routes would have had multiple layers of meaning, many of which may no longer be understood by archaeologists. Differentiating between the sacred and the profane on roads or trails is not an easy exercise when only a small part of the paths survive today, and archaeological teams may not understand a basic "to" or "from." Some past peoples lined their roads with bricks, stone or wood, working to keep them clear of debris, while others allowed human or animal traffic to trample paths flat. Trails, paths, and roads also vary in width and length (Argotte-Espino and Chavez 2005), and modern reuse may present the greatest challenge for remote sensers to locate "ancient" paths from space. Meaning in landscape is closely connected to the meaning of past paths and trails, as they would likely have been closely connected to major landscape features.

In southeast Utah, an archaeological study using IKONOS and Earlybird (another high resolution satellite image), detected a series of 10 m wide Pueblo trails in a network extending for 100 km. On the ground, the paths could only be visible to the well-informed eye. The trails connected many ancestral pueblo settlements, but could have predated the houses. They consisted of straight roads that did not pass around canyons or hills, but instead, traveled through them. Use of the IR band helped to identify the trails the best. The team could not connect any one meaning to the trails, as they were likely associated with trade, social interactions, politics, and general communication. Whether the trails had a religious purpose could not be determined. Locating archaeological features along the trails proved difficult because of issues with general destruction, animal grazing, erosion, bikes, and off-roading (Williamson *et al.* 2002).

Detecting trails or paths in densely vegetated areas with satellite imagery is another archaeological challenge, especially in rainforest areas. In the Arena region of Costa Rica, Mayan occupation in areas further north was not dense. This affected human impact on the landscape. With low human occupation density, there was more of a reliance on community feasting and wild food gathering. In the Arenal region, a separation existed between cemeteries and villages. Understanding how the people of this area ascribed meaning along routes between the cemeteries and villages became one of the central foci of a satellite archaeology study. The study used color infrared imagery, IKONOS, RADAR, Landsat, SRTM, and TIMS imagery with range between 8.2 and 12.2 μm, which detected temperature differences on the ground. Black and white aerial photography detected some paths prior to a 1973 mudslide. RADAR imagery detected many anomalies but had too much noise. Landsat imagery helped to pick out moisture differences, while pan sharpening the IKONOS imagery and using PCA, band combinations, filtering, and contrast enhancements helped to visualize the paths. Draping the imagery over SRTM data allowed 3D visualization (Figure 5.11).

Starting in ca. 500 BC, the people of the Arenal region altered the landscape with the construction of paths, found to be 2 m or more in-depth, and constructed of earth and stone. These linear footpaths allowed the perpetuation of social memory, yet there were problems differentiating between modern paths and ancient ones. The "proper" way to reach a cemetery was along an entrenched straight path, thus creating a form of social memory connected to a sense of monumentality. Radiocarbon dating occurred with samples of tephra from the paths, as the Arena volcano has erupted 10 times over the past 4000 years (Lambert 1997; Sheets 2004; Sheets and Sever 2006, 2007).

Locating canals and other linking bodies of water depends on what the bodies of water linked. Some may have been natural transportation or trading routes (thus providing the impetus for constructing the canal in the first place), while others may have facilitated more political contacts. The purpose and function of canals would have changed through time. Canals that lay unused in one period may be reused by another ruler, and thus dug out again. Dams and reservoirs would have altered these linking routes. Detecting past bodies of water from space requires virtually identical techniques as the alluvial chapter section, although higher resolution imagery may need to be obtained if the canals were not wide. Past land use practices would have affected usage of linking

Figure 5.11 Arenal region of Costa Rica (scale 1:2196 m) note extensive cloud cover in imagery, arrow points to Arenal Volcano, 2008 image courtesy of Google Earth™ Pro.

bodies of water, which is why a broad remote sensing and GIS approach is required (Niknami 2004).

Temporary/border

Waystations, caravanserai, frontier posts and border forts, quarries and mines, trading centers, inscriptions (rock types)

What constitutes the "fringe" of any culture will change through time as borders shift according to changing political situations. Associated border architecture will follow these shifts. How and why borders expand and contract through time is not necessarily something that remote sensing will be able to detect, as it is more closely connected to political or power changes. Environmentally connected border changes (i.e. fortress abandonment due to drought or lack of natural resources) may be detectable from space, especially if a major water source has disappeared. Trading routes will open up as cultures expand and as resources are secured. What constitutes a border area is not limited to land-locked sites: Coastal settlements are, by nature, along the frontier of any ancient culture.

One question not examined yet with satellite archaeology is how remotely sensed imagery might be able to detect areas with rock inscriptions or carvings. Inscriptions could be left for religious purposes, as warnings (which would be located in more visible areas), or as a way to share information about an expedition (military or to obtain natural resources). Carved statues in rocky outcroppings could have religious meaning or be some

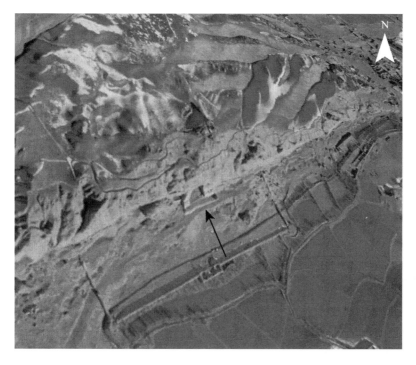

Figure 5.12 Bamiyan Buddhas, Afghanistan (scale 1:65 m), from space one can view the destruction of the Buddhas caused by the Taliban, image courtesy of Google Earth™ Pro.

other type of cultural signifier (Figure 5.12). Using hyperspectral satellite imagery such as ASTER, archaeologists could classify landscapes with known inscription information or associated carvings. These may appear at a certain elevation or in a specific geological formation, both of which can be detected from space. Modeling landscapes with SRTM data in conjunction with the ASTER analysis can give clues about potential paths past peoples might have taken to and from marginal regions. These paths may be formed by "connecting the dots" of known and newly discovered inscription data.

Studying ancient quarries reused in modern times can be problematic, but associated material culture found during ground-truthing will help define a modern mine as "ancient." Vegetation can be studied as a possible aquifer indication, and flow models can be created in a GIS. Old paths to and from mines can be created through digital elevation models, so archaeologists can gain a bird's eye view of how peoples may have planned their expeditions (Vermuelen 1998). Satellite imagery can aid in reconstructing past mining landscapes under threat of development. Egypt's ancient quarries are being mapped through the Quarryscapes project, which is using Landsat imagery and Google Earth™ to show ancient mines either being reused or under threat of reuse (Bloxam and Storemyr 2002). In Yemen, 70 km to the northeast of Sana'a, a detailed geological study of the region took place using multiple Landsat images, SPOT, and Quickbird imagery draped over digital elevation model data. The project took place in Jalabi, which was known for silver mining in the 9th century AD. This study located mines in specific geological types and at specific heights. The Quickbird data revealed ancient terraces (with palm trees and water sources) described by Al-Hamdani in ca. AD 1000. When in the field, the team studied archaeometallurgy, and analyzed the abandonment of the mines (Deroin *et al.* 2006). Ancient resource areas can be identified from space using their spectral signatures, which may aid locating the sites during survey (Martinez-Navarrete *et al.* 2005).

One example of a culture's border area, constituted by multiple landscape types, includes coastal port areas. These would have been major centers for trade, travel, and all forms of political and economic exchange. Multiple satellite images would be required to analyze coastal landscapes as they represent a confluence of landscape types. Rivers flow into larger bodies of water; port sites may be on the edge of rockier terrain, and may have moved over time through sedimentation of river mouths. Along the Ambracian Gulf in Epirus, Greece, Landsat SPOT, RADARSAT, and ASTER imagery, combined with coring and sedimentological data, detected river mouth changes through time as part of the Nikopolis project (Stein and Cullen 1994; Sarris *et al.* 1996). Marine cycles would have exposed the submerged surface, which the archaeological team analyzed to detect buried areas and change processes. Archaeological sites could be buried, landlocked, or destroyed, and this project was able to time past changes and their extent. The project allowed for variable rates of change. PCA and NDVI allowed the archaeologists to detect physical characteristics in the landscape, as well as overall landscape brightness, greenness, and wetness. PCA found more humid sediments, coastlines, lagoons, paleochannels, and swamp deposits, while the SAR data found likely meander scars. This allowed past landscape reconstruction in conjunction with the site coring (Vining and Wiseman 2006).

Resource management systems

Dams and reservoirs, resource areas (forests, fishing grounds, salt pans)

These features are generally found in association with settlements, with resource areas being difficult to detect using remote sensing. Fishing and hunting areas are not easy to define, and would have taken place near most water sources or rural areas with animals. Reservoirs could have dried up over time, and would be detectable using the same remote sensing techniques to find rivers (Stafford *et al.* 1992; Bhattacharya 2004).

Installation

Hunting or game preserves, zoological parks, botanical gardens

Studying ancient installations from space is not something that has, to date, received any attention from archaeologists. Detecting game or hunting preserves, if located close to settlements, will probably not be possible, even with high-resolution satellite imagery. How past people may have defined their game preserves is not an easy question to answer even with detailed archaeological or historical data from landscape changes. Botanical gardens would have been supported by the elite and may be located in association with elite installations. This would be difficult to differentiate from an agricultural plot.

Agriculture

Fields and plow marks

Detecting past agricultural practices from space depends entirely on how much modern practices have affected landscape evolution. Thousands of years of continuous and intensive cultivation may erase traces of past agriculture. Deposits from rivers and weathering may also work to obliterate former traces of fields. Urbanization or changing landscape practices over the past 30 years make using past satellite imagery or aerial photographs essential for landscape reconstruction (Supajanya 1989; Harrower 2002). Some places, such as the UK or mainland Europe, are known for having better preserved field systems. Other places where one might expect such preserved systems to exist, such as Egypt, have virtually no traces of previous agricultural zones.

Every region in the world will require different approaches to the detection of past agricultural areas using remote sensing. In the southeast Crimea of Ukraine, an area on the World Monument Fund's list of 100 most endangered monuments, the Chora of Chersonesos, was studied with Corona and Landsat imagery through a GIS. The team used stereo pairs of Corona imagery to create digital elevation models. Comparing the Corona imagery with classified Landsat imagery from 1988 and 1992 showed an increase in urbanization of 7 percent (Trelogan *et al.* 1999). Levelled landscapes can also prove difficult to assess. Although an archaeological team may detect hidden ridges and furrows with remote sensing, and medieval landscapes using digital terrain models, others could not be detected due to leveling of the region by farmers (Sittler and Schellberg 2006).

Landscape palimpsests present additional problems (Beck *et al.* 2002). Just because a landscape was farmed in the past does not mean it was farmed throughout history. Areas can lie fallow for generations before being farmed again. Perhaps fields in a floodplain area were salted by Romans following an attack, and not used for 50 years. Instead, past people may have used the area to build homes, or animal pens. As the salts were washed out by inundations or rainfall and the nutrients were replaced, farming may have returned to that area. Archaeologists must think of landscapes in individual periods of time (Wilkinson *et al.* 2005) and as affected by ongoing political, economic, and environmental factors. Local field systems would have been intimately connected to local population sizes, which were, in turn, affected by economic and ecological constraints (Wilkinson *et al.* 1994). This necessitates a holistic approach to landscapes.

Corona imagery is the best imagery available to detect past changes in the Middle East, due to its high resolution and low cost. It can be compared with more modern imagery to assess overall landscape changes over the past 40 years. Archaeologists need to think about other ways of detecting past field systems, whether through testing for manure or additional inorganic remains that may be remains of fertilizing (Wilkinson 1989). Using SRTM data to detect areas of settlement in floodplain regions may be difficult, as modern towns can cover past ancient sites (Sheratt 2004; Menze *et al.* 2006) or even field systems.

Modern agriculture in inundated areas still allows the detection of large mounds, but the total area of past agricultural practices will not be possible to see with satellite images. Water sources connected to past fields are another story. Signatures of earthworks and canals may aid in reconstructing past agricultural patterns in areas with significant water resource management (Parry 1992). Even in areas where intensive agriculture has

Figure 5.13 West Delta, Delta, Egypt (scale 1:36000), Alexandria is the large city along the western coast, 2008 image courtesy of Google Earth™ Pro.

drastically altered past landscapes, satellite remote sensing can detect past water sources for settlements and agriculture. These studies can also help anthropologists understand present land use practices (Badea *et al.* 2002). Using Landsat imagery, SRTM data, and aerial photographs, a team of scientists detected parts of the Canopic channel in the northwest Delta of Egypt. The 36 km trace and the 20 km trace were part of the larger channel that provided fresh water to Alexandria and other ancient settlements (Figure 5.13). The most recent channeled segment of the Canopic flowed north to the archaeological site of Herakleion in the 1st century AD. With the lowering of the western Delta and accumulation of sediments, a new course of the Canopic channel developed. A total of six bends could be seen along the traces of the ancient channel. The ancient coastline shifted south at a rate of 22.5 km a year, with the channels extending 6 km north of the current shoreline, due to sea levels rising and sedimentation. The study also examined the Idelu Lagoon, now converted to agricultural land to support part of Egypt's rapidly expanding population (Stanley and Jorstad 2006).

Past fields or field systems can be detected in similar ways to past settlements, through either cropmarks or frostmarks. Corona, Quickbird, or IKONOS imagery may all reveal past field systems with visual detection (in the case of Corona), or through the use of the IR band with filtering. LIDAR imagery also works well in detecting past field systems, in addition to settlements. A good understanding of the chemical properties of soil, weather patterns, and, most importantly, planting seasons, will aid in the detection of past fields, which may appear better in areas with crops than bare fields (Shell 2002).

Mortuary

Graves and tombs, general mortuary architecture, shrines

Detecting mortuary features is not an area that has, to date, received as much attention from satellite archaeology if there is not associated monumental architecture. Certainly, mortuary areas form an integral part of most settlement areas. If they are not a part of those settlement areas, then they will probably be located nearby. Some mortuary features will be easily detectable from space, while others will not. For example, bodies deeply buried in a stone shaft tomb might be able to be detected from space if there is a stone superstructure or other related architecture. Bodies buried beneath a home will not be able to be detected, for obvious reasons. Graves will be different shapes and sizes in each archaeological region, and will vary depending on the status of the individual (Figure 5.14). Mortuary superstructures will also vary.

How archaeologists detect mortuary features from space depends on what they hope to find. Do ancient cemeteries have their own distinct spectral signatures? This is something to be determined by remote sensing analysis. If the tombs are built from the same material as associated houses, and the cemetery has a similar stratigraphy to the settlement area, then the same techniques one would use to find ancient settlements would apply. This includes running classifications, PCA, and filtering on Landsat, SPOT, ASTER, and Quickbird imagery. It remains to be seen if dozens or hundreds of bodies in the same grave would affect the surrounding soil's spectral signature. What about exposed areas of bones atop archaeological sites? As observed by the author on the ground, the "hill of bones"

Figure 5.14 Arlington National Cemetery (scale 1:108 m), the small white dots are gravestones, 2008 image courtesy of Google Earth™ Pro.

at the site of Mendes in the northeast Delta would be large enough to be detected by high-resolution data. How the bone-covered small mound would be detected would, as in all remote sensing, be affected by moisture conditions.

Smaller mortuary remains, including tombs or shrines, could be detected, but this would depend on their size. The naos at Mendes is easy to see on Quickbird imagery, while smaller shrines or stelae may not be visible. What about tombs such as in the Valley of the Kings? Entrances have been enlarged for tourism, and protective walls around the tomb entrances prevent floodwaters from entering the tombs. These can be detected on Quickbird imagery, yet the typical or smaller tomb entrances cannot be detected. Could high resolution thermal imagery detect potential buried tomb entrances? A study of the thermal patterns of the Valley of the Kings' tombs from space has not yet been attempted by archaeologists. Dense numbers of tourists and the general heat in the Valley of the Kings may affect this study. Other tombs would be too deeply buried beneath debris to be detected from space. Applying higher resolution SAR imagery may help detect tombs in future.

Religion

Temples, chapels, sacred areas (architecture vs. landscapes)

Archaeologists may debate what constitutes a religious place, as many natural areas have served important roles in religious practice in the past. Today, as in the past, one may be in the presence of their god(s) or goddess(es) by being outside. This section will deal with using satellite imagery to detect physical religious structures. Satellite imagery can aid in understanding temple orientation or building placement, as well as the relationship of religious structures to settlements and the rest of landscape (Fowler 1996b). Sacred buildings can drastically alter surrounding landscapes, especially when they are large in size. Areas such as Giza (i.e. the area with the most famous pyramids in Egypt) can be transformed from an expanse of desert to a region imbued with religious meaning. From space, it is far easier for archaeologists to visualize the meaning of past places, and see the geological formations that may have contributed to their construction.

Satellite archaeology allows for a "virtual phenomenology," or the experience of totality of archaeological place. When visiting an archaeological site today, an archaeologist cannot fully appreciate the long-term changes through time that one can see from space. Satellites allow archaeologists to work back in time, to reconstruct past landscapes as close as possible to when religious structures might have been built. There are physical and metaphysical reasons for constructing religiously charged structures, and both are closely tied into a past culture's integration of landscape into religious belief systems.

Remote sensing has contributed to understanding past patterns relating to religion and power. Using Quickbird satellite imagery, one archaeological team attempted to answer the question of how the people of Easter Island transported the moai over rugged terrain. Using composite sets of imagery Quickbird imagery from April 2003, December 2002, and February 2003, the team pan sharpened and smoothed the imagery to find extensive road networks (Figure 5.15). Even in 1919, people had noted some of these ancient tracks, but archaeologists did not document them. The remote sensing analysis discovered 32 km of roads, suggesting independent groups moved the statues around the 17 km^2 island. Old roads were differentiated from the modern roads during ground

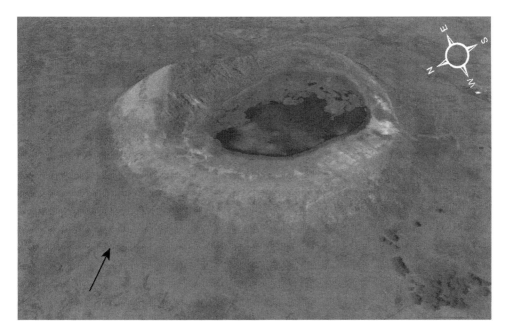

Figure 5.15 Rapa Nui (Easter Island), Chile (scale 1:130 m), the faint paths surrounding the volcano are the paths used to drag the stones used for the Moai, 2008 image courtesy of Google Earth™ Pro.

survey. Many of the roads looked like spokes emerging from the Rano Ranaku quarry and were used mainly for the purpose of statue transportation. Unfortunately, many modern activities have destroyed the roads (Hunt and Lipo 2005).

Archaeologists need to understand temple placement according to local cultural choices. In China, Feng Shui led to the placement of temples and other monuments. Knowing how Feng Shui was applied aided archaeologists in mapping the Tang Mausoleum in X'ian, China, over an area of 5000 km^2. Archaeologists used Landsat, SPOT, KVR-1000, and IKONOS imagery to visualize the landscape, with the Huiling Mausoleum visible mainly on the visible IKONOS imagery (Boehler *et al.* 2004). When the orientation, size, and materials of temples are known, archaeologists can select the remote sensing methods and satellites most likely to detect additional temple or religious sites. This may work well in desert areas, such as the region of Tuna el-Gebel, Middle Egypt, where larger religious structures may be buried just beneath the ground surface (Figure 5.16).

Ceremonial

Centers (such as Stonehenge), inscribed landscapes

Ceremonial features and inscribed landscapes remain closely connected to religious beliefs, yet are different in terms of how satellites might detect them from space. Ceremonial centers will be connected to trails, mountains, and other natural features,

Figure 5.16 Tuna el-Gebel, Egypt (scale 1:178 m), note numerous buried structures just beneath the desert sands, which are visible from space, 2008 image courtesy of Google Earth™ Pro.

with a journey often required to reach them. Total landscapes could be sacred, along with more regular aspects of landscapes associated with agricultural patterns (Kidder and Saucier 1991). SPOT imagery, digital elevation models, and GIS aided archaeologists in analyzing possible ritual unity amongst Minoan peak sanctuaries dating to ca. 2300–1500 BC (Soetens *et al.* 2002). Depending on where centers are placed, the landscape type can be studied for the purposes of quantifying elevations, center size, and relationship to known settlements. For example, in the northern basin of the Rio Grande in Peru, a digital terrain model aided archaeologists in understanding geoglyph placement (Reindel *et al.* 2006). These geoglyphs would normally only be detectable on high-resolution satellite imagery. Detecting religious centers can have other purposes as well. Archaeological remote sensing work in Poverty Point used Landsat data to detect site ridges and the main plaza area (Figure 5.17). In this case, remote sensing aided the archaeologists in examining technology and how it affects cultural interpretation and public outreach (Williamson and Warren-Findley 1991).

How much can satellites detect?

Coring, excavation, and subsurface archaeological detection methods remain the only way, at present, to gain highly detailed information about archaeological material below the current surface. Until more time- and cost-efficient ways of detecting archaeological

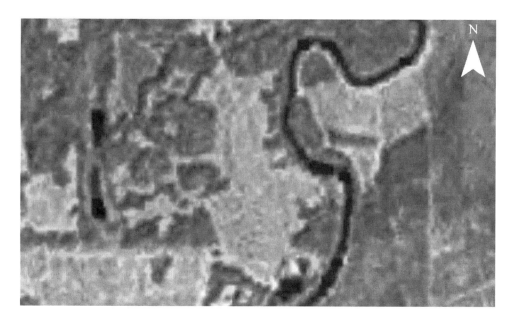

Figure 5.17 Poverty Point, Louisiana, Landsat image in pseudocolor, image courtesy of NASA World Wind.

Figure 5.18 Photograph of coring in Middle Egypt, image by Sarah Parcak.

material appear, archaeologists will need to rely on initial, broader landscape analyses with remote sensing, followed by one of the aforementioned methods for more detailed investigation. How long would this type of coring approach take? Despite the feasibility of wide-scale systematic coring across the Nile floodplain (Figure 5.18) coring would be an excessively expensive and time-consuming method of locating buried sites. For example, concerning the 2450 km^2 area of the author's fieldwork work in the East Delta and Middle Egypt, if one placed cores 500 m apart (looking for medium to large buried sites), with a full day required to sink a seven meter deep core (as experienced by the author) it would take 4898 days (13.4 years) to complete this survey. With excavation seasons in Egypt averaging two months, or 48 workdays per season, a similar floodplain coring survey would take 102 years. Sadly, there is neither enough funding nor trained personnel to carry out these studies.

Such a project would undoubtedly reveal numerous buried archaeological sites and would be invaluable for landscape evolution studies, not only in Egypt, but if similar approaches were applied at other sites around the world. Owing to current cost and time constraints for such a coring survey, perhaps a smaller series of random cores should be placed between known surface sites until more efficient technology exists to perform subsurface landscape scans. Hyperspectral satellite images such as ASTER can detect far more subtle landscape changes than SPOT or Landsat satellite images and may aid in revealing potential subsurface sites. CASI and LIDAR hold great promise for the future of revealing slightly buried or obscured archaeological remains. Understanding the vagaries of each landscape and feature type will help archaeological teams to plan for their remote sensing projects to gain the best results possible, no matter what the project goals or constraints.

6

CASE STUDIES

Overview

Case studies are invaluable for illustrating how specific archaeological projects have implemented satellite remote sensing work in reaction to specific regional issues. This chapter features six remote sensing and survey projects in different regions that contain broad landscape types and diverse archaeological features. These examples appeared appropriate owing to their in-depth approaches to archaeological remote sensing and their placement of satellite archaeology in broader archaeological contexts. By discussing the different approaches each project took, this section will explore how and why each study was successful in its specific context. The studies occur in regions where many remote sensing studies are already taking place and include The Peten (Guatemala), Angkor Wat (Cambodia), Xi'an (China), Ubar (Oman), Homs (Syria), The Delta and Tell-el-Amarna (Egypt). Three of the studies chosen represent regional remote sensing studies in the Middle East. Ubar is representative of desert remote sensing studies. In the cases of Egypt and Syria, one might initially consider them to yield similar floodplain environments, yet each region is ultimately distinct and hence require different approaches. Many ancient cities emerged in floodplains, and with a long history of regional archaeology in the Ancient Near East, an examination of Homs, Syria, emphasizes approaches to studying a single multi-period site in a broader regional content. In Egypt, the case study is broader in scale and compares and contrasts how settlement pattern studies can be conducted in different floodplain regions of the same river system. It is only through generating a detailed discussion of broader projects that other archaeologists can gain insights into how they might model their own remote sensing survey projects.

The Peten, Guatemala

Features on ground in rainforest regions across the world, such as the Peten, Guatemala, may be difficult or virtually impossible to see let alone traverse. This leaves satellite remote sensing as one of the only viable tools for locating previously unknown sites and features. Such limitations and difficulties have encouraged archaeological remote sensing work in the Peten region of Guatemala (Figure 6.1) by William Saturno and his team. Satellite remote sensing allowed a much better understanding of the region surrounding one of the most important Mayan archaeological sites, San Bartolo. A pyramidal structure at San Bartolo contained painted decoration that represented the oldest known Maya

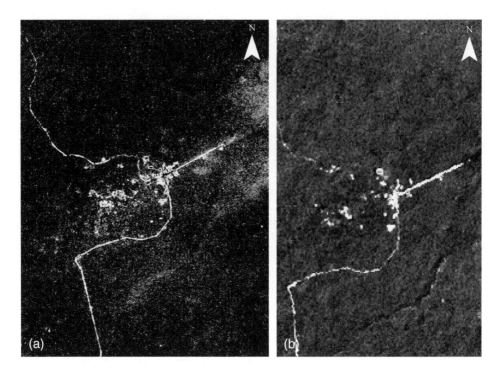

Figure 6.1 Tikal, Guatemala: (a) ASTER imagery NDVI; (b) Landsat NDVI (scale 1:2393 m), images courtesy of NASA.

hieroglyphic writings. The remains dated to the late Preclassic period (400 BC–AD 200), and more specifically, 200–300 BC (Saturno *et al.* 2006).

Saturno and his team faced several problems in their efforts to gain a better understanding of San Bartolo in its regional context. First, the Peten, Guatemala measures some 36,000 km², covered in sense vegetations, and represents a vast undertaking for any survey work. Second, half of the region had been deforested since the 1970s, destroying many archaeological sites as they are exposed to looters and unscrupulous developers. Third, the remaining area is threatened by a lack of conservation measures and could disappear in the next 10–20 years if they are not implimented, making satellite remote sensing absolutely crucial for discovering and recording archaeological data shown in Figure 6.2. This potential broad scale loss has major implications for Mayan archaeology as there are numerous archaeological sites remaining to be discovered in the dense forest regions. If Saturno's work at one site alone (San Bartolo) is any indication of the potential richness of undiscovered sites, then the archaeological sites awaiting future discovery in the Peten could prove to be just as, if not more, important.

For more than 170 years, archaeological surveys have proven to be nearly impossible in the dense and virtually impassible Central American rainforests. Through a Space Act Agreement, in essence an accord allowing the sharing of satellite datasets, the University of New Hampshire and NASA's Marshall Space Flight Center negotiated a joint effort to implement a settlement survey in the Maya lowlands. The archaeological

Figure 6.2 The Peten, Guatemala, Landsat (scale 1:41700 m), image courtesy of NASA.

goals included identifying ritual, economic, demographic, and environmental factors in the Preclassic environment surrounding San Bartolo. NASA's objectives focused on studying settlement patterns via hydrology, examining the regional geology, locating bajos, and linear features, and mapping drainage patterns. NASA also wished to create vegetation maps to analyze subsistence strategies, and generate climate models of the region (Saturno *et al.* 2007).

By using a combination of satellite data, particularly Landsat TM, IKONOS, Quick-bird, Urban STAR-3 (an X-band system used for reflecting surface topography), and AIRSAR, the project succeeded in locating archaeological sites, roadways, canals, reservoirs, and bajos. Although the remote sensing analysis identified archaeological sites, specific spectral signatures have not yet been isolated. In some cases, such as Lindbergh's early surveys, sites have been found in the northeast Yucatan. However, the dense vegetation remains an obstacle to most survey work (Figure 6.3). Tom Sever's surveys in the mid-1980s adopted supervised and unsupervised classifications for Landsat TM imagery, as well as TIMS and infrared (IR) photography, but found no correlation between vegetation patterns and archaeological sites. Instead, IKONOS imagery proved to be the best archaeological site indicator when pan sharpened and passed through a Brovey transform. Here, vegetation signatures were correlated during ground navigation to the unknown sites. On the ground, the survey verified past human activity, recorded temples, causeways, reservoirs, and agricultural areas. The project incorporated all the data into a GIS for further analysis (Saturno *et al.* 2007).

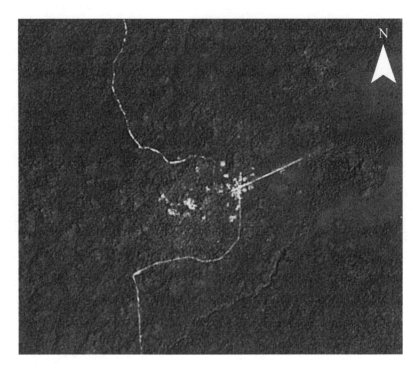

Figure 6.3 Tikal, Guatemala (scale 1:2393 m), 2008 image courtesy of Google Earth™ Pro.

These archaeological sites appear to be creating a microenvironment, with chemical leeching in the soils from the limestone masonry and limestone plasters. Vegetation is clearly being affected by the underlying archaeological structure, although the exact mechanisms are not completely understood and further analysis is needed. Some questions requiring further assessment include: Is there an optimum month in which a spectral signature will be reflected most strongly? Which different remote sensing methods will work best in detecting the sites? The on-going project is applicable for other parts of Central America, especially the Peten and northern Belize regions where the bulk of excavation work in Maya archaeology is currently concentrated. Saturno's investigations have the potential to save other research projects a great deal of time and money, not just in Central America, but worldwide where rainforests obscure ancient settlement sites and features (Saturno *et al.* 2007). Archaeological remote sensing analysis incorporates site and feature detection as a first step to answering larger ecological questions, which Saturno, Tom Sever, and others have already demonstrated (Figure 6.4).

A further line of inquiry focuses on whether the Maya used the bajo islands (seasonally flooded swamps) for agriculture? This issue is debated among Maya archaeologists. Errin Weller (2006) notes that bajo islands make up 40 percent of Guatemala's landscape, making them likely candidates for at least some agricultural usage. Weller used Landsat, SAR, SRTM, and IKONOS satellite data to examine bajo islands surrounding the well-known archaeological sites of Tikal and Yaxha, more specifically Bajo La Justa and Bajo Santa Fe. In satellite data analysis, band combinations 4-3-1 and 4-3-2 showed a yellow signature that might be connected with the decay of limestone. Principal components analysis

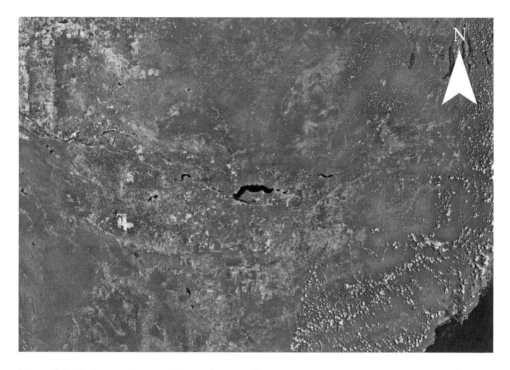

Figure 6.4 The Peten, Guatemala, Landsat pseudocolor (scale 1:250 m), image courtesy of NASA World Wind.

(PCA) found additional bajo islands, while combining the IKONOS, Landsat, and SRTM data showed a number of larger bajos. Edge detection techniques, however, did not manage to isolate any features, which had previously enhanced canals and causeways. In Sante Fe, 87 bajos appeared with 209 water features. Weller argued that the bajos should to be considered as communities, either for agriculture or settlement (Weller 2006). The debate continues as research proceeds, but at this stage the data illustrate just how important environmental factors are in affecting past communities in Central America.

Angkor Wat, Cambodia

Angkor Wat is one of the best-known monumental archaeological sites in Southeast Asia, occupied from the 9–15th centuries AD. It is the largest and most elaborate urban complex in the pre-industrial world, and courts many thousands of tourists each year (Figure 6.5). Conversely, its fame makes it one of the most targeted sites for looting in Southeast Asia—particularly during the recent civil war, with the antiquities market financing the purchase of weaponry. Satellite remote sensing, however, has contributed to a better archaeological understanding of Angkor Wat, and has enabled archaeologists to collaborate with the Cambodian government to create better site management maps. Satellites imagery analysis has provided surprising insights into past water management strategies at Angkor, and revealed a much broader urban complex around the temple

Figure 6.5 Angkor Wat, Cambodia, Landsat image (scale 1:250 m), image courtesy of NASA World Wind.

area, which now demonstrates that in size and complexity Angkor Wat far exceeds previous estimates (Figure 6.6).

Modern archaeological investigations began at Angkor Wat with the use of RADAR data and aerial photography (Moore and Freeman 1997, Moore *et al.* 1998), and 3D modeling using aerial photography (Sonneman *et al.* 2006), which elucidated traces of a complex network of artificial water systems at the site and throughout its hinterland (Moore 1989). SIR-C data traced ancient fields, canals, and reservoirs that had remained otherwise unidentified (James 1995). AIRSAR and TOPSAR data revealed barays, a form of artificial basin, demonstrating the continued importance of more-aerial based remote sensing (Freeman *et al.* 1999). This has led to additional AIRSAR scanning of Angkor, which promises to revolutionize further how archaeologists viewed this site and its hinterland.

In September of 2000, AIRSAR scanned an area of 3000 km^2 surrounding Angkor, and revealed that the main core covered an area measuring 1000 km^2, while the temple complex spread out over an area of 2000 km^2. The latter area also contained local shrines, and showed that associated settlements generally lay in low density regions. The archaeological project in Cambodia was a collaboration between the French government, the Australian Government, the World Monuments Fund, the Mekong River Commission, and NASA's Jet Propulsion Laboratory, all of whom recognized the need for an integrative approach to site conservation, management, and public presentation. Although AIRSAR did not actually reveal any previously unknown monuments, it allowed for a holistic view of the total area and showed changes through time (Fletcher and Evans 2002).

It is noteworthy that the AIRSAR imagery allowed archaeologists to see through 98 percent cloud cover, surpassing the capabilities of conventional satellite imagery.

Figure 6.6 Angkor Wat, Cambodia, Landsat pseudocolor image (scale 1:250 m), image courtesy of NASA World Wind.

Ultralight aircraft also helped take lower elevation aerial photographs, which were especially helpful for inaccessible parts of the site that were dotted with anti-personnel mines. The overall project results revealed distinct anthropogenic changes to the landscape reservoir, showing that the water system incorporated an interconnecting system of channels and soil embankments (Figure 6.7). The ancient ponds offered a sufficiently efficient agricultural system that the Cambodian people are reusing them today (Evans *et al.* 2007). Additional ground systems emerged in three-band color composite imagery, which illuminated the overall urban layout and ancient forest clearance to accommodate the city's hydrological network. Today, satellite imagery also reveals that, erosion and flooding pose major threats to the ancient city. Hence, remote sensing analysis will also aid in monitoring and mitigating threats to Angkor as a cultural resource (Fletcher and Evans 2002).

The work at Angkor has progressed to form part of the Greater Angkor Project (GAP), combining AIRSAR data with SIR-C/X-SAR data. Research reveals that, originally, artificial moats and dykes allowed Angkor to develop into a great city (Pottier 2002). Once the populace controlled land and water resources, which formed the roots of Khmer culture, wealth began to accumulate. The construction of temples and affiliated religious structures coincided with the integral establishments of supporting water control systems. Although the floodplain had many advantages, being particularly fertile and good for cultivation, it was vastly altered and augmented to serve the people of Angkor. Further analysis, focusing on the C, L, and P bands in AIRSAR, in conjunction with old maps and aerial photographs, examined a 1500 km^2 mosaic, finding surface variations relating to moisture and vegetation. Hence, archaeologists have determined that the Khmer culture was intimately familiar with the hydraulic cycles on a local scale.

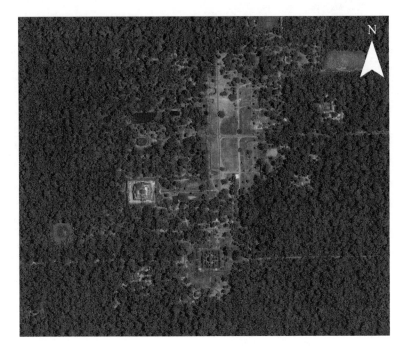

Figure 6.7 Angkor Wat, Cambodia, note high resolution of temple complex (scale 1:491 m), 2008 image courtesy of Google Earth™ Pro.

They understood the full importance of controlling water sources in the rainy season versus the dry season through significant terrain alteration. Remote sensing has also allowed archaeologists to understand better how the Khmer defined their political organization (via landscape use and settlement patterns), and has redefined our understanding of power and place in a Khmer setting. Furthermore, it has clarified the role of multiple sites in relation to and in isolation from Angkor (Moore *et al.* 2007).

Angkor Wat's isolation and location in a densely vegetated rainforest area has partly protected it and partially endangered it from looters, while various revolutionary groups have disrupted the tourist industry through kidnappings and massacres. In such dangerous and difficult circumstances, satellites have emerged as invaluable aids in modeling Angkor Wat to design and implement safer management strategies. Many of the same techniques that archaeologists have used successfully to locate archeological sites in Central America should be able to locate previously unknown sites in other parts of Cambodia. However, two major problems emerged, namely cloud cover and standing water. Although there are cloudless days over Angkor and elsewhere in Cambodia, like all rainforests, the prevalence of clouds can make finding cloud-free satellite imagery (outside of AIRSAR) much harder. It remains to be seen what sensors, such as LIDAR, reveal about the landscapes at Angkor, as they can be flown on cloudless days or even in the space of a few cloudless hours. Hence, LIDAR and AIRSAR could allow archaeologists to review the Cambodian landscape more frequently and with greater affect: Perhaps more reservoirs, temples, and settlement sites remain to be found, and indeed, protected for future generations of archaeologists, tourists, and the Cambodians themselves.

Figure 6.8 Xi'an, China, Landsat image (scale 1:574 m), 2008 image courtesy of NASA World Wind.

Xi'an, China

In China, aside from the Great Wall, there is no archaeological site or feature more famous than the terracotta warriors of Xi'an (Figure 6.8). Thousands of life-sized models of soldiers compose the guard for the tomb of Emperor Qinshihuang, who lived ca. 259–210 BC, and who unified China in 221 BC. Each solder displays individual hair styles, facial features, coloring (which does not last when exposed to air), and detailed equipment and uniforms related to their rank and function. The power and wealth Emperor Qinshihuang held to command the creation of such an army was not inconsiderable. With more than 8000 terracotta horses and over 40,000 bronze weapons known from pits to the east of the Mausoleum, Xi'an attracts hundreds of thousands of visitors each year. The beautiful bronze armor and wagons, popularly reconstructed in the Hollywood movie *Hero*, attest to the high level of craftsmanship during Emperor Qinshihuang's reign (Wenlie 1998).

One of the main questions that archaeologists have attempted to answer using satellite remote sensing analysis is whether or not the tomb complex of Qinshihuang is still mostly intact. According to ancient sources, the "tomb" complex contained nothing less than a complete underground city, replete with a river of "flowing mercury," and held many precious and semiprecious jewels. Tracing the entire complex would likely represent the most significant archaeological "find" in the history of archaeology, surpassing the 1922 discovery of Tutankhamen's tomb by Howard Carter. Unlike the uncovering of Tutankhamen's tomb, this find is vastly larger and is much more slowly revealing its secrets; archaeologists still only have a general idea of what it is meant to contain. The biggest remaining question is to what extent is it preserved, having been intended to exist as a model universe for the Emperor (Rawson 1996).

The question of the potential looting of Qinshihuang's tomb though can be gauged by monitoring artifacts appearing on the illegal antiquities market. If looters had robbed the tomb in the past two centuries, one would assume that similar funerary pieces would already have appeared in museum collections or private published collections. China has only been open to foreign tourists for the past 30 years, so most looting would likely have occurred at a local level. The significance of the area was not even known to the local population until 1974, when the Chinese government intensified archaeological excavations in the area. The whole complex remains closely guarded due to its importance to China's tourism industry, and also the role it plays in Chinese national pride. The Shaanxi Provincial Cultural Relics Bureau and the Management of Qinshihuang Mausoleum Museum manage the site; the latter takes responsibility for excavating and publishing site data. Fortunately, the Lintong District Government has banned construction projects within the protection zone around the Mausoleum, described in an annual report to UNESCO (Anon. 2003).

The use of satellite remote sensing has already aided archaeologists in understanding the construction and state of preservation of the Qinshihuang Mausoleum (Xiaohu 2004). It should be noted that, in comparison to the other case studies, relatively few publications exist in English discussing the application of satellite remote sensing to this region. Combining the Mausoleum and the adjacent terracotta army pits (the densest archaeological area) gives a total area of 19.63 km^2, or an area large enough to be analyzed coarser resolution satellite data. The tomb itself measures 1014 m east–west by 2228 m north–south in an oblong shape, and rises to 65 m tall, in a total area of 2.26 km^2 (Anon. 2003). The landscape surrounding the site is not even, and combines farmland and urban structures.

Archaeologists have applied a number of satellite and remote sensing techniques to analyze the Qinshihuang Mausoleum, including airborne and geophysical applications. The study allowed comparisons between aerial photographs from 1956 and 1974 to assess general landscape changes. Prior to 2005, archaeologists had not conducted any hyperspectral studies on Chinese archaeological sites. An OMIS2 spectrometer analyzed a 60 km^2 area, and carried out both daytime and nighttime scanning, as well as recording general temperatures, humidity, and spectrum measurements of the ground surface. Stone stays relatively cool during the day, but becomes warmer by nightfall due to thermal inertia, or the absorption of heat. This thermal inertia is detected by remote sensing analysis. Hence, the slopes of the Mausoleum facing the sun would absorb more energy since variations in topography and surface angles to the sun mean differential heating. It was hoped that this would reveal additional information about the Mausoleum's architecture.

For example, a higher temperature was indeed connected to the 21 million m^3 of rammed earth composing the Mausoleum, since more compact soil has better conductivity. In general, trees blossomed better on the archaeological site, and were better able to resist freezing due to the conducted geothermal energy, while reduced crop growth was connected with underlying ash pits at the site. Some soil removal was observed beneath the Mausoleum, but archaeologists calculated that the preserved tunnel was not deep enough to breech the underground palace complex that had been observed via "thermal anomalies." Remote sensing has also observed eastern and western tomb entrances. In order to assess this complex and its hinterlands, archaeologists created a digital terrain model for a 3 km radius surrounding the tomb (Figure 6.9) (Kelong *et al.* 2004; Tan *et al.* 2006).

Figure 6.9 Xi'an, China (scale 1:168 m), note distortion in imagery, 2008 image courtesy of Google Earth™ Pro.

This author's conversations with Chinese archaeologists have revealed that the Mausoleum is unlikely to be opened any time in the near future. Chinese archaeologists assert that current archaeological methods are insufficiently advanced to handle the most important tomb in China, and wish to excavate it using best techniques possible. They are worried about preservation, which the present work on the terracotta warriors has proven to be problematic. Hence, the true extent of the tomb awaits more detailed probes and more advanced 3D subsurface scanning. Perhaps subsurface scanning will become more widely available and will advance to the point where archaeologists can map an entire site without excavation. Cutting tiny boreholes enables limited viewing to retrieve information about the surviving material culture within the tomb.

In the meantime, many more questions exist about the extent of the surrounding army. How much have the buried terracotta warriors affected spectral signatures inherent in surrounding soils and vegetation, as seen in Figure 6.10? What type of satellite sensors may be able to detect the buried remains outside of hyperspectral data? One wonders if Quickbird or IKONOS imagery would be able to detect the vegetation differences in their IR bands. The seasonality of the optimum satellite imagery is another issue that needs to be studied for this region in particular. Perhaps there are additional associated terracotta warrior groups that are waiting to be discovered. Hence, the current and developing satellite technology need not wait for a farmer to dig a well to discover

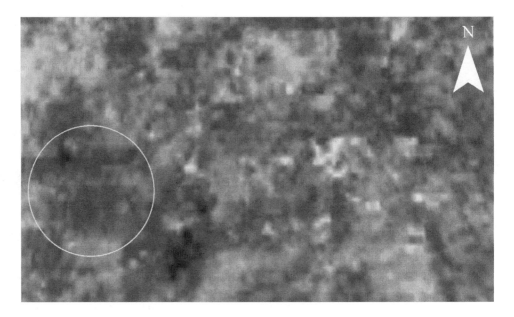

Figure 6.10 Xi'an, China, Landsat pseudocolor (scale 1:168 m), note different reflectance when compared to Figure 6.8, image courtesy of NASA World Wind.

the complex. Having already detailed the Mausoleum, the Chinese government has already begun to protect and preserve China's most important archaeological site.

Ubar, Oman

One of the more "romantic" remote sensing studies uncovered the famed city of Ubar in the so-called Arabian empty quarter of Oman (Figure 6.11). Ubar formed a key component in a series of desert caravanserai (or a roadside rest house), facilitating trade in frankincense and myrrh, perhaps as early as ca. 2000 BC and continuing until AD 200. The general region around Ubar was mentioned in the writings of Ptolemy, the Koran, and the *Thousand-and-One Arabian Nights*. Pliny noted that there were "octoman-siones" (octagonal-shaped stations) along the frankincense route, providing an invaluable architectural and aerial clue. Ubar's legendary placement in a vast desert, however, made it virtually impossible to relocate using more conventional remote sensing studies (Welzenbach 1995; Clapp 1996; Fisher and Fisher 1999).

In 1930, the British explorer Bertram Thomas mentioned a track of some sort, which was rediscovered in the 1950s. Problems with dunes, however, made traversing this road too difficult. Archaeologists and explorers contacted NASA's Jet Propulsion laboratory after reading about the results of a SIR-A mission in Egypt, and thought a similar approach might aid in re-discovering Ubar. With more data scheduled to be collected from SIR-B in 1984, they wanted to know if it was possible to have imagery taken over the "empty quarter." This proved to be possible. The team obtained Landsat TM, illustrated in Figure 6.12, SPOT 10 m data, as well as SIR-C imagery for analysis before conducting their ground-truthing and potential excavation seasons.

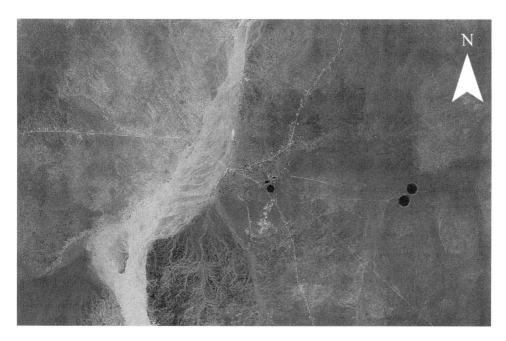

Figure 6.11 Ubar, Oman (scale 1:8608 m), 2008 image courtesy of Google Earth™ Pro.

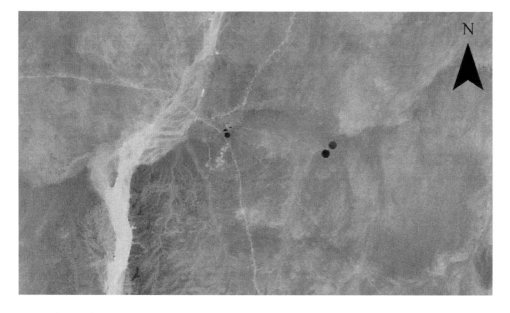

Figure 6.12 Ubar, Oman, Landsat image (scale 1:8608 m), image courtesy of NASA World Wind.

Many remote sensing methods were used in the analysis. Edge detection filters proved to be the most useful on the SIR-C data, which found a series of older tracks in the area Ptolemy called the "Omanum Empirium." Other methods attempted included band combinations, contrast enhancements, spatial filtering, edge enhancement, and Landsat band ratio composites. Principal components analysis (PCA) also aided in detecting potential tracks beneath the dunes, while direct band ratioing, helped the team to differentiate between ancient and modern tracks. During the analysis, an L-shaped feature appeared, which seemed somewhat narrow. The team used a helicopter to reach the site, which proved to be a natural shallow depression and the site of a major Neolithic settlement.

In general, the remote sensing analysis allowed this project to eliminate large areas from their ground survey, and provided small areas for visual assessment before conducting surface reconnaissance. An archaeological surface team followed the paths found via the filtered SIR-C data, and found a potential candidate for the location of Ubar near the modern village of Shisr. Excavation over three seasons yielded a number of potsherds, oil lamps, and Iron Age material from Rome, India, Persia, and Greece, dating to between 800 BC–AD 400. Excavation also produced a possible towered fortress, which the team connected to Pliny's "octomansiones" (Blom *et al.* 1997, 2000, 2007). Circumstantial evidence suggests that this site represents the city of Ubar, but other considerations need to be assessed. Perhaps "Ubar" did not represent a single site, but was instead a region, or series of places caravanserai could meet for trade. Chemical analyses (i.e. residue analysis) on the pottery and other areas might have aided the team in connecting the site to the frankincense trade. This site, however, was rather small, and has some difficulty fulfilling all of the requirements of fabled Ubar, including an inability to support large numbers of people due to minimal water sources. In other regards, however, the project proved the successes of applying RADAR data in desert regions, documenting the ability of satellite remote sensing to locate sites using good scientific and historical data.

Homs, Syria

The modern Middle East includes the broad area composing the ancient Near East (which included mostly Egypt, Turkey, Syria-Palestine, Iraq, and Iran) and is an important region in which many surveys and remote sensing studies have taken place, or are currently ongoing (McAdams 1981; Wilkinson 2001, 2002; Alizadeh *et al.* 2004; Wilkinson *et al.* 2004). It is necessary to discuss a number of modern landscape analysis issues before introducing the case study about Homs in Syria. Throughout the area composing the ancient Near East, modern agriculture has often obscured past remains, especially deep plowing that has destroyed many ancient levees and low-lying sites. Scholars have also noted a diversity of terrain, which can obscure sites. Additionally, different vegetation types may mask sites in various ways. The issue of site visibility on the ground also makes aerial reconnaissance necessary (Banning 1996). Other important features, however, may be hard to identify from space. The locations of levees and settlements have a long history in the ancient Near East, and have changed greatly over time, leaving a complicated network of former river-channels and sites throughout Mesopotamia. Satellite imagery and SRTM data have helped to link levee usage with adjacent archaeological sites, as well as including distinguishing past sequences of levees from different time periods (Hritz and Wilkinson 2006).

Figure 6.13 Homs, Syria, Landsat image (scale 1:22812 m), note how ancient water systems are visible even on coarse resolution imagery, image courtesy of NASA World Wind.

Many landscape types occur across the modern Middle East, spanning deserts, scrubland, floodplains, lowlands, mountainous terrain, coastlines, and submerged past landscapes (Figure 6.13). Many remote sensing projects have advocated a variety of approaches for the study of these current and past landscapes, while in particular desert environments require more intricate procedures regarding landscape analysis issues. In southern Arabia, Landsat data has yielded visible remains from ancient oases, especially in Yemen, where some larger buildings and older field systems survive (Brunner 1997). Landscape changes present additional challenges. At the archaeological site of al-Raqqua in north central Syria, archaeologists compared Landsat TM, SPOT, and Corona imagery scanned at 1200 and 4000 dpi. The site is known to have settlements from the Neolithic onwards, with 20 identified structural complexes, and was abandoned in AD 1250 until the 1940s. However, rapid urbanization has occurred here since the 1960s. The study noted a marked difference in the four types of satellites imagery: Corona data revealed medieval river channels and past meanderings across the floodplain. Corona imagery also detected that 45 percent of landscape had been unaffected by urbanization (Challis *et al.* 2002). In addition, Corona imagery detected the shrinking of Lake Qatina in Syria due to modern agricultural expansions (Philip, Jabar *et al.* 2002).

Modernization has affected landscape changes and satellite image analysis in different ways. For instance, dam construction and reservoirs in the Middle East make it an urgent priority to conduct archaeological surveys in areas that will soon be submerged. A satellite remote sensing survey in Turkey focused along the river course behind the construction of the Birecik Dam, which was completed in 2000, close to the border with Syria. In this circumstance, SPOT, Corona, Landsat, and KVR-1000 satellite images were used instead of aerial photography, as permission was not granted by the military to use aircraft in this broader sense. The analysis and work took place before the rising waters could cover a number of sites. Large-scale maps were created, allowing the researchers to map ancient quarries, past roads, and mounds (mainly via Corona imagery). Problems were noted with erosion and deposition, as well as deep plowing, which had scattered material culture from small sites (Comfort 1997a, 1998, 1999; Comfort *et al.* 2000; Comfort and Ergec 2001).

Other ancient features altered by modernization may appear only when viewed from space. When examining ancient settlement development in the North Jazeira, specialists noted hollow ways (or ancient spoke-like roads emerging from ancient sites, visible from space as slight depressions) becoming visible in both aerial photographs and high-resolution satellite images, with the subsequent collection of past ceramic material yielding a 500-year span in this area (Emberling 1996). Archaeological sites may also appear quite unexpectedly. Using Landsat ETM+ and ASTER imagery, an archaeological team detected what was postulated to be a late Holocene meteorite impact crater, known as the "Umm al-Binni structure" in the marshlands of southern Iraq. This appeared only when the marshlands were drained, and may be connected to larger issues related to global climate change around ca. 2200 BC (Master and Woldai 2004).

In the floodplains of the Middle East archaeologists can utilize satellite imagery to map what are known as "signature landscapes," or landscapes dating to a specific period of time. Corona imagery revealed Sassanian period (ca. AD 224–642) landscapes in northwestern Iran, in the region of the Mughan Steppes (Alizadeh and Ur 2007). The study synthesized data from the satellite imagery and ground survey, and identified transportation routes, nucleated settlements, and irrigation areas. Some areas contained settlement resources or features to encourage resettlement, while other areas did not. In general, a palimpsest model has been advocated (Wilkinson 2003), as settlements wax and wane, being affected by cyclical weather patterns and larger environmental changes. In contrast, nomadic landscapes were found to be difficult to locate, but could be traced by Corona imagery, which also revealed fortified settlement complexes. In areas of low undulating topography, small scatters of material culture survived, but most of these clusters were found to be more modern rather than ancient (Alizadeh and Ur 2007).

Having illustrated various approaches to Middle Eastern landscapes, this section will focus more heavily on the work taking place at the site of Homs, Syria. This project used a combination of Corona, Landsat (Figure 6.14), IKONOS, and Quickbird imagery to assess the landscape broadly and to examine long-term human–environment interactions. Archaeological sites appeared as tells with low relief soil marks, with remains ranging from small walls less than 1 m wide to large multi-period settlements. In general, Landsat imagery proved useful for environment characterization and for visualizing rates of change, but as not good for site detection and mapping due to its coarser resolution in comparison to IKONOS and Quickbird. Like all remote sensing projects, teams must consider the size of the features they hope to detect as well as their associated landscape features. The Homs project, at its start, had no database of remains, or any aerial photography coverage in its 630 km^2 study area and needed a site targeting system. By using visual bands on Landsat, the project compared how Landsat and Corona detected ancient remains. Ancient field systems, seen on Figure 6.15, appeared on the Corona imagery. In this case, visual detection aided the team more than any

Figure 6.14 Homs, Syria, Landsat pseudocolor (scale 1:4240 m), image courtesy of NASA World Wind.

Figure 6.15 Homs, Syria (scale 1:2281 m), note cropmarks in the fields showing older water courses, 2008 image courtesy of Google Earth™ Pro.

detailed processing of Landsat imagery data due to the visually changed landscapes (Donoghue *et al.* 2002; Philip, Beck and Donoghue 2002).

Corona imagery detected non-multi-period sites otherwise not visible in the IKONOS imagery. The study compared site detection techniques by examining the relationships between ground moisture, grain size of the soil, soil iron oxide content, geology, vegetation, and image and absorption reflection factors (Wilkinson *et al.* 2006). Corona imagery taken in the minimum and maximum crop growth periods also contributed to site visibility. The Corona imagery proved somewhat problematic for the analysis, however, as the team encountered difficulties finding landmarks that correlated with recognizable coordinates today, thus making georeferencing somewhat inaccurate. Overall, the team noted a high density of features, yet subsequent landscape modification was a major problem for the team. For example, some sites had been visible in the IKONOS imagery but did not appear clearly on the ground owing to more recent extensive plowing.

The team relied mainly on visual interpretation of the satellite imagery, as they concluded that it would not be possible to create a number of spectral signatures that would work in their study environment. They emphasized the need for further remote sensing research in areas with similar conditions. The IKONOS imagery produced an error rate of greater than 25 m. The team compiled ground control points using a handheld GPS, but found it difficult to identify archaeological sites that had been cut into and then backfilled with the same material. Regarding their experiences, team cautioned future researchers about limitations of satellite imagery applications for survey work (Beck *et al.* 2007).

One wonders what results might have been obtained using multispectral analysis. For instance, more positive results might emerge from material culture being examined in similar environments, such as floodplains. Tells are broadly similar in form and general composition across the ancient Near East, especially in areas where mudbrick structures dominate. Similar remote sensing methods may work in identifying tells in different parts of the world in related landscape types such as floodplains. Although spectral signatures for sites may vary due to differences in mudbricks, ancient technologies, potsherds, and soil matrixes, many tells will likely absorb higher amounts of water than their adjacent landscapes and will have higher organic debris contents. It is crucial to recognize what differences and similarities occur in the analysis of satellite imagery for archaeological site discovery, but one should also try to apply a full range of available, albeit continuously emerging, analytical techniques. Spectral reflectance charts may aid in analyzing other imagery types such as ASTER. Multispectral analysis may detect varying crop types growing over archaeological sites, which may, in-turn, indicate specific site types (e.g. an occupation mound versus an overgrown fortress). Such destructions might be identified though normalized difference vegetation indexes (NDVI), PCA, classification, band ratioing, or other techniques. Soil identification might be another way to detect past areas of settlement. The Homs projects team did note that marl clays could be better identified through histogram manipulations, but this is only one of many other potentially successful remote sensing techniques.

The Homs projects also encountered cost limitations. They mention spending of US$44,000 on IKONOS imagery for a total area of 650 km², at a cost of US$68 per km². For future work, it might be more cost effective to purchase Quickbird imagery. Today, even purchasing corrected IR imagery from Digital Globe via tasking satellites, namely, obtaining new imagery, would cost US$36.00 per km², half the project cost and with a slightly better resolution. Despite this project's limited application of and success with satellite image data analysis, it demonstrated how valuable visual detection is for broad-scale landscape analysis and for ground-truthing in multiple terrains. Given their impressive success using visual detection, it is not hard to imagine what results multispectral analysis will yield for broad-scale archaeological feature detection.

In the Middle East, predictive modeling for ancient sites is still problematic. Archaeologists have noted that there is no statistical advantage to using regularly spaced spatial units for landscape analysis, as there are problems with spatial autocorrelation (Hodder and Orton 1976: 174–83). Looking for anomalies, or "noise," on images via visual detection or spectral signature analysis is far more likely to lead to archaeological site identification on the ground than randomly picking places. However, potential and real ground-based problems must be recognized first. Archeological features, such as field systems, walls, terraces, tracks, and tumuli, cluster in variable ways around various archaeological sites. How to identify different field patterns needs more refinement, especially in areas where there has been reuse: Aerial archaeology may aid in further reconstructing field systems. Undulating and difficult terrain hampers effective survey work, and creates obstacles in collecting data in a meaningful way and connecting it to the larger archaeological picture. However, these are problems that archaeologists are overcoming through the ongoing testing of multiple remote sensing methods.

The Delta and Middle Egypt

Ancient Egypt represents one of the best-known and most productive archaeological landscapes across the globe, yet regional surveys represent a fairly insignificant part of Egyptological research in the past 200 years (Kessler 1981; Kemp and Garfi 1993; Jeffreys and Tavares 1994; Jeffreys and Tavares 2001; Jeffreys 2003). Intrasite survey is another issue: Subsurface archaeological detection has become increasingly important over the past few decades (Herbich 2003; Mumford et al. 2003), detecting a number of mortuary and culture features that many projects have subsequently excavated. A few broader remote sensing projects have concentrated around the pyramid region near Cairo (Yoshimura et al. 1997). One such mission utilized Quickbird satellite imagery to map the Abusir pyramid fields, focusing on the general position and topology of the areas. This study found that the color of buried limestone blocks was easier to detect on Quickbird imagery, and encouraged combining surface detection, magnetometer survey and remote sensing analysis (Barta and Bruna 2005). Another desert-based study used Landsat and ASTER imagery to create digital elevation models and to map early to mid-Holocene landscapes in the Western desert, when conditions were more humid. Using topographic, hydrological, and geological information, the study predicted areas where Holocene sites were most likely to be detected along ancient water sources. These potential target sites were then surveyed to survey the existence of past human activity (Bubenzer and Bolten 2003; Bolten et al. 2006; Bubenzer and Riemer 2007).

Egypt's heritage faces many threats in the face of a rapidly increasing population, urbanization, and looting (see Chapter 8), which is a problem faced elsewhere across the Middle East (Schipper 2005), and the world as a whole. Decorated and inscribed wall faces are currently flaking off temples in Luxor due to rising salinity levels (Brand 2001a, 2001b), while agricultural developments have harmed and continue to threaten archaeological sites. When Napoleon visited Egypt in the early 1800s, as illustrated in *The Description of Egypt* (Jomard 1829), Egypt's floodplain landscapes were covered with ancient mounds, or "tell" sites (Edwards 1891). In the early 1900s, archaeologists had already noted the widespread destruction of these mounds, which farmers had begun to mine for fertile Nile silt and mud, known as *sebbakh* (Kelsey 1927). Egypt's landscape continues to change: Egyptian farmers are reclaiming desert lands for agriculture (Giddy and Jeffreys 1992), while growing settlements on or beside archaeological sites also threaten to engulf and destroy many archaeological sites.

Regional archaeological surveys form the only way to detect the surviving surface sites before they too are lost or engulfed. In addition, landscape geomorphology issues can best be understood from a spatially based perspective (Coutellier and Stanley 1987; Said 1988, 1990; Hassan 1997). With so many new discoveries being made on known archaeological sites, changing the way Egyptologists frame the history of ancient Egypt, it remains to be seen what regional settlement patterns can contribute via the subfield of settlement pattern studies, which is otherwise virtually non-existent in Egyptian archaeology. Settlement archaeology has become increasingly important in Egyptology (Kemp 1972) while the diverse landscapes composing Egypt make it necessary to approach settlement pattern studies using satellite archaeology. This author's study area in the East Delta was chosen initially to investigate the regional settlements surrounding Tell Tebilla (Mumford 2002, 2003), where the author had spent several years excavating under the auspices of the Survey and Excavation Projects in Egypt (SEPE), directed by Gregory Mumford of the University of Alabama at Birmingham. The subsequent Middle Egypt survey, shown in Figure 6.16, grew from a desire to examine regional settlement patterns in relationship to the well-known late Dynasty 18 site of Tell el-Amarna, where excavation has been undertaken for over a century by a succession of British and German missions, and most recently under the direction of Barry Kemp (Cambridge University).

Defining the limits of the overall survey area was problematic for the East Delta, while historical and geographical factors made it much easier to choose survey boundaries in Middle Egypt. A 50 × 60 km area was selected somewhat arbitrarily around Tell Tebilla, while a 15 × 30 km area was segregated within the area enclosed by Akhenaton's boundary stelae (defining the agricultural lands belonging to Akhetaten, or modern Tell el-Amarna) (Figure 6.17). Due to the broad survey area and initial limited funding, the author decided to test the capabilities of coarser resolution ASTER, Corona, SPOT, and Landsat 7 imagery in the detection of previously unknown ancient features. Some archaeologists may argue that Landsat and SPOT imagery can be too coarse (i.e. 30 m pixel resolution) to detect archaeological features in floodplain areas (Wilkinson 2002), but they are right only when smaller features, such as cropmarks, need to be found. A wide range of techniques could be tested on known sites in the Delta (Butzer 1975), where many surveys and excavations had already taken place, and confirmed via Corona imagery. At the time of this Delta research, Google Earth™ only offered SPOT 20 m imagery for the Delta, where more surveys have been conducted. Middle Egypt was quite different, as the last major survey to cover the West Bank opposite Tell el-Amarna took under the Napoleonic Survey of Egypt in 1798–1802.

In the Delta, the most appropriate satellite imagery appeared to be Landsat and SPOT imagery dating to the wettest months (the winter), as moisture content seemed likeliest to aid in isolating archaeological sites. Many previous surveys had taken place in the East Delta (Bietak 1975; Van den Brink 1987; Chlodnicki *et al.* 1992, Butzer

Figure 6.16 Middle Egypt, showing high tell in the middle of a town during 2004 Middle Egypt
Survey Project, photograph by Sarah Parcak.

2002), while the work of the Egyptian Exploration Society's Delta survey also proved
invaluable for checking historical excavation and survey data. In the last two decades
Egypt's Supreme Council for Antiquities (SCA) has placed an increasingly high priority
on Delta archaeology through the Egyptian Antiquities Information Service (EAIS)
recording teams, halting most new work south of Cairo and encouraging more projects
in the Delta (Cashman 2001; El-Ghandour 2003). One hundred and nineteen known
surface sites have been recorded in the East Delta survey area, being known through
excavations and surveys, but also provided a base for testing varying remote sensing
methods (Parcak 2003). Other earlier satellite studies in the Delta had not been as
successful in differentiating between modern settlements and the ancient sites they
covered partially or completely (Brewer *et al.* 1996).

   Likewise, this author's initial tests, using band combinations, band ratioing, and
supervised and unsupervised classifications, did not work in detecting a high percentage
of the known archaeological sites in the East Delta. However, the problem proved to
be the spectral signatures of the known sites: They could not be readily distinguished
from the spectral signatures of the towns and buildings on top of them. This problem
was solved when a PCA was processed for a 4-3-2 RGB Landsat 7 image using six principal components. This technique enabled more subtle landscape variations to appear.
It succeeded in detecting 90 percent of the already known archaeological sites, and
detected 44 previously unknown sites with the same spectral signatures. The validity

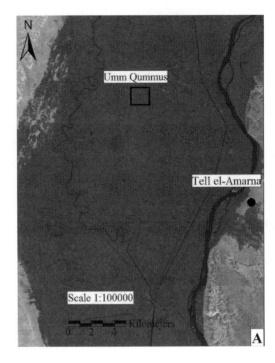

Figure 6.17 Middle Egypt, overall Landsat image (scale 1:100000 m) of 2004 survey area, image courtesy of NASA.

of these "new" sites was also confirmed independently with Corona imagery prior to fieldwork in the summer of 2003, which visited 62 known, poorly known, or previously unknown sites. Overall, the remote sensing techniques and subsequent survey attained a 93 percent success rate for detecting previously unknown archaeological sites. The survey located and recorded surface material culture for comparison to the already known survey and excavation materials (Parcak 2004a).

The Middle Egypt survey project applied the same types of satellite datasets, and, with additional funding, also used Quickbird data. Unlike the Delta survey, the exact location of other ancient sites was not known in the floodplain across the Nile from Tell el-Amarna (Lepsius 1859). Hence, remote sensing techniques were tested on the nearest known site at el-Ashmunein (Spencer 1982, 1989, 1993), shown in Figure 6.18, a large, multi-period tell located 10 km to the north of the intended survey area. Running an unsupervised classification on a 4-3-2 RBG Landsat image clarified the spectral signature of the known archaeological part of el-Ashmunein, seen in Figures 6.19a and 6.19b, and detecting a surprising 70 additional "ancient site" signatures (27 of which had already been recognized through brief mentions in past publications, but had never been surveyed in detail; see Kemp 2005). The remaining 43 previously unknown site surfaces that appeared were confirmed in both the Corona and Quickbird data. Ground truthing took place in Spring 2004, visiting 69 of the 70 sites found in the remote sensing study (one site could not be visited due to lack of a bridge across a canal), which located

Figure 6.18 Ashmunein, Middle Egypt, photograph by Sarah Parcak.

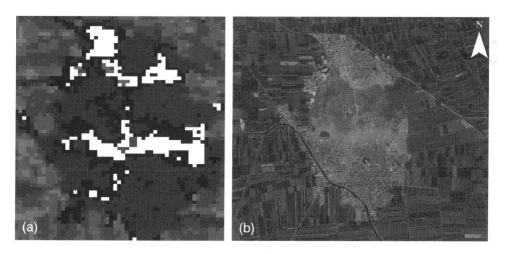

Figure 6.19 Ashmunein, Middle Egypt: (a) classified Landsat 4-3-2 image (scale 1:875 m), the white pixels represent archaeological material, while the darker pixels represent mixed archaeological debris; and (b) the modern town of Ashmunein, compare it with the 2008 Quickbird image (scale 1:806 m) of Ashmunein, images courtesy of NASA and Google.

ancient material culture at 98 percent of the previously unknown sites (Parcak 2005, 2007b).

The higher pixel value associated with the "ancient site" signatures sites detected in the remote sensing analysis seems connected to the relative overall moisture content of the soil. For instance, tell sites in Egypt, and the Middle East, in general, are formed by a complex series of processes (Schiffer 1987; Steadman 2000), and are normally covered with layers of eroded clay and silty soil, beneath which lies higher concentrations of mudbrick, the main building material for the ancient Egyptians. This soil is full of organic material, which alters its ability to retain moisture. Compounds called hummous colloids are created from chemicals. These compounds change the vegetation's vigor, and then transform chemically the moisture on the mound (Davidson and Shackley 1985; Limp 1992b: 34; Rapp and Hill 1998; French 2002). It appears to be this chemically altered moisture that is being detected by the PCA in the East Delta survey region (after the spectral redundancy has been removed from the image) and by classification techniques in the Middle Egypt survey area. The success of these two different techniques shows how recognizing and implementing different methods of detection can work in similar environments (i.e. floodplains) along the same river system, relating no doubt to changing weather patterns, atmospheric conditions, and longer term anthropomorphic changes.

Hence, the remote sensing project work in Egypt has answered questions relating to human–environment interaction throughout Egyptian history, yet much work remains to be done through future survey seasons. The overall remote sensing and ground survey results provided much data on long-term settlement changes in the East Delta, some of which appear far more connected to environmental shifts than previously thought (Parcak 2004b). Detailed ceramic analysis in Middle Egypt revealed mostly late Roman occupation on the West Bank, and indicated intensive trade between this region and Aswan, Libya, Alexandria, and other parts of the Mediterranean. Ongoing coring work in Middle Egypt is helping to reconstruct past shifts in the Nile's courses and related settlement placement and changes. Future research will be conducted via the RESCUE project (for Remote Sensing and Coring of Uncharted Egyptian Sites), which aspires to detect all of the Delta's previously unknown surface sites, beginning in summer 2009. This project will conduct detailed coring, mapping, and survey, seen in Figure 6.20, ideally before the sites are destroyed. If the Middle Egypt and Delta survey results are any indication, then there are thousands of ancient surface settlement sites awaiting discovery in Egypt's floodplain regions, viewed in Figures 6.21a and 6.21b. Regarding the unknown subterranean sites that lie beneath the current detection range of satellite imagery, future detection must await the release and development of better technology.

Conclusion

The studies presented here have shown how various archaeologists have approached satellite archaeology research designs in different landscapes. Each study has had its own challenges to overcome, whether it is the landscape type, issues with funding, ground survey difficulties, or general data synthesis. These and other projects will naturally have individual needs according to regional landscape types, project funding, team makeup, overall team expertise, and the overall project goals. By discussing both the

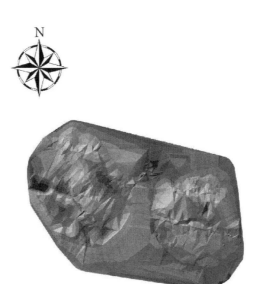

Scale 1:12000

Figure 6.20 Middle Egypt Survey 2005, the site of Kom el-Ahmar, mapped using a differential GPS, photograph courtesy of Sarah Parcak.

Figure 6.21 Tell Sheikh Masara: (a) Quickbird image; and (b) photograph, note how the sheikh's tomb looks from space, images courtesy of Google Earth™ Pro and Sarah Parcak.

positive and negative aspects of each project's approaches, it is hoped that archaeologists working in similar geographic areas or landscape types will be able to model their projects accordingly. Satellite archaeology is ever changing and evolving, thus, as new satellite imagery appears with improved spatial and spectral resolutions, project designs will change as well. Regarding the subsequent chapter, how projects can approach the collection of archaeological data on the ground forms the next logical step in research design.

7

REMOTE SENSING AND SURVEY

Overview

Without detailed ground surveys, information collected from remotely sensed satellite images loses much of its potential meaning. Studies can be conducted with reference to the application of specific techniques with great success, only if the archaeological situation is known in detail. For example, if 90 percent of the settlement sites from a particular region are known to date to the Roman period, and satellite remote sensing specialists locate 100 additional possible archaeological sites, it is likely that the majority of the new sites would also date to the Roman period. One would not normally, question such a supposition in an archaeological publication. When publishing reports, archaeologists risk conjecture if their studies have not implemented ground-truthing or previous survey work risk due to the error rates typical in all remote sensing analysis. It is hoped that, when attempting different applied remote sensing analytical methods, some will work, while it is anticipated that others will not. Techniques of analysis that do not work are still very useful to remote sensing archaeologists, as it is through understanding why particular techniques do not work that one can identify techniques for future work that could help to locate additional archaeological features of interest. Understanding this from a ground-based perspective is invaluable.

This chapter outlines the key factors for archaeological ground surveying (or "ground-truthing") of data collected from remotely sensed images. To what extent can satellite remote sensing surveys be considered as different to more typical ground based archaeological surveys (Aufrecht 1994; Given *et al.* 1999; Orton 2000; Blakely and Horton 2001; Kardulias 2002; Piro and Capanna 2006; Campana 2007)? They may outwardly appear to be virtually identical: During survey work, a team will often walk set transects (i.e. linear paths) across individual sites (Figure 7.1), or follow geological or natural features, pending landscapes differences, looking for, and often recording and collecting material culture. Ground surveys for satellite imagery, however, differ greatly from typical archaeological surveys. In these circumstances archaeologists will have pinpointed in advance specific areas for archaeological reconnaissance. Rather than conducting a typical survey using arbitrary 100, 200, 300, or more meter transects across a landscape with teams of people (Knapp 2000), a ground-truthing team will have pre-selected "archaeological signatures" for verification, thus increasing survey efficiency. How the archaeological teams want to conduct the survey on the ground will vary depending on numerous factors (Alcock and Cherry 2004), which will be discussed here in detail.

Figure 7.1 Delta survey, Egypt, showing geoarchaeologist Larry Pavlish doing a pacing survey, photograph by Sarah Parcak.

The very purpose of archaeological remote sensing work affects how and why archae-ologists record specific features on the ground. Different types of archaeological survey must also be evaluated, compared to and contrasted with satellite remote sensing ground-truthing. Any subsequent survey work will depend on the overall goal of the archaeological exploration: Remote sensing work might aim to locate new archaeological sites, establish cultural resource management, monitor archaeological sites under threat, assess general landscape risks (e.g. urban sprawl), or locate significant geomorphological features. Each type of remote sensing ground survey, like all surveys in archaeology, would require a different type of approach.

In contrast to traditional ground survey, the remote sensing specialist must record everything on the ground (i.e. all vegetation, soils, and water sources) for later comparison with the satellite imagery to determine why a particular area yielded an "archaeological" signature. One should not only be concerned with locating archaeological sites, but also underlying archaeological site markers, which may vary widely depending on landscape geomorphology. These will include types of vegetation, water, soil, and local geological features. How any past land usage changed will also be of great interest, as key changes (especially in the past 30 years, encompassing multispectral remote sensing) will affect pixel values in land use land cover change analyses. Landscape characterization from space is entirely different: One may think the satellite imagery shows one thing (such as an open field), but finds it to be something else on the ground (such as low scrub forest). This is more often the case in areas not previously surveyed.

Satellite remote sensing survey requires a full landscape analysis. Archaeologists must consider past, present, and possible future land-use practices at the ground-truthing stage. Evaluating the capabilities of certain satellite types in terms of what they can and cannot see on the ground is a key component of remote sensing in archaeology. Misinterpretation of satellite imagery is a more frequent remote sensing issue but can be corrected with later analyses based on ground results. In some cases, premature overexcitement at having found a "long-lost" feature or site without ground verification can lead to poor science, hype, and misinformation, detracting from the field. This is where a full survey becomes important: If one takes into account all the past and present factors affecting landscapes, information gained from remote sensing analysis (including aerial photography and different satellite imagery types) can be tested on the ground, and applied to a broader area. Good science is the ultimate aim of remote sensing, in order to reconstruct past historical and environmental events as well as landscape use changes.

New developments in satellite technology require modified approaches to surveying and excavation. What previously could not be seen or detected on the ground due to spatial or spectral resolution might now be seen from space (Figure 7.2). Increasing refinement of spatial and spectral resolution in satellite imagery allows archaeologists to pinpoint and visit previously unknown features on the ground. In turn, such improvements will enable survey to be further refined. The need for survey work in rapidly changing landscapes affects how archaeologists use and interpret satellite imagery, and how they adapt known remote sensing techniques to their purposes. Currently, few

Figure 7.2 Middle Egypt, showing reverse cropmarks (the dense mudbrick architecture is preventing the growth of the cotton), 2008 image courtesy of Google Earth™ Pro.

archaeologists have the technical skills to program their own algorithms and remote sensing programs, nor, at this stage is it generally needed, but like other disciplines (geology, atmospheric science and health) that have advanced to this stage, archaeology will, in time, adapt this and subsequent technological advances.

One of the main issues for discussion is the overall role of remote sensing in archaeology: Although remote sensing is not yet a standard tool for archaeological surveys, it will become so in 5–10 years. With many archaeology and anthropology graduate programs now offering, if not requiring, some form of GIS and remote sensing in their curriculum, students have adapted their programs accordingly to such recent needs. The growth in researchers and students utilizing remote sensing has caused a new way of thinking in archaeology. While the specific remote sensing methodology faces continuous development, surveys will only continue to improve based on new ways of interpreting satellite imagery. Remote sensing is used far less to detect singular features on single sites for subsequent excavation, but this, too, is quickly changing (Parcak 2007a). At the very least, visually interpreted satellite imagery can aid mapping, artifact plotting, and identifying correlations between archaeological and geological features for surveys, which requires limited technical skill and training other than the use of a graphics design program.

As the field of archaeological remote sensing is still relatively young, it is prone to trial and error, especially when applying methodologies in the field. This is where the recording part of the ground survey becomes so critical. Many parts of the world are underserved by existing remote sensing work; and even less so with the applied remote sensing work required for archaeology. Hence, any attempts at analytical remote sensing methods may be devoid of any local reference points.

Worldwide, in general, each region and sub-region will pose problems for remote sensing and archaeological survey work due to the nature of satellite imagery analysis. Here it is essential to know what satellites can and cannot detect (e.g. ancient canals or buried walls). Paying close attention to the additional factors affecting recording can help with initial survey work. Developing specific survey forms for each region is crucial (Figure 7.3), and will be discussed in detail in this chapter. Each team can adapt such survey forms to their own needs, but the suggested format provides a good starting point already tested during a number of remote sensing ground survey seasons in floodplain environments in Egypt.

Cost–benefit analysis should be central to any discussion of how remote sensing can aid regular survey. How much can a single survey gain from using remote sensing as opposed to a regular foot survey? This author's own research in Middle Egypt furnished one example. It is important to demonstrate the specific advantages and disadvantages of incorporating satellite imagery over a sole reliance on traditional survey techniques. Thirty-five years ago, before the adoption of satellite remote sensing in general, one would need to compile lists of known archaeological sites in the survey areas and place them onto modern maps. In the case of the current study, the parameters for choosing the survey area included selecting Middle Egypt because it remained mostly poorly studied from the perspective of analyzing settlement patterns through time (Kemp 2005). Instead of evaluating satellite remote sensing techniques, one can test more general ground surveying techniques: Pacing set distances such as 100 m transects, or randomly choosing areas (quadrants) for more intensive searching. Even using aerial photographs, many surface sites could not be located, being buried beneath modern

Figure 7.3 Sarah Parcak using a differential GPS during the Middle Egypt Survey Project 2005 season, photograph by Sarah Parcak (using a tripod).

towns and villages. For the sake of direct comparison, in this hypothetical study only one person would be responsible for locating the sites, accompanied by an Egyptian inspector from the Supreme Council for Antiquities (SCA), a driver and a policeman (Figure 7.4).

In initiating foot surveys without the benefit of pre-selected target sites, one immediately runs into various problems. For example, approaching a surface survey of Middle Egypt, one is faced with a former floodplain region characterized by a vast area of rice, cotton, and sugarcane cultivation (Figure 7.5). The first question is where should one begin? In regards to security issues, any current archaeological survey team would be permitted to visit only six places in one day and must tell the police exactly where they are going 24 hours in advance. The study area in Middle Egypt spans 15 × 30 km, much of which is inaccessible to field walking since large tracts of cultivation often lie beneath water. Furthermore, one cannot walk in fields without obtaining each owner's permission, while parasites in irrigation water offer serious health hazards. Navigation problems arise through the numerous canals and channels obstructing potential walking routes. This leaves main and secondary road connecting towns and villages for the actual survey route.

Other problems arise. Where would a traditional survey team look for sites in modern towns and what would they hope to find? A number of modern settlements in Middle Egypt are large enough to represent small cities. Unless an exact area within a town is

Figure 7.4 Middle Egypt Survey Project team (driver and policeman), 2004, photograph by Sarah Parcak (using a tripod).

Figure 7.5 Fields in Middle Egypt, photograph by Sarah Parcak.

known to contain archaeological remains, one could spend days, if not weeks or months, wandering through it and finding nothing. Perhaps questioning the local inhabitants of towns or villages could reveal the location of archaeological features, or indeed entire ancient towns. Local people may often deny the presence of antiquities, fearing confiscation of land or other official interference, or may simply remain ignorant of ancient remains other than for well-known sites. Even if an elderly man or woman remembers a free-standing archaeological site, they might not remember its exact location. Such detailed questioning and verification require additional time. If the archaeological site proved to be in the vicinity of modern agricultural fields, it could take many hours or days of searching along dirt roads or footpaths, often traveling on foot since few tracks in fields are wide enough to accommodate cars and trucks. Not knowing the exact coordinates of an archaeological site introduces another problem: By being even several hundred meters off track, one can easily enter an unproductive field system and miss the most knowledgeable farmers who are aware of the existence of ancient remains.

An additional consideration represents the time needed for traditional surface survey work. Aside from the area covered by the fields, over 160 towns and villages lie in the Middle Egypt survey area (Figure 7.6). If one could visit six places per day for one hour each it would take 27 days to see every town and village, including traveling time. Unfortunately, the range of town sizes would require from one hour to at least one week to search every street thoroughly for archaeological remains (40 hours of work, entailing walking up and down streets and speaking to local people). Hence, it would take a minimum of five full-time months to visit every town in the survey region. A survey of this nature would have already become quite costly, especially considering that

Figure 7.6 Urban surveying, Egypt, note the steep angle of the parked car, photograph by Sarah Parcak.

179

less than one percent of the survey area is classified as "urban", leaving over 300 times the area and time required to complete a full foot survey with 100 percent coverage (See Table 7.1). Assuming one could visit field systems, problems of accessibility and transportation might obscure any potential results. On foot, one could reasonably, albeit less extensively, search a 2×2 km quadrant in an eight-hour day, assuming that the fields were connected by good footpaths. It would thus take a minimum of 112 workdays to field walk the entire survey region (measuring 450 km^2), which is 4.5 months. Thus, to survey both the urban and field areas on foot using traditional survey methods would take a minimum of 9.5 months. Adding in typical survey delays and a break on Fridays, problems with transportation and bureaucracy, the survey would likely take about one year. In contrast, the Middle Egypt Survey Project had obtained pre-selected target areas from satellite images analyzed and surveyed from the same region in only two weeks (14 days), which represents a savings in time of 2600 percent. This does not include the time spent prior to the survey season analyzing the satellite imagery, preparing for the survey, or processing the collected archaeological material culture, but all surveys must spend time on such activities (minus the imagery analysis).

Cost is also a major consideration for large-scale surveys, but the overall purpose of the actual survey cannot be forgotten. Typical surveys must pay for a driver, vehicle, accommodation, food, workmen (if needed), salaries for officials or specialists, supplies and equipment. Being able to survey 26 times more efficiently allows for more time in the field with additionally much reduced costs, as well as decreased wear on technical equipment. This is, however, representative of regional surveys searching for large sites or features, whose goals remain very different than the goals of most field walking teams. Remote sensing survey is different in this respect: Satellites cannot, at this moment in time, detect small sherd or lithic scatters in fields. Tiny objects detected with the naked eye represent major differences between satellite imagery analysis and the power of the human eye. Small scatters of objects found across landscapes add up to a much bigger landscape picture, addressing more subtle landscape usages. Ideally, both types of surveys can be carried out in an area, but as shown by the Middle Egypt example, "typical" ground surveys are not always possible, or easy, depending upon the local terrain.

Once teams have located larger sites or features through a remote sensing survey, it is possible for future teams to return to those areas to conduct more typical field walking in the areas across and surrounding these places. Future intensive ground survey may be advisable, especially if additional features appear on the ground that did not appear during the satellite imagery analysis. Sherd(s) and lithic scatters, or remnants from earlier sites and features, will likely appear in the areas surrounding the relocated archaeological sites (Figure 7.7). This represents an ideal marriage of field walking and remote sensing survey. This is most useful in larger landscapes that are difficult to traverse, or where typical ground surveys are not possible to conduct, such as desert regions, where sites often cluster around surviving (and ancient) water sources possibly detectable from space. Additional site features not detected by satellite imagery analysis will take more time for the ground survey teams, and must be carefully plotted, to address why they did not appear during the original analysis. These unexpected features can be just as valuable as located features, as they force the team to consider running alternative analytical remote sensing techniques to isolate them, which, if successful, may allow an even greater number of features to be detected in future survey seasons.

Figure 7.7 Sherd scatters in a field, Middle Egypt Survey Project 2004, photograph by Sarah Parcak.

During ground surveys, teams must consider the anthropological side of survey work just as seriously as the remote sensing itself. Local interactions can provide the most fruitful information exchanges, especially regarding landscape use changes, archaeological site destruction, and future land-use practices. Initially, it is suggested that a team identifies and meets the leaders of a village or group of individuals, and discusses the survey project with them. Honesty is the best policy, and it may be that the survey team can aid local farmers with detailed hydrological maps or maps showing places where wells can be drilled. Although this may take a considerable amount of time at the outset, building good relationships may streamline work permits or may enable further survey work in otherwise forbidden areas. With remote sensing, plans change, and you do not always know where you will go. Information travels quickly via local networks in rural locations, which is why time needs to be set aside into the survey schedule for consulting local people. At no point should money exchange hands, unless a specific service was rendered (i.e. car fixed, tools purchased, etc.). Issuing gratuities will foster increasing expectations and costs to survey seasons, and may encourage local people to pillage sites and antiquities to earn extra money, thereby setting a dangerous precedent. People should be thanked, but only in culturally acceptable ways. Knowing what is and is not culturally acceptable prior to a survey season will help. Small gifts of tea, fruit, or sweets are always appropriate if a local person takes significant time to show an archaeological site or feature. Carrying a Polaroid camera will allow an immediate gift of photographs, which are always much appreciated by people who often lack photos of their families. Building trust is far more crucial, especially in areas where local politics can interfere with work progress. In all of the survey work the author has conducted,

Figure 7.8 Middle Egypt Survey Project 2004, children who helped survey, photograph by Sarah
    Parcak (using a tripod).

no individual has ever asked for money for taking time to aid in the survey process. In several instances, individuals actually made it clear that they did not want or expect any money, and that they appreciated interest in their cultural heritage. Returning in subsequent years to conduct coring or additional survey work, this author found that entire villages would come out to greet her. In several cases, local people gave intact ancient pots to the author (who turned them over immediately to the Egyptian SCA), saying they had been found during the construction of their homes.

Elderly adults represent only one group of people that should be questioned during remote sensing ground-survey. Children are often the best resource for locating smaller features that may not have been noted on the satellite imagery (Figure 7.8). If accompanied by government officials, children tend to be shooed away. Small bribes of sweets (again, remembering cultural appropriateness) work wonders during foot surveys, especially in larger towns that may cover a site or feature partially. Asking children directly for help has assisted this author and many of her colleagues during surveys, as children tend to know each nook and cranny of a town. Posing the right questions to local individuals can be difficult, as each person will have their own version of local history. This is to be expected: Each place will have multiple "histories" from multiple perspectives. How each individual signifies change to a landscape is also important to note, and will change depending on their position.

Additional questioning of locals will vary depending on what the team wishes to find. People are open about how landscapes and crop pattern have changed over time, and may be willing to show things that have appeared in fields or close to their homes. Farmers are also likely to know about cropmark patterns, and may be able to comment

Figure 7.9 Tell ed-Da'ba, East Delta (scale 1:99 m), note extensive cropmarks in the field, 2008
image courtesy of Google Earth™ Pro.

on how well they appear in certain types of crops. In Egypt, cotton and rice paddies
show buried mudbrick walls clearly, whereas fields of corn show walls less clearly (from
the ground). Different crops will grow higher or lower pending the buried archaeological features, and studying cropmark patterning in other parts of the world (seen in
Figure 7.9) will aid in this process if there are no previous cropmark records in a particular survey area. The wet time of year may show brief snapshots of buried walls in desert
environments, especially as plants grow quickly over a short period of time. In Jordan,
for example, Nabatean fields have appeared in the deserts during the brief wet season
(Glueck 1965).

Visiting the local or regional land-use or agricultural office may assist with learning
about general landscape changes. They may have records regarding field boundaries
changes, site names, crop usage, population density, and urbanization changes over the
past 200 years, or more, which will change across regions in the same country: Each
area has its own distinct, individual history depending on resource allocation, growth,
expansion, and collapse over time. This stretches beyond the roughly 50-year time
span of local living memory, which may or may not be necessary depending on the
needs of the survey team. Geology or water-management departments in universities
represent additional points of contact for survey teams. These offices often have access to
high-quality maps and aerial photographs. Questions should be asked of the antiquities
authorities regarding how much can be sampled from surveying sites, stored locally, or
transported abroad. This will affect general survey collection strategies, and shows the
importance of partnering with local institutions who might be able to store or study

items in more detail, and may be able to save money by conducting scientific analyses in the host country.

For any survey, archaeologists must question the reliability of information collected from local individuals regarding recent landscape change as well as archaeological site location. Even when conducting fieldwork with precise GPS coordinates for archaeological sites, it can be difficult orienting oneself on the ground. Roads may have changed or have gone out of use. In-field directions to archaeological sites can be highly problematic, and this is not surprising. Imagine if a stranger or group of strangers, accompanied by officials and police, were to stop and knock on your door, asking for directions to a specific place known only to your community. Perhaps this place is sacred (e.g. a shrine or cemetery covering an archaeological mound), or perhaps it is a place you, your family, friends, or neighbors rely on for income for food and clothing. Why would you feel obligated to direct the group of foreigners to the exact location? There are always multiple layers and internal or external pressures and factors that we do not or cannot realize that may affect the veracity of information received. Aside from speaking the local language, following local customs, or hiring local workers, which all aid survey work, this is a reality that archaeologists must respect and understand from the perspective of local groups.

In the majority of cases, however, local people remain the most valuable resource for archaeological remote sensing surveys. One is most likely to encounter farmers in rural areas, and what better people to make inquiries regarding landscape changes, land-use practices and crop usage at different times of year? Farmers know their own land and its immediate history better than any local or regional government organization. Asking what types of fertilizers were used, or when fields were irrigated, will also aid in the post-processing of satellite imagery data. It may be that such factors influence whether certain types of archaeological sites appear in satellite imagery. Farmers have taken the author to numerous archaeological sites not otherwise discovered in her initial remote sensing analysis, which, in turn, assisted with locating sites with further imagery analysis (Figure 7.10). Farmers also know a great deal about the archaeological material on their land. In some cases, they can discuss to what time period a particular site might date (i.e. Roman versus earlier), and why they think it dates to that period of time, with great accuracy.

Ethical issues abound when conducting ground surveys, especially regarding the illegal antiquities trade. In addition, maintaining colonial or ethnocentric views can lead to mistrust and even obstacles regarding what locals may or may not have recovered on their land or nearby. If locals claim to have discovered "treasure" (e.g. 500 jade masks from a particular site in Central America), it is likely that significant leg-pulling is occurring. However, if people claim they found more mundane items, such as concentrations of broken pottery (Figure 7.11) and bones in an adjacent field, this is more readily believable. Conversely, if someone were to inform an archaeological team about locally found objects (e.g. statuary, complete vessels, etc.), the local inhabitants could easily become suspicious when the foreigners ask to see such objects stored (illegally) in their homes. Gaining access to such objects may take years of building trust, but what is the survey team legally bound to do from an ethical perspective should this happen? Theoretically, archaeologists should follow a strict ethical code regarding the looting and illegal antiquities trade. Yet stopping this trade cannot happen overnight. Convincing local people about the potential employment opportunities from future

Figure 7.10 Farmer, Middle Egypt, photograph by Sarah Parcak.

Figure 7.11 Pottery, Middle Egypt, photograph by Sarah Parcak.

excavations being conducted on a previously undiscovered archaeological site may not outweigh the money they might receive from plundering and selling items to dealers. Discovering a previously unknown archaeological site through remote sensing, which then proves to be looted, may also have undesirable consequences for the survey team.

This should be discussed with local authorities (which may not be possible if they are involved with the looting) or assessed by speaking to trusted local sources. How to proceed in such circumstances will require discussion and rigorous debate, especially as the field of archaeological remote sensing develops.

Ethnoarchaeology also has applications to remote sensing surveys. Where land use practices have not changed much over the millennia, interviewing people about their farming practices and observing these techniques might contribute towards understanding past land-use strategies. One pertinent example comes from the site of Angkor Wat (as discussed in Ch. 6), where radar survey has revealed the site to be significantly larger than previously thought (Evans *et al.* 2007). Water management issues have not diminished in significance over time, as past water distribution systems observed from space and confirmed on the ground appeared to follow more "modern" strategies. Answering these and related questions can be just as important as locating archaeological sites. Studying modern land-use practices can help understanding of how and why past sites might appear during the satellite imagery analysis, which can, in turn, help to locate additional sites and features.

Discussing landscapes with local people and sharing survey data with them requires a degree of caution. Military regulations differ between countries and while Google Earth™ is publicly available for sensitive areas it is not always wise to carry around wide-format printouts of satellite imagery. This will vary across the world, but it is always wise to err on the side of caution during surveying. For example, during a 2002 survey of South Sinai, this author, accompanied by her survey team, a driver, and an Inspector from the SCA (required by the Egyptian government for all foreign expeditions), nearly got arrested for entering an unmarked security zone. The inspector, who had worked in South Sinai for 15 years, knew the survey area fairly well: He avoided variously marked military areas and compounds, following what appeared to be a non-military road into a large wadi, where we commenced with a survey atop a ridge overlooking the wadi. During a search for ancient material culture, we noted a group of uniformed, armed men running towards the car, and decided to return to the car. Our inspector was having a heated discussion with an officer, and he instructed us to "get into the car." We kept our maps, cameras, and GPS units concealed so as not to worsen the situation. The officer looked briefly into the car, noticed nothing, and let us go. Our inspector subsequently explained that we had entered an unmarked military area, of which he had been unaware, and that he had convinced the officers that we were nothing more than simple tourists who did not know any better. We narrowly avoided being arrested, but if they had found our survey equipment, we would certainly have encountered more serious ramifications, despite our antiquities permission to survey in this region. This unforeseeable situation was fortunately remedied by a highly competent and quick thinking Egyptian colleague. We would not have surveyed there had we known it was a military area.

Coordinating with local authorities sensitively is crucial to avoid this and other situations, given all the irregularities of ground-truthing. Advance planning for all contingencies can minimize any potential problems. A survey is not worth risking the life, career, or health of any team member, and all team members must be advised of all possible ramifications of fieldwork. Dog whistles are critical, given the large numbers of stray dogs (with rabies) that reside near archaeological sites. In another survey region in Central America, Tom Sever's team was held up at gunpoint (Sever 1998: 158). They, too, had luck on their side. Every remote senser in archaeology has a story to tell about the adventures and perils of fieldwork, and it would be beneficial to collect these stories into a compendium of "what not to do" to prevent problems in future survey efforts. Additional publications, online forums, blogs, and courses can also pass on this information, but more is needed to promote good survey practices in archaeological remote sensing.

Along with knowing the potential dangers inherent in conducting ground-truthing, timing is also critical for carrying out surveys, regarding both time of year and time of day. Surveys should, if possible, coincide with the season and time of day the satellite took the original imagery. Features may not be visible on the ground during other times of the day or year without test trenching, which may not prove feasible during surveys. Dry or wet conditions may prove optimal depending on the survey's global location. Either condition may allow for additional features to be observed by the survey team. Local planting cycles may allow or prevent survey work, especially in areas inundated once or more times per year. This would thwart the collection of material culture in fields. The dry season would be best for conducting surveys in southeast Asia. For example, daily torrential rainstorms do not permit the use of non-waterproof equipment, or may interfere with GPS signals in rainforest environments (in addition to the overlying foliage). Cloudy days may also cause reception problems for satellite receiving stations. Issues that affect normal foot surveys, such as extreme temperatures, affect ground-truthing surveys in a similar, but not entirely related way: Typical ground collection survey may work, for example, from 6 a.m.–2 p.m. in certain regions, with post-processing occurring in the afternoons at the nearest convenient or proper facility. Satellite survey work is less predictable: Even though a survey team may know the general area where it will be working, and may have selected a set number of sites to be visited on a particular day, vehicular problems, washed out roads, or bureaucratic delays may all combine to make the work day significantly longer and less productive than expected.

Given that satellite remote sensing will have detected a certain number of "new" features or sites in a given region, the goal of the survey team will be to visit as many places as possible. This is one way that ground-truthing of satellite imagery differs markedly from foot survey: One seldom knows exactly what will appear in a transect survey, including even the general size of a site (despite predictive modeling), whereas remote sensing enables one to estimate the general size of features located on the ground (Figure 7.12). During ground survey, given that team members will be walking in set transects across a landscape, one can estimate the general area to be covered over a day or over the course of a survey season. With ground-truthing, everything changes when teams begin to search for sites on the ground. Although they may know exactly where to go to locate the site signatures, the specific things generating such data remain unknown and need to be verified. Striving for efficiency in surveying must be balanced against a myriad of unknown variables and obstacles to be encountered. Even in areas already visited by ground-truthing, the one common factor in archaeological surveys across the globe is to expect the unexpected. For example, on a tragic note, Bedouin bandits murdered explorer Captain Palmer during his survey work in the Sinai Peninsula in the late 1800s (Wilson 1976).

Figure 7.12 East Delta survey, cemetery originally appeared as a modern town covering an ancient site during imagery analysis, photograph by Sarah Parcak.

A less dramatic, but pertinent example, occurred in October 2007, when the author participated in a documentary on environmental change in ancient Egypt. As part of the footage, the documentary team filmed the author prospecting a large archaeological site in the northeast Delta, examining surface potsherds, essentially showing how archaeologists collect surface data to show periods of settlement. During the initial summer 2003 survey, thousands of sherd(s) (dating to multiple time periods) covered the site to such an extent it proved impossible to see the silt surface in many places. However, under different weather conditions, only thick Roman period sherd(s) appeared, with 2–3 inches of light silt covering most of the site. It did not seem likely that thousands of sherd(s) had simply disappeared. One needs to think about general micro-landscape changes due to seasonality: For instance, October is a time of transition in the northeast Delta and throughout much of Egypt. Having completed the summer and early fall harvests, farmers burn their fields to ready them for the next planting cycle. August and September are dry months, and with many fires in the fields, dust and ash can be thick in the air, and aid in the accumulation of a loose surface layer on higher ground (Figure 7.13). This is why few sherd(s) appeared on the surface of the survey site: Buried beneath few inches of powdery surface silt, the sherd(s) would not reappear until after the winter rains (which would either wash away the silt or delineate the subsurface pottery).

It took this visit to realize just how crucial a spring to mid-summer visit is to carry out an effective ground survey on large multi-period settlement sites in Egypt. In contrast, the winter rain turns archaeological sites into mud and makes survey unpleasant if

Figure 7.13 Tell Sharufa, East Delta 2003 Delta survey, note dense vegetation covering the site, photograph by Sarah Parcak.

not impossible. This is a good lesson for carrying out ground-truthing in other regions: Seasonality can make the difference between a successful and unsuccessful season. Regardless of the success in locating archaeological sites or remains, remote sensers in archaeology cannot accept at face value the current status of traditional survey results for a given region. Just because archaeological survey reports may claim something does not exist within a given region does not mean it is not actually there.

More critical thinking is required. Archaeological remote sensers must conceptualize a greater range of landscape possibilities. As an example, the author has viewed crop-marks surrounding the site of Tanis in Egypt's East Delta, which suggest the multiperiod archaeological landscape in the vicinity to be 20 times its current size. Confirmation of such remote sensing work naturally awaits ground-truthing. Other remote sensing has located environmental features in Central America that have helped archaeologists to understand how the Maya flourished, and ultimately, how they might have collapsed (Saturno *et al.* 2007). No result in archaeological remote sensing analysis is too insignificant or odd to investigate. A strange signature on a satellite image might represent a modern village, or it might represent an archaeological feature heretofore unknown in a particular region. This does not mean that remote sensing specialists should be prone to flights of fancy: Satellite imagery analysis is a scientific exercise that requires rigorous testing and close examination of any potential false positives. The full range of possibilities must be considered, as remote sensing has already revealed just how little we actually know about ancient landscapes and landscape usage. The results of such analysis affect the choices ground survey teams can make in planning sufficient survey seasons.

Remote sensing changes traditional ground survey by allowing the team to locate and choose which sites to visit in advance. Thus, how does remote sensing aid in general pre-survey planning? If one has a good idea of the types of sites to be visited, and hence the types of features to be encountered, a team can bring appropriate surveying equipment into the field. Surveying schedules can be made, and specialists can be brought accordingly. Ideally, each site can be field walked, with a topographic plan generated rapidly by total stations or a differential GPS. Coring, if possible, should be initiated to understand the full date-range of the site, and ideally excavation of a few test trenches. All of these steps take significant time, but if carried out, may allow only one site to be visited each day. This is why advance planning becomes so important: How the team wishes to approach each site may be different, with some sites selected as "key" targets (perhaps displaying the largest or most readily apparent features) that require more intensive examinations. Other sites may be threatened by modern development, and need to be surveyed in greater detail before the information is lost. Collection and surveying strategies abound, and everything depends on the specific region where a team is working. There is no one right way to survey, although different archaeologists may debate this topic at great length. Each situation will determine the most appropriate specialized approach. In addition, it may not be possible to collect material culture at each site for analysis, due to significant restraints on time. Other situations may not allow detailed interviewing of local people. However, knowing where to go in advance of the survey provides a good starting point, while plans for future surveying seasons will affect the approaches a team may take in the initial season.

Although each survey will have individual needs based on landscape types, the size of the recording team, and the specific archaeological circumstances encountered, it is an essential to adapt a basic archaeological ground-truthing form for recording survey data. While consistency is a key component in recording the ground-collected data, it is assumed that each team will adapt their forms to any local in-field needs, as well as refine them over subsequent surveying seasons. In the course of three survey seasons in Egypt, the author made numerous changes to her forms, and foresees additional changes in future seasons. Landscapes are consistent only in their ability to remain in flux with modernization and global warming, and subsequently archaeologists need to remain flexible in their approach to recording them.

In the process of preparing for the ground-truthing survey, the team will need to determine how large an area to tackle. Part of this decision will depend on the budget, timing, team size, the amount of detail the team wishes to extract from the survey region, and the permission granted by the government in question. One of the major issues with archaeological satellite remote sensing is that it is relatively easy to analyze in comparison to the time it takes to survey, especially with larger area imagery such as Landsat or SPOT. The normally more costly Quickbird imagery, ordered in advance by the team, often limits the survey region to smaller areas. As in all remote sensing analyses, it may transpire that a team only wishes to investigate a small number of features or anomalies appearing in the imagery in question. In these cases, assessing the overall area is not as essential. Remote sensing allows for a larger geographic coverage to be investigated given that a team can visit specific locations rather than conducting a random intensive search. However, attempting to cover too large an area can affect survey quality. Biting off more than one can chew in an initial survey season can be a beneficial for gauging future survey logistics. Only by an initial survey season can a team learn and plan from how much can be done in a set amount of time with limited resources, and a certain number of team members, and potential unknown variables, which include host government restrictions, weather and unpredictable transportation. Each host nation and region will differ, and specific survey timing depends on the individual goals of each survey team. Once a team learns its specific limitations and in-field problems, future surveys can be conducted with greater efficiency.

Large areas of negative space may appear in the remote sensing analysis, and it is up to each team to decide how much time should be spent testing areas where no apparent archaeological surface features are indicated. Further time should be devoted to answering why a particular area is devoid of sites. In addition, researchers should test the validity of the remote sensing analysis, but it is also expected that remote sensing will not identify 100 percent of the surface features during the first season, or indeed, in any season. In some cases, what may appear to be definite archaeological features may reflect something else entirely, shown in Figure 7.14. Farmers have used soils from archaeological sites as fertilizers for a long period of the time in the Middle East, hence "false" signatures may not reveal distinct archaeological sites, but instead may reflect how land-use practices have changed. Until survey has begun, one will not know the total limitations of initial remote sensing analysis, and there will always be limitations.

Figure 7.14 East Delta Survey, what appeared to be vegetation on the satellite image turned out to be crops covering an archaeological site, photograph by Sarah Parcak.

Concerning the establishment of a survey area's size, one example is provided in Egypt's East Delta. Testing the results from a wide number of site types over a large region (50 × 60 km) allowed the refinement of a similar remote sensing surface survey methodology in the subsequent Middle Egypt Survey Project. The Delta survey experience enabled improvements in the overall Middle Egypt Survey Project approach and results, which was necessary given tighter police restrictions. The smaller 15 × 30 km area in Middle Egypt also permitted a more intensive recording of each site. Instead of looking for sites that previous surveys had identified, the Middle Egypt Survey Project located and focused mainly on previously unknown archaeological sites. Given the problems encountered with site location in the Delta survey (e.g. issues with map accuracy, blocked roads, and a much larger area), the author restructured the Middle Egypt survey appropriately, choosing the order of sites to be visited in advance. This allowed for greater coordination with the required police escorts, which needed to liaise in advance and coordinate with other police escorts in an adjacent province partially covered by the author's survey. Instead of simply prohibiting the author from conducting her survey in different jurisdictions, the police kindly pre-approved the list each evening, and even supplied an exceptionally bright officer to assist the author with her GPS readings.

Once a team decides on the overall survey area, it is useful to generate detailed maps by draping contours over satellite imagery on ArcView®/ArcGIS®, which can then be printed in large format. Information from local maps, if available, can also be digitized and added to the georeferenced satellite maps. Each located site or feature in question will thus already be placed on the map, and can even be labeled in the potential order to be visited. The local antiquities office, or government agency in charge of archaeological permit granting, should also receive a copy. Hence, team members will then have access to an up-to-date reference tool, which is otherwise lacking or unavailable commercially in many parts of the world and which is indispensable for quality ground-truthing.

While ground-truthing, pending access to electricity, or a portable generator, it may be easier to record directly into a handheld palm desk accessory (PDA). Hard copy recording may be preferable, and is suggested in combination with PDA recordings given the likelihood of electronic failure in rural areas, or issues with excess heat and moisture in the field. One of the advantages of a handheld PDA recording is being able to import data to and from a database in ArcGIS® while examining the satellite data. One can also mark off specific locations previously visited during the survey. Highly durable computers for tough field conditions are now publicly available, but their higher cost may be prohibitive for modest project budgets. Printing facilities would also provide the survey data in a hardcopy format, enabling multiple bound copies for ease of comparison during the course of the season.

Recording sheet overview

Regarding the format of the recording sheets and booklet, each team may have personal preferences, but two pages (double-sided) per site usually allows for sufficient detailed recording. The author utilized this format, with the first page being graph paper (permitting a rough surface survey sketch), with, if possible, the outline of the site or feature in question pre-drawn to-scale (Figure 7.15). If one can print out the appropriate part of the satellite image containing each site or feature, with an accompanying modern map

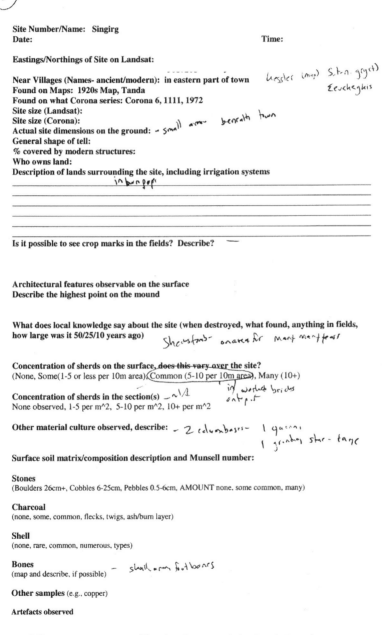

Site Number/Name: Singirg
Date: **Time:**

Eastings/Northings of Site on Landsat:

Near Villages (Names- ancient/modern): in eastern part of town   *Kessler (map) Seten. gryet)*
Found on Maps: 1920s Map, Tanda   *Zeucheghis*
Found on what Corona series: Corona 6, 1111, 1972
Site size (Landsat):
Site size (Corona):
Actual site dimensions on the ground: *- small area - beneath town*
General shape of tell:
% covered by modern structures:
Who owns land:
Description of lands surrounding the site, including irrigation systems
                        in bun pops

Is it possible to see crop marks in the fields? Describe?

Architectural features observable on the surface
Describe the highest point on the mound

What does local knowledge say about the site (when destroyed, what found, anything in fields,
how large was it 50/25/10 years ago)   *Sherustras- onarea for many manyears*

Concentration of sherds on the surface, does this vary over the site?
(None, Some(1-5 or less per 10m area), Common (5-10 per 10m area), Many (10+)
                                                                  in worked bricks
Concentration of sherds in the section(s) *- N/A*   *outp.t*
None observed, 1-5 per m^2, 5-10 per m^2, 10+ per m^2

Other material culture observed, describe: *- 2 columbases- 1 quern*
                                                1 grinding star - tang

Surface soil matrix/composition description and Munsell number:

Stones
(Boulders 26cm+, Cobbles 6-25cm, Pebbles 0.5-6cm, AMOUNT none, some common, many)

Charcoal
(none, some, common, flecks, twigs, ash/burn layer)

Shell
(none, rare, common, numerous, types)

Bones
(map and describe, if possible)   *- skull, arm foot bones*

Other samples (e.g., copper)

Artefacts observed

Figure 7.15 Middle Egypt Survey workbook, photograph by Sarah Parcak.

(if available), this will facilitate directions to the site and surface recording of features and material culture. The next page represents the main recording page, treating the archaeological site in a similar fashion to archaeological loci (each included section is discussed below). The third page is intended for recording specific comments about the site in question, while the last page facilitates sketching material culture collected during the survey.

The following section describes each subsection on the survey description page, which can be augmented further by each survey team. In some cases, data can be circled for ease of data recording. In all cases, nothing should be too unimportant to note. One might assume they will remember a seemingly unimportant observation later on in the same day, only to realize later it was a significant piece of data that was omitted as other sites and new data required entry. In the lab several months later, one might be asking why certain sites appear on the satellite imagery, only to realize for example that critical information regarding vegetation patterns was not recorded. Thus, consistency and detail remain the most important parts of ground-truthing recording, applying form recording sheet numbers similar to archaeological site forms. Recording details are also dependent on the time one has to survey a particular site or feature. Naturally, maximum information retrieval using the best possible methods is needed, but the limitations of a particular survey, or day, should also be described for later acknowledgement of survey limitations. The team may not be able to collect data, or may not be able to analyze it in-situ. Archaeological sites might also not be able to be photographed due to neighboring military restrictions. Some combination of the above situations might be possible on any given day. A team may not be able to reach a site or region. Additional sites or features might be found on the ground, or be shown to a team by local individuals, thereby throwing off the survey timing (unless teams have built in extra time foreseeing delays). Each subsection is described in full, noting the particular data one might record and why.

Date/time of day visited

While dates are always essential to record during archaeological work, time of day is equally important. This enables subsequent analyses to correlate what the team viewed on the ground during a certain time of day with the specific time at which the satellite imagery was generated. Every satellite image is taken at a set time of day, and it may emerge that certain features are viewable only during that time. For example, mud-brick architecture in the Middle East is relatively easy to distinguish from silt deposits in the summer (when many teams work in the field) until around noon, due to the ability of mudbrick to absorb moisture. In the afternoon, the ground on multi-period archaeological sites tends to become quite hard and dry, thus rendering the mudbrick architecture more difficult to view unless one has a practiced eye. Quickbird satellite images are taken at 10.40 a.m. each day coinciding with the optimum viewable point for mudbrick architecture. Thus, for site features detected by Quickbird imagery, a survey team would be best advised to visit them in the morning hours. Conversely, some site ground features may emerge best in the afternoon outside the viewing period for satellite imagery. Additional remote sensing algorithms may make such features clearer. Additionally, one might coincide the time of day spent at each site with the digital photos taken. It is too easy to mix up photos from similar sites after weeks of survey work, while pre-arranging site and image timeframes aids in keeping editing photographic files for each site.

Site name(s)—ancient and modern

Most town names change over time. If a team is lucky enough to have the ancient name of an archaeological site in question, it can be pre-recorded on forms for in-field comparison to historical name changes. Specific archaeological sites are sometimes still called by their ancient names or their derivatives by local people, or a related variant. Archaeologists may recognize a site by a ancient particular name, but it is essential to realize most local people have an entirely different and usually modern name for it. Knowing both ancient and modern toponyms is essential for excavation at the site/feature.

Original GPS points/site directions

This represents the eastings and northings of the site or feature, ideally reflecting a central point, taken during the remote sensing analysis. Aiming for a central point maximizes the location of a site on the ground using a GPS unit with a +/- error range.

Actual northings and eastings

Satellite images can be incorrectly georeferenced, or can sometimes be georeferenced in relation to old maps with inaccurate town coordinates. These coordinates can be later corrected with specific ground control points taken at the features/sites in question. Ideally ground-control points should be taken of large, unmovable, and "permanent" features, such as at a corner of a school, a local monument, a church or mosque (if permitted), a large landmark like a factory, or a cluster of structures on or near the archaeological site.

Original published information about site

In some cases, there may be existing published data discussing the sites or features in question. Not all archaeological remote sensing covers previously unknown sites: Many archaeologists have conducted large-scale surveys where little is known about an archaeological site other than assessments such as "possible site(?)." In various state archaeology registers, there may be incorrect data on the current state of an archaeological site. All of the known data on the site should be collected in a database format for comparison with the satellite imagery analysis. Past comments may aid in interpreting ground-truthing data.

What maps/surveys does it appear on, if any

Some areas of the world have been extensively ground-surveyed without the use of satellite imagery, and require revisiting. Others have not been surveyed, but are in regions well covered by modern maps (Figure 7.16). Every government- or foreign-produced map will be different, and may emphasize alternative features depending on the map's focus (e.g. farm boundaries; road maps, etc.). Gathering as many maps as possible of

Figure 7.16 Modern Delta maps, photograph by Sarah Parcak.

the region in question will aid in the remote sensing analysis, especially concerning vegetation and geology. A number of maps show archaeological sites/features that previous surveys have ignored. All the data can be scanned and imported into an ArcGIS® database.

How large is the area in question on the ground

Each type of satellite image records different data, whether it be spectral, spatial, or temporal data. Satellite images from different times of year may show slightly different data (Parcak 2005, 2007a), so the actual size of the sites/features on the ground may differ from the original analysis. How and why the ground-data differs is also an interesting discussion point, and will help in later analyses.

How does this compare to the different satellite image information

Each study will rely on a variety of satellite imagery, and it is useful to discern how each image type portrayed the archaeological site/features compared to what the team observes on the ground.

Towns and cities closest to site (and location in relation to these sites)

This category is also crucial. As some modern maps have been shown to be unreliable, it is helpful to have actual directions to the archaeological site or feature from the closest towns. If one becomes lost during the survey process, does not have access to maps, or there are issues with a GPS unit, a set of directions can remedy this situation. Published directions for future teams or government organizations are also helpful (e.g. take the large road heading north from such and such a town, take the second right to town Y, and then take first left. The site is approximately 250 m NW from the turnoff).

Who owns the land on which the site is located

Many archaeological sites and features may be located on privately owned land. If possible, it can be useful to have the name of the individual community members who own the land in question. Inquiries can be made of the landowners to see what additional archaeological features may have been visible in the past. Any inquiries should be made with caution and discretion since it may be illegal in some nations as digging and may be regarded as destroying an archaeological site, albeit through plowing or other indirect activity, or a government may be able to seize the land. This is a sensitive issue and should be dealt with carefully.

Shape of site or what is left (if anything)

Things can change quickly on the ground, even over the course of several years (i.e. the time-span between the date of the satellite imagery and the subsequent survey). Features noted in the generated satellite image data may no longer exist by the time the survey is conducted. It is also possible that additional features may have emerged depending on the time of year in which the survey is conducted. Even if a site is "destroyed" (i.e. usually being levelled to modern ground level), cropmarks may still indicate significant subsurface features. The actual surviving shape of the site or feature is important to describe, and plot (via a GPS) on the ground. It may differ greatly from what appeared during the satellite imagery analysis, and the remote sensing team needs to address why and how. For example, crops may cover a large part of a site, obscuring it from space, but a slightly higher crop or topographic elevation may make a mostly subsurface site viewable at ground level.

Description of local vegetation

This section facilitates detailed discussions of the surrounding field systems (if any). Dialogues with farmers or landowners will aid in this process. Crop patterns can change each year via crop rotation, and will affect how features do or do not appear in the satellite imagery. Fertilizers in the soil may also affect the spectral signatures of landscapes, but would yield a widespread and more field-boundary aligned signature than an archaeological site. Certain types of vegetation will grow on top of archaeological features in different parts of the world. For example, in coastal areas of Costa Rica, as shown by student research as part of the author's introductory remote sensing course, palm trees are drawn to shell middens, due to the large concentration of calcium carbonate in the soil. In particular circumstances, concentrations of these trees detected by satellite imagery may tend to indicate the presence of shell middens (pers. comm. B. Arnold, April 2008). Archaeological soils and associated structures also influence the spectral signature of imagery. Other patterns and association with archaeological remains undoubtedly exist in other parts of the world.

Figure 7.17 Tanis, Egypt (scale 1:1000 m), note extensive cropmarks to the east of the site, 2008 image courtesy of Google Earth™ Pro.

Can you see crop marks or any shape or size on the ground surrounding the site?

This is more specific to the archaeology of crop regions. Walls thinner than 60 cm fall below the pixel size detected with high-resolution Quickbird satellite imagery (Figure 7.17), may or may not appear on satellite imagery at certain times of year. Crop rotation and vegetation growth patterns change each year. Cropmarks appear most clearly during the initial growth phases of grass and crops due to thermal immersion patterns (Shell 2002). Hence, timing one's tasking of satellite imagery to the optimum time of year to detect features through crop marks is crucial, but may not be realized until the initial investigation season. However, once a team is fully attuned to their study region, future imagery purchases can be adjusted accordingly.

Are there any architectural features on the surface of the site?

Features observed in the satellite imagery should be correlated with anything observed on the ground. Some circular, spiral, rectilinear, or other-shaped features may appear on satellite imagery but not on the ground, or vice versa. This may reflect the time of year of the imagery used, weather patterns, the period of the survey, or the general wetness or dryness of a given feature or site. The specific time of the survey may need to be adjusted to maximize recording capacity.

What are the irrigation systems or current/past water sources
surrounding the site (describe in detail: Size of canals/lakes/rivers,
amount of water, when it/they are high or low, when is the area dry)?

Water is the primary source that affects how archaeological features can be viewed from space. Many features show up in either wet or dry periods of the year, and knowing in what seasons soil and other surface coverage may be affected by relative moisture levels will assist in further imagery analysis. Human influence is another key to water source management. Governments may release water from dams at set times of year (e.g. Aswan). This should be noted during ground survey work. The overall size of water sources or former (or current) water sources may also affect how archaeological sites can be viewed. With lake and river beds in desert regions drying up over long periods of time, archaeological sites can often be found by examining concentric rings of former, higher, lake edges (Figure 7.18) (Bubenzer and Bolten 2003), or the banks of former rivers (Wendorf *et al.* 1987). Additional deep wells or dense vegetation may also indicate former water sources and thereby associated archaeological sites (Mumford and Parcak 2002).

Where is the highest point of the archaeological site?

Higher parts of archaeological sites generally indicate areas of better preservation, or denser archaeological debris. Surveying the site with a differential GPS will allow for a 3D rendering of the area, which the imagery specialist can then use for draping over

Figure 7.18 Kharga Oasis, Egypt (scale 1:410 m), 2008 image courtesy of Google Earth™ Pro.

the satellite imagery. Further imagery analysis in the higher area may reveal additional features or signatures worthy of investigation.

What is the concentration of sherd(s) for each area?

If an archaeological site is covered with a sufficiently dense quantity of potsherds (e.g. Umm el-Qaab at Abydos, Egypt), these could affect the signature of the site. No previous remote sensing publications appear to discuss this factor. Sherd(s) may reflect more strongly in a particular part of the spectrum or may be viewed in a similar fashion to geological features. Observing and testing the signatures obtained from such concentrations of ceramic material within or covering archaeological sites will aid in refining the satellite imagery analysis. On higher-resolution imagery, sherd clusters may not have a significantly different spectral signature, but may have their own digital number range, which may vary slightly from the rest of the image to an extent where they can be isolated and pinpointed on other archaeological sites. This may work particularly well in imagery programs where individual pixels can be isolated outside of running classification algorithms.

What other material culture remains can be observed?

Isolating additional material culture remains may aid in interpreting satellite imagery, especially higher-resolution imagery. For instance, subsurface metalworking areas, ovens, kilns, middens, and simple graves in cemeteries may yield their own spectral signatures within a site, due to the different ways they affect the soil.

What does local knowledge have to say about the site and its history?

Consulting indigenous records, officials, and private individuals near or on site may aid in elucidating further details and local traditions of one's study region in contrast to the published archaeological data.

Site photograph notes

As many features as possible should be digitally photographed, with description and locational comments added to each image entered into the field computer at the end of each workday. Having a catalogue of local vegetation types, soils, and geology will aid in later analyses of the satellite imagery, and it is also helpful to have a running photographic record for later comparative purposes (Figure 7.19a and 7.19b). Taking video footage of the area, perhaps panning slowly for 360 degrees from the site center (when possible), will also aid in later analysis, as it can help the team both to document and "revisit" the site, allowing additional features to be noted photographically.

What preliminary observations can be made about the sherd(s) and material culture remains in an area?

Initial thoughts by a team about the ceramic material or material culture, in general, will aid in forming a more definite impression of a site's nature, date, span, and other aspects. It is recognized that much early observation can be speculative, while firm

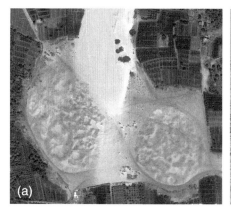

Figure 7.19 Kom el-Ahmar, Middle Egypt: (a) Quickbird image (scale 1:200 m); and (b) photograph, note the density of the pottery scatters on the site surface, darker shaded areas
on the Quickbird image represent these sherd scatters, images courtesy of Google
Earth™ Pro (2008) and photograph by Sarah Parcak.

conclusions are not usually realized before conducting rigorous archaeological analysis
(i.e. drawing sherd(s), cutting thin sections, conducting lab analyses, radiocarbon dating,
and analyzing material culture from secure contexts). It may be more helpful to formulate
a series of questions about the newly found site or feature (e.g. "From surface material
culture, the site appears to be occupied only during the Old Kingdom—is that the case
for all sites in the region?"). Additional research is generally necessary in most cases when
one locates an unusual feature or site. Considering various questions on the ground at
the newly located site will further the research agenda, since many questions will need
to be answered at the site and cannot rely on memory after departing the site. This is
where it is advantageous to survey with several members, to general dialogue and foster
as many questions and answers as possible.

Example recording sheet (from 2004 Middle Egypt Survey Project)

Site Number/Name: Tell Sheikh Masara
Date: March 6
Eastings/Northings of Site on Landsat: 2853205
(note: 1 km+offset included in each reading) 3063285
Near Villages (Names—ancient/modern): Mallawi
Original Published information about site: None previously known
Found on Maps: 1920s Map, Mallawi
Found on what Corona series: Corona 1111 series, 1972
How large is the area in question on the ground: 80 × 80 m
How does this compare to the different satellite image information:
Site size (Landsat): 90 × 90 m (small pixel cluster)
Site size (Corona): Small (does not appear to be much larger than 90 × 90 m)

Towns and cities closest to site (and location in relation to these sites):
Located in fields 2 km south of Mallawi

Who owns the land on which the site is located: Not known, inquiries to farmers did not yield any answers

Description of local vegetation: To the east, sugarcane and fields, to the south clover, to the north and west more sugarcane

Shape of site or what is left (if anything): Semi-square

Can you see crop marks or any shape or size on the ground surrounding the site? None seen surrounding site

Are there any architectural features on the surface of the site? Old brick structure, probably modern

What are the irrigation systems or current/past water sources surrounding the site (describe in detail: Size of canals/lakes/rivers, amount of water, when it/they are high or low, when is the area dry)? None observed save modern irrigation channels

Where is the highest point of the archaeological site? Sheikh's tomb and modern bricks

What is the concentration of sherd(s) for each area? Mixed concentration, denser concentrations next to modern pits and around the edges of the site

What other material culture remains can be observed? Silty surface, some pottery, modern mudbricks, and halfa grass, not much else on surface

What does local knowledge have to say about the site and its history? One man said: "Since my grandfather's time the site has been like this, but much bigger, many feddans larger."

Site photograph notes: Photo numbers 1–18 for the day.

What preliminary observations can be made about the sherd(s) and material culture remains in an area?
The survey went to visit an old sheikh's tomb and it turned out to be on top of an ancient *tell* site, initially discovered in the remote sensing analysis. It rises 4m above the surrounding fields, and is covered in halfa grass, dried sugarcane and several piles of sherd(s) that likely came from the robbers' trench in the middle of the site. This trench also reveals a corner of a red brick structure. The sherd(s) seem Late Roman in date, with one potential Islamic sherd seen. It once was a very large site, as many sherd(s) were seen in the fields walking to and from the site. Another sheikh's tomb on the site had collapsed. According to locals, the sheikh's coffin was burned, but many people had come here because it was a "sacred area." The pottery dates to ca. AD 400–800.

Conclusion

Ultimately, when doing remote sensing survey, it is the number and appropriateness of questions one asks about the archaeology and surrounding landscape that generate the most useful data for the post-processing stage. As a survey is ongoing, all completed archaeological sites and features should be noted and mapped according to the spatial

Table 7.1 Survey times based on relative town sites during 2003/4 Egypt surveys

Relative town size	Time per site (h)	Time total (h)	Time in months
85 villages	1	85 hours	–
40 small towns	5	200 hours	–
20 medium towns	10	200 hours	–
10 large towns	20	200 hours	–
5 cities	40	200 hours	–
160 towns	–	685 hours	5 months, 4 days

and temporal subdivisions of the survey. Additional logical places for site locations (e.g. predictive modeling) that may not appear during the imagery analysis should be included, such as caves or overhanging rock formations. Site deflation occurs in desert regions, while floodplains and mound formations may bury and obscure earlier archaeological site levels from imagery analysis. Each landscape type, whether it is desert, jungle, floodplain, urban, coastal, forested or mixed, offers diverse "typical" global environments. These types and the work conducted within them will be affected by local conditions, time of year, and the experience of the remote sensing and survey teams, vary markedly.

Given the broad results one can obtain from combining ground survey and remote sensing, and the confusion which can result from landscape destruction, it appears that the entire field of ground survey and field-walking needs to be reconsidered. A study carried out in the heavy clay soils of South Tuscany compared remote sensing, aerial photography, ground survey and excavation (Campana and Francovich 2005). It noted that an integrated approach was needed due to issues of landscape interpretation and recording: 50 percent of Tuscany is covered in forests, while the rest contains cultivated heavy soils. In addition, the authors observed that the best areas for visibility in South Tuscany represent alluvial plains, but encountered problems with alluvial thickness and development. The study also recorded major differences between surface collection and excavation, with two sample areas of 470 km^2, using oblique aerial photographs and Quickbird and IKONOS imagery. Using the IKONOS imagery, the team located 84 features on the ground, with 39 new sites appearing. Older aerial photographs revealed some features that could not be observed in the present day due to poor IKONOS imagery. Anomalies appeared in the infrared part of the spectrum only. The capture time of the satellite imagery proved to be an issue, with a delay of five to six weeks. Quickbird imagery covering an area of 200 km^2, with a delay of 15 days in acquisition time, was also used for feature detection. The team noted that one pixel of multispectral IKONOS imagery equaled 32.65 pixels of Quickbird pan-sharpened imagery. One way to augment these results would be to pan-sharpen the IKONOS imagery, or priority order their Quickbird imagery (with only a delay of 24 hours).

Widespread destruction of landscapes via growing settlements, agricultural holdings, and other projects, has become an archaeological surveyor's nightmare. Archaeologists must reconsider the distinct processes that are affecting site destruction and encroachment in different parts of the world, and incorporate these areas and forthcoming threatened areas to the areas one hopes to evaluate using satellite remote sensing analysis and ground survey. Destructive processes change over time, and will vary given the amount of alteration each landscape has undergone in the past thousands of years (depending on a survey time period). The team in Tuscany used mobile PDAs to conduct a real-time comparison by creating a real-time virtual landscape, but noted many data collection problems. The team recorded 1000 sites on 10,000 oblique photographs, with an additional 9000 sites recorded in the field, but had significant difficulties in interpreting the data as it was incomplete with post-depositional processes obscuring many areas. Observing things on the ground during survey work would have made for an incomplete landscape analysis. Remote sensing, however, allowed the team to evaluate past and present land-use patterns, to see how broadly modernization had affected landscape usage.

Archaeological survey and remote sensing can no longer be considered as disparate entities. Globalization requires more time- and cost-efficient ways of conducing surveys in areas threatened by development and looting, while global warming is becoming a significant threat to field research, especially in coastal areas. How many archaeologists can claim that the excavations and surveys they conduct today are not salvage work? Satellite remote sensing can contribute immeasurably to the process of survey and site preservation, while remote sensing in and of itself should not be conducted in a vacuum. Both approaches require new perspectives and new strategies, which will continue to be refined as satellite imagery and techniques of analysis improve. Additional resources must be created to address the issue of communicating remote sensing survey strategies, whether through blogs, list-serves, annual symposia, or other media. As the world changes even more rapidly, archaeologists will need to devise improved surveying strategies no matter where they are working. Considering the full range of archaeological remote sensing applications to survey provides a good start.

CONSERVATION, HERITAGE MANAGEMENT, AND THE ETHICS OF REMOTE SENSING FOR ARCHAEOLOGY

Overview

Remote sensing in archaeology should not be considered from the sole perspective of archaeological site location. Studying any features and landscape changes from space necessitates a broader perspective, and one that addresses long-term issues with global implications. "Preserve the past for future generations" is an oft-repeated message in archaeology, yet how does remote sensing fit into longer-term planning for site and feature preservation? It is a difficult question to address, especially considering how remote sensing has become a public activity with global participation possibilities. As remote sensing is at a crossroads of many fields and subfields, remote sensing analysis can detect the effects of tourism, development, and global warming at archaeological sites around the world. Natural and non-natural factors affect archaeological site preservation simultaneously. Archaeological remote sensing can detect both of these factors in tandem so archaeologists can plan future management strategies. This is not an easy task, and is becoming more difficult with rapid globalization, thus necessitating alternative strategies that should include local remote sensing training initiatives and better data sharing practices.

The very nature of archaeological remote sensing data makes remote sensing ethics and the law a central point for debate and discussion. Do the ethics of remote sensing fit within the debate over archaeological ethics, in particular the ethics statements adopted by the Society for American Archaeology (SAA), the Archaeological Institute of America (AIA), and other learned archaeological societies around the world? Archaeological remote sensing discourse necessitates an alternative ethics statement, and one that brings together archaeological and remote sensing ethics.

Education is another critical factor with archaeological remote sensing, considering the usage of Google Earth™ by millions of people around the globe. Archaeological discovery and exploration are no longer restricted activities: When people first download Google Earth™, the first places generally visited (following one's own home) include the Giza Pyramids, Machu Picchu, the Great Wall of China, and the Taj Mahal (Figure 8.1), creating a form of desk-based tourism. Amateur remote sensers have located numerous "strange" anomalies, which are often communicated to professional archaeologists via email. In a recent *National Geographic News* article (Handwerk 2006), archaeologist Scott Madry discussed how he had located Roman-period villas on the ground in France, communicated to him by French people who found them using Google Earth™.

Figure 8.1 Taj Mahal, India (scale 1:180 m), 2008 image courtesy of Google Earth™ Pro.

Google Earth™ is now in the classroom, and also available to looters, who have most likely incorporated it into their looting plans.

Education is the only way forward with regards to responsible archaeological usage of these emerging technologies (Kligman 2006), but until governments make heritage and conservation national priorities, and implement stricter policies for the sale of all antiquities, the looting will continue. Pressure from universities, museums, public and private groups around the world seems to be working in some cases: Recent government crackdowns have led to the arrest of several high-profile antiquities trackers, such as the US case against Fredrick Schultz involving Egyptian antiquities (and a subsequent conviction under the United States National Stolen Property Act) as well as the ongoing Italian case against Getty Museum curator Marion True. This puts a higher priority on educating the public and students in the ethics of using remote sensing, as all public information regarding newly discovered archaeological features is probably examined in-depth by those who are destroying the archaeological record.

While governments do their best to guard known archaeological sites and lock museums, looters rob poorly guarded known sites and non-guarded unknown sites every day, thus fueling the international illegal antiquities trade. How archaeologists can detect, protect and preserve the tens (if not hundreds) of thousands of unknown archaeological sites around the world to prevent this looting is an ongoing debate in archaeology, especially regarding resource management. Satellite remote sensing, in combination with aerial photography, allows, at present, for the fastest detection of larger archaeological sites across broad landscapes, due to the presence of many shallowly buried ancient features that enrich sites with organic or magnetic debris. However, once archaeologists publish remote sensing results, looters can purchase their own satellite imagery and attempt the same methods of analysis. Having the resources to ground-truth the located sites and features, as well as protect the sites, from such looters is another matter entirely. Governments should place heritage higher on their list of priorities: Archaeological heritage is closely tied in with national pride, and more interest in the heritage of a particular country can bring in tourist money as well as money from foreign archaeological expeditions. Ecotourism (which includes visits to archaeological sites) is a thriving industry, and having more identified and secure sites in beautiful locations will aid local economies. The employment of local people on archaeological expeditions is another way to improve the economies of poor villages and towns. Ultimately, working with foreign governments, if possible, to train their archaeologists as well as learn from them, is the best way to implement good archaeological remote sensing practice. This encourages good archaeological practice, which aids in conservation and heritage management initiatives.

The conservation of archaeological sites via remote sensing is a multifaceted issue affected by both natural and anthropomorphic factors (Williamson 1998; Bertocci and Parrinello 2006). Modern landscapes change quickly and at ever-increasing rates, which may or may not affect archaeological site preservation. These broad changes affect local and regional climates, biodiversity, soil degradation, and general human vulnerability. How quickly this change affects archaeological sites can be considered as a separate but related issue. Archaeologists should evaluate the overall rate of change per archaeological site type and features within a landscape, while comparing it to as many variables as possible. This includes the site or feature's distance from population centers, roads

Figure 8.2 Karnak Temple, Egypt (scale 1:267 m), note proximity of the temple complex to the town, 2008 image courtesy of Google Earth™ Pro.

(Figure 8.2), agricultural and industrial development zones, and general landscape changes caused by weather and natural disasters. The threat of destruction or partial removal for certain sites should be explored, especially regarding overall rates of change through land use land cover analyses. Using the full range of tools available for the remote sensing analysis is necessary but not always possible due to a lack of maps, aerial photography, or perhaps high quality satellite imagery. Comparing past and present landscapes makes it possible to assess future archaeological landscapes, which may or may not be available for more detailed exploration. Identifying, via remote sensing, where to work and how much time remains for more detailed archaeological analysis contributes towards a form of archaeological triage: If archaeologists do not know where to look, they cannot even begin to make plans for archaeological conservation. Addressing natural changes within landscapes is the first logical step towards conserving archaeological sites and their associated landscapes.

Conservation and heritage management

Natural forces affecting archaeological site preservation are numerous and vary according to landscape type. Change can occur over a single day or over thousands of years. Varying types of natural factors affect archaeological sites and features, which is why remote sensing can aid in untangling the web of change possibilities. Desertification, rapid rainforest growth, flooding, vegetation changes due to global warming or cooling, forest regrowth, and earthquakes are but a few of the natural changes that can affect landscapes and archaeological sites. Archaeologists can assess entire archaeological landscapes from space to prevent natural disasters from damaging monuments, but how much can these measures help? In 1994, a massive and unexpected flood hit the Valley of the Kings in Egypt, damaging dozens of tomb interiors. Now, the Egyptian government has placed floodwalls in front of the tombs of Sety I and Ramesses I (Figure 8.3), yet how well these will combat future flooding remains a point of contention. If archaeologists had carried out a detailed remote sensing analysis, it is possible that predictive models could have assisted in better placing the floodwalls along the desert mountaintops to divert the floodwaters, such as what Jordanian archaeologists employed at Petra using a combination of SPOT imagery and GIS analysis (Akasheh 2002). Only a real future flood will test the effectiveness of the measures, but it underscores the necessity of using all available technologies at hand to protect major monuments such as the Valley of the Kings and other threatened sites.

Natural disasters can be expected in archaeological landscapes near fault lines, or in locations where humans have employed measures to make uninhabitable land habitable. New Orleans represents such a location. The San Born Company mapped New Orleans over 200 times between 1876 and 1994, making it one of the most well mapped cities in the world. One project placed each map as a layer within a GIS to examine overall land use and land cover changes (Berry 2003). Now, large parts of the city remain deserted following the major flooding in 2006, a situation that is not likely to change in the next 5 to 10 years. Archaeologists should learn a great deal from this disaster: Even well mapped cities in modern landscapes are quickly abandoned in ways that cannot be readily understood without examining local land management practices. How and why parts of the city remain inhabited can be tied in with complicated social, economic, and political factors, which, outside of direct natural affects, remain at the heart of landscape

Figure 8.3 Valley of the Kings, Luxor, Egypt (scale 1:171 m), 2008 image courtesy of Google Earth™ Pro.

changes. Human inhabitation in these high-risk zones provides clues to remote sensing specialists to how and why groups may have abandoned areas or returned to them.

Past maps may be the only resource available with information about landscapes affected by natural and anthropomorphic factors. In Germany, the Danube Valley represents a landscape largely altered by these factors. Archaeologists assessed the Heuneberg early Iron Age topography over a 20 km^2 area using LIDAR, creating a detailed digital elevation model (DEM). They located a number of mounds and some rampart systems evident on an industrial map from the 1920s, but did not locate a ditch still visible in the same map (Bofinger *et al.* 2006). This clearly shows that modern disturbances had long since eroded the ancient landscape, and that even the most advanced remote sensing systems are not capable of detecting the entirety of disturbed landscapes. Ancient texts such Herodotus (reprint 2003) can aid in either relocating lost sites or providing details about the destruction of cities, but these are restricted to larger cities in historic times. Approaching damaged landscapes dating to non-historic or non-literate times can prove even more difficult.

Areas under threat from natural disasters or anthropomorphic affects can be mapped with high-resolution imagery, but the decision to protect a region resides with the national government or international bodies. India has several examples of these sites. The Agra, or Taj Mahal, is one of the world's best known architectural achievements, yet it remains under threat from pollution. Remote sensing specialists used IKONOS imagery to classify the land cover surrounding the Taj, and have proposed the area to

Figure 8.4 Southeast India in Tamil Nadu along the Mahabalipuram, Landsat image, image courtesy of NASA World Wind.

UNESCO as a heritage zone (Dayalan 2006). Larger areas already classified as a world heritage site, such as the coastal system in southeast India in Tamil Nadu along the Mahabalipuram (Ramasamy *et al.* 1992), shown in Figure 8.4, dating to between 600–700 BC, face constant threats from both biophysical and anthropogenic effects. The river system is 1000 km long, composed of 46 rivers with a catchment system of 171,000 km^2, populated by 5.8 million fishermen. There are significant problems arising from urbanization, overpopulation, tectonic changes, sea level rises, and coastal erosion from natural factors (Krishnamoorthy *et al.* 2002). How can international bodies with limited resources such as UNESCO protect such a large area with a dense population? The issues extend far beyond the capabilities of a single organization. A single archaeological site can be guarded, while an entire heritage zone requires much broader thinking and planning when thinking about longer term management plans.

Landscapes and archaeological sites within those landscapes can be altered to the point where remote sensing analysis can no longer detect their existence. Archaeologists have long argued that no matter how destroyed an archaeological site might be, there will always be a way for archaeologists to detect its existence, whether through geological, chemical, or technical analysis (Renfrew and Bahn 2008). Do we need to reconsider this statement? Modernization has altered landscapes to the point where advanced remote sensing analysis via high-resolution imagery and Airborne P-band SAR can no longer detect the presence of known archaeological sites (Chapoulie *et al.* 2002). Ground cover and weather patterns combine to obscure ancient sites, which may not be detectable via ground-based remote sensing techniques due to issues with timing and cost. Even the speed and character of overall site degradation is only beginning to be understood. Using a combination of Quickbird and IKONOS satellite imagery and chemical sampling (i.e. finding phosphate, iron and zinc levels in the ground), a team sampled a 1 × 11 km area in Rygge Municipality, Norway, over a flat and hilly landscape. The team compared the error in detected anomalies versus known anomalies, finding likely archaeological sites versus "real" sites. Although the study located 30 previously unknown archaeological sites (mounds and some ancient houses), only 458 sites appeared during the survey, which the team estimated to be 1000 too few, with many thousands of additional likely sites not detected (Gron *et al.* 2004). How much people transform landscapes can only be understood using both chemical and air-based methods as entire archaeological landscapes are lost entirely each year. How much more is lost with the construction of towns, and accompanying pipelines, roads, buildings, factories, as well as mechanical plowing, needs more study, before landscapes can no longer be characterized by any archaeological means.

Countries such as China undergoing more rapid development have recognized the heritage and conservation-related problems that go along with urbanization. Environmental problems in China are also coupled with a major rise in tourism. The Chinese Center for Remote Sensing in Archaeology has studied this problem in detail, and had found a contradiction between conservation and utility development. Although sites can be affected by development, they are also aided by the general improvement of a region (i.e. areas can better serve tourists and archaeological teams) (Shupeng 2004). Difficult questions remain surrounding the development of Beijing for the 2008 Olympics. Dozens of historic hutongs no longer exist due to the increase in number of 4- and 5-star hotels, and one wonders what lies beneath the city, much like in Rome or Athens, which is now lost to archaeological exploration. Similar development issues have affected the archaeological remote sensing exploration of the Great Wall and nearby mausoleums. Out of the 600 known mausoleums, only 113 can be found with remote sensing, while one-third of the known Ming wall sections have disappeared. Over the past hundreds of years, locals have removed bricks from these sections for houses, roads, and pig sties (Shuren *et al.* 2004). Laws protecting archaeological sites need to be followed on a local level, but laws (if in place) do not always mesh with development needs. Changes in politics and government policies become just as important to study as landscape changes and history.

How global warming affects population movement, crop cycles and general governmental environmental decisions is closely tied into heritage and preservation issues. In Central America, the production of milpus, an important crop, is linked to the global climate: A hotter climate shortens the dry season, thus preventing slash and burn agriculture, while a cold front delays the wet season planting (Gunn *et al.* 1995). Farmers using slash and burn agricultural practices have destroyed large tracts of rainforest across Guatemala, exposing archaeological sites to looting (Saturno *et al.* 2007). How do similar practices affect archaeological landscapes across the globe, and how can they be detected with remote sensing analysis? Many archaeological landscapes located in dense forested areas remain to be discovered, including numerous Islamic cities located along the east Africa coast, seen in Figure 8.5 (Chittick 1974). Loggers and developers are unlikely to report finding a city in the jungle, as it would only delay construction or shipment dates. Poor education contributes to this destruction: Deforestation in rainforest is often illegal, with those who practice slash and burn agriculture not realizing that sustainable practices would support their families to a far greater extent (Martini and Souza 2002). With changing climates, countries employ alternative agricultural practices, thus further altering landscapes. In addition, millions of people are now displaced

Figure 8.5 Takwa, Kenya (scale 1:77 m), an important coastal trading site, 2008 image courtesy of Google Earth™ Pro.

persons due to war and famine. How can we justify the intersection between human need and protecting the past?

This debate extends to the construction of dams. Rivers with unpredictable annual flooding can be dammed (with accompanying social and political issues), but the cost to archaeological heritage is enormous. Any time large tracts of land surrounding a water source that has been in use for thousands of years become submerged, it is logical to assume that hundreds or thousands of archaeological sites will disappear, many of which will not be known. Archaeologists and anthropologists have fought against the rising waters of the Three Gorges Dam project, and dams across the Middle East (especially the Ataturk dam in Turkey), to record sites before their submersion. In the case of the Aswan High Dam in the 1960's and 1970's, a call from UNESCO prompted an international team of archaeologists to aid in the complete excavation of large number of sites (Adams 1979) or the removal of temples to higher ground. Similar dam construction in other countries has not met with the same broad international efforts. Archaeologists have studied how dams have affected landscapes using Landsat, SPOT, and Corona satellite imagery (Comfort 1998). One study examined settlement change in the late Neolithic in the Murhgab River Delta region of Turkmenistan over a 20,000 km^2 area using Landsat and Corona satellite imagery. The team found that a dam constructed following World War II had destroyed many archaeological sites, with subsequent irrigation works and desertification combining to eliminate additional sites from the landscape (Cerasetti and Massino 2002). Although surveys are ongoing in Sudan's Fourth Cataract region, where the Sudanese government is constructing a dam along the Nile, archaeologists are not using remote sensing to model or map the landscape, instead using foot survey to map the thousands of likely unknown sites, which will soon be underwater. These issues extend far beyond heritage to political disagreements over water, which will become a bigger problem as global warming continues.

If developers have caused deforestation or destruction in a known archaeological landscape, archaeologists may benefit from studying these landscapes before further changes occur. Forested landscapes in Europe can be studied with LIDAR (Doneus and Briese 2006), but this is not feasible over large areas due to cost. Bare landscapes may reveal archaeological features if non-mechanized farming is in practice. Using Landsat imagery from 1987 and 2002, one team examined 24 Iron Age burial cairns in Scotland using NDVI, and found higher NDVI values in the later imagery (Barlindhaug et al. 2007), showing denser vegetation. Some countries have strict forest regrowth policies, or have implemented stricter policies over the past 20 years. These policies should be examined, as vegetation and archaeological site discovery are closely connected. Each country will also have specific policies dealing with archaeological site protection: Many governments have specific policies that dictate an area must be surveyed by an archaeological team prior to land development. The policies will differ per country and many laws may not be followed.

Archaeological site management and conservation plans should reflect the many ways natural and anthropomorphic affect landscapes surrounding archaeological features. Each landscape will present a different set of problems. SPOT and Landsat satellite imagery have examined marsh reclamation and sedimentation surrounding Mont St. Michel, seen in Figures 8.6a and 8.6b (Deroin and Verger 2002), which will continue to worsen as sea levels rise. Coastal archaeological sites can be monitored with satellite imagery datasets to monitor monthly or yearly changes, which also include tourism. A totality of approach using environmental data, aerial photography, GIS, maps, education, and public outreach remains to best approach to preserve these landscapes (Dingwall et al. 2002).

This is not a realistic approach in the majority of the world's landscapes, especially in areas where site guards are poorly paid (if they exist), and where tourists are allowed to touch tomb walls or even take away pieces of the monuments. At the Acropolis in Athens (as seen by the author), site guards spread marble chips on the ground each morning, as many tourists take "a piece of ancient Greece" home with them. How does tourism affect the actual spectral signatures of archaeological sites? This is a subject that remains to be studied. How general tourism can be monitored from space is not something easily studied: Archaeologists and heritage specialists generally rely on number counts of visitors to sites. What can be studied, however, is how the landscape surrounding the archaeological sites has changed, whether through enlarged towns, newly constructed hotels, and how much these hotels create pressure on the local ecological systems. With ecotourism companies creating trips to more far-flung locations, more archaeological sites are under threat of destruction. In locations such as Egypt's Western Desert, archaeological sites once known only to archaeologists are now covered in off-road vehicle tracks, while tourists scatter surface (and often in-situ) archaeological remains. Educating tourist companies is now just as important as educating to tourists who flock to remote locations. While some companies practice ethical tourism, booking only "green hotels" using local products, and promoting good tourism practices, the cost is generally prohibitive for the average tourist.

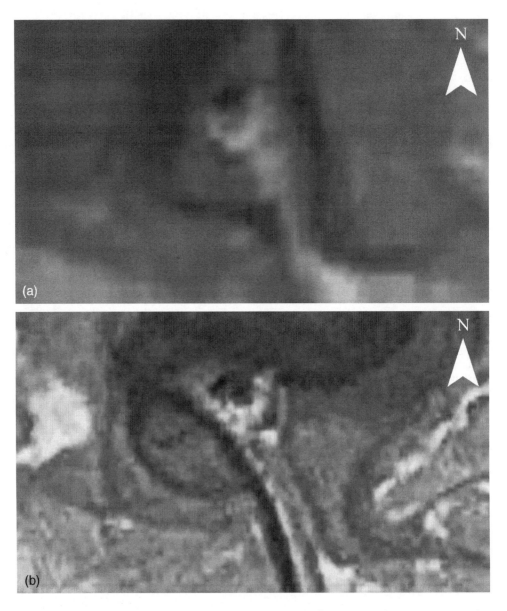

Figure 8.6 Mont St. Michel, France: (a) 1990 Landsat; and (b) 2000 Landsat images, note the better resolution of the later image, images courtesy of NASA World Wind.

Evaluating significant changes in Egypt's landscapes brought about by tourism and natural factors provides a useful case study analysis for comparative purposes. Tourism is the main economic source of the Egyptian economy, so preserving and conserving archaeological sites is of interest to the Egyptian government. However, population growth at over 2 percent per year, combined with major urbanization and coastal development, pose significant threats to Egypt's archaeological sites. Remote sensing studies outside archaeology have contributed to our understanding of how quickly these changes are taking place. Egypt's population is projected to reach 111 million people by 2030, with 90 percent occupying less than 5 percent of the land, chiefly in the Delta and along the Nile (Sultan *et al.* 1999). Landsat satellite imagery has shown that cities and large villages in the Delta grew 37 percent in size from 1972–1990, while small villages grew 77 percent, with an overall urbanization rate of 58 percent (Sultan *et al.* 1999). Urban expansion represents an even greater threat to archaeological site preservation. The overall area occupied by cities and towns reflects a doubling of urban areas every 20–30 years, as shown by Landsat MSS imagery, and with a constant growth rate urban areas could cover 12 percent of the Delta by 2010 (Lawrence *et al.* 2002). It is most concerning that the majority of unknown archaeological sites in Egypt are located next to or beneath smaller villages and towns. Changes in sea levels and the increasing salinity also affects many sites in the Delta, along with accretion and erosion along the Delta's coastline, analyzed using Landsat and SPOT satellite imagery (Frihy *et al.* 1994; El-Raey *et al.* 1995; Frihy *et al.* 1998). Coastal development along the Red Sea is another problem. The Red Sea coastal zone is a unique natural resource, with both natural and archaeological resources under threat from development (Peacock 1993). The Eastern and Western Deserts cover such large areas, the Egyptian government cannot protect them from looters who regularly deface or cut away Pharaonic or prehistoric rock inscriptions (Darnell 2002).

Additional environmental problems in the Delta and Nile Valley include increased salinity, shorter fallow periods, loss of alluvial deposits, and no nutrient replacement (El-Baz 1989; El-Raey *et al.* 1999; El-Gamily *et al.* 2001). These factors explain why so many archaeological sites are threatened: Farmers use the nutrient-rich archaeological site soils with high phosphate levels as fertilizers, to meet rising needs for cultivation (Lenney *et al* 1996). Often, brick factories (which use archaeological debris to create modern bricks) can be located atop archaeological sites, with up to 10 brick factories observed on one site (Van den Brink 1987). On a local level, officials remove non-registered archaeological sites to make way for farmland, schools, cemeteries, and housing, shown in Figures 8.7a and 8.7b (Parcak 2007b). If the rates of urban development continue in the Delta it is possible that all agricultural lands and associated archaeological sites are at risk of being lost in 70 years (Salem *et al.* 1995). In addition, Egypt is facing rising salinity levels in the soil, causing the encroachment and subsuming of archaeological sites for cultivation (Goossens and Van Ranst 1998). Development is the single largest threat to the discovery of previously unknown archaeological sites in Egypt, which number in the many thousands. If archaeologists have excavated less than one-hundredth of 1 percent of all known archaeological sites in the Egyptian Delta, the amount of information to be gained from archaeological site preservation initiatives is staggering (Parcak 2008).

Urbanization is a factor that governmental policies may be able to control, unlike war, which allows looting and archaeological site damage to occur at unprecedented rates. It is difficult for archaeologists to assess the exact amount of damage war has caused to archaeological sites, as higher resolution satellite imagery is available only from 2002 onwards, and aerial photography may not exist or be possible to obtain. Coverage of the area in question may not exist at all, or a comparative analysis may not be possible with only one higher resolution image available. Cultural heritage preservation is not generally part of an invading army's agenda. Destroying the history and culture of an

Figure 8.7 Ismu al-Arus, Middle Egypt, note: (a) cropmarks in photograph compared to (b) Quickbird image (scale 1:90 m), arrow points to the areas seen in the photograph, photograph by Sarah Parcak and 2008 Quickbird image courtesy of Google Earth™.

occupied country only aids demoralization and asserts the so-called "superiority" of the invading group, as evidenced by the destruction of the Bamiyan Buddahs by the Taliban. Environmental byproducts of war, such as the oil soaked deserts sands of Kuwait from the first gulf war, can be detected from space (Anon. 1992). These byproducts of war aid in the obscuring of ancient landscapes. The embargo and subsequent inflation in Iraq led to additional lands under cultivation plus looting, with over 8500 objects missing from regional museums and bomb craters at known sites (Nashef 1990, 1992).

Ongoing looting of archaeological sites has turned large archaeological mounds in Iraq into the equivalent of waffles, with looting pits covering the entirety of sites. At present, the main group guarding archaeological sites in Iraq is the Italian Carabinieri, but at what point does the potential loss of human lives outweigh the protection of cultural heritage? After drug and gun smuggling, the looting of archaeological sites is the third-largest factor funding the insurgency in Iraq (Bogdanos 2005), so protecting archaeological sites is critical to the ongoing efforts there. Can remote sensing aid in preventing the looting (Figure 8.8) and smuggling in Iraq, Afghanistan, and other locations in the world? Satellite imagery analysis can, at best, monitor and detect likely border crossings where smuggled objects are likely to appear, aiding in mapping key places, like the Iraq National Museum, to be protected prior to an invasion. Protecting cultural heritage is now a Department of Defense (DoD) priority, with the DoD employing archaeologists (Anon. 2004) to discuss prevention and preservation strategies. Until heritage is a global priority, and the international illegal antiquities markets are shut down in Switzerland, Japan, and in well-known international auction houses, the destruction of archaeological and cultural remains will remain an unfortunate byproduct of war.

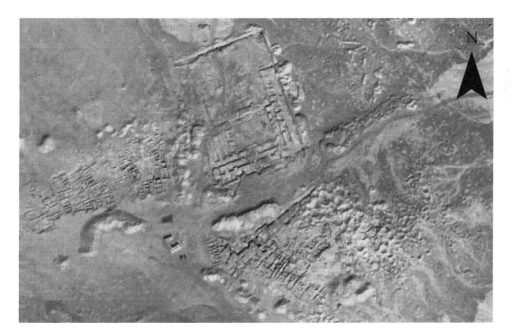

Figure 8.8 Jokha, Iraq (scale 1:118 m), note the looting pits, 2008 image courtesy of Google Earth™ Pro.

Protecting heritage using satellite remote sensing prompts more questions than it provides answers. If archaeologists monitor thousands of known archaeological sites with remote sensing, whose responsibility does it become to protect these sites? Is it the responsibility of the country where the site is located, where funding may be an issue, or is it responsibility of the group monitoring the site? What about any previously unknown archaeological sites detected from space? Some archaeologists assert that a facility to handle all world heritage sites is everyone's responsibility, and that a global GIS database should be created (Holcomb 2002). Every country in the world has different heritage management policies (if such exist), with international organizations with their own specific projects and priorities. Ultimately, protecting archaeological heritage occurs at a local level, whether through international organizations based locally, or through individual government employees (Hadjimitsis *et al.* 2006). Having concern for archaeological heritage occurs at a global level, and is a global responsibility to the extent that it is international organizations that can provide resources and training to local people to promote conservation.

An international multilateral heritage agreement, the equivalent to the Kyoto Accord (Peter 2002), would aid in setting global priorities, but it is not probable that heritage could attract as much attention on a global scale as global warming. Each country has specific planning permission guidelines for development, but the European Union guidelines merit discussions. The EU Planning Policy Guidance 10, set in 1990, requires evaluation for archaeological remains from aerial photography at a 1:2500 scale, and ground-based investigation. The cost of the analysis is born by the developers (Palmer 2002a, 2002b). Should other countries or regions adopt this same aerial approach? It would appear to be time- and cost-efficient, as using higher resolution satellite imagery or aerial photography from Google Earth™ would require minimal training. Individual country or region priorities remain at the heart of the matter.

Remote sensing is playing an increasing role in heritage initiatives at international levels. UNESCO promotes remote sensing to protect both cultural and natural resources, and has numerous partner organizations. In order for an archaeological site to be nominated as a world heritage site, a lengthy process is undergone whereby a detailed site description plan is submitted to UNESCO. In addition to information about the archaeological site, a detailed site management plan is required by UNESCO, which describes how a site will be protected. This requires maps showing areas of the site most threatened by natural or anthropomorphic features. In 2000, the site of Merv, seen in Figure 8.9, a world heritage site in Turkmenistan, was named as one of the world's 100 most threatened archaeological sites. Archaeologists used IKONOS imagery to create a base map for future conservation efforts (Ziebart *et al.* 2002). Satellite imagery needs to be used within a GIS framework in order to create a buffer zone surrounding the archaeological site. Land use and land cover change analysis must be created, in order to create predictive models for the landscape surrounding the nominated archaeological site (De Maeyer *et al.* 2002), so they can be protected and preserved.

Education and outreach will aid in the more widespread usage of remote sensing in archaeology for heritage and conservation. There is increased interest from the general public for remote sensing in archaeology, especially with the advent of Google Earth™. How archaeologists should design remote sensing courses for their own students, colleagues, the general public, and international archaeology bodies, will differ according to the need and level of computing backgrounds. Funding from USAID

Figure 8.9 Merv, Turkmenistan, broader landscape surrounding site showing intensified agriculture, 2008 image courtesy of Google Earth™ Pro.

allowed Elizabeth Stone to set up a remote sensing training school for Iraqi archaeologists at Stonybrook University (Stone 2008), but this is not possible in every situation with more limited funding. Distance learning for satellite technology in archaeology (Birnbacher and Koudelka 2002) is not feasible. Person to person contact is critical for teaching satellite remote sensing in a classroom, while technical training requires long-term commitments to both the classroom and the remote sensing laboratory. More generalized outreach education should not be difficult, while accompanying ethics training for students in archaeological remote sensing classes should be mandatory.

One wonders if growing up with Google Earth™ in the classroom will change the perspectives of future generations of archaeologists. The author grew up anticipating *National Geographic* each month, and first "visited" many of the world's archaeological sites through the photos therein. Children can visit archaeological sites with connected photos on Google Earth™ any time of the day, and pursue websites for more detailed information. UNESCO is promoting outreach activities, via their program for Global Learning and Observations to Benefit Environment, for secondary school teachers and scientists (Ishwaran and Stone 2002). Will the wonder of archaeological discovery be dampened for future generations? The technology of remote sensing is advancing too quickly for this to occur. Students enter the field of archaeology with a better understanding of how they can apply remote sensing to their research, which will aid in applying future versions of remote sensing technology.

International initiatives to promote teaching remote sensing aid in promoting archaeological site conservation. At the central campus of the International Space University in

219

Figure 8.10 Supreme Council for Egyptian Antiquities, Cairo, during 2004 training, photograph by Sarah Parcak.

Strasbourg, a two-month summer session teaches satellite remote sensing to international graduate and undergraduate students of archaeology (Farrow *et al.* 2002). During the 2007 session, students created a manual for remote sensing usage in archaeology as a summer project with an accompanying field school (pers. comm., Williamson 2007). A similar field school program exists in Italy, based at Rome University "La Sapienza." Students receive training in basic archaeological method, landscape theory, GIS, applied satellite remote sensing, landscape modeling, and GIS database creation, with the courses taught by an international team of archaeologists. Survey forms an integral part of many international archaeological field schools, but remote sensing is not yet taught as part of survey training. International field schools should be designed to reflect the needs of each targeted group or organization. The author taught an intensive three-day remote sensing course, seen in Figure 8.10, to members of Egypt's Supreme Council for Egyptian Antiquities (SCA), in the office of the Egyptian Antiquities Information Service (EAIS) (funded through the US State Department Ambassador's Fund for Cultural Preservation), focusing on the major archaeological conservation and preservation issues for Egyptian archaeology. The author noted an increased usage of satellite remote sensing by the EAIS and SCA following the course.

Ethics

Ethical usage of remote sensing for archaeology is a topic that has not undergone significant discussion amongst scholars. How to approach the issue of ethics in archaeological remote sensing is not clear, due to the overlap between the statements of ethical usage of remote sensing and ethical archaeological practices. How can archaeologists using remote sensing walk the line between ethical archaeological practice and ethical remote sensing practice, while protecting sites against looting and preserving them against modern development? It is necessary to review and discuss both types of ethics statements, examining all of the ethical issues relating to remote sensing usage in archaeology. This promotes the creation of a specific archaeological remote sensing ethics statement, which will encourage good remote sensing practice while discouraging data sharing that can lead to looting. It is up to each individual archaeological remote sensing specialist to put these statements in practice.

The first ethics statement to be examined is the "Code of Ethics of the American Society for Photogrammmetry and Remote Sensing," approved in 1975. This is a major body of remote sensing specialists. The statement has existed for nearly 35 years (nearly as long as multispectral remote sensing), and remains fully relevant today. The statement can be found on the American Society for Photogrammmetry and Remote Sensing website, http://www.asprs.org:

> Honesty, justice and courtesy form a moral philosophy which, associated with mutual interest among people, should be the principles on which ethics are founded.
>
> Each person who is engaged in the use, development, and improvement of the mapping sciences (photogrammetry, remote sensing, GIS, and related disciplines) should accept these principles as a set of dynamic guides for conduct and a way of life rather than merely for passive observance:

Code of Ethics
Accordingly, each person…shall…

1. Be guided in all professional activities by the highest standards and be a faithful trustee or agent in all matters for each clients or employee.
2. At all times function in such a manner as will bring credit and dignity to the mapping sciences profession
3. Not compete unfairly with anyone who is engaged in the mapping sciences profession by:

    a. Advertising in a self-laudatory manner;
    b. Monetarily exploiting one's own or another's employment position;
    c. Publicly criticizing another person's working in or having an interest in the mapping sciences;
    d. Exercising undue influence or pressure, or soliciting favors through offer monetary inducements

4. Work to strengthen the profession of mapping sciences by:

    a. Personal effort directed toward improving personal skills and knowledge
    b. Interchanges of information and experience with other persons interested in and using a mapping science, with other professions, and with students and the public;

c. Seeking to provide opportunities for professional development and advancement of persons working under his or her supervision;

d. Promoting the principle of appropriate compensation for work done by persons in their employment

5. Undertake only such assignments in the use of mapping sciences for which one is qualified by education, training and experience...

6. Give appropriate credit to other persons and/or firms for their professional contributions

7. Recognize the proprietary, privacy, legal, and ethical interests and right of others. This not only refers to the adoption of these principles in the general conduct of business and professional activities, but also as they relate specifically to the appropriate and honest application of photogrammetry, remote sensing, geographic information systems, and related spatial technologies. Subscribers to this code shall not condone, promote, advocate, or tolerate any organization's or individual's use of these technologies in a manner that knowingly contributes to:

a. deception through data alternation;

b. circumvention of the law;

c. transgression of reasonable and legitimate expectation of privacy.

This ethics statement recognizes the scientific nature of remote sensing. Inappropriate data manipulation in remote sensing, like any scientific field, can occur easily, thus necessitating a discouragement of this practice. Data alteration is, however, difficult to detect, especially without ground-truthing to confirm project results. Remote sensing is a highly interdisciplinary field, requiring multiple levels of human interactions to facilitate and implement discoveries or research. The issue of "undertak(ing) only such assignments in the use of mapping sciences for which one is qualified by education, training and experience," is a more difficult issue. Who decides who is a qualified remote sensing specialist? One can become a member of a learned international society, or take training courses from remote sensing companies to gain a certificate, but determining who is and is not qualified to do remote sensing work is not a straightforward matter. One might assume that a PhD in some area of remote sensing might qualify an individual to do remote sensing work, but then what of MA students who specialize in geospatial studies, or undergraduates with geography degrees and several years of remote sensing to project experience? How do professors who learn about remote sensing later in their careers fit into the overall experience picture, or laypeople with backgrounds in science who take university or community college courses, not to mention professional certification courses? Google Earth™ adds another dimension: All Google Earth™ users take part in remote sensing, and many users have discovered new features on the Earth's surface. The process of peer-review aids in determining what should and should not be published, but who qualifies as an "expert" and what that level of expertise allows with regards to remote sensing research is not well understood. The question of the "appropriate and honest application of photogrammetry, remote sensing, geographic information systems, and related spatial technologies" is another issue that requires discussion as it applies to archaeological practices.

Ethical applications of general remote sensing belong more in a legal realm, yet international remote sensing law is still a developing field. For example, an Indian court was asked to ban Google Earth in the wake of the late 2008 terrorist attacks in Mumbai, with lawyers claiming that Google Earth was used for planning purposes by the terrorists (Anon. 2008). What about the dozens of companies in the USA and across the globe who offer slightly higher-resolution data at a premium cost? Anyone with money anywhere in the world can purchase high-resolution satellite imagery. Although companies request the purchaser describe how and why the satellite imagery will be used, it seems any "reasonable" description is accepted. Though this data is not free, it is publicly available. Each government restricts information in a different way, yet data is easy to share, and easy to import via a handheld PDA. For example, during fieldwork, a prototype mobile application could support transfer of updated maps and data back to the PDA's using compact flash (CF) cards. Broadband satellite access points allow for international data communication via the Internet to a university-hosted database and web map server application. There will only be additional international ramifications for the increasing spatial resolution of satellite imagery and data-sharing.

Remote sensing laws in the USA address some of the complicated issues relating to ethics in remote sensing. The Land Remote Sensing Policy Act 1992 authorizes the Secretary of Commerce to issue licenses for the operation of private Earth remote sensing space systems, with the authority delegated to NOAA. It is illegal for an organization to launch a system without a license. An act entitled The National Defense Authorization Act 1997, restricts remote sensing data distribution for Israel, which is interesting given that that the author has not come across a single multispectral satellite archaeology case study from Israel. Regarding major remote sensing policies, there is an interagency memorandum of agreement between the Departments of Commerce, State, Interior and the CIA, which provides for shutter control on private remote sensing satellites and other technical issues. In 2003, the USA instituted a commercial remote sensing policy, whereby NOAA has to publish, develop and review remote sensing policies. It encourages the development of space systems in the USA, but an FCC license is needed for the satellite frequencies and to launch the satellites. Additional information about space and law can be found online at the University of Mississippi School of Law's National Center for Remote Sensing, Air, and Space law at: http://www.spacelaw.olemiss.edu/index.html

Legal ramifications of the usage of satellite imagery extend to archaeology. There are some contradictions between the ASPRS ethics statement and the ethics statement adopted by the Society for American Archaeology (Lynott and Wylie 1995). It is recognized that a number of international archaeological learned bodies have ethics statements. The SAA ethics statement covers a broad spectrum of issues, and is the ethics statement most cited by American archaeologists in the classroom or at conferences. Each statement will be cited and discussed with regards to how they can be connected to remote sensing practice for archaeologists. Six main principles found the SAA ethics statement: Stewardship; accountability; commercialization; public education and outreach; intellectual property; and public reporting and publication.

The first principle, that of stewardship, states:

1. It is the responsibility of all archaeologists to work for the long-term conservation and protection of the archaeological record by practicing and promoting stewardship of the archaeological record ... they should use

the specialized knowledge they gain to promote public understanding and support for its long-term preservation.

Conservation and protection of the archaeological record are the primary concerns of archaeological remote sensers, and looting fits into both of these categories. Looting prevention is recognized as a significant issue across the globe, and looters will use any tools at their disposal to gain information about archaeological sites or to obtain knowledge about the locating of possible items they could sell. How remote sensing might aid in looting is a major topic for consideration, especially as satellite imagery improves in resolution and more becomes publicly available. Looters frequently follow archaeological expeditions, or pay family members to "spy" on activities. The author worked on a Roman-Crusader fortress along the Mediterranean, when the team uncovered a marble capitol in the late afternoon. Only the team had seen the capitol, and they reburied it for removal the following day. The capitol had disappeared by early the next morning, and it became clear that people would visit the site each evening and probe the trench to see if the team had uncovered anything of interest. Many archaeologists tell similar stories.

Given all of the problems with archaeological looting, how is remote sensing contributing to the international illegal antiquities market? Remote sensing helps and hinders looters at the same time. Archaeologists can monitor sites using high resolution imagery, but the cost of this activity becomes quickly prohibitive. Free programs such as Google Earth™, and World Wind make it fairly easy to zoom in on known archaeological sites free from modern vegetation. Individuals have the right to place a bookmark with uploaded photographs anywhere in the world, thus giving anyone the right to give coordinates and images of previously unknown archaeological sites and features. Someone living next to such an area might not think anything of it, or might somehow want to attract a network of looters to their town for personal gain. Looters can use these programs to plan routes to and from sites, and to pick the best places to dig for antiquities.

Fortunately and unfortunately, free imagery programs online frequently allow the discernment of subsurface architecture. Looters can also choose the best places to hide their goods, plotting points to avoid such as police checkpoints. Remote sensing may become more automated in the future, making it possible for people with no remote sensing skills to locate previously unknown sites from their soil or vegetation signatures. Training local authorities on free imagery programs can help to prevent looting via detection of likely places where looters might strike, but computer access is not always guaranteed. Images on free viewing programs can be outdated. High-resolution images would be able to record robber holes between excavation seasons, but would likely do little to stop destruction of sites as looting often takes place in areas where archaeological site guards are poorly paid (if any exist in the first place). Many parts of the world do not yet have high-resolution data available on these programs, but they will within a few years, when even higher-resolution data may be visible.

Stewardship extends to protecting sites for future generations, but what is the responsibility of the archaeologists towards the individuals living on or by archaeological sites? During surveys, people can be afraid to report any archaeological remains on their property for fear that their homes and land may be confiscated. Archaeologists specializing in remote sensing must think deeply about how their survey data may affect the lives of people on the ground. Illegal home construction and agricultural reclamation goes on

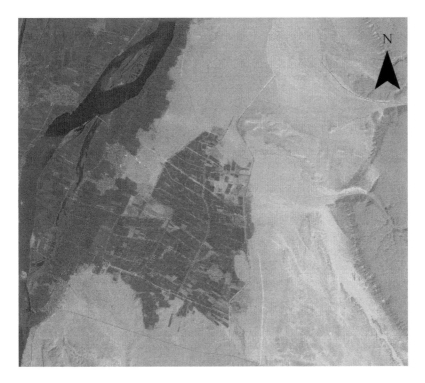

Figure 8.11 Tell el-Amarna, Egypt (scale 1:2678 m), showing agricultural expansion, 2008 image courtesy of Google Earth™ Pro.

near or on archaeological sites around the world, yet what choices do people have when their families need to be fed and housed and corrupt officials allow this to occur? At Tell el-Amarna, a Pharaonic capitol city in Middle Egypt dating to ca. 1300 BC (Kemp and Garfi 1993), over 90 hectares of the city have been lost in the past 30 years due to agricultural expansion and urban development, detected through satellite imagery analysis (Parcak 2005). In 2006, officials came in and bulldozed a number of homes illegally constructed atop the city. There was no warning to the inhabitants of the illegal housing. If the agricultural expansion is not stopped, however, most of the city will be gone in 25 years (Figure 8.11). Can local officials monitor things year by year, as another 30 or 40 feet of desert are added to people's agricultural plots? This is not likely, as remote sensing has shown how much this is affecting one of Egypt's best-preserved cities. On the West Bank of Luxor, people had built dozens of homes atop elite tombs in the village of Qurna. Authorities bulldozed these homes in 2007, many of which were used to mask the theft of antiquities from the tombs below (observed by the author in 1999).

Issues of protecting sites and looting are rooted in global issues like poverty, access to medical care, and food. In Egypt, international aid agencies often have little choice but to build hospitals, schools, or water treatment plants atop archaeological sites, as it is the only land free from cultivation or development. Do archaeologists have the right to stop this type of development when it enhances the lives of poor people? Over one-third of the archaeological site of Tell Tebilla, a Late Period (ca. 600 BC) site (Mumford 2003, 2004), was removed for the construction of a water plant by USAID. No information is available about the area of the site removed, and it took over 20 years for the water plant to become semi-operational. The people in the surrounding villages, however, now have access to clean water. More coordination is needed between these aid agencies and archaeological organizations in countries around the world. Every country will have their own policy regarding the survey of sites before potential removal, but when so much is at stake of being lost, more could be done using satellite imagery. Moral issues of global access to healthcare, education, food, and water are serious issues that, at present, clearly conflict with the idea of preserving heritage and protecting sites.

The next category of the SAA's statement of ethics deals with the issue of accountability:

> 2. Accountability requires an acknowledgement of public accountability, so consult actively with the affected groups ...

These affected groups include the people or groups where the archaeological work is taking place as well as the archaeologists conducting the excavation or survey work. As satellites improve in their spectral and spatial resolutions, many issues concerning people's rights to privacy will become relevant. Additional issues involving ownership of data, in particular archaeological data, will need to be debated. At present, the author can publish on any remote sensing topic in archaeology. Although her colleagues might be somewhat confused to see her name on a remote sensing publication involving horse burial sites in the Russian Steppes, or Andean elite housing in Peru, as long as she had used sound remote sensing and archaeological method, the papers would likely be accepted via the process of peer-review. Any remote sensing specialist in archaeology has the right to publish following this process. The press, however, does not employ this method of critique. Thus, what will happen to the process of archaeological discovery when any individual can order high-resolution satellite imagery of ongoing excavations and publish the results prior to the end of an excavation season? Everything in archaeology is naturally context based: People examining a feature from space will not be able to examine material culture or radiocarbon dates to assess the overall importance of an excavated feature. The general public, however, would comprehend the significance of uncovering of a new temple at a well-known site.

The right to publish the data on newly discovered features would become a topic of debate closely connected to the idea of accountability. Would the individual or group who "discovered" the newly excavated features from space be credited with the discovery, or would the credit for discovery rightfully remain with the group of excavators on the ground? Publication of archaeological excavations can take years: Should an embargo be placed on the publications of all archaeological data that is not written by the individuals in charge of the excavation? This is not something that would be accepted by the larger archaeological community, as scholars frequently publish old excavation reports long after the initial excavators have died. While the process of peer review would prevent the publication of archaeological material by amateurs who "discovered" the features or sites in question, the press would not adhere to these standards. Credit for archaeological discovery does not always come from scholarly publications, as it is attributed generally to those who grab the headlines. This is a topic that requires serious consideration, and is one that could readily become out of hand.

Figure 8.12 Mt. Ararat, Turkey (scale 1: 3456 m), 2008 image courtesy of Google Earth™ Pro.

Already, educated laypeople are making spurious claims of archaeological discovery from space (Taylor 2007), such as the so-called "discovery" of Noah's Ark, to which the press and reputable publications gave serious consideration. According to the team in charge of this work, "ship shaped objects" appeared atop Mt. Ararat in Turkey (seen in Figure 8.12) on IKONOS imagery, which the team then compared to a copper plated illustration from the 1600s to prove the object was indeed Noah's Ark. This unfortunate usage of remote sensing for archaeological discovery had significant flaws. No proper remote sensing analysis or specialist can be associated with the "discovery" of this feature. Geologists have stated that the anomaly is a fairly common geological formation (a rock ledge covered in ice) thus exposing the find to be more in the realm of science fiction than science (Cline 2007).

Once again, hype and the "story" triumphed over archaeological method. Both the press and archaeologists are accountable to the general public. Proper remote sensing, as shown by many hundreds of peer-reviewed publications cited in this book, requires rigorous scientific analysis followed by thorough ground-based testing, survey, and excavation. Similar stories to the one described will always gain excessive attention in the media due to their very nature: Combining space technology and the Bible, in addition to other legendary accounts, will undoubtedly yield future stories with little science to support claims of an extraordinary nature. Only making the science of satellite archaeology more accessible to the general public can prevent pseudoarchaeology from triumphing over good practice. In addition to the process of peer-review, archaeologists should contribute stories to local newspapers, or publish newsletters. Good project websites receive a great deal of attention from school groups, while visits to local schools promote the practice of good science. Publishing accessible material promotes this practice as well as promoting archaeological accountability.

The third area of discussion covers commercialization, an area of ongoing debate, especially as pertains to the publishing of items known to be looted.

3. Archaeologists should avoid, whenever possible, activities that enhance the commercial value of archaeological objects.

Archaeological remote sensers not careful with their data dissemination can inadvertently support looting. Suspicious individuals frequently contact the author and her colleagues requesting detailed information regarding their survey work, so clearly looters have recognized the potential for using satellite imagery in their efforts. This problem extends to large conferences as well, with likely looters attending and posing as other scholars or students. Some scholars tell stories of being followed by individuals at conferences pressuring them for copies of maps and other information. Thus, people working in the field of archaeological remote sensing should not respond to anyone they feel is making unusual requests for data.

What happens when archaeologists using remote sensing discover previously unknown archaeological sites where significant looting has taken place? Does this enhance the value of looted items with a known provenience? The majority of looted objects lose their provenience. People's financial gains from these previously unknown sites, however, cannot be understated, and are closely connected with larger global issues (including war). In a study examining drainage canals along the Holmul River in Guatemala using Landsat TM and ETM imagery, IKONOS, and STAR-3-DEM imagery, archaeologists noted that deforestation has contributed the illegal antiquities trade. Looting is estimated to bring in US$10 million dollars a month (Sever and Irwin 2003). This is in a well-known area. How many ancient objects from Central America can be located on Ebay®, or in antique stores in Paris, Geneva, and London? Many objects are fakes, but a surprising number of real objects make it onto the public market. Looting is also connected to more "major" crimes, as seen by the situation in Iraq.

Elizabeth Stone's research using Quickbird satellite imagery found 16 km^2 of looting holes in 101 km^2 of archaeological sites located in southern Iraq, which was the equivalent to four times the total excavated area in the past 100 years. She noted that looting took place in the mid-1990s during a time of extreme poverty, and in 2003 during the insurgency (Stone 2008). Only a concerted international effort between government agencies, archaeologists, and the general public will stop this and related looting, which makes organizations such as Saving Antiquities For Everyone (SAFE, see http://www.savingantiquities.org) all the more valuable to archaeology.

Public education and outreach, the fourth category, are the main ways that archaeological sites can be protected against looting and conserved, as well as getting public support for the stewardship of archaeological record.

4. Archaeologists should reach out to, and participate in cooperative efforts with others interested in the archaeological record with the aim of improving the preservation, protection, and interpretation of the record. In particular, archaeologists should undertake to: (1) enlist public support

for the stewardship of the archaeological record; (2) explain and promote the use of archaeological methods and techniques in understanding human behavior and culture; and (3) communicate archaeological interpretations of the past ...

Explaining and promoting the use of archaeological methods and techniques in understanding human behavior and culture is the job of all archaeologists. Remote sensing and its usage also help to communicate archaeological interpretations of the past. How each individual will use this information is not something any archaeologist can predict. Educating the public on the ethics of archaeology would be just as important as educating them on how archaeologists assists with interpreting the past. Unfortunately, not all individuals can be trusted.

An ongoing recent case involves a US army warrant officer based in Heliopolis in Cairo. Egyptian authorities recorded 370 objects as missing from the Maa'di museum. The officer sold 90 objects to a Texas-based art dealer for $21,000, claiming the objects passed to him from his grandfather, who had worked in Egypt in the 1930s and 1940s. The dealer then supposedly consigned these pieces to collectors and galleries in Manhattan, London, Zurich and Montreal (El-Aref 2008). While the case is still ongoing, it underscores the fact that the temptation to steal or loot can affect those often charged with protecting a country's cultures and heritage. These can include archaeological site guards, who make very little money, or site workers themselves, as well as individuals living on top or next to archaeological sites. Educating the individuals who would have easiest access to material from archaeological sites would aid in stopping looting. This starts at the level of local agencies that deal with water or land management.

The fifth and sixth topics, those of intellectual property and public reporting and publication, are very closely related areas. The first, intellectual property, is a topic which applies more readily to archaeological excavations than archaeological remote sensing:

5. If there is a compelling reason, and no legal restrictions or strong countervailing interests, a researcher may have primary access to original materials and documents for a limited and reasonable time, after which there materials must be made available to others.

Archaeological inventories are the first area that may cause problems. In the USA, a national inventory of archaeological sites was not yet complete in 1987 (Williamson 1987), and is not something that is publicly accessible today. Technology transfer is an important issue in preservation management, yet do countries have the computer equipment and related facilities to store this data (Campana and Frezza 2006), and if they do, how well-guarded would it be from theft by looters? The best place for looters to work is within the government system. The USA, supposedly one of the more data-protection conscious nations in the world, frequently has data-theft issues, seen frequently on the news. Information does not appear to be safe in any format. Working closely with foreign archaeological bodies to ensure data protection may help. Looting may not threaten archaeological sites as much as ongoing development, so sharing information and maps is necessary to help government agencies with site management. Ultimately, no databases are secure.

Data sharing and data access are additional ethical issues within archaeological remote sensing which tie into the sixth category of the SAA ethics statement:

6. An interest in preserving and protecting in-situ archaeological sites must be taken into account when publishing and distributing information about their nature and location.

Many satellite datasets are freely available over the Internet, while higher resolution satellite imagery datasets have additional costs associated with them if they are to be used by more than one individual. Is it ethical for archaeologists to share higher resolution data with international colleagues (who could not afford such imagery datasets) without paying higher costs to commercial companies? At present, such agreements are based on an honor system, yet data-sharing is a common practice.

Overall access to archaeological site data is an additional issue for debate, especially as many funding agencies demand public access to any data generated from projects through websites or published data. This remains a necessity, but the information should be made available in such a way that it protects archaeological sites. Non-specific site location data should be available on the Internet or on specific site pages. Most archaeological journals are available only in research libraries or centers on campuses, where the individuals who have access are limited. JSTOR and other online reference journal databases tend to be available only on campus networks, with a three to four-year gap in the most recent publications featured. Ultimately, archaeologists must consider the most important factors in determining what information should be made available. If looters want access to archaeological site data and publications, and have an extensive (and well-funded) international network, it is likely that they will be able to get some of the information they require.

Following data-protection models from other fields will help to protect archaeological sites. In the fields of Public Health and Medicine, the US Government requires that patient data is geocoded to protect the rights of each individual patient. GIS plays an important role in the geocoding that makes this possible. For example, individual data points are given numbers/codes, and the data is further hidden through generalizations made about broader areas (city blocks, or 1 km zones). The same information should be applied to archaeological sites found through remote sensing analysis. No specific GPS coordinates should be given for any data found through satellite remote sensing analysis and subsequent survey. The data can be masked through publishing more generalized maps that contain points, perhaps with some type of error or offset introduced to confuse potential looters. Actual site data points might be accessible via a secure online network, or in person-to-person contact.

Satellite imagery will appear more over time in court cases dealing with property disputes or other illegal activities, and it remains a question if archaeological projects that publish exact coordinates of archaeological sites of features that are later looted or defaced should be held liable. It is the responsibility of each archaeological project to protect, to the best of their ability, the places where they excavate or survey. Previous knowledge that looters will use any and all information to loot or harm sites should be a key consideration. This is why a specific archaeological remote sensing code of ethics should be developed, to promote data sharing and publishing of archaeological remote sensing data in a responsible way. Should international organizations that harm archaeological sites, either advertently or inadvertently, be held responsible as well? At this stage, it is too early to answer this question.

This is closely connected to international wars or internal country conflicts. The US Department of Defense now has heritage as a priority, educating servicemen and servicewomen to be sent abroad in the heritage of both Afghanistan and Iraq. Funding for these activities is aimed mainly at the Middle East: What about other threatened parts of the world? Archaeologists may wrestle with the idea of helping the Department of Defense with their efforts abroad, citing either political or moral issues. If US government agencies express an interest in preserving the heritage of foreign countries, however, it is not an opportunity to be missed. The DoD has a number of archaeologists and museum curators supporting their efforts, showcased at several major archaeology conferences including the Archaeological Institute of America and the World Archaeology Conference. It is hoped that this will support future heritage and conservation efforts abroad. One wonders what is happening to the cultural heritage of countries under severe internal pressures such as Zimbabwe, shown in Figure 8.13, Burma, or North Korea.

Only through the creation of an independent set of ethics guidelines for archaeological remote sensing can the conflicts between the ASPRS and SAA statements of ethics be resolved as well as emphasizing the positive similarities. This ethics statement draws on both sets of guidelines. It is hoped that archaeologists practicing remote sensing will

Figure 8.13 Great Zimbabwe, Zimbabwe (scale 1:113 m), circular structures are in the central part of the image and are partially obscured by vegetation, 2008 image courtesy of Google Earth™ Pro.

adhere to a similar ethics statement. There is no international body (as of yet) to promote the usage of or adherence to these guidelines.

1. Archaeological remote sensers shall not publish data that could potentially harm archaeological sites, features, related material culture, or the people surrounding the archaeological sites and features.
2. Archaeological remote sensers should, to the best of their abilities, promote good remote sensing practice in the field, classroom and other applicable situations
3. Archaeologists will not create false satellite remote sensing data to their personal benefit (either for monetary gain or for press coverage).
4. When publishing their data or putting data on the Internet, archaeologists using remote sensing will geocode data points for unknown or little-known archaeological sites and features, or they will introduce error into their maps to discourage looting and to protect sites.
5. When publishing their data, archaeologists will discuss techniques that do and do not work, and will strive to disseminate their results as broadly and as responsibly as possible.
6. Archaeological remote sensers should promote the usage of remote sensing in foreign countries through training, outreach, and data sharing.
7. During ground-truthing, archaeologists testing satellite imagery during ground-truthing shall not undertake activities that risk the health and safety of their team members or affect local groups of people.

The question of who will enforce these proposed ethical guidelines remains a question. Conference organizers, granting agencies, and article reviewers can all support them, but every group of individuals will have a vested interest in a particular approach. How the proposed ethical guidelines should be debated is another issue, and there may be additional topics that will be included in future as landscape issues evolve with globalization. There is still much to discuss on the topic of archaeological remote sensing and how it is connected to conservation, preservation, and ethics. Using a wide range of satellite image types discussed in this volume will allow the monitoring and protecting of known and unknown past sites and features through defining their specific spectral profiles. Future developments with higher resolution data and real time data will introduce additional topics for debate and discussion. While education and outreach remain the best ways to share satellite archaeology data, they need to be done in such a way that archaeological sites are not harmed. The ultimate goal of archaeology, after all, is not the discovery of past archaeological remains: It is to protect and preserve them for future generations.

9

CONCLUSION

The previous chapters have illustrated the present state of affairs in archaeological remote sensing. It remains for me to introduce, however, the potential new directions that satellite remote sensing is taking, and additional ways satellite remote sensing might contribute to the broader field of anthropology. Remote sensing programs will undoubtedly improve over time, and more specific programs for archaeological work may be developed. More advanced computer programming is needed to improve specific algorithms, but we are a long way from obtaining, if ever, any "automated" satellite archaeology: To realize this objective, innumerable sets of conditions and different signatures would need to be identified and put into remote sensing programs—not impossible, but quite far reaching. Each region of the world requires specific approaches that change according to weather patterns and each satellite image. If satellite imagery analysis cannot be made "automatic" in the foreseeable future, will ongoing computer programs require less training, or will specific programs for archaeologists be developed? Imagery programs may become more user friendly, but, like all advanced computer programming, will require coursework and training for interpretation. Remote sensing programs are not restricted to any one field, as the same techniques that can locate past archaeological sites can be used in every remote sensing subfield, including forestry, geology, physics, biology, and many others.

The field of satellite archaeology will almost certainly offer more information to archaeologists, through additional resources, free satellite imagery, blogs, discussion boards, and, as time passes, additional written and electronic resources. As more discoveries are made, increasing information will appear on the Internet, with project websites discussing surveying strategies. Archaeologists will need to rethink their surveying and excavation strategies in light of this new information, especially as sub-meter satellite images become commercially available. It seems likely that satellite archaeology will no longer remain in the domain of "technical" researchers: Archaeological applications are becoming just as broad and important as the techniques themselves. Hence, satellite archaeology, as a field, is clearly in its infancy.

Archaeologists, then, are left to ponder what the future might hold for satellite archaeology, and how it will affect excavation and survey work. Graduate students across the USA and elsewhere are now emerging with increasing levels of technical training and experience that will affect how they conduct their own research projects. Many archaeological and anthropological positions now require a background in GIS and remote sensing: Increasingly universities in the USA are hiring recent doctoral graduates with such backgrounds. These skills are becoming an indispensable tool to many graduate and undergraduate curriculums across the globe, thus perpetuating the cycle of training in remote sensing (many archaeology classes now include GIS and remote sensing).

Satellite archaeology has already earned its place as a sub-specialization of archaeology. However, there appear to be few courses at present with a sole focus on satellite archaeology, which normally falls under the broader study of "landscape archaeology." In future, course programs will need to incorporate remote sensing, GIS, geophysical science, and landscape archaeology, advocating a broader approach to the analysis of past landscapes. Mastering these approaches is necessary to recover as complete a picture as possible of past cultures and their environmental settings. However, more collaboration is needed between natural and social sciences: Archaeology is generally considered a social science, with some aspects falling in the natural sciences (e.g. DNA testing, radiocarbon dating, etc.), and remote sensing falls more strongly within the natural or applied sciences (e.g. physics, computer science, etc.). Applied satellite archaeology is more of a natural science, while the broader implications of satellite archaeology place it within the social sciences. Both fields play equally strong roles in satellite archaeology, which is why students of archaeology should be encouraged to take courses in physics, computer science, geology, and geography. Those courses will only enhance the ability of the next generation of satellite archaeologists.

Broadening traditional satellite archaeology, namely research dealing with more historical periods, will facilitate its application in other areas of archaeology and anthropology (Couzy 1985; Kruckman 1987; Davenport 2001). For example, in Olduvai Gorge (Figure 9.1), archaeologists used GPS points to map layers of ash sediment, using geological strata to trace associated hominid remains deposited throughout the landscape (Ebert and Blumenschine 1999). If there are consistencies in hominid deposition layers, then satellites should be able to detect similar spectral signatures elsewhere in landscapes revealing additional hominid deposition layers. Digital elevation models would help physical anthropologists better map such landscapes. Satellite imagery can also detect past water sources, which in turn could yield evidence for adjacent early human activity. Similar approaches could be attempted for paleontology, where dinosaur bones appear in specific geological strata (Figure 9.2).

Satellite imagery analysis has the potential to assist with larger anthropological and archaeological questions relating to past migrations through Africa, Europe, and the Americas by applying landscape reconstruction. Can past human behavior truly be mapped with satellites? So many anthropological questions relate to how and why human beings chose to live in a particular location. Satellite image data, especially those dealing with land use and land cover change, can facilitate ethnoarchaeological approaches to past landscape use with regards to crop patterns, field organization, and the use of local water sources for irrigation (e.g. the potential for past Mayan land use practices to be applied today).

How human beings interact with their landscapes is a crucial question for anthropologists and archaeologists, and satellites offer a slightly different perspective on anthropomorphic landscape relationships. An ethnoarchaeological study of people living in a rainforest can assess how deforestation or climate changes may have affected their relationships with the land and how they adapted to changing climate conditions. Such studies also have implications for past and future climate change adaptations.

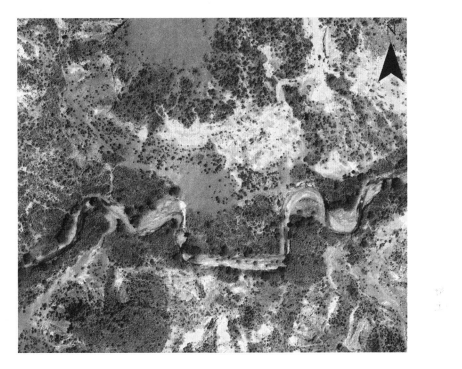

Figure 9.1 Olduvai Gorge, Tanzania (scale 1:175 m), 2008 image courtesy of Google Earth™ Pro.

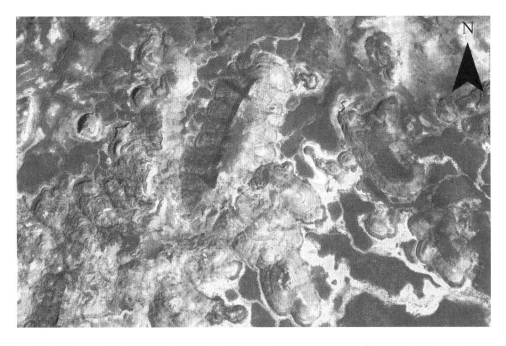

Figure 9.2 Kill Site, Montana (scale 1:301 m), 2008 image courtesy of Google Earth™ Pro.

Evaluating animal habitats from space may be useful for subsistence pattern studies, and certainly ties into broader strategies for cultural and natural resource management.

One of the areas that will revolutionize the field of satellite archaeology is the improvement of spatial and spectral resolutions. By early 2009, 30 cm pixel (one foot) resolution satellite imagery will be available commercially via the same company now selling IKONOS imagery. This doubles the present Quickbird imagery resolution, while Digital Globe is planning for a 30 cm resolution satellite to be launched in 2009. This essentially equals the highest resolution found in aerial photography. Satellites offering 30 cm resolution will make it far easier to detect buried walls and buildings, and refine our perception about how narrow bands of soil and vegetation may be affected by buried structures. Archaeologists will also be better able to use this new imagery in the mapping and planning of existing sites in a GIS.

It will not be much longer before a 10 cm resolution (4 inch) satellite will be launched, perhaps by 2011. Like all computer-related technologies, satellite technology is advancing at ever-faster rates. There are not many archaeological features (excluding material culture remains) smaller than 10 cm, while aircraft born LIDAR has a resolution of 3 cm. New strategies for analyzing higher-resolution archaeological data will emerge over time. Archaeologists can only speculate, at this moment in time, how good satellite data will become in 20 or 30 years. Perhaps we will be able to zoom in from space on individual potsherds and other small material culture remains, analyzing them in situ, making archaeologists completely rethink how surveys are conducted. Ground-based remote sensing will continue to improve as well, giving archaeologists ever-clearer images of buried architecture. Satellite and ground-based remote sensing may allow full 3D reconstructions of above- and below-surface architecture and features, enabling archaeologists to maximize their excavation efforts in the most significant areas. Then, and only then, will the gap between "dirt archaeologists" and remote sensers be bridged (Johnson 1996, 2005). Archaeologists will also be able to request high-resolution imagery of their own archaeological sites at the end of an excavation season, getting an aerial view of a site when kite or balloon aerial photography might otherwise be restricted or unavailable.

The resolution of SAR imagery is improving along with multispectral satellite imagery. Currently, archaeologists can purchase 2 m resolution SAR imagery, although the imagery is expensive, and has not yet been applied to archaeological exploration. Future SAR imagery will allow archaeologists to visualize buried architecture for the first time, as current SAR data is too coarse to define most architectural features. Smaller canals, channels, or even field boundaries may be detectable with higher resolution SAR data, which will certainly affect future work in satellite archaeology. Additional features, which currently lie too deeply buried beneath modern debris, towns, or in floodplains, might be discernable by future SAR images.

Spectral resolution is another area that will only improve over time. Hyperspectral datasets, such as those offered by ASTER, are finally being applied to more satellite archaeology studies, with other hyperspectral data (some of which requires a sensor to be installed in a plane) also allowing more versatile analysis. Future hyperspectral satellites will offer far better spatial resolution. There is not, at present, a spectral database of archaeological features for each region of the world. Although spectral databases do exist for specific geological formations or chemicals, ancient structures may often utilize different types of stones and other materials during construction or subsequent modifications.

Figure 9.3 Moundville, Alabama (scale 1:251 m), 2008 image courtesy of Google Earth™ Pro.

On archaeological sites, the presence of stone buildings among less substantial structures and materials signify a highly stratified society, or suggest a general purpose and function for the buildings. Archaeologists can target even more specific bands for archaeological analysis, since the bands that detect ancient canals in Thailand will be different from the bands that detect ancient Mississippi culture mounds in the southern USA (Figure 9.3). Archaeological spectral databases will allow archaeologists to determine that not only that they have found a feature, but may further define what exactly the feature is. This will be extra beneficial to regions where ground-truthing is impossible, or, in the case of turbulent areas, may help in monitoring sites under threat of looting.

Will the refinement and identification of spectral signatures advance to the point where their reflectance of an archaeological site, and areas within a site, determine a rough date for the site? This would appear unlikely given how much mixed debris often cover site surfaces, or how frequently ancient buildings have been modified in later phases of the archaeological record. However, if the satellite imagery can distinguish multiple signatures for debris specific to certain periods of time (e.g. including volcanic ash layers from Pompeii seen in (Figure 9.4)), multiple site dates might be obtainable. In later periods where more specialized technologies are used, a combination of certain materials might make dating a site from space possible. For example, Roman period lime kilns are distinct, and used large amounts of limestone (e.g. Mendes, East Delta, Egypt). Subsurface signatures indicating concentrations of limestone surrounding burnt-brick would likely prove to be Roman in date in areas where such technology normally reflects Roman activity. By isolating specific activities and their

Figure 9.4 Pompeii, Italy (scale 1:234 m), 2008 image courtesy of Google Earth™ Pro.

material expression that characterizes certain periods, one might be able to detect both cultural and temporal signatures through remote sensing.

How quickly archaeologists are able to obtain high-resolution remote sensing data is another factor that should only improve over time. At the moment, much free coarser resolution data can be downloaded at will from websites, while high-resolution data can require payment and a waiting time of weeks to several months for tasking or delivery. Even companies offering a 24-hour "rush" data option prioritize their services to government agencies or companies paying for large data orders. In contrast, ordering imagery from data libraries is a relatively quick process, with delivery taking only several days. Such services will only improve and companies will only develop online databases for customers to purchase and download satellite data. A subscription charge may accompany this, depending on the overall quality of the imagery being ordered.

Until much higher spatial and spectral resolution satellite data becomes available, it will take a long time for the current high-resolution satellite data to become much less expensive in what has become a very lucrative industry. For instance, the present "cutting edge" satellite imagery, such as Quickbird and IKONOS, will eventually become much cheaper. Today, to purchase the minimum sized land area (25 km^2) for archived Quickbird imagery costs US$10.00 per km^2, which is well within the affordable range for most archaeological excavations and graduate students. For infrared Quickbird imagery the cost rises to US$18.00 per km^2, thus amounting to US$450.00 for minimum area coverage, also well within most modest archaeological budgets. Once again, these costs will undoubtedly decrease once commercially available resolutions improve and additional discounts are offered to academic researchers. Regulations on data sharing may also change: At present, researchers are required to inform Digital Globe of whether other individuals will have access to their satellite data. The cost increases for each additional user. Although archaeologists can share high-resolution data, they are ethically bound to maintain their initial contract with Digital Globe. As in the computer industry, these image sharing rules and regulations are not likely to change drastically, since companies are project-driven and rely on payments for high-resolution data, regardless of the individual purchaser's intent, be it educational or commercial.

Is satellite technology advancing faster than archaeologists' ability to learn, apply, and analyze the data and programs, and all the inherent implications? Each time new satellite imagery programs appear on the market, there can be a delay before an archaeological publication emerges discussing the application of the new satellite data. This is more a function of archaeological practice than the ability of archaeologists to recognize and apply fully new technology. Archaeologists usually must obtain grants to purchase costly new satellite imagery, and once they have analyzed the satellite imagery, need to ground-truth, or field test, their results. Once an article or monograph is submitted, it may take as long as one year before the data is published. The entire process can take two to three years before an article appears discussing new applications of imagery. In the meantime, archaeological teams may very well have adopted another satellite image or a more advanced remote sensing technique in conjunction with ground-truthing. It is therefore recommended that archaeologists start an online journal for archaeological remote sensing. This will decrease the lag time between paper submission and publication, and will allow the publication of higher resolution color photographs that do not generally appear in conventional archaeological journals.

Using aircraft, such as ultralights, has tremendous potential for the field of remote sensing in archaeology. Ultralights are sufficiently inexpensive (through rental), have enough carrying capacity to support LIDAR scanners, and often require less complicated permits than aircraft. Many ultralights operate around tourist areas, and are not seen as much of a security risk. Archaeologists have the advantage of contracting for ultralights more spontaneously than aircraft (pending budget restrictions), and can test flying missions closer to the ground. LIDAR can be combined with lower flying aerial photography at the end of excavation seasons, or survey seasons, where the team can direct the ultralight to exact locations of previously unknown archaeological sites. Not only can the team receive the modeling data from the satellite imagery analysis, but they can integrate additional levels of data for a more complete landscape model.

Archaeological looting is one of the most important areas issues that satellite archaeology can help address. Real-time satellite monitoring may not be possible right now, but may be in another few decades. International cultural authorities may, someday, be able to train satellites on culturally rich regions, hiring security specialists to monitor them remotely. Using high-resolution data, archaeologists or national antiquities organizations can currently monitor specific threatened archaeological sites on a monthly basis, but this is still too expensive and not effective enough; Many looted sites lie in inaccessible regions of the world (e.g. Iraq, as shown in Figure 9.5, and Afghanistan). Archaeological looting needs to be recognized as a more serious crime by governments, and international police forces (Interpol), who represent the only organizations sufficiently equipped to pursue and prosecute offenders at local to international levels. Another option may be to task satellites to spot check threatened sites regularly, and conduct specialist analyses via blogs. This may only aid looters, however, who have gotten smarter through time and adapt their looting strategies accordingly.

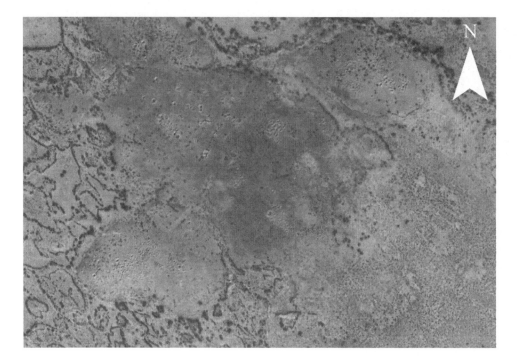

Figure 9.5 Umma, Iraq (scale 1:144 m), note extensive looting pits, 2008 image courtesy of Google Earth™ Pro.

Future archaeologists and heritage protection agencies will need to do the same thing to protect the past sufficiently.

With regards to advancing satellite technologies, all remote sensing specialists need to refine constantly their methods of analysis, and need to continue to learn new programs throughout their careers. One of the best methods is through teaching: I continuously learn about remote sensing analysis from articles and commercial websites, and often speak to people in the satellite industry to learn about new directions. Even though I direct a remote sensing laboratory with health research as a major component (a focus of my university), this has only enhanced my ability to do archaeological remote sensing research. Remote sensing analytical techniques are similar no matter what the subdiscipline, and, at the end of the day, remote sensers model environments to fit their research questions. Both health and archaeology use remote sensing to visualize anthropomorphic and environmental patterns and how they change through time. By teaching students in diverse disciplines (public health, medicine, physics, biology, and many other areas), I am forced to think outside my archaeological box, to address diverse questions and research interests. Looking through lenses colored by different fields has actually helped focus my personal research questions, while broadening my remote sensing approaches.

The field of satellite remote sensing, like archaeology, will always advance, becoming broader as satellite technology improves and the general public becomes more aware of its existence. The overall quality of science applied in archaeology improves annually with further education and training, but the applicability of applied satellite technologies for archaeology remains an issue. Although the techniques and methods of analysis will improve through time, the mentality of how archaeologists approach satellite archaeology should remain generally the same: Having an open mind and a desire to promote the best possible science and ethical practices.

It is likely that press coverage remote sensing in archaeology will increase with additional advances and associated discoveries. With recent features in *National Geographic News* (Handwerk 2006), Scientific American (Hvestendahl 2008), The Economist (Anon. 2003), PBS-NOVA, the Discovery Channel, and foreign papers (Heimlich 2004), the public is becoming increasingly aware of how satellites can contribute to archaeological research. In more affluent nations around the globe, children are now being raised with satellite technology, while most computer literate people are aware of Google Earth™. Uploaded photographs of archaeological sites on Google Earth™ offer multiple perspectives to interested viewers. People no longer need to rely on picture-perfect photographs, such as those in publications like *National Geographic*, to gain a greater appreciation for past landscapes.

Interpreting imagery for the purposes of past archaeological discovery is closely connected to how human beings can be influenced by the power behind imagery. Images can be controversial, powerful, and painful all at once (Steiner 1987). The responsibility of interpreting or indeed manipulating important imagery generally falls into a few hands, which are not always unbiased (Pursnell 1991: 918–20). Satellite imagery, with multispectral capabilities, has the ability to convey much more information than a typical photograph. Although a series of photographs over time can be effective, satellite imagery (which already has global coverage) can show broader changes over time for the past three to four decades, thus allowing each viewer to take an active role in determining the implications of these and future changes. A picture may be "worth a thousand words," but satellite imagery can be worth a million dollars: Politicians and international aid agencies have used sequential satellite images to raise millions of dollars in the aftermath of the December 2006 tsunami in southeast Asia, emphasizing the damage based on pre- and post-tsunami effects. During the August 2006 flooding in New Orleans, the sign "help" someone had painted atop a building could be seen from 700 miles in up space, underscoring the individual human component in the disaster. Images of ancient cities and architectural features seen from space will certainly not inspire the same emotional response as images of global tragedies, but the power of wonder and curiosity should not be underestimated.

Climate change will affect archaeological sites somewhat differently than urbanization and increasing populations, but is still an important factor to consider when studying archaeological landscapes. Regarding our current climate, change will probably be much greater in the lives of our grandchildren, depending on how quickly things advance over the next 30 years. The rate of population growth and changes in land use practices will affect future archaeological site destruction and preservation more than any other factor. It is essential to promote global education initiatives aimed at local and government tourism, heritage, and antiquities organizations, since only these institutions will be able to interfere effectively with the local populace to promote heritage preservation (if possible), which otherwise exceeds the mandate of foreign surveying projects.

Satellite remote sensing projects carried out by archaeologists with backgrounds in both remote sensing and archaeology have much to offer, but satellite archaeology is not always a substitute for archaeological excavation or survey work: It is one of a number of tools that archaeologists can apply in their research. Archaeologists should be skeptical of any technology that appears to promise a solution to "all problems." Unfortunately, satellite archaeology is a tool that can easily be abused if one lacks sufficient training in either remote sensing or archaeology. Satellite remote sensing has its own inherent problems, many of which have been detailed above, that should be recognized before starting a satellite archaeology project. Everything will depend on the interests, background, and needs, of the archaeologist and their research team, and the restrictions of their specific research location.

This treatment has aimed to make satellite remote sensing for archaeology more accessible and comprehensible for people with an interest in the subject, whether they are lay people, undergraduate students captivated by the possibilities of Google Earth™, graduate students who aspire to carry out their own survey projects, or professional archaeologists who wish to venture into satellite remote sensing for archaeology. This book has avoided any attempts to be an advanced technical manuscript. Should a reader be more interested in satellite remote sensing after perusing this book, they are recommended to take a university course or examine any of a number of existing remote sensing manuals (referenced in the introduction).

Satellite remote sensing for archaeology should not be viewed as an inaccessible science, nor should it be viewed as something that can be picked up "over the weekend." It requires dedicated study for those who wish to become proficient in its application, and, above all, an open and willing mind for the constant advances in both remote sensing technologies and archaeology. Our world and technology are changing far faster than we can observe and keep up with individually, and, with so many thousands of archaeological sites and features left to find and protect, satellite archaeology does not entail a race to see who can find the most archaeological sites, or a "lost" ancient city. Instead, it is one method of many to model past landscapes, to answer where we came from, and to see far better where we are going.

BIBLIOGRAPHY

Adams, R. and Wood, E. (1982) "Ancient Maya canals: grids and lattices in the Maya jungle," *Archaeology*, 35 (6): 28–35.

Adams, R.E.W., Brown, W.E. and Culbert, J.P. (1981) "Radar mapping, archaeology, and ancient Maya land use," *Science*, 213: 1457–63.

Adams, W. (1979) "On the Argument from Ceramics to History: A Challenge Based on Evidence from Medieval Nubia," *Current Anthropology*, 20: 727–744.

Agache, R. (1968) "Essai d'utilisation aérienne et au sol d'émulsions spectrozonales, dites infrarouges couleurs," *Society Prehistorique de France*, 65: 198–201.

Akasheh, T.S. (2002) "Ancient and modern watershed management in Petra," *Near Eastern Archaeology*, 65 (4): 220–4.

Alcock, S. and Cherry, J. (2004) *Side by Side Survey: Comparative Regional Studies in Mediterranean Survey*, Oxford: Oxbow Books.

Aldenderfer (2003) "Preliminary stages in the development of a real-time digital recording system for archaeological excavation using ArcView GIS," *Journal of GIS in Archaeology*, 1: 1–22.

Alizadeh, A., Kouchoukos, N., Wilkinson, T., Bauer, A. and Mashkour, M. (2004) "Human–environment interactions on the Upper Khuzestan Plains, Southwest Iran, recent investigations," *Paleorient*, 30: 69–88.

Alizadeh, K. and Ur, J. (2007) "Formation and destruction of pastoral and irrigation landscapes on the Mughan Steppe, north-western Iran," *Antiquity*, 81 (311): 148–60.

Allan, J. and Richards, T. (1983) "Use of Satellite Imagery in Archaeological Surveys," *Libyan Studies*, 14: 4–8.

Altaweel, M. (2005) "The use of ASTER satellite imagery in archaeological contexts," *Archaeological Prospection*, 12: 151–66.

Anon. (1992) "Satellite imagery reveals secrets of the past: using Landsat and Seasat in archaeology," *Photonics Spectra*, 26 (8): 114.

Anon. (1995) "Angkor by satellite," *Athena Review,* 1: 12–13.

Anon. (2003) "Archaeology: what lies beneath?," *The Economist,* 369: 75–6.

Anon. (2004) "SERDP projects advance state of the science for detecting archaeological sites," *SERDP Information Bulletin*: 2.

Anon. (2005) NASA Worldwind forums, Worldwind vs. Google Earth Beta, online at http://forum.worldwindcentral.com/, accessed Sep. 15th, 2008.

Anon. (2008) Indian court asked to ban Google Earth, from *The Times* online, December 10, 2008, http://technology.timesonline.co.uk/tol/news/tech_and_web/the_web/article5314085.ece, accessed Jan 8th, 2008

Argotte-Espino, D. and Chavez, R.E. (2005) "Detection of possible archaeological pathways in Central Mexico through digital processing of remote sensing images," *Archaeological Prospection*, 12 (2): 105–14.

Arnold, J.B.I. (1993) "Matagorda Bay surveys: Applications of inexpensive satellite navigation," *International Journal of Nautical Archaeology*, 22 (1): 79–87.

Aufrecht, W.E. (1994) *Archaeological Survey of the Kerak Plateau, Conducted During 1978–1982 Under the Direction of J.M. Miller and J.M. Pinkerton*, by J.M. Miller. Reviewed in: *Journal of the American Oriental Society*, 114 (1): 133.

Ayuga, J.G.R., Mozota, F.B., Lopez, R. and Abadia, M.F. (2006) "Application of hyperspectral remote sensing to the Celtiberian city of Segeda," in S. Campana and M. Forte (eds) *From Space to Place: 2nd International Conference on Remote Sensing in Archaeology*, Oxford: British Archaeology Reports.

Badea, A., Reif, A. and Rusdea, E. (2002) "The remote sensing imagery as support of the thematic data within the 'Apuseni' project," in B. Warmbein (ed.) *Proceedings of the Conference Space Applications for Heritage Conservation*, Strasbourg: European Space Agency.

Bailey, D.W., Tringham, R., Bass, J., Stevanovich, M., Hamilton, M., Neumann, H., Angelova, I. and Raduncheva, J. (1998) "Expanding the dimensions of early agricultural tells: Podgoritsa archaeological project," *Journal of Field Archaeology*, 25 (4): 373–96.

Balaji, K., Suresh, L.S., Raghavswamy, V. and Gautam, N.C. (1996) "The use of remote sensing in monitoring changes in and around archaeological monuments: a case study from Hyderabad, Andhara Pradesh," *Man and Environment*, 21 (2): 63–70.

Ballard, R. (2007) "Archaeological oceanography," in J. Wiseman and F. El-Baz (eds) *Remote Sensing in Archaeology*, Interdisciplinary Contributions to Archaeology book series, New York: Springer.

Banks, E.P. (1995) "Remote sensing and the archaeology of the silk road," *Current Archaeology*, 36 (3): 520.

Banning, E.B. (1996) "Highlands and lowlands: problems and survey frameworks for rural archaeology in the Near East," *Bulletin of the American Schools of Oriental Research*, 301: 25–45.

Barasino, E. and Helly, B. (1985) "Remote sensing and archaeological research in Thessaly (Greece) New prospects in 'archaeological landscape,' " in S. Campana and M. Forte (eds) *From Space to Place: 2nd International Conference on Remote Sensing in Archaeology*, Oxford: British Archaeology Reports. *Proceedings of the EARScL/ESA Symposium European Remote Sensing Opportunities* Strasbourg, March 31-April 3, ESA SP-233.

Barcelo, J.A., Forte, M. and Sanders, D.H. (2000) "The diversity of archaeological virtual worlds," in J.A. Barcelo, M. Forte, and D.B. Sanders (eds) *Virtual Reality in Archaeology*, Oxford: Archaeopress.

Barlindhaug, S., Holm-Olsen, M. and Tommervik, H. (2007) "Monitoring archaeological sites in a changing landscape-using multitemporal satellite remote sensing as an early warning method for detecting regrowth processes," *Archaeological Prospection*, 14: 231–44.

Barta, M. and Bruna, V. (2005) "Satellite imaging in the pyramid fields," *Egyptian Archaeology*, 26: 3–6.

Beazeley, G.A. (1919) "Air photography in archaeology," *The Geographical Journal*, 53: 330–5.

Beazeley, G.A. (1920) "Surveys in Mesopotamia during the war," *The Geographical Journal*, 55: 109–23.

Beck, A. (2006) "Google Earth and World Wind: remote sensing for the masses?," *Antiquity*, 80 (308). Online. Available HTTP: <http://antiquity.ac.uk/ProjGall/beck/> (accessed 10 September 2008).

Beck, A., Philip, G., Abdulkarim, M. and Donoghue, D. (2007) "Evaluation of Corona and Ikonos high resolution satellite imagery for archaeological prospection in western Syria," *Antiquity*, 81 (311): 161–75.

Beck, A., Philip, G., Donoghue, D. and Galiatsatos, N. (2002) "Evaluation of integrated high and medium scale satellite imagery to archaeology in semi-arid environments," in B. Warmbein (ed.) *Proceedings of the Conference Space Applications for Heritage Conservation*, Strasbourg: European Space Agency.

Becker, H. (2001) "Duo- and quadro- sensor configuration for high-speed/high-resolution magnetic prospecting with caesium magnetometry," *Magnetic Prospecting in Archaeological Sites*, ICOMOS: Paris, 20–25.

Becker, H. and Fassbinder, J. (1999) "In search of Piramesses – the lost capital of Ramses II in the Nile Delta (Egypt) by caesium magnetometry," *Archaeological Prospection, 6*(4) 108: 146–50.

Becker, H. and Fassbinder, J. (2001) "In search for the city wall of Homer's Troy-development of high-resolution caesium magnetometry, 1992–1994," in K.H. Hemmeter, J.W.E. Fassbinder, W.E. Irlinger, M. Petzet and J. Ziesemer (eds) *Magnetic Prospecting in Archaeological Sites*, Munchen: Lipp Verlag.

Behrens, C. and Sever, T. (eds) (1991) *Applications of Space-age Technology in Anthropology*, Stennis Space Center, MS: NASA.

Belvedere, O., Papa, M.A., Ceraulo, A., Lauro, D. and Burgio, A. (2006) "GIS and Web mapping of S. Leonardo Valley and Alesa Hinterland," in S. Campana and M. Forte (eds) *From Space to Place: 2nd International Conference on Remote Sensing in Archaeology*, Oxford: British Archaeology Reports.

Ben-Dor, E., Portugali, J., Kovachi, M., Shionim, M. and Vinitzki, L. (1999) "Airborne thermal video radiometry and excavation planning at Tel Leviah, Golan Heights, Israel," *Journal of Field Archaeology*, 26 (2): 117–27.

Ben-Dor, E., Kovachi, M., Vinitzki, L., Shionim, M. and Portugali, J. (2001) "Detection of buried ancient walls using airborne thermal video radiometry," *International Journal for Remote Sensing*, 22 (18): 3689–702.

Berry, J. (2003) "Historic Sanborn maps in the digital age: city of New Orleans," *Journal of GIS in Archaeology*, 1: 73–8.

Bertocci, S. and Parrinello, S. (2006) "The Flaminian way in Umbria: an integrated survey project for the study and conservation of the historical, architectural, and archaeological features," in S. Campana and M. Forte (eds) *From Space to Place: 2nd International Conference on Remote Sensing in Archaeology*, Oxford: British Archaeology Reports.

Bevan, A. and Conolly, J. (2002) "GIS, archaeological survey, and landscape archaeology on the Island of Kythera, Greece," *Journal of Field Archaeology*, 29 (1–2): 123–38.

Bewley, R. (2001) "Understanding England's historic landscapes: an aerial perspective," *Landscapes*, 2 (1): 74–84.

Bewley, R. and Raczkowski, W. (2002) (eds) *Aerial archaeology: developing future practice. NATO Science Series*, New York: Springer.

Bewley, R. and Musson, C. (2006) "Culture 2000 project. European Landscapes: past present and future," in S. Campana and M. Forte (eds) *From Space to Place: 2nd International Conference on Remote Sensing in Archaeology*, Oxford: British Archaeology Reports.

Bewley, R., Crutchley, S. and Shell, C. (2005) "New Light on an Ancient Landscape: LIDAR survey in the Stonehenge World," *Antiquity*, 79: 636–47.

Bezori, G., Astori, B. and Guzzetti, F. (2002) "GPS and photogrammetric methodologies for an archaeological survey," in B. Warmbein (ed.) *Proceedings of the Conference Space Applications for Heritage Conservation*, Strasbourg: European Space Agency.

Bhattacharya, A. (2004) "Applications of remote sensing and GIS for locating archaeological sites in quaternary alluvial terrain," in C. Wang (ed.) *International Conference on Remote Sensing Archaeology*, Beijing: Chinese Center for Remote Sensing Archaeology.

Bietak, M. (1975) *Tell el-Dab'a II, der fundort im rahmen einer archaologisch-geographischen untersuchung uber das agyptische Ostdelta*, Vienna: Academie der Wisseschaften.

Bintliff, J. and Snodgrass, A. (1988) "Off-site pottery distributions: a regional and interregional perspective," *Current Anthropology*, 29 (3): 506–13.

Birnbacher, U. and Koudelka, O. (2002) "Available satellite technology for distributing educational programmes," in B. Warmbein (ed.) *Proceedings of the Conference Space Applications for Heritage Conservation,* Strasbourg: European Space Agency.

Blakely, J.A. and Horton, F. (2001) "On site identifications old and new: the example of Tell el-Hesi," *Near Eastern Archaeology,* 64 (1–2): 24–36.

Blank, J.E. (1973) *The Impact of the Natural Sciences on Archaeology,* by T.E. Allibone (ed.) Reviewed in: *American Anthropologist,* 75 (6): 1930–1.

Blom, R., Zairins, J., Clapp, N. and Hedges, G.R. (1997) "Space technology and the discovery of the lost city of Ubar," *1997 IEEE Aerospace Conference Proceedings,* 1: 19–28.

Blom, R.G. (1992) "Space technology and the discovery of Ubar," *Point of Beginning,* August–September: 11–20.

Blom, R.G., Chapman, B., Podest, E. and Murowchick, R. (2000) "Applications of remote sensing to archaeological studies of early Shang civilization in Northern China," *Proceedings of the IGARSS 2000 Geoscience and Remote Sensing Symposium,* 6: 2483–5.

Blom, R.G., Crippen, R.E., Zairns, J. and Hedges, G.R. (2000) "Remote sensing, shuttle radar topographic mapper data, and ancient frankincense trade routes," *Proceedings of the IGARSS 2000 Geoscience and Remote Sensing Symposium,* 6: 2477–9.

Blom, R.G., Crippen, R., Elachi, C., Clapp, N., Hedges, G. and Zarins, J. (2007) "Southern Arabian Desert trade routes, frankincense, myrrh, and the Ubar legend," in J. Wiseman and F. El–Baz (eds) *Remote Sensing in Archaeology,* Interdisciplinary Contributions to Archaeology book series, New York: Springer.

Bloxam, E. and Storemyr, P. (2002) "Old Kingdom basalt quarrying activities at Widan el Faras, northern Fayum deserts," *Journal of Egyptian Archaeology,* 88: 23–36.

Blumberg, D.G. (1998) "Remote sensing of desert dune forms by polarimetric synthetic aperture radar (SAR)," *Remote Sensing of Environment,* 65: 204–216.

Blumberg, D.G., Freilikher, V., Fuks, I., Kaganovskii, Yu., Maradudin, A.A. and Rosenbluh, M. (2002) "Effects of roughness on the retroreflection from dielectric layers," *Waves in Random Media,* 12 (3): 279–292.

Boehler, W., Heinz, G., Qiming, G. and Shenping, Y. (2004) "The progress in satellite imaging and its application to archaeological documentation during the last decade," in C. Wang (ed.) *International Conference on Remote Sensing Archaeology,* Beijing: Chinese Center for Remote Sensing Archaeology.

Bofinger, J., Kurz, S. and Schmidt, S. (2006) "Ancient maps–modern data sets different investigative techniques in the landscape of the Early Iron Age Princely Hill Fort Heuneburg, Baden-Württemberg, Germany," in S. Campana and M. Forte (eds) *From Space to Place: 2nd International Conference on Remote Sensing in Archaeology,* Oxford: British Archaeology Reports.

Bogdanos, M. (2005) "The casualties of war: the truth about the Iraq museum," *American Journal of Archaeology,* 109: 477–526.

Bolten, A., Bubenzer, O. and Darius, F. (2006) "A digital elevation model as a base for the reconstruction of Holocene land-use potential in arid regions," *Geoarchaeology,* 21 (7): 751–62.

Bourgeois, J. and Marc, M. (eds) (2003) *Aerial Photography and Archaeology 2003: A Century of Information,* Gent: Academia Press.

Box, P. (2003) "Safeguarding the Plain of Jars: megaliths and unexploded ordnance in the Lao People's Democratic Republic," *Journal of GIS in Archaeology,* 1: 90–102.

Bradford, J.S.P. (1956) *Mapping Two Thousand Tombs from the Air: How Aerial Photography Plays its Part in Solving the Riddle of the Etruscans,* London: Illustrated London News.

Brand, P. (2001a) "Rescue epigraphy in the Hypostyle Hall, a postscript to 'A forest of columns: the Karnak Great Hypostyle Hall Project', by William J. Murnane," *KMT: A Modern Journal of Ancient Egypt,* 12 (3): 59.

Brand, P. (2001b) "Rescue epigraphy in the Karnak Hypostyle Hall," *Egyptian Archaeology,* 19: 11–13.

Brewer, D., Wenke, R., Isaacson, J. and Haag, D. (1996) "Mendes regional archaeological survey and remote sensing analysis," *Sahara*, 8: 29–42.

Brivio, P.A., Pepe, M. and Tomason, R. (2000) "Multispectral and multiscale remote sensing data for archaeological prospecting in an alpine alluvial plain," *Journal of Cultural Heritage*, 1: 155–64.

Brophy, K. and Cowley, D. (2005) *From the Air: Understanding Aerial Archaeology*, Stroud: The History Press.

Broucke, P.B.F.J. (1999) *Virtual Archaeology: Re-Creating Ancient Worlds*, by Maurizio Forte and Alberto Siliotti and *Marmaria: Le sanctuaire d'Athena a Delphes*, by J. Bommelaer. Reviewed in: *American Journal of Archaeology*, 103 (3): 539–40.

Brunner, U. (1997) "Geography and human settlements in ancient southern Arabia," *Arabian Archaeology and Epigraphy*, 8 (2): 190–202.

Bubenzer, O. and Bolten, A. (2003) "In Egypt, Sudan, and Namibia, GIS helps compare human strategies of coping with arid habitats," *Archnews*, Summer 2003: 13–14.

Bubenzer, O. and Riemer, H. (2007) "Holocene climatic change and human settlement between the central Sahara and the Nile Valley: archaeological and geomorphological results," *Geoarchaeology*, 22 (6): 607–20.

Buettner-Januch, J. (1954) "Use of infrared photography in archaeological work," *American Antiquity*, 20: 84–7.

Bugayevskiy, L. and Snyder, J (1995) *Map Projections: A Reference Manual*, London: Taylor & Francis.

Butzer, K. (1975) "Delta," *Lexikon der Agyptologie*, 1: 1043–52.

Butzer, K. (1976) *Early Hydraulic Civilization in Egypt: A Study in Cultural Ecology,* Chicago: University of Chicago Press.

Butzer, K. (2002) "Geoarchaeological implications of recent research in the Nile Delta," in C.M. van den Brink and T.E. Levy (eds) *Egypt and the Levant: Interrelations from the 4th Through the Early 3rd Millennium BCE*, Leicester: Leicester University Press.

Campana, S. (2002) "High resolution satellite imagery: a new source of information to the archaeological study of Italian landscapes? Case study of Tuscany," in B. Warmbein (ed.) *Proceedings of the Conference Space Applications for Heritage Conservation,* Strasbourg: European Space Agency.

Campana, S. (2007) "Understanding archaeological landscapes: steps towards an improved integration of survey methods in the reconstruction of subsurface sites in South Tuscany," in J. Wiseman and F. El-Baz (eds) *Remote Sensing in Archaeology*, New York: Springer.

Campana, S. and Forte, M. (eds) (2006) *From Space to Place: 2nd International Conference on Remote Sensing in Archaeology*, Oxford: British Archaeology Reports.

Campana, S. and Frezza, B. (2006) "A proposal for the digital storage and sharing of remotely sensed archaeological data," in S. Campana and M. Forte (eds) *From Space to Place: 2nd International Conference on Remote Sensing in Archaeology*, Oxford: British Archaeology Reports.

Campana, S. and Francovich, R. (2005) *Seeing the Unseen. Buried Archaeological Landscapes in Tuscany*, Taylor & Francis, The Netherlands.

Campana, S., Francovich, R. and Marasco, M. (2006) "Remote sensing and ground-truthing of a medieval mound (Tuscany-Italy)," in S. Campana and M. Forte (eds) *From Space to Place: 2nd International Conference on Remote Sensing in Archaeology*, Oxford: British Archaeology Reports.

Campbell, K.M. (1981) "Remote Sensing: Conventional and Infrared Imagery for Archaeologists," *University of Calgary Archaeology Association*, 11: 1–8.

Cantral, R.D. (1975) "A Satellite Perspective of the Yucatan Peninsula," *Proceedings of the Central States Anthropological Society*, 1: 83–94.

Capper, J.E. (1907) "Photographs of Stonehenge as seen from a war balloon," *Archaeologia*, 60: 571.

Carr, T. and Turner, M. (1996) "Investigating regional lithic procurement using multispectral imagery and geophysical exploration," *Archaeological Prospection*, 3: 109–27.

Cashman, J. (2001) "Egypt's new archaeological database," *Archaeology Computing Newsletter*, Spring: 48–9.

Castleford, J. (1992) "Archaeology, GIS and the time dimension: an overview," in G. Lock and J. Moffett (eds) *Computer Applications and Quantitative Methods in Archaeology*, Oxford: Tempus Reparatum.

Caton-Thompson, G. (1929) "Zimbabwe," *Antiquity*, 3: 424–33.

Caton-Thompson, G. (1931) "Kharga Oasis," *Antiquity*, 5: 221–6

Cerasetti, B. and Massino, M. (2002) "The Murghab delta palaeochannel: reconstruction on the basis of remote sensing from space," in B. Warmbein (ed.) *Proceedings of the Conference Space Applications for Heritage Conservation*, Strasbourg: European Space Agency.

Challis, K. (2006) "Airborne laser altimetry in alluviated landscapes," *Archaeological Prospection*, 13 (2): 103–27.

Challis, K. and Howard, A.J. (2006) "A review of trends within archaeological remote sensing in alluvial environments," *Archaeological Prospection*, 13 (4): 231–40.

Challis, K., Howard, A.J., Moscrop, D., Gearey, B., Smith, D., Carey, C. and Thompson, A. (2006) "Using airborne LIDAR intensity to predict the organic preservation of waterlogged deposits," in S. Campana and M. Forte (eds) *From Space to Place: 2nd International Conference on Remote Sensing in Archaeology*, Oxford: British Archaeology Reports.

Challis, K., Priestnall, G., Gardner, A., Henderson, J. and O'Hara, S. (2002) "Corona remotely-sensed imagery in dryland archaeology: the Islamic city of al-Raqqa, Syria," *Journal of Field Archaeology*, 29 (1–2): 139–53.

Changlin, W. and Ning, Y. (2004) "Environmental study and information extraction of archaeological features with remote sensing imagery in arid areas of Western China," in C. Wang (ed.) *International Conference on Remote Sensing Archaeology*, Beijing: Chinese Center for Remote Sensing Archaeology.

Chapman, H. (2006) *Landscape Archaeology and GIS*, Stroud: The History Press.

Chapoulie, R., Martinaud, M., Paillou, P. and Dreuillet, P. (2002) "New airborne synthetic aperture RADAR for a new method of archaeological prospection of buried remains," in B. Warmbein (ed.) *Proceedings of the Conference Space Applications for Heritage Conservation*, Strasbourg: European Space Agency.

Chevallier, R., Fontanel, A., Grau, G. and Guy, M. (1970) "Application of optical filtering to the study of aerial photography," *Photogrammetria*, 26: 17–35.

Chittick, N. (1974) *Kilwa: An Islamic Trading City on the East African Coast. Volume I: History and Archaeology*, Nairobi: British Institute of Eastern Africa.

Chlodnicki, M., Fattovich, R. and Salvatori, S. (1992) "The Italian archeological mission of the C.S.R.L. Venice of the eastern Nile Delta: a preliminary report of the 1987–1988 field seasons," *Cahier de Recherches de l'Institut de Papyrologie et d'Egyptologie de Lille*, 14: 45–62.

Clapp, N. (1996) *The Road to Ubar*, New York: Mariner Books.

Clark, C.D., Garrod, S.M. and Pearson, P. (1998) "Landscape archaeology and remote sensing in Southern Madagascar," *International Journal of Remote Sensing*, 19 (8): 1461–77.

Cleave, R.W.L. (1985) "Satellite mapping and the interpretation of 'false color,' " *The Biblical Archaeologist*, 48 (3): 160–1.

Cline, E. (2007) *From Eden to Exile: Unraveling Mysteries of the Bible*, Washington, DC: National Geographic.

Cole, J., Feder, K, Harrold, F., Eve, R., and Kehoe, A. (1990) "On folk archaeology in anthropological perspective," *Current Anthropology*, 31 (4): 390–4.

Coleman, D.F., Ballard, R.D. and Gregory, T. (2003) "Marine archaeological exploration of the Black Sea," *Proceedings of OCEANS 2003*, 3: 1287–91.

Comer, D. (1999) "Discovering archaeological sites from space: using shuttle radar at Petra, Jordan," *CRM*, 21(5): 9–11.

Comer, D. and Blom, R. (2002) Detection and identification of archaeological sites and features using RADAR data acquired from airborne platform. Online. Available HTTP: <http://airsar.jpl.nasa.gov/documents/workshop2002/papers/N1.pdf> (accessed 4 September 2008)

Comer, D. and Blom, R. (2007) "Detection and identification of archaeological features using synthetic aperture radar (SAR) data collected from airborne platforms," in J. Wiseman and F. El-Baz (eds) *Remote Sensing in Archaeology*, Interdisciplinary Contributions to Archaeology book series, New York: Springer.

Comfort, A. (1997a) *Mission Archeologique de Zeugma, satellite remote sensing and archaeological survey on the Euphrates: remote sensing and archaeological survey on the Euphrates report*, Luxembourg: Comfort, A.

Comfort, A. (1997b) "Satellite remote sensing and archaeological survey on the Euphrates," *Archaeological Computing Newsletter*, 48: 1–8.

Comfort, A. (1997c) "Satellite remote sensing and archaeological survey on the Euphrates," *Aerial Archaeology Research Group News*, 14: 39–46.

Comfort, A. (1998) *Mission Archeologique de Zeugma, satellite remote sensing and archaeological survey on the Euphrates: remote sensing and archaeological survey on the Euphrates report*, Luxembourg: Comfort.

Comfort, A. (1999) *Mission Archeologique de Zeugma, satellite remote sensing and archaeological survey on the Euphrates: remote sensing and archaeological survey on the Euphrates report*, Luxembourg: Comfort.

Comfort, A. and Ergec, R. (2001) "Following the Euphrates in antiquity: north–south routes around Zeugma," *Anatolian Studies*, 51: 19–49.

Comfort, A., Abadie-Reynal, C. and Ergec, R. (2000) "Crossing the Euphrates in antiquity: Zeugma seen from space," *Anatolian Studies*, 50: 99–126.

Conant, F. (1990) "1990 and beyond: satellite remote sensing and ecological anthropology," in Emilio F. Moran (ed.) *The Ecosystem Approach in Anthropology from Concept to Practice*, Ann Arbor: University of Michigan Press.

Condit, H.R. (1970) "The spectral reflectance of American soils," *Photogrammetric Engineering*, 36, 955–66.

Connah, G. and Jones, A. (1983) "Aerial archaeology in Australia," *Aerial Archaeology*, 9: 1–23.

Conolly, J. and Lake, M. (2006) *Geographical Information Systems in Archaeology*, Cambridge Manuals in Archaeology book series, Cambridge: Cambridge University Press.

Conroy, G., Anemone, A., Regenmorter, J. and Addison, A. (2008) "Google Earth, GIS, and the Great Divide: A new and simple method for sharing paleontological data," *Journal of Human Evolution*, 2008, in press.

Conyers, L. (2004) *Ground-Penetrating Radar for Archaeology (Geophysical Methods for Archaeology)*, Lanham, MD: AltaMira Press.

Conyers, L. (2007) "Ground-penetrating radar for archaeological mapping," in J. Wiseman and F. El-Baz (eds) *Remote Sensing in Archaeology*, Interdisciplinary Contributions to Archaeology book series, New York: Springer.

Cooper, F., Bauer, M. and Cullen, B. (1991) Satellite spectral data in archaeological reconnaissance in western Greece, in T.S.C. Behrens (ed.) *Applications of Space-Age Technology in Anthropology*, Stennis Space Center: NASA.

Coutellier, V. and Stanley, D. J. (1987) "Late Quaternary stratigraphy and paleogeography of the eastern Nile Delta," *Marine Geology*, 27: 257–75.

Couzy, A. (1985) "Environmental studies using satellite imagery," *Studies in the History and Archaeology of Jordan*, 2: 287–90.

Cox, C. (1992) "Satellite imagery, aerial photography and wetland archaeology: an interim report on an application of remote sensing to wetland archaeology: the pilot study in Cumbria, England," *World Archaeology*, 24 (2): 249–67.

Crashaw, A. (2001) "Some history of the captured German WWII photography," *Aerial Archaeology Research Group Newsletter*, 22: 45–9.

Crawford, O.G.S. (1923a) "Stonehenge from the air: course and meaning of 'The Avenue'," *Observer*: 13.

Crawford, O.G.S. (1923b) "What air photography means to the future of archaeology," *Christian Science Monitor*: 9.

Crawford, O.G.S. and Keillor, A. (1928) *Wessex from the Air*, London: Clarendon Press.

Custer, J., Eveleigh, T., Klemas, V. and Wells, I. (1986) "Application of LANDSAT Data and synoptic remote sensing to predictive models for prehistoric archaeological sites: an example from the Delaware coastal plain," *American Antiquity*, 51: 572–88.

Darnell, J. (2002) *Theban Desert Road Survey in the Egyptian Western Desert .Volume 1: Gebel Tjauti Rock Inscriptions 1–45 and Wadi el-Hôl Rock Inscriptions 1–45*, Chicago: Oriental Institute Publications.

Davenport, G.C. (2001) "Remote sensing applications in forensic investigations," *Historical Archaeology*, 35 (1): 87–100.

Davidson, D. and Shackley, M. (1985) *Geoarchaeology: Earth Science and the Past,* London: Duckworth.

Davis, J.L. (1993) *Interpreting Space: GIS and Archaeology*, by K.M.S. Allen, S.W. Green and E.B.W. Zubrow. Reviewed in: *American Journal of Archaeology*, 97 (2): 357–9.

Dayalan, D. (2006) "The use of remote sensing and GIS in the management and conservation of heritage properties at the Agra," in S. Campana and M. Forte (eds) *From Space to Place: 2nd International Conference on Remote Sensing in Archaeology*, Oxford: British Archaeology Reports.

De Laet, V., Pulissen, E. and Waelkens, M. (2007) "Methods for the extraction of archaeological features from very high-resolution Ikonos-2 remote sensing imagery, Hisar (Southwest Turkey)," *Journal of Archaeological Science*, 34 (5): 830–41.

De Maeyer, P., Bogaert, P., de Man, J., de Temmerman, L., Gamanya, R., Binard, M. and Muller, F. (2002) "Cartography and land use change of world heritage areas and the benefits of remote sensing and GIS for conservation," in B. Warmbein (ed.) *Proceedings of the Conference Space Applications for Heritage Conservation*, Strasbourg: European Space Agency.

Deegan, A. and Foard, G. (2008) *Mapping Ancient Landscapes in Northamptonshire*, London: English Heritage.

Dengfeng, C. and Dengrong, Z. (2004) "Modeling and rending realistic terrain from photographs," in C. Wang (ed.) *Proceedings of the International Conference for Remote Sensing Archaeology*, Beijing: Center for Remote Sensing Archaeology.

Deo, S.G. and Joglekar, P.P. (1996) "Satellite remote sensing in archaeology," *Man and Environment*, 21 (2): 59–62.

Deroin, J.P. and Verger, F. (2002) "Application of remote sensing to monitor the Mont-Saint-Michel Bay (France): natural and cultural heritage aspects," in B. Warmbein (ed.) *Proceedings of the Conference Space Applications for Heritage Conservation,* Strasbourg: European Space Agency.

Deroin, J.P., Tereygeol, F., Benoit, P., Al-Thari, M., Al-Ganad, I.N., Heckes, J., Hornschuch, A., Peli, A., Pillault, S. and Florsch, N. (2006) "Archaeological remote sensing in Yemen, the Jabali test site: from large scale survey to field investigation," in S. Campana and M. Forte (eds) *From Space to Place: 2nd International Conference on Remote Sensing in Archaeology*, Oxford: British Archaeology Reports.

Deuel, L. (1973) *Flights into Yesterday: The Story of Aerial Archaeology*, Harmondsworth: Penguin.

Dingwall, L., Barratt, G., Fitch, S. and Huckerby, C. (2002) "The use of remotely-sensed imagery in cultural landscape characterization at Fort Hood, Texas," in B. Warmbein (ed.) *Proceedings of the Conference Space Applications for Heritage Conservation,* Strasbourg: European Space Agency.

Dolphin, L., Moussa, A. and Mokhtar, G. (1977) *Applications of Modern Sensing Technology to Egyptology*, Menlo Park: SRI International Radio Physics Laboratory.

Doneus, M. (2001) "Precision mapping and interpretation of oblique aerial photographs," *Archaeological Prospection*, 8: 13–27.

Doneus, M. and Briese, C. (2006a) "Digital terrain modeling for archaeological interpretation within forested areas using full-waveform laserscanning," in M. Ioanides, D. Arnold, F. Niccolucci and K. Mania (eds) *The 7th Symposium on Virtual Reality, Archaeology, and Intelligent Cultural Heritage VAST 2006*, Wellesley, MA: AK Peters.

Doneus, M. and Briese, C. (2006b) "Full-waveform airborne laser scanning as a tool for archaeological reconnaissance," in S. Campana and M. Forte (eds) *From Space to Place: 2nd International Conference on Remote Sensing in Archaeology*, Oxford: British Archaeology Reports.

Donoghue, D.N.M. and Shennan, I. (1987) "Remote sensing of Morton Fen, Lincolnshire: summary of recent work," *Fenland Research*, 4: 46–53.

Donoghue, D.N.M. and Shennan, I. (1988) "The application of multispectral remote sensing techniques to wetland archaeology," in P. Murphy and C. French (eds) *The Exploitation of Wetlands,* Oxford: British Archaeological Reports.

Donoghue, D.N.M., Galiatsatos, N., Philip, G. and Beck, A.R. (2002) "Satellite imagery for archaeological applications: a case study from the Orontes Valley, Syria," in R.H. Brewley and W. Raczkowski (eds) *Aerial Archaeology: Developing Future Practice*, NATO Science book series, vol. 1, Amsterdam: IOS Press.

Dorsett, J., Gibertson, D., Hunt, C. and Barker, G. (1984) "The UNESCO Libyan Valleys survey VIII: image analysis of Landsat data for archaeological and environmental surveys," *Libyan Studies*, 15: 71–80.

Drager, D.L. (1983) "Projecting archaeological site concentrations in the San Juan Basin, New Mexico," in D.L. Drager and T. R. Lyons (eds) *Remote Sensing in Cultural Resource Management,* Washington, DC: National Park Service.

Dubois, J.M.M. (1996) *Archaeology, Volcanism, and Remote Sensing in the Arenal Region. Costa Rica*, by P.D. Sheets and B.R. McKee (eds). Reviewed in: *International Journal of Remote Sensing*, 17 (1): 214–15.

Ebert, J.I. (1976) "Remote sensing within an archaeological research framework: methods, economics, and theory," in T.R. Lyons and R.K. Hitchcock (eds), *Remote Sensing Techniques in Archaeology*, Albuquerqe, NM: Chaco Center, National Park Service, University of New Mexico.

Ebert, J.I. and Blumenschine, R. (1999) "Bones and stones," *GPS World*, 10: 20–29.

Ebert, J.I. and Gutierrez, A. (1979) "Relationships between landscapes and archaeological sites in Shenandoah National Park: a remote sensing approach," *Bulletin of the Association for Preservation Technology*, 11 (4): 69–87.

Ebert, J.I. and Lyons, T.R. (1980a) "Remote sensing in archaeology, cultural resources treatment and anthropology: The United States of America in 1979," *Aerial Archaeology*, 5: 1–19.

Ebert, J.I. and Lyons, T.R. (1980b) "The detection, mitigation, and analysis of remotely-sensed, 'ephemeral' archaeological evidence," in T.R. Lyons and F.J. Mathien (eds) *Cultural Resources Remote Sensing*, Washington, DC: National Park Service.

Ebert, J.I., Lyons, T.R. and Drager, D.L. (1979) "Comments on 'Application of orthophoto mapping to archaeological problems,' " *American Antiquity*, 44 (2): 341–5.

Edeine, B. (1956) "Une méthode praqtique pour la détection aérienne des sites archaéologiques, en particulier par la photographie sur films en coleurs et sur films infrarouges," *Bulletin de la Société Préhistorique Fracaise*, 53: 540–546.

Edwards, A. (1891) *Pharaohs, Fellahs, and Explorers*, London: McIlvane and Co.

Edwards, D.A. and Partridge, C. (1977) *Aerial Archaeology*, London: Aerial Archaeology Foundation.

Eichhorn, B., Hendricks, S., Riemer, H. and Stern, B. (2005) "Desert roads and transport vessels from late Roman-Coptic times in the Eastern Sahara," *Journal of African Archaeology*, 3 (2): 213–239.

Eisenbeiss, H. and Zhang, L. (2006) "Comparison of DSMs generated from mini UAV imagery and terrestrial laser scanner in a cultural heritage application," *International Archives of Photogrammetry, Remote Sensing and Spatial Information Sciences*, 36 (5): 90–6.

Eisenbeiss, H., Lambers, K. and Sauerbier, M. (2006) "Photogrammetric recording of the archaeological site of Pinchango Alto (Peru), using a mini helicopter (UAV)," in A. Figueiredo and G.L. Velho (eds) *The World is in Your Eyes– Proceedings of the 33rd CAA Conference, Tomar, Portugal*, Lisbon: Instituto Portuges de Arquelogia.

Eisenbeiss, H., Lambers, K., Sauerbier, M. and Zhang, L. (2005) "Photogrammetric documentation of an archaeological site (Palpa, Peru) using an autonomous model helicopter," *International Archives of Photogrammetry, Remote Sensing and Spatial Information Sciences*, 34 (5): 238–243.

Elachi, C. (1982) "Radar images of earth from space," *Scientific American*, 247: 46–53.

El-Aref, N (2008) "Home from the range," *Al-Ahram*, 25–31 December 2008 Issue No. 927, online at http://weekly.ahram.org.eg/2008/927/he1.htm, accessed Jan 8th, 2008.

El-Baz, F. (1980) "Narrative of the journey," *The Geographical Journal*, 146 (1): 51–9.

El-Baz, F. (1984) "The desert in the space age," in F. El-Baz (ed.) *Deserts and Arid Lands*, The Hague: Martinus Nijhoff Publishers.

El-Baz, F. (1989) "Monitoring Lake Nasser by space photography," in A. Rango (ed.) *Remote Sensing and Large Scale Global Processes*, Baltimore: International Association of Hydrological Sciences.

El-Baz, F., Robinson, C. and Al-Saud, T.S.M. (2007) "Radar images and geoarchaeology of the eastern Sahara" in J. Wiseman and F. El-Baz (eds) *Remote Sensing in Archaeology*, Interdisciplinary Contributions to Archaeology book series, New York: Springer.

El-Etr, H., Yousif, M. and Dardir, A. (1979) "Utilization of 'Landsat' images and conventional aerial photographs in the delineation of some aspects of the geology of the central eastern desert, Egypt," *Annals of the Geological Survey of Egypt*, 9: 136–62.

El-Gamily, H., Nasr, S. and E-Raey, M. (2001) "An assessment of natural and human-induced changes along Hurgada Ras Abu Soma coastal area, Red Sea," *International Journal of Remote Sensing*, 22: 2999–3014.

El-Ghandour, M. (2003) *New Regulations to Foreign Missions*, Cairo: Egyptian Supreme Council for Egyptian Antiquities, Ministry of Culture, distributed through the American Research Center in Egypt.

El-Raey, M., El-Din, M.S., Khafagy, A. and Zed, A. (1999) "Remote sensing of beach erosion/accretion patterns along Damietta-Port Said shoreline, Egypt," *International Journal of Remote Sensing*, 20: 1087–1106.

El-Raey, M., Frihy, O., Nasr, S. and El-Hattab, M. (1995) "Change detection of Rosetta promontory over the last forty years," *International Journal of Remote Sensing*, 16 (5): 825–34.

El-Rakaiby, M., Ashmawy, M., Yehia, M., and Ayoub, A. (1994) "In-situ reflectance measurements and TM data of some sedimentary rocks with emphasis on white sandstone, southwestern Sinai, Egypt," *International Journal for Remote Sensing*, 15 (18): 3785–97.

Emberling, G. (1996) *Settlement Development in the North Jazira, Iraq: A Study of the Archaeological Landscape*, by T.J. Wilkinson and D.J. Tucker. Reviewed in: *American Antiquity*, 61 (4): 820.

Empereur, J. (2000) *Alexandria rediscovered*, New York: George Braziller.

Engelbach, R. (1929) "The aeroplane and Egyptian archaeology," *Antiquity*, 3 (12): 47–73.

Ernenwein, E.G. and Kvamme, K.L. (2008) "Data processing issues in large-area GPR surveys: correcting trace misalignments, edge discontinuities and striping," *Archaeological Prospection*, 15: 133–49.

Estrada-Belli, F. and Koch, M. (2007) "Remote sensing and GIS analysis of a Maya city and its landscape: Holmul, Guatemala," in J. Wiseman and F. El-Baz (eds), *Remote Sensing in Archaeology*, New York: Springer.

Etaya, M., Sudo, N. and Sakata, T. (2000) "Detection of subsurface ancient Egyptian remains utilizing optical and microwave satellite data," *Proceedings of the IGARSS 2000 Geoscience and Remote Sensing Symposium*, 6: 2480–2.

Evans, D. and Farr, T.G. (2007) "The use of interferometric synthetic aperture radar (InSAR) in archaeological investigations and cultural heritage preservation," in J. Wiseman and F. El-Baz (eds) *Remote Sensing in Archaeology*, Interdisciplinary Contributions to Archaeology book series, New York: Springer.

Evans, D., Pottier, C., Fletcher, R., Helmsley, S., Tapley, I., Milne, A. and Barbetti, M. (2007) "A comprehensive archaeological map of the world's largest preindustrial settlement complex at Angkor, Cambodia," *Proceedings of the National Academy of Sciences of the United States*, 104 (36): 14277–82.

Fagan, B.M. (1989) "The backward-looking curiosity: a glance at archaeology in the year of our Lord 1989," *American Journal of Archaeology*, 93 (3): 445–9.

Failmezger, V. (2001) High resolution aerial color IR, multispectral, hyper-spectral, and SAR imagery over the Oatlands Plantation archaeological site near Leesburg, Virginia," in S. Campana and M. Forte (eds) *Remote Sensing in Archaeology*, Florence: All' Insegna Del Giglio.

Farley, J., Limp, W. and Lockhart, J. (1990) "The archaeologist's workbench: integrating GIS, remote sensing, EDA and database management," in K. Allen, S. Green and E. Zubrow, *Interpreting Space: GIS and Archaeology*, Bristol, PA: Taylor and Francis.

Farrow, J., Becker, F., Allenbach, B. and Clandillon, S. (2002) "Practical remote sensing activities in an interdisciplinary masters-level space course," in B. Warmbein (ed.) *Proceedings of the Conference Space Applications for Heritage Conservation,* Strasbourg: European Space Agency.

Fassbinder, J. and Hetu, R. (1997) "Bibliographic research on aerial archaeology an archaeological prospection," *Aerial Archaeology Research Group News*, 14: 49–51.

Fedick, S.L. and Ford, A. (1990) "The prehistoric agricultural landscape of the central Maya lowlands: an examination of local variability in a regional context," *World Archaeology*, 22 (1): 18–33.

Fedick, S.L., Morrison, B.A., Andersen, B.J., Boucher, S. and Acosta, J.D. (2000) "Wetland manipulation in the Yalahau region of the northern Maya lowlands," *Journal of Field Archaeology*, 27 (2): 131–52.

Ferrarese, F., Mozzi, P., Veronese, F. and Cervo, F. (2006) High resolution DTM for the geo-morphological and geoarchaeological analysis of the city of Padua (Italy)," in S. Campana and M. Forte (eds) *From Space to Place: 2nd International Conference on Remote Sensing in Archaeology*, Oxford: British Archaeology Reports.

Fiennes, R. (1991) *Atlantis of the Sands: The Search for the Lost City of Ur*, London: Bloomsbury.

Fisher, J. and Fisher, B. (1999) "The use of KidSat images in the further pursuit of the frankincense roads to Ubar," *Geoscience and Remote Sensing*, 37 (4): 1841–7.

Fletcher, R. and Evans, D. (2002) "The extent and settlement patterns of Angkor, Cambodia: preliminary results of an AirSAR survey in September 2000," in B. Warmbein (ed.) *Proceedings of the Conference Space Applications for Heritage Conservation,* Strasbourg: European Space Agency.

Folan, W., Marcus, J. and Miller, W.F. (1995) "Verification of a Maya settlement model through remote sensing," *Cambridge Archaeological Journal*, 5 (2): 277–83.

Foley, B. (2008) "Greek Deepwater Survey" *American Journal of Archaeology*, in press.

Forte, M. (1993) "Image processing applications in archaeology: classification systems of archae-ological sites in the landscape," in J. Andressen, T. Madsen and I. Scollar (eds) *Computing the Past: Computer Applications and Quantitative Methods in Archaeology*, Aarhus: Aarhus University Press.

Forte, M. (1998) "Il Progetto Valle del Belice: applicazioni GIS e di remote sensing su dati archeologici," *Archeologia e Calcolatori*, 9: 291–304.

Forte, M. (2000) "Archaeology and virtual micro-topography: the creation of DEMs for reconstructing fossil landscapes by remote sensing and GIS applications," in G. Locke (ed.) *Beyond the Map*, Amsterdam: IOS Press.

Forte, M. (2002) "GIS, aerial photographs and microtopography in archaeology: methods and applications," in R.H. Brewley and W. Raczkowski (eds) *Aerial Archaeology: Developing Future Practice*, NATO Science book series, vol. 1, Amsterdam: IOS Press.

Fowler, M. (1993) "Stonehenge from space," *Spaceflight*, 35: 130–2.

Fowler, M. (1994a) "Danebury and its environs from 830 kilometers," *Hampshire Field Club and Archaeological Society Section Newsletter*, 21: 26–30.

Fowler, M. (1994b) "Ground cover mapping from multispectral satellite imagery," *Aerial Archaeology Research Group News*, 9: 11–19.

Fowler, M. (1994c) "Stonehenge from a new perspective: the detection of archaeological features on multispectral satellite imagery," *Aerial Archaeology Research Group News*, 10: 8–16.

Fowler, M. (1994d) "Satellite image processing for archaeologists," *Archaeological Computing Newsletter*, 39: 2–8.

Fowler, M. (1995a) "High resolution Russian satellite imagery," *Aerial Archaeology Research Group News*, 10: 29–32.

Fowler, M. (1995b) "Detection of archaeological features on multispectral satellite imagery," *Aerial Archaeology Research Group News*, 10: 7–14.

Fowler, M. (1996a) "Declassified intelligence satellite photographs," *Aerial Archaeology Research Group News*, 13: 30–35.

Fowler, M. (1996b) "High resolution satellite imagery in archaeological applications: a Russian satellite photograph of the Stonehenge region," *Antiquity*, 269: 667–71.

Fowler, M. (1997a) "Declassified intelligence satellite photographs—an update," *Aerial Archaeology Research Group News*, 14: 47–8.

Fowler, M. (1997b) "It may not be done well ... but it could be the best that is available," *Aerial Archaeology Research Group News*, 15: 33–5.

Fowler, M. (1999) "High resolution satellite imagery from the Internet," *Aerial Archaeology Research Group News,* 17: 29–32.

Fowler, M. (2004) "The archaeological potential for Kh-7/9 intelligence photographs," *Aerial Archaeology Research Group News*, 26: 11–16.

Fowler, M. and Curtis, H. (1995) "Stonehenge from 230 kilometers," *Aerial Archaeology Research Group News*, 11: 8–16.

Fowler, M. and Darling, P. (1988) "Archaeological applications of imaging radar," *Aerial Archaeology Research Group News*, 16: 14–19.

Fowler, M.J.F. and Fowler, Y.M. (2005) "Detection of archaeological crop marks on declassified Corona KH-4B intelligence satellite photography of southern England," *Archaeological Prospection*, 12 (4): 257–64.

Fowler, W., Estrada-Belli, F., Bales, J., Reynolds, M. and Kvamme, K. (2007) "Landscape archaeology and remote sensing of a Spanish-conquest town: Ciudad Vieja, El-Salvador," in J. Wiseman and F. El-Baz (eds) *Remote Sensing in Archaeology*, Interdisciplinary Contributions to Archaeology book series, New York: Springer.

Franco, L. (1996) "Ancient Mediterranean harbours: a heritage to preserve," *Ocean and Coastal Management*, 30 (2–3): 115–51.

Freeman, A., Hensley, S. and Moore, E. (1999) "Analysis of radar images of Angkor, Cambodia," *Proceedings of the IGARSS 1999 International Geoscience and Remote Sensing Symposium*, 5: 2572–4.

French, C. (2002) *Geoarchaeology in action: studies in soil micromorphology and landscape evolution*, London: Routledge.

Frihy, O., Dewidar, K., Nasr, S. and El-Ray, M. (1998) "Change detections of the northeast Nile Delta of Egypt: shoreline changes, spit evolution, margin changes, of the Manzala lagoon and its islands," *International Journal of Remote Sensing,* 19 (10): 1901–12.

Frihy, O., Nasr, S., El-Hattab, M. and El-Raey, M. (1994) "Remote sensing of beach erosion along Rosetta promontory northwestern Nile delta, Egypt" *International Journal of Remote Sensing*, 15 (8): 1649–60.

Ganzin, N. and Mulama, M. (2002) "Evaluation of forage resources in semi-arid Savannah environments with satellite imagery: contribution to the management of protected areas: a case study on the Nakuru National Park, Kenya (Preliminary Version)," in B. Warmbein (ed.) *Proceedings of the Conference Space Applications for Heritage Conservation*, Strasbourg: European Space Agency.

Garbuzov, G.P. (2003a) "Archaeological investigations and satellite remote sensing," *Rossiiskaia Arkheologiia*, 2: 45–55.

Garbuzov, G.P. (2003b) "The use of space remote sensing for archaeological mapping of the Tarman Peninsula, Russia," *Archaeologia Polona*, 14: 176–7.

Gatsis, I., Pavlopoulos, A. and Parcharidis, I. (2001) "Geomorphological observations and related natural hazards using merged remotely sensed data: a case study in the Corinthos Area (NE Peloponnese, S. Greece)," *Geografiska Annaler. Series A, Physical Geography*, 83 (4): 217–28.

Giddy, L. and Jeffreys, D. (1992) "Memphis 1991," *Journal of Egyptian Archaeology*, 79: 1–11.

Gillion, D.A. (1970) "Use of infrared photography in archaeology," *Colorado Anthropologist*, 2: 13–19.

Given, M., Knapp, A.B., Meyer, N., Gregory, T.E., Kassianidou, V., Noller, J.S., Wells, L., Urwin, N. and Wright, H. (1999) "The Sydney Cyprus Survey Project: an interdisciplinary investigation of long-term change in the North Central Troodos, Cyprus," *Journal of Field Archaeology*, 26 (1): 19–39.

Glueck, N. (1965) *Deities and Dolphins: the Story of the Nabataeans*, New York: Farrar, Straus and Giroux.

Godja, M. (2004) "Aerial archaeology in Central Europe: current state of the Czech project," in C. Wang (ed.) *Proceedings of the International Conference for Remote Sensing Archaeology*, Beijing: Center for Remote Sensing Archaeology.

Going, C. (2002) "A neglected asset. German aerial photography of the Second World War period," in R.H. Bewley and W. Raczowski (eds) *Aerial Photography: Developing Future Practice*, NATO Science Series 1: Life and Behavioural Sciences book series, vol. 337, Amsterdam: IOS Press.

Golchale, P. and Bapat, S. (2006) "Reconstructing the ancient republics (janapadas) of the Indian sub-continent," in S. Campana and M. Forte (eds) *From Space to Place: 2nd International Conference on Remote Sensing in Archaeology*, Oxford: British Archaeology Reports.

Goodchild, R.G. (1950) "Roman Tripolitania: reconnaissance in the desert frontier zone," *The Geographical Journal*, 115: 4–6.

Goodman, D., Schneider, K., Piro, S., Nishimura, Y. and Pantel, A. (2007) "Ground penetrating radar advances in subsurface imaging for archaeology," in J. Wiseman and F. El-Baz (eds) *Remote Sensing in Archaeology*, Interdisciplinary Contributions to Archaeology book series, New York: Springer.

Goossens, R. and Van Ranst, E. (1998) "The use of remote sensing to map gypsiferous soils in the Ismailia Province (Egypt)," *Geoderma*, 87: 47–56.

Goossens, R., de Wulf, A., Bourgeois, J., Gheyle, W. and Willems, T. (2006) "Satellite imagery and archaeology: the example of Corona in the Altai Mountains," *Journal of Archaeological Science*, 33 (6): 745–55.

Gore, P. (2004) "Archaeological site prediction: a multispectral approach," in C. Wang (ed.) *International Conference on Remote Sensing Archaeology*, Beijing: Chinese Center for Remote Sensing Archaeology.

Goskar, T., Carty, A., Cripps, P., Brayne, C. and Vickers, D. (2003) "The Stonehenge Lasershow," *British Archaeology*, 73 (4): 9–15.

Gould, R. (1987) "Archaeological survey by air: a case from the Australian Desert," *Journal of Field Archaeology*, 14 (4): 431–443.

Green, N.E. (1957) "Aerial photographic interpretation and the social structure of the city," *Photogrammetric Engineering*, 23: 89–96.

Gron, O., Aurdal, L., Christensen, F. and Loska, A. (2004) "Mapping and verifying invisible archaeological sites in agricultural fields by means of multi-spectral satellite images and soil chemistry," in C. Wang (ed.) *International Conference on Remote Sensing Archaeology*, Beijing: Chinese Center for Remote Sensing Archaeology.

Gron, O., Christensen, F., Orlando, P., Baarstad, I. and MacPhail, R. (2006) "Hyperspectral and multispectral perspectives on the prehistoric cultural landscape: the ground-truthed chemical character of prehistoric settlement and infrastructure identified from space," in S. Campana and M. Forte (eds) *From Space to Place: 2nd International Conference on Remote Sensing in Archaeology*, Oxford: British Archaeology Reports.

Gumerman, G.J. and Lyons, T.R. (1971) "Archaeological methodology and remote sensing," *Science*, 172 (3979): 126–32.

Gumerman, G.J. and Neely, J.A. (1972) "An archaeological survey of the Tehuacan Valley, Mexico: a test of color infrared photography," *American Antiquity*, 37 (4): 523–7.

Gumerman, G.J. and Schaber, G. (1969) "Infrared scanning images: an archeological application," *Science*, 164 (3880): 712–13.

Gunn, J.D., Folan, W.J. and Robichaux, H.R. (1995) "A landscape analysis of the Candelaria Watershed in Mexico: insights into paleoclimates affecting upland horticulture in the southern Yucatan Peninsula semi-karst," *Geoarchaeology*, 10 (1): 3–42.

Gupta, R.D., Rai, G.K. and Bhaskar, C.B. (2004) "GIS based user interactive system for management of archaeological data of Kaushambi site," in C. Wang (ed.) *International Conference on Remote Sensing Archaeology*, Beijing: Chinese Center for Remote Sensing Archaeology.

Guy, M. (1993) "SPOT and archaeology," *SPOT Magazine* (June): 19–21.

Hadjimitsis, D.G, Themistocleous, K., Ioannides, M. and Clayton, C. (2006) "The registration and monitoring of cultural heritage sites in the Cyprus landscape using GIS and satellite remote sensing," in M. Ioannides, D.B. Arnold, F. Niccolucci and K. Mania (eds) *Proceedings of CIPA/VAST/EG/EuroMed 2006: 37th CIPA International Workshop dedicated on e-Documentation and Standardization in Cultural Heritage*, Aire-la-Ville, Switzerland: Eurographics.

Hafner, K. and Rai, S. (2005) "Governments tremble at Google's bird's-eye view," *New York Times*, 20 December.

Hagerman, J.B. and Bennett, D.A. (2000) "Construction of digital elevation models for archaeological applications," in K.L. Wescott and R.J. Brandon (eds) *Practical Applications of GIS for Archaeologists: A Predictive Modeling Kit*, London: Taylor & Francis.

Hailey, T.I. (2005) "The powered parachute as an archaeological aerial reconnaissance vehicle," *Archaeological Prospection*, 12 (2): 69–78.

Hakobyan, H. and Palmer, R. (2002) "Prospects for aerial survey in Armenia," in R.H. Brewley and W. Raczkowski (eds) *Aerial Archaeology: Developing Future Practice*, NATO Science book series, vol. 1, Amsterdam: IOS Press.

Halkon, P. (2006) "Reconstructing an Iron Age and Roman Landscape- new research in Foulness Valley, East Yorkshire, England," in S. Campana and M. Forte (eds) *From Space to Place: 2nd International Conference on Remote Sensing in Archaeology*, Oxford: British Archaeology Reports.

Hamilton, D. (2007) *Remote Sensing in Archaeology: An Explicitly North American Perspective*, by J.K. Johnson (ed.) Reviewed in: *Archaeological Prospection*, 14: 149–50.

Hamlin, C.L. (1977) "Machine processing of LANDSAT data: an introduction for anthropologists and archaeologists," *MASCA Newsletter*, 13 (1–2): 1–11.

Handwerk, B. (2006) Google Earth satellite maps boost armchair archaeology. Online. Available HTTP: <http://news.nationalgeographic.com/news/2006/11/061107-archaeology.html>.

Hardy, D.D. (1983) "An overview of remote sensing: remote sensing in peat and terrain resource surveys," *Symposium of IPS Commission*, Aberdeen, Scotland.

Harp, E. (ed.) (1975) *Photography in Archaeological Research*, School of American Research Advanced Seminar Seroes, Albuquerque: University of New Mexico Press.

Harp, E.J. (1966) "Anthropology and remote sensing," Bedford, Mass., Office of Aerospace Research, Air Force Cambridge Research Laboratories, Terrestrial Sciences Laboratory.

Harrower, M., McCorriston, J. and Oches, E.A. (2002) "Mapping the roots of agriculture in southern Arabia: the application of satellite remote sensing, global positioning system, and geographic information system technologies," *Archaeological Prospection*, 9 (1): 35–42.

Hassan, F.A. (1997) "The dynamics of a riverine civilization: a geoarchaeological perspective on the Nile Valley, Egypt," *World Archaeology*, 29 (1): 51–74.

Heimlich, R. (2004) "Archaologie aus dem All Satellitenbilder geben Hinweise auf antke Statten Vor neun Jahren gb US-Prasident Clinton Spionagebilder frei- eine Fundgrube fur die Agyptologen," *Kolner Stadt-Anzeiger and Frankfurter Rundschau*, Koln: Frankfurt.

Helly, B., Bravard, J. and Caputo, R. (1992) "La plaine orientale de Thessalie (Grece): mobilite des paysages historiques et evolution tecto-sedimentaire," *Actes du colloque dur l'evolution de paysages historiques dans les pays Mediterraneens*, Colloque de Ravello, 35: 1–90.

Herbich, T. (2003) "Archaeological geophysics in Egypt: the Polish contribution," *Archaeological Polonia*, 41: 13–56.

Hererra, J. H., Trejo, D. and Covarrubias, M. (2002) "The creation of a GIS archaeological site catalogue in Yucatan, Mexico: a tool to preserve its cultural heritage," in B. Warmbein (ed.) *Proceedings of the Conference Space Applications for Heritage Conservation*, Strasbourg: European Space Agency.

Herodotus (2003) *The Histories*, London: Penguin Classics.

Hijazi, J.H. and Qudah, O. (1997) "Use of SPOT satellite data for the mapping of floods in the archaeological site of Petra," *Studies in the History and Archaeology of Jordan*, 6: 51–5.

Hirata, M., Koga, N., Shinjo, H., Fujita, H., Gintzburgery, G. and Mayiazak, A. (2001) "Vegetation classification by satellite image processing in a dry area of north-eastern Syria," *International Journal for Remote Sensing*, 22(4): 507–16.

Hixson, D.R. (2005) "Measuring a Maya metropolis," *Institute of Maya Studies Newsletter*, 34 (1): 1–3.

Hodder, I. and Orton, C. (1976) *Spatial Analysis in Archaeology*, Cambridge: Cambridge University Press.

Hoffman, M.A. (1983) *Remote Sensing: A Handbook for Archaeologists and Cultural Resource Managers*, by T.R. Lyons and T.E. Avery; *Remote Sensing: Practical Exercises on Remote Sensing in Archaeology. Supplement No. 1*, by T.E. Avery and T.R. Lyons; *Remote Sensing: Instrumentation for Non-destructive Exploration of Cultural Resources. Supplement No. 2*, by S.A. Morain and T.K. Budge; *Remote Sensing: Aerial Anthropological Perspectives: A Bibliography of Remote Sensing in Cultural Resource Studies. Supplement No. 3*, by T.R. Lyons, R.K. Hitchcock and W.H. Wills; *Remote Sensing: A Handbook for Archaeologists and Cultural Resource Managers Basic Manual Supplement. Supplement No. 4*, by M. Aikens, W.G. Loy, M.D. Southard and R.C. Hanes; *Remote Sensing: Multispectral Analyses of Cultural Resources: Chaco Canyon and Bandelier national Monument. Supplement No. 5*, by T.R. Lyons (ed.); *Remote Sensing: Archaeological applications of Remote Sensing in the North Central Lowlands. Supplement No. 6*, by C. Baker and G.J. Gumerman; and *Remote Sensing: Aerial and Terrestrial Photography for Archaeologists. Supplement No. 7*, by T.E. Avery and T.R. Lyons. Reviewed in: *American Antiquity*, 48 (1): 203–4.

Hoffman, P. (2001) "Detecting informal settlements from Ikonos images using methods of object oriented image analysis—an example from Cape Town, South Africa," in C. Jurgens (ed.) *Remote Sensing of Urban Areas*, Regensberger: Geographische Schriften.

Holcomb, D. (1992) "Shuttle imaging radar and archaeological survey in China's Taklamakan Desert," *Journal of Field Archaeology*, 19: 129–38.

Holcomb, D. (2002) "Remote sensing and GIS technology for monitoring UNESCO World Heritage Sites: a pilot project," in B. Warmbein (ed.) *Proceedings of the Conference Space Applications for Heritage Conservation,* Strasbourg: European Space Agency.

Holcomb, D. and Shingiray, I.L. (2007) "Imaging radar in archaeological investigations: an image processing perspective," in J. Wiseman and F. El-Baz (eds) *Remote Sensing in Archaeology,* Interdisciplinary Contributions to Archaeology book series, New York: Springer.

Holden, N., Horne, P. and Bewley, R. (2002) "High resolution digital airborne mapping and archaeology," in R.H. Brewley and W. Raczkowski (eds) *Aerial Archaeology: Developing Future Practice,* NATO Science book series, vol. 1, Amsterdam: IOS Press.

Holladay, J.S. (1986) "The stables of ancient Israel: functional determinants of stable construction and the interpretation of pillared building remains of the Palestinian Iron Age," in L.T. Geraty and L.G. Hertt (eds) *The Archaeology of Jordan and Other Studies Presented to Siegfried H. Horn.* Berrien Springs, MI: Andrews University Press.

Holley, G.R., Ritina A., Dalan, P. and Smith, A. (1993) "Investigations in the Cahokia site Grand Plaza," *American Antiquity,* 58 (2): 306–19.

Hritz, C. and Wilkinson, T. (2006) "Using shuttle radar topography to map ancient water channels in Mesopotamia," *Antiquity,* 80: 415–24.

Huadong, G. and Changlin, W. (2004) "Remote sensing archaeology in China: status and progress," in C. Wang (ed.) *International Conference on Remote Sensing Archaeology,* Beijing: Chinese Center for Remote Sensing Archaeology.

Hunt, T. and Lipo, C. (2005) "Mapping prehistoric statue roads on Easter Island," *Antiquity,* 79: 158–68.

Hurcom, S. and Harrison, R. (1998) "The NDVI and spectral decomposition for semi-arid vegetation abundance estimation," *International Journal for Remote Sensing* 19(16): 3109–25.

Hvistedahl, M. (2008, May 23) "The space archaeologists." *Popular Science.* Online. Available HTTP: <http://www.popsci.com/scitech/article/2008-05/space-archaeologists> (accessed 10 September 2008).

Ishwaran, N. and Stone, R.I. (2002) "Heritage learning and data collection: biodiversity and heritage conservation through collaborative monitoring and research," in B. Warmbein (ed.) *Proceedings of the Conference Space Applications for Heritage Conservation,* Strasbourg, France.

James, J. (1995) "Shuttle radar maps ancient Angkor," *Science,* 267 (5200): 965.

Jeffreys, D. (2003) "Introducing 200 years of ancient Egypt: modern history, ancient archaeology," in D. Jeffreys, (ed.) *Views of Ancient Egypt since Napoleon Bonaparte: Imperialism, Colonialism, and Modern Appropriation,* London: UCL Press.

Jeffreys, D. and Tavares, A. (1994) "The historic landscape of Early Dynastic Memphis," *Mitteilungen des Deutschen Archaologischen Instituts Abteilung Kairo,* 50: 143–73.

Jeffreys, D. and Tavares, A. (2001) "An integrated mapping project for the Saqqara plateau and escarpment," in M. Barta and J. Krejc' (eds) *Abusir and Saqqara in the Year 2000.* Archive Orientalni: Praha.

Jennings, J. and Craig, N. (2003) "Using GIS for politywide analysis of Wari imperial political economy," *Journal of GIS in Archaeology,* 1: 33–46.

Jensen, J. (1996) *Introductory Digital Image Processing: A Remote Sensing Perspective,* Upper Saddle River: Prentice Hall.

Jensen, J. (2000) *Remote Sensing of the Environment: An Earth Resource Perspective,* New York: Prentice Hall.

Jingjing, Y.L. (2006) "Applications of remote sensing archaeology technologies in China," in S. Campana and M. Forte (eds) *From Space to Place: 2nd International Conference on Remote Sensing in Archaeology,* Oxford: British Archaeology Reports.

Johnson, A. (2005) *Plane and Geodetic Surveying: The Management of Control Networks,* London: Routledge.

Johnson, G.R. and Platt, R.R. (1930) *Peru from the Air,* London: American Geographical Society.

Johnson, J. (1950) "The Dura air photographs," *Archaeology*, 3: 158–9.

Johnson, J.K. (1996) *Delta Digitizing: GIS and Remote Sensing in Northwest Mississippi. New Methods, Old Problems: Geographic Information Systems in Modern Archaeological Research*, Carbondale, IL: Center for Archaeological Investigations, Southern Illinois University.

Johnson, J.K. (ed.) (2006) *Remote Sensing in Archaeology: An Explicitly North American Perspective*, Tuscaloosa: University of Alabama Press.

Jomard, E.F. (1829) "Description des Antiquities d'Athribis, de Thumis, et de Plusiers nomes du Delta Oriental," in C.L.F. Panckoucke (ed.) *Memoires de Description de l'Egypte IX,* Paris.

Jorde, L.B. and Bertram, J.B. (1976) "Current and future applications of aerospace remote sensing in archaeology: a feasibility study," *Reports of the Chaco Center*, 1: 11–67.

Joyce, C., Fuller, D. and Noel, M. (1992) "Archaeology takes to the skies," *New Scientist*, 133 (1805): 42.

Kamei, M. and Nakagoshi, N. (2002) "Assessing integrity in cultural landscape: a case study from Japan," in B. Warmbein (ed.) *Proceedings of the Conference Space Applications for Heritage Conservation*, Strasbourg: European Space Agency.

Kardulias, P.N. (2002) *The Sydney Cyprus Survey Project: Social Approaches to Regional Archaeological Survey*, by Michael Given and A. Bernard Knapp. Reviewed in: *Journal of Field Archaeology*, 29 (3–4): 483–6.

Karnieli, A., Gabai, A., Ichoku, C., Zaady, E. and Shachak, M. (2002) "Temporal dynamics of soil and vegetation spectral responses in a semi-arid environment," *International Journal for Remote Sensing*, 23 (19): 4073–87.

Kelong, T., Yuqing, W., Qingbo, D., Xiaohu, Z., Dewen, W. and Xinlong, N. (2004) "Remote sensing archaeological research of the first emperor mausoleum in Qin Dynasty (Qinshihuang's Mausoleum)," in C. Wang (ed.) *International Conference on Remote Sensing Archaeology*, Beijing: Chinese Center for Remote Sensing Archaeology.

Kelsey, F. (1927) "Les foules et les livres," *Chronique D'Egypte*, 3: 78–9.

Kemp, B. (1972) "Temple and town in ancient Egypt," in P. Ucko, R. Tringham and G.W. Dimbleby (eds), *Man, Settlement and Urbanism*, London: Duckworth.

Kemp, B. (2005) "Settlement and landscape in the Amarna area in the Late Roman Period," in J. Faiers (ed.) *Late Roman Pottery at Amarna and Related Studies*, London: Egypt Exploration Society.

Kemp, B. and Garfi, S. (1993) *A Survey of the Ancient City of El-'Amarna*, London: Egypt Exploration Society.

Kennedy, A. (1925) *Petra: Its History And Monuments*, London: Country Life.

Kennedy, D. (1995) "Water supply and use in the southern Hauran, Jordan," *Journal of Field Archaeology*, 22 (3): 275–90.

Kennedy, D. (1997) "Roman roads and routes in northeast Jordan," *Levant*, 29: 71–93.

Kennedy, D. (1998) "Declassified satellite photographs and archaeology in the Middle East: case studies from Turkey," *Antiquity*, 72: 553–61.

Kennedy, D. (2002) "Aerial archaeology in the Middle East: the role of the military: past, present ... and future?," in R.H. Brewley and W. Raczkowski (eds) *Aerial Archaeology: Developing Future Practice*, NATO Science book series, vol. 1, Amsterdam: IOS Press.

Kennedy, D. and Bewley, R. (2004) *Ancient Jordan from the Air*, London: Council for British Research in the Levant.

Kenyon, J.L. (1991) *Air Photography and Archaeology*, by D.N. Riley. Reviewed in: *American Antiquity*, 56 (1): 163–4.

Kessler, D. (1981) *Historische Topographie der Region zeischen Mallawi und Samalut. Beihefte zum Tubinger Atlas des Vorderen Orients 30*, Wiesbaden: Wiesbaden Press.

Khawaga, M. (1979) "A contribution to the fractal pattern of the Abu Tartar plateau: Western Desert, Egypt," *Annals of the Geological Survey of Egypt*, 9: 163–71.

Kidder, A.V. (1929) "Air exploration of the Maya country," *Bulletin of the Pan-American Union*, 63: 1200–5.

Kidder, A.V. (1930) "Five days over Maya country," *Scientific Monthly*, 30: 193–205.

Kidder, T. and Saucier, R. (1991) "Archaeological and geological evidence for proto-historic water management in northeast Louisiana," *Geoarchaeology*, 6 (4): 307–35.

Kligman, D.M. (2006) "Teaching and using remote sensing in Argentine archaeology: evaluating the University of Buenos Aires curriculum and the graduation theses of the last decade," in S. Campana and M. Forte (eds) *From Space to Place: 2nd International Conference on Remote Sensing in Archaeology*, Oxford: British Archaeology Reports.

Knapp, A.B. (2000) *Approaches to Landscape*, by Richard Muir. Reviewed in: *Journal of Anthropological Research*, 56 (3): 420–2.

Knisely-Marpole, R. (2001) "Kite aerial photography in Egypt's Western Desert," *Aerial Archaeology Research Group News*, 23: 33–7.

Kouchoukos, N. (2001) "Satellite images and Near Eastern Landscapes," *Near Eastern Archaeology*, 64 (1–2): 80–91.

Krishnamoorthy, R., Bharthi, G.S., Periakali, P. and Ramachandran, S. (2002) "Remote sensing and GIS applications for protection and conservation of World Heritage Site and ecosystems on the coastal zone of Tamil Nadu, India," in B. Warmbein (ed.) *Proceedings of the Conference Space Applications for Heritage Conservation*, Strasbourg: European Space Agency.

Kruckman, L. (1987) "The role of remote sensing in ethnohistorical research," *Journal of Field Archaeology*, 14 (3): 343–51.

Komatsu, G, Olsen, J, Ormö, J, di Achille, G., Kring, D., Matsui, T. (2006) "The Tsenkher structure in the Gobi-Altai, Mongolia: Geomorphological hints of an impact origin," *Geomorphology*, 74, (1–4): 164–180.

Kvamme, K.L. (2007) "Integrating multiple geophysical datasets," in J. Wiseman and F. El-Baz (eds) *Remote Sensing in Archaeology*, Interdisciplinary Contributions to Archaeology book series, New York: Springer.

Kvamme, K.L. (2008) "Archaeological prospecting at the Double Ditch State Historic Site, North Dakota, USA," *Archaeological Prospection*, 15(1): 62–79.

Ladefoged, T.N., McLachlan, S.M., Ross, S.C.L., Sheppard, P.J. and Sutton, D.G. (1995) "GIS-based image enhancement of conductivity and magnetic susceptibility data from Ureturituri Pa and Fort Resolution, New Zealand," *American Antiquity*, 60 (3): 471–81.

Lambers, K., Eisenbaiss, H., Sauerbier, M., Kupferschmidt, D., Gaisecker, T., Sotoodeh, S. and Hanusch, T. (2007) "Combining photogrammetry and laser scanning for the recording and modeling of the Late Intermediate Period Site of Pinchango Alto, Palpa, Peru," *Journal of Archaeological Science*, 34 (10): 1702–12.

Lambert, D.P. (1997) *GPS Satellite Surveying*, by Alfred Leick. Reviewed in: *Annals of the Association of American Geographers*, 87 (2): 401–3.

Lambin, E.F., Walkey, J.A. and Petit-Maire, N. (1995) "Detection of Holocene Lakes in the Sahara using satellite remote sensing," *Photogrammetric Engineering and Remote Sensing*, 61 (6): 731–7.

Landis, K. (2004) "Testing history: 200 years ago, Lewis and Clark mapped the West with crude tools and little technology. How close did they get to the truth? Even NASA wants to know," *Boy's Life*, 94: 30–4.

Lasaponara, R. and Masini, N. (2006a) "Performance evaluation of data fusion algorithims for the detection of archaeological features by using satellite QuickBird data," in S. Campana and M. Forte (eds) *From Space to Place: 2nd International Conference on Remote Sensing in Archaeology*, Oxford: British Archaeology Reports.

Lasaponara, R. and Masini, N. (2006b) "Identification of archaeological buried remains based on the normalized difference vegetation index (NDVI) from QuickBird satellite data," *Geoscience and Remote Sensing Letters*, 3 (3): 325–8.

Lasaponara, R. and Masini, N. (2007) "Detection of archaeological crop marks by using satellite QuickBird multispectral imagery," *Journal of Archaeological Science*, 34 (2): 214–21.

Lawrence, W., Imhoff, M., Kerles, N. and Stutzer, D. (2002) "Quantifying urban land use and impact in Egypt using diurnal imagery of the earth's surface," *International Journal for Remote Sensing*, 23: 3921–37.

Lemmens, J.P.M.M., Stancic, Z. and Verwaal, R.G. (1993) "Automated archaeological feature extraction from digital aerial photographs," in J. Andressen, T. Madsen and I. Scollar (eds) *Computing the Past: Computer Applications and Quantitative Methods in Archaeology: Proceedings of the 20th CAA Conference Held at Aarhus University*, Aarhus: Aarhus University Press.

Lenney, M., Woodcock, C., Collins, J. and Hamdi, J. (1996) "The status of agricultural lands in Egypt: the use of multispectral NDVI features derived from Landsat TM," *Remote Sensing of the Environment*, 56: 8–20.

Lepsius, K. (1859) *Denkmaler aus Aegypten und Aethiopien*, Berlin: Nicolai.

Leucci G. (2002) "Ground penetrating radar survey to map the location of buried structures under two churches," *Archaeological Prospection*, 9: 217–28.

Leucci, G., Negri, S. and Ricchetti, E. (2002) "Integration of high resolution optical satellite imagery and geophysical survey for archaeological prospection in Hierapolis (Turkey)," *Proceedings of the IGARSS 2002 Geoscience and Remote Sensing Symposium*, 4: 1991–3.

Li, X., Ruixia, Y. and Jian, X. (2004) "The remote sensing foundation research into the spatial information of ancient ruins and their numerically emulational conjectures," in C. Wang (ed.) *International Conference on Remote Sensing Archaeology*, Beijing: Chinese Center for Remote Sensing Archaeology.

Lillesand, R., Kiefer, R. and Chipman, J. (2004) *Remote Sensing and Image Interpretation*, New York: John Wiley and Sons.

Limp, W. (1989) *The Use of Multispectral Satellite Imagery in Archaeological Investigations*, Fayetteville: Arkansas Archaeological Survey.

Limp, W. (1992a) Applications of multispectral digital imagery in Southeastern archaeological investigations, in J. Johnson, (ed.), *Method and Theory in Southeastern Archaeology*, Tuscaloosa: University of Alabama Press.

Limp, W. (1992b) *The Use of Multispectral Digital Imagery in Archaeological Investigations*, Arkansas Archaeological Survey Research Series book series, vol. 34, Fayetteville, Arkansas: Kansas Archaeological Survey.

Limp, W. (2000) *Anthropology, Space and Geographic Information Systems*, by Mark Aldenderfer and Herbert D.G. Maschner. Reviewed in: *Journal of Field Archaeology*, 27 (2): 223–6.

Lindbergh, C.A. (1929a) "Colonel and Mrs. Lindbergh aid archaeologists," in *Carnegie Institute Reports*, New York: Carnegie Institute.

Lindbergh, C.A. (1929b) "The discovery of the ruined Maya cities," *Science*, 70, 12–13.

Liu, L., Chen, X., Lee, Y.K., Wright, H. and Rosen, A. (2002) "Settlement patterns and development of social complexity in the Yiluo Region, North China," *Journal of Field Archaeology*, 29 (1–2): 75–100.

Lorenza, H., Hernandez, M.C. and Cuellar, V. (2002) "Selected radar images of man-made underground galleries," *Archaeological Prospection*, 9: 1–7.

Lunden, B. (1985) "Aerial thermography: a remote sensing technique applied to detection of buried archaeological remains at a site in Dalecarlia, Sweden," *Geografiska Annaler. Series A, Physical Geography*, 67 (1–2): 161–6.

Lynott, J. and Wylie, A. (eds) (1995) *Ethics and Archaeology: Challenges for the 1990s*. Washington, DC: Society for American Archaeology.

Lyons, T.R., B.G. Pouls, and Hitchcock, R.K. (1972) "The Kin Bineola irrigation study: An experiment in the use of aerial remote sensing techniques in archaeology," *Proceedings of the Third Annual Conference in Remote Sensing in Arid Lands*. Tuscon: Office of Arid Land Studies, University of Arizona.

MacDonald, R. (1995) "Corona: success for space reconnaissance, a look into the cold war, and a revolution for intelligence," *Photogrammetric Engineering and Remote Sensing*, 61(6): 689–720.

McAdams, R. (1981) *Heartland of Cities: Surveys of ancient settlement and land use on the central floodplain of the Euphrates*, Chicago: University of Chicago Press.

McCauley, J., Schaber, G., Breed, C., Grolier, M., Haynes, C., Issawi, B., Elachi, C. and Blom, R. (1982) "Subsurface valleys and geoarchaeology of the eastern Sahara revealed by shuttle radar," *Science*, 218: 1004–20.

McGovern, P., Sever, T.L., Myers, J.W., Myers, E.E., Bevan, B., Miller, N.F., Bottema, S., Hongo, H., Meadow, R.H., Kuniholm, P.I., Bowman, S.G.E., Leese, M.N., Hedges, R.E.M., Matson, F.R., Freestone, I.C., Vaughan, S.J., Henderson, J., Vandiver, P.B., Thuesen, C.S. and Sease, C. (1995) "Science in archaeology: a review," *American Journal of Archaeology*, 95 (1): 79–142.

McHugh, W., Breed, C., Schaber, G., McCauley, J. and Szabo, B. (1988) "Acheulian sites along the 'Radar rivers,' southern Egyptian Sahara," *Journal of Field Archaeology*, 15: 361–79.

McHugh, W., McCauley, J., Haynes, C., Breed, C. and Schaber, G. (1988) "Paleorivers and geoarchaeology in the southern Egyptian Sahara," *Geoarchaeology*, 3 (1): 1–40.

McHugh, W., Schaber, G., Breed, C. and McCauley, J. (1989) "Neolithic adaptation and the Holocene functioning of Tertiary palaeodrainages in southern Egypt and northern Sudan," *Antiquity*, 63: 320–36.

McKinley, A.C. (1921) *Photos of the Cahokia Mounds. Exploration and fieldwork of the Smithsonian Institution in 1921*, Washington, DC: Smithsonian Institution.

McManus, K., Donoghue, D., Brooke, C. and Marsh, S. (2002) "Airborne thermography of the vegetation-soil interface for detecting shallow ground disturbance," in B. Warmbein (ed.) *Proceedings of the Conference Space Applications for Heritage Conservation,* Strasbourg: European Space Agency.

Madry, S. and Crumley, C. (1990) "An application of remote sensing and GIS in a regional archaeological settlement pattern analysis: the Arroux River Valley, Burgundy, France," in K. Allen, S. Green and E. Zubrow (eds) *Interpreting Space: GIS and Archaeology*, Bristol, PA: Taylor and Francis.

Mahanta, H.C. (1999) "Applications of satellite remote sensing in archaeological research," *Bulletin of the Department of Anthropology, Dibrugarh University*, 27: 46–60.

Marcolongo, B. and Bonacossi, D.M. (1997) "L'abandon du systeme d'irrigation qatabanite dans la vallee du wadi Bayhan (Yemen): analyse geo-archeologique," *Comptes Rendus de l'Academie des Sciences—Series IIA—Earth and Planetary Science*, 325 (1): 79–86.

Marcolongo, B., Ninfo, A. and Simone, M. (2006) "'Valle d'Agredo': a paleoenvironmental and geoarchaeological reconstruction based on remote sensing analysis," in S. Campana and M. Forte (eds) *From Space to Place: 2nd International Conference on Remote Sensing in Archaeology*, Oxford: British Archaeology Reports.

Martinez-Navarrete, M.I., J. Vincent-Garcia, P. Lopez-Garcia, J. Lopez-Saez, I Zavala-Morencos, and P. Diaz Del Rio, "Metallurgy at Kargaly and reconstruction of environment," *Rossijskaâ Arheologiâ*, 4: 84–91.

Martini, P.R. and Souza, I.M. (2002) "Satellite remote sensing as a tool to monitor Indian reservation in the Brazilian Amazonia," in B. Warmbein (ed.) *Proceedings of the Conference Space Applications for Heritage Conservation,* Strasbourg: European Space Agency.

Masini, N. and Lasaponara, R. (2006a) "Evaluation of the spectral capability of QuickBird imagery for the detection of archaeological buried remains," in S. Campana and M. Forte (eds) *From Space to Place: 2nd International Conference on Remote Sensing in Archaeology*, Oxford: British Archaeology Reports.

Masini, N. and Lasaponara, R. (2006b) "Investigating the spectral capability of QuickBird data to detect archaeological remains buried under vegetated and not vegetated areas," *Journal of Cultural Heritage*, 8 (1): 53–60.

Masini, N. and Lasaponara, R. (2007) "Satellite-based recognition of landscape archaeological features related to ancient human transformation," *Journal of Geophysics and Engineering*, 3: 230–5.

Master, S. and Woldai, T. (2004) *The Umm Al-Binni Structure in the Mesopotamian Marshlands Of Southern Iraq, as a Postulated Late Holocene Meteorite Impact Crater: Geological Setting and New Landsat ETM+ and Aster Satellite Imagery*, Johannesburg: University of Witwatersrand, Economic Geology Research Institute (EGRI).

Mathys, T. (1997) "The use of declassified intelligence satellite photographs to map archaeological sites and surrounding landscape in the upper Syrian Jezira region," in *International Symposium on Remote Sensing Applications in Archaeology*, Minneapolis: St. Cloud State University.

Meats, C. (1996) "An appraisal of the problems involved in the three-dimensional ground penetrating radar imaging of archaeological features," *Archaeometry*, 38: 359–81.

Meats, C. and Tite, M. (1995) "A ground penetrating radar survey at Rowbury Copse Banjo enclosure," *Archaeological Prospection,* 2(4): 229–236.

Menze, B.H., Ur, J.A. and Sherratt, A.G. (2006) "Detection of ancient settlement mounds: archaeological survey based on the SRTM terrain model," *Photogrammetric Engineering and Remote Sensing*, 72: 321–7.

Merola, P., Allegrini, A., Guglietta, D. and Sampieri, S. (2006) "Using vegetation indices to study archaeological areas," in S. Campana and M. Forte (eds) *From Space to Place: 2nd International Conference on Remote Sensing in Archaeology*, Oxford: British Archaeology Reports.

Mindell, D. (2007) "Precision navigation and remote sensing for underwater archaeology," in J. Wiseman and F. El-Baz (eds) *Remote Sensing in Archaeology*, Interdisciplinary Contributions to Archaeology book series, New York: Springer.

Montufo, A. (1997) "The use of satellite imagery and digital image processing in landscape archaeology, a case study from the Island of Mallorca, Spain," *Geoarchaeology*, 12: 71–85.

Moore E. and Freeman, A. (1997) "Radar, scattering mechanisms and the ancient landscape of Angkor," *Remote Sensing Society Archaeology Special Interests Group Newsletter*, 1: 15–19.

Moore, E. (1989) "Water management in early Cambodia: evidence from aerial photography," *The Geographical Journal*, 155 (2): 204–14.

Moore, E., Freeman, T. and Hensley, S. (1998) "Circular sites at Angkor: a radar scattering model," *Journal of the Siam Society*, 85 (1–2): 107–19.

Moore, E., Freeman, T. and Hensley, S. (2007) "Spaceborne and airborne radar at Angkor: introducing new technology to the ancient site," in J. Wiseman and F. El-Baz (eds) *Remote Sensing in Archaeology*, Interdisciplinary Contributions to Archaeology book series, New York: Springer.

Morozova, G.S. (2005) "A review of Holocene avulsions of the Tigris and Euphrates Rivers and possible effects on the evolution of civilizations in Lower Mesopotamia" *Geoarchaeology*, 20 (4): 401–23.

Moshier, S. and El-Kalani, A. (2008) "Late Bronze Age paleogeography along the ancient Ways of Horus in Northwest Sinai, Egypt," *Geoarchaeology*, 23 (4): 450–73.

Moussa, A., Dolphin, L. and Mokhtar, G. (1977) *Applications of Modern Sensing Technology to Egyptology*, Menlo Park: SRI International.

Mumford, G. (2002) "Reconstructing the ancient settlement at Tell Tebilla (East Delta)," *Bulletin of the American Research Center in Egypt*, 182: 18–23.

Mumford, G. (2003) "Reconstruction of the temple at Tell Tebilla (East Delta)," in G. Knoppers and A. Hirsh (eds) *Egypt, Israel and the Ancient Mediterranean World: Studies in Honour of Donald B. Redford*, Leiden: Brill.

Mumford, G. and Parcak, S. (2002) "Satellite imagery analysis and new fieldwork in South Sinai, Egypt (El-Markha Plain)," *Antiquity*, 76 (4): 953–4.

Mumford, G. and Parcak, S. (2003) "Pharaonic ventures into South Sinai: El-Markha Plain Site 346," *Journal of Egyptian Archaeology*, 89: 83–116.

Mumford, G., Pavlish, L. and D'Andrea, C. (2003) "Geotechnical survey at Tell Tabilla, north-eastern Nile Delta, Egypt," in Z. Hawass (ed.) *Egypiology at the Dawn of the Twenty-First Century: History, Religion: Proceedings of the Eighth International Congress of Egyptologists, Cairo, 2000*, Cairo: The American University in Cairo Press.

Myers, J.W. (1989) "Science in archaeology: a review," *American Journal of Archaeology*, 93 (4): 599.

NASA (2005) "NASA Worldwind forums> Worldwind v Google Earth Beta," in NASA (ed.) *NASA Worldwind Forums*, NASA.

Nashef, K. (1990) "Archaeology in Iraq," *American Journal of Archaeology*, 94 (2): 259–89.

Nashef, K. (1992) "Archaeology in Iraq," *American Journal of Archaeology*, 96 (2): 313–23.

Niknami, K.A. (2004) "Application of remote sensing and geographic information (GIS) for the study of prehistoric archaeological site locations: case study from Garrangu River Basin, northwestern, Iran," in C. Wang (ed.) *International Conference on Remote Sensing Archaeology*, Beijing: Chinese Center for Remote Sensing Archaeology.

Okayasu, T., Muto, M., Jamsran, U. and Takeuchi, K. (2007) "Spatially Heterogeneous Impacts on Rangeland after Social Systems Change in Mongolia," *Land Degradation and Development*, 18 (5): 555–66.

Okin, G., Roberts, D., Murray, B. and Okin, W. (2001) "Practical limits on hyperspectral veg-etation discrimination in arid and semi-arid environments," *Remote Sensing of the Environment*, 77 (2): 212–25.

Orton, C. (2000) *Sampling in Archaeology*, Cambridge: Cambridge University Press.

Ostir, K. and Nuninger, L. (2006) "Paleorelief detection and modeling: a case of study in eastern Laguedoc (France)," in S. Campana and M. Forte (eds) *From Space to Place: 2nd International Conference on Remote Sensing in Archaeology*, Oxford: British Archaeology Reports.

Ostir, K., Kokalj, Z. and Sprajc, I. (2006) "Application of remote sensing in the detection of maya archaeological sites in South-Eastern Campeche, Mexico," in S. Campana and M. Forte (eds) *From Space to Place: 2nd International Conference on Remote Sensing in Archaeology*, Oxford: British Archaeology Reports.

Owen, G. (1993) "Looking down at Amarna," *Aerial Archaeology Research Group News*, 6: 33–7.

Palmer, R. (1978) "Computer transcriptions from air photographs: an explanation," *Aerial Archaeology* 2: 5–8.

Palmer, R. (1993) "Remote sensing and archaeology," *Aerial Archaeology Research Group News*, 7: 18–19.

Palmer, R. (1995) "Integration of air photo interpretation and field survey projects," *Archaeological Prospection*, 2: 167–76.

Palmer, R. (2002a) "A poor man's use of Corona images for archaeological survey," in Armenia in B. Warmbein (ed.) *Proceedings of the Conference Space Applications for Heritage Conservation*, Strasbourg: European Space Agency.

Palmer, R. (2002b) "Air photo interpretation and mapping to guide fieldwork in commer-cial archaeology in England," in R.H. Brewley and W. Raczkowski (eds) *Aerial Archaeology: Developing Future Practice*, NATO Science book series, vol. 1, Amsterdam: IOS Press.

Parcak, S. (2003) "New methods for archaeological site detection via satellite image analysis: case studies from Sinai and the Delta," *Archaeologia Polonia*, 41: 243–5.

Parcak, S. (2004a) "Egypt's Old Kingdom 'Empire'(?): A case study focusing on South Sinai," in A. Hirsch and G. Knoppers (eds) *Egypt, Israel and the Ancient Mediterranean World: Studies in Honour of Donald B. Redford*, Leiden: Brill.

Parcak, S. (2004b) "Finding new archaeological sites in Egypt using satellite remote sensing: case studies from Middle Egypt and the Delta, in C. Wang (ed.) *International Conference on Remote Sensing Archaeology*, Beijing: Chinese Center for Remote Sensing Archaeology.

Parcak, S. (2004c) "Satellite Remote Sensing Resources for Egyptology," *Gottinger Mitzellen*, 198: 63–78.

Parcak, S. (2005) "Satellites and Survey in Middle Egypt," *Egyptian Archaeology*, 29: 28–32.

Parcak, S. (2007a) "Going, going, gone: towards a satellite remote sensing methodology for monitoring archaeological tell sites under threat in the Middle East," *Journal of Field Archaeology*, 42: 61–83.

Parcak, S. (2007b) "The Middle Egypt Survey Project: 2005/6 season report," *Journal of Egyptian Archaeology*, 92: 3–8.

Parcak, S. (2008) "Survey in Egyptology," in R. Wilkinson (ed.) *Egyptology Today*, Cambridge: Cambridge University Press.

Parcak, S. (2009) "The skeptical remote senser," in S. Ikram and A. Dodson (eds) *Beyond the Horizon: Studies in Egyptian Art, Archaeology and History in Honour of Barry J. Kemp,* Cairo: American University in Cairo Press.

Parker, A.G., Preston, G., Walkington, H. and Hodson, M.J. (2006) "Geomorphological and geoarchaeological studies from the lower gulf region of southeastern Arabia are increasing our knowledge of hydrological, ecological, and aeolian changes during the Holocene. Preliminary analyses of sediment records from two palaeolakes," *Arabian Archaeology and Epigraphy*, 17 (2): 125–130.

Parrington, M. (1983) "Remote Sensing," *Annual Review of Anthropology*, 12: 105–124.

Parry, J. (1992) "The Investigative role of Landsat TM in the examination of pre- and proto-historic water management sites in Northeast Thailand," *Geocarto International*, 4: 5–24.

Parssinen, M., Salo, J. and Rasanen, M. (1996) "River floodplain relocations and the abandonment of aborigine settlements in the Upper Amazon Basin: a historical case study of San Miguel de Cunibos at the Middle Ucayalia River," *Geoarchaeology*, 11 (4): 345–59.

Pavlish, L. (2004) "Archaeometry at Mendes, 1990–2002," in G. Knoppers and A. Hirsh (eds) *Egypt, Israel and the Ancient Mediterranean World: Studies in Honour of Donald B. Redford*, Leiden: Brill.

Pavlish, L., Weeks, K. and D'Andrea, C. (2004) "Forthcoming Results of a magnetic survey over the remains of the Mortuary Temple of Amenophis I and surrounding environs," in H. Kars and E. Burke (eds) *Proceedings of the 33rd International Symposium on Archaeometry, April 22–26, 2002,* Geoarchaeological and bioarchaeological studies book series, vol. 3, Amsterdam: Institute for Geo- and Bioarchaeology, Vrije Universiteit.

Peacock, D. (1993) "The site of Myos Hormos: a view from space," *Journal of Roman Archaeology* 6: 226–32.

Peebles, C.S. (2007) Review of *Remote sensing in archaeology: an explicitly North American perspective*, University of Alabama Press: Tuscaloosa, in *Choice*, 44 (10): 1798.

Peter, N. (2002) "Supporting environmental treaties with remote sensing data: an example of the application of a multilateral environmental agreement: The Kyoto Protocol," in B. Warmbein (ed.) *Proceedings of the Conference Space Applications for Heritage Conservation*, Strasbourg: European Space Agency.

Peterman, G.L. (1992) "Geographic Information Systems: Archaeology's Latest Tool," *The Biblical Archaeologist*, 55 (3): 162–7.

Philip, G., Beck, A. and Donoghue, D. (2002) "The contribution of satellite imagery to archaeological survey: an example from western Syria," in B. Warmbein (ed.) *Proceedings of the Conference Space Applications for Heritage Conservation*, Strasbourg: European Space Agency.

Philip, G., Jabour, F., Beck, A., Bshesh, M., Kirk, A. and Grove, J. (2002) "Settlement and landscape development in the Homs Region, Syria: research questions, preliminary results 1999–2000 and future potential," *Levant*, 34: 1–23.

Piovan, S., Peretto, R. and Mozzi, P. (2006) "Palaeohydrogrpahy and ancient settlements in the Adige River Plain, between Rovigo and Adria (Italy)," in S. Campana and M. Forte (eds) *From Space to Place: 2nd International Conference on Remote Sensing in Archaeology*, Oxford: British Archaeology Reports.

Piro, S. and Capanna, M.C. (2006) "Multimethodological approach to study the archaeological park of Maalga Karthago (Tunis) using remote sensing, archaeology, and geophysical prospecting methods," in S. Campana and M. Forte (eds) *From Space to Place: 2nd International Conference on Remote Sensing in Archaeology*, Oxford: British Archaeology Reports.

Poidebard, A. (1929) *Les Révélations archéologiques de la Photographie aérienne-une nouvelle méthode de Recherches et d'observations en région de Steppe*, Paris: Editions Plon.

Poidebard, A. (1931) Sur les traces de Rome-exploration archéologique aérienne en Syria, *L'illustration*.

Poidebard, A. (1934) *La trace de Rome dans le desert de Syrie*, Paris: Paul Geunther.

Posnansky, M. (1982) "African archaeology comes of age," *World Archaeology*, 13 (3): 345–58.

Pope, K. and Dahlin, B. (1989) "Ancient Maya wetland agriculture: new insights from ecological and remote sensing research," *Journal of Field Archaeology*, 16: 87–106.

Pope, K.O., Dahlin, B.H. and Adams, R.E.W. (1993) "News and short contributions," *Journal of Field Archaeology*, 20 (3): 379–83.

Pottier, C. (2002) "Mapping Angkor, for a new appraisal of the Angkor region," in B. Warmbein (ed.) *Proceedings of the Conference Space Applications for Heritage Conservation*, Strasbourg: European Space Agency.

Pouls, B.G., Lyons, T.R. and Ebert, J. (1976) "Photogrammetric mapping and digitization of prehistoric architecture: techniques and applications in Chaco Canyon National Monument," in T.R. Lyons (ed.) *Remote Sensing Experiments in Cultural Resource Studies: Non-Destructive Methods of Archaeological Exploration, Survey, and Analysis*, Albuquerqe: National Park Service, University of New Mexico.

Powesland, D. (2006) "Redefining past landscapes: 30 years of remote sensing in the Vale of Pickering," in S. Campana and M. Forte (eds) *From Space to Place: 2nd International Conference on Remote Sensing in Archaeology*, Oxford: British Archaeology Reports.

Powesland, D., Lyall J. and Donoghue, D. (1997) "Enhancing the record through remote sensing: the application and integration of multi-sensor, non-invasive remote sensing techniques for the enhancement of the sites and monuments record. Heslerton Parish Project, N. Yorkshire, England," *Internet Archaeology*, 2. Online. Available HTTP: <http://intarch.ac.uk/journal/issue2/pld_toc.html> (accessed 10 September 2008).

Powesland, D., Lyall, J., Hopkinson, G., Donoghue, D., Beck, B., Harte, A. and Stott, D. (2006) "Beneath the sand–remote sensing, archaeology, aggregates, and sustainability: a case study from Heslerton, the Vale of Pickering, North Yorkshire, U.K," *Archaeological Prospection*, 13 (4): 291–9.

Pursell, C. (1991) "Preservation technologies: as answers get easier, questions remain hard," *The Public Historian*, 13 (3): 113–16.

Qingjiu, T. and Jianqiu, H. (2004) "Hyperspectral Remote Sensing Archaeology for Shell Mound Site in Jiangsu," in C. Wang (ed.) *International Conference on Remote Sensing Archaeology*, Beijing: Chinese Center for Remote Sensing Archaeology.

Rabeil, T., Mering, C. and Ramousse, R. (2002) "Using GIS and remote sensing in the management of protected areas in West Africa; the example of the W National Park in Niger," in B. Warmbein (ed.) *Proceedings of the Conference Space Applications for Heritage Conservation*, Strasbourg: European Space Agency.

Rajamanickam, M., Chandrasekar, N. and Saravanan, S. (2004) "GIS–Based Shoreline Change Detection Between Kallar and Vembar Coast," in C. Wang (ed.) *International Conference on Remote Sensing Archaeology*, Beijing: Chinese Center for Remote Sensing Archaeology.

Ramasamy, S.M., Venkatasubramanian, V., Abdullah, S.R. and Balaji, S. (1992) "The Phenomenon of River Migration in Northern Tamil Nadu: Evidence from Satellite Data, Archaeology, and Tamil Literature," *Man and Environment*, 7 (1): 13—26.

Rapp, G. and Hill, C. (1998) *Geoarchaeology: The Earth-Science Approach to Archaeological Interpretation*, New Haven: Yale University Press.

Rapp, Jr., G. (1975) "The geologist," *Journal of Field Archaeology*, 2 (3): 229–37.

Rawson, J. (1996) "Sculpture for tombs and temples," in J. Rawson (ed.) *The British Museum Book of Chinese Art*, New York: Thames and Hudson.

Rees, L.W.B. (1929) "The Transjordan Desert," *Antiquity*, 3: 389–407.

Reindel, M., Cuadrado, J. and Lambers, K. (2006) "Altares en el desierto: Las estructuras de piedra sobre los geoglifos Nasca en Palpa". *Arqueología y Sociedad*, 17, 179–222.

Renfrew, C. and Bahn, P. (2000) *Archaeology: Theories, Method, and Practice*, New York: Thames and Hudson.

Renfrew, C., Dixon, J. and Cann, J. (1966) "Obsidian and Early Cultural Contact in the Near East," *Proceedings of the Prehistoric Society*, 32: 30–72.

Richardson, B. and Hritz, C. (2007) "Remote sensing and GIS use in the archaeological analysis of the central Mesopotamian Plain," in J. Wiseman and F. El-Baz (eds) *Remote Sensing in Archaeology*, Interdisciplinary Contributions to Archaeology book series, New York: Springer.

Riccetti, E. (2001) "Remotely Sensed and Geophysical Data for Nondestructive Archaeological Prospection," *Proceedings of the IGARSS 2001 Geoscience and Remote Sensing Symposium*, 7: 3084–6.

Riccetti, E. (2004) "Application of Optical High Resolution Satellite Imagery for Archaeological Prospection over Hieropolis (Turkey)," *Proceedings of the IGARSS 2004 Geoscience and Remote Sensing Symposium*, 6: 3898–901.

Riley, D. (1982) *Aerial Archaeology in Britain*, Princes Risborough, Buckinghamshire: Shire.

Riley, D. (1992) "Aerial Photography in Israel," *Current Archaeology*, 136: 139–142.

Risbol, O., Gjersten, A.K. and Skare, K. (2006) "Airborne laser scanning of cultural remains in forests: some preliminary results from a Norwegian project," in S. Campana and M. Forte (eds) *From Space to Place: 2nd International Conference on Remote Sensing in Archaeology*, Oxford: British Archaeology Reports.

Rizzo, E., Chianese, D., Lapenna, V. and Piscitelli, S. (2003) Integration of Magnetometric, GPR, and Geoelectric Measurements Applied to the Study of the New Viggiano Archaeological Site (Southern Italy), *Geophysical Research Abstracts*, 5: 02111.

Roberts, A. (1990) *An Analysis of Classic Lowland Maya Burials*, by W.B.M. Welsh. Reviewed in: *American Antiquity*, 55 (2): 440–1.

Robinson, C. (2002) "Application of satellite radar data suggests that the Kharga Depression in southwestern Egypt is a fracture rock aquifer," *International Journal of Remote Sensing*, 23 (19): 4101–14.

Romano, D.D and Schoenbrun, B.C. (1993) "A Computerized Architectural and Topographical Survey of Ancient Corinth," *Journal of Field Archaeology*, 20 (2): 177–190.

Roosevelt, A.C. (2007) "Geophysical Archaeology in the Lower Amazon: A Research Strategy," in J. Wiseman and F. El-Baz (eds) *Remote Sensing in Archaeology*, Interdisciplinary Contributions to Archaeology book series, New York: Springer.

Rossi, C and Ikram S. (2002) "Surveying the North Kharga Oasis," *KMT*, 13 (4): 72–9.

Roughley, C. (2001) "Understanding the Neolithic landscape of the Carnac region: a GIS approach," in Z. Stancic and T. Veljanovski (eds), *Proceedings of the Computer Applications and Quantitative Methods in Archaeology Conference*, BAR International Series 931, Oxford, Archaeopress.

Roughley, C. (2002) "Les monuments de Bougon, partie integrante du paysage," in J.P. Mohen and C. Scarre (eds), *Les Tumulus de Bougon: Complexe Megalithique du Ve au IIIe Millenaire*, Paris: Errance.

Roughley, C. (2004) "Views of Carnac: applications of visibility analysis and dynamic visualisation for understanding the Neolithic monuments of Southern Brittany," *Internet Archaeology*, 16. Online. Available HTTP: <http://intarch.ac.uk/journal/issue16/roughley_index.html> (accessed 8 September 2008).

Roughley, C., Sherratt, A. and Shell, C.A. (2002) "Past records new views: Carnac 1830–2000," *Antiquity*, 76 (291): 218–23; reprinted in T.C. Darvill and C. Malone (eds) (2003) *Megaliths from Antiquity*, Colchester: Antiquity Publications.

Rowlands, A. and Sarris, A. (2007) "Detection of exposed and subsurface archaeological remains using multi-sensor remote sensing," *Journal of Archaeological Science*, 34 (5): 795–803.

Rowlands, A., Sarris, A. and Bell, J. (2006) "Airborne multi-sensor remote sensing of exposed and subsurface archaeological remains at Itanos and Roussolakkos, Crete," in S. Campana and M. Forte (eds) *From Space to Place: 2nd International Conference on Remote Sensing in Archaeology*, Oxford: British Archaeology Reports.

Said, R. (1988) *Geological Evolution of the Nile Valley*, New York: Springer.

Said, R. (1990) *The River Nile: Geology, Hydrology, and Utilization*, New York: Pergamon Press.

Salem, B., El-Cibahy, A. and El-Raey, M. (1995) "Change detection of land cover classes in agro-ecosystems of northern Egypt by remote sensing," *International Journal of Remote Sensing*, 16(14): 2581–94.

Sarris, A. (2005) "Use of remote sensing for archaeology: state of the art," *Proceedings of the International Conference on the Use of Space Technologies for the Conservation of Natural and Cultural Heritage*, Campeche, Mexico.

Sarris, A. and Jones, R. (2000) "Geophysical and related techniques applied to archaeological survey in the Mediterranean: a review," *Journal of Mediterranean Archaeology*, 13 (1): 3–75.

Sarris, A., Dunn, R.K., Rife, J.L., Papadopoulos, N., Kokkinou, E. and Mundigler, C. (2007) "Geological and geophysical investigations in the Roman cemetery at Kenchreai (Korinthia), Greece," *Archaeological Prospection*, 14 (1): 1–23.

Sarris, A., Topouzi, S., Chatziiordanou, E., Liu, J. and Xu, L. (2002) "Space technologies in archaeological research and CRM of semi-arid and desertification affected regions: examples from China and Greece," in B. Warmbein (ed.) *Proceedings of the Conference Space Applications for Heritage Conservation*, Strasbourg: European Space Agency.

Sarris, A., Vafidis A., Mertikas S., Guy M., Vrontaki E., Manakou M. and Kalpaxis T. (1998) "Ancient Itanos (Erimoupolis, Lasithi): an archaeological site as a remote sensing laboratory," *Proceedings of the 31st International Symposium of Archaeometry, 1998, Budapest, Hungary*, Oxford: British Archaeological Reports.

Sarris, A., Weymouth J., Cullen B., Stein C. and Wiseman J.T. (1996) "The Nikopolis Project – integration of geophysical prospection, satellite remote sensing, and GIS techniques in the study of Epirus, Greece," *Proceedings of the 30th International Symposium of Archaeometry*, Urbana, Illinois.

Saturno, W., Sever, T., Irwin, D., Howell, B. and Garrison, T. (2007), "Putting us on the map: remote sensing investigation of the ancient Maya landscape," in J. Wiseman and F. El-Baz (eds) *Remote Sensing in Archaeology*, Interdisciplinary Contributions to Archaeology book series, New York: Springer.

Saturno, W., Stuart, D. and Beltrán, B. (2006) "Early Maya writing at San Bartolo, Guatemala," *Science*, 311 (5765): 1281–3.

Schaedel, R. P. (1951) "The lost cities of Peru," *Scientific American*, 185(2): 18–24.

Schiffer, M. (1987) *Site Formation Processes of the Archaeological Record*, Albuquerque: University of New Mexico Press.

Schipper, F. (2005) "The protection and preservation of Iraq's archaeological heritage, Spring 1991–2003," *American Journal of Archaeology*, 109(2): 251–72.

Schmidt, A. (2001) *Geophysical Data in Archaeology: A Guide to Good Practice*, London, Oxbow Books.

Schmidt, H. and Karnieli, A. (2002) "Analysis of the temporal and spatial vegetation patterns in a semi-arid environment observed by NOAA AVHRR imagery and spectral ground measurements," *International Journal for Remote Sensing*, 23 (19): 3971–90.

Scollar, I. (1963) "International colloquium on air archaeology," *Antiquity*, 37: 296–7.

Scollar, I. (2002) "Making things look vertical," in R.H. Brewley and W. Raczkowski (eds) *Aerial Archaeology: Developing Future Practice*, NATO Science book series, vol. 1, Amsterdam: IOS Press.

Scollar, I., Tabbagh, A., Hesse, A. and Herzog, I. (1990) *Archaeological Prospecting and Remote Sensing: Topics in Remote Sensing*, Cambridge, Cambridge University Press.

Sever, T. (1995) "Remote sensing," *American Journal of Archaeology*, 99: 83–4.

Sever, T. (1998) "Validating prehistoric and current social phenomena upon the landscape of the Peten, Guatemala," in D. Liverman, E. Moran, R. Rindfuss and P. Stern (eds) *People and Pixels: Linking Remote Sensing and Social Science*, Washington, DC: National Academy Press.

Sever, T. and Wagner, D. (1991) "Analysis of prehistoric roadways in Chaco Canyon using remotely sense digital data," in C. Trombold (ed.) *Ancient Road Networks and Settlement Hierarchies in the New World*, Cambridge, Cambridge University Press.

Sever, T. and Wiseman, J. (1985) *Remote sensing in Archaeology: Potential for the Future, Report on a Conference*, March 1–2, 1984, Earth Resources Laboratory, NSTL, Mississippi.

Sever, T.L. and Irwin, D.E., (2003) "Remote-sensing investigation of the ancient Maya in the Peten rainforest of northern Guatemala," *Ancient Mesoamerica*, 14: 113–22.

Sheets, P. (2004) The Origins of Monumentality in Ancient Costa Rica, Revealed by Satellite and Aircraft Remote Sensing (Invited Paper), in C. Wang (ed.) *International Conference on Remote Sensing Archaeology*, Beijing: Chinese Center for Remote Sensing Archaeology.

Sheets, P. and Sever, T. (1988) "High tech wizardry," *Archaeology*, 41: 28–35.

Sheets, P. and Sever, T. (1991) "Prehistoric footpaths in Costa Rica: transportation and communication in a tropical rainforest," in C. Trombold (ed.) *Ancient road networks and settlement hierarchies in the New World*, Cambridge, Cambridge University Press.

Sheets, P. and Sever, T. (2006) "3-D Visualization of Ancient Professional Landscapes in Costa Rica," in S. Campana and M. Forte (eds) *From Space to Place: 2nd International Conference on Remote Sensing in Archaeology*, Oxford: British Archaeology Reports.

Sheets, P. and Sever, T. (2007) "Creating and perpetuating social memory across the ancient Costa Rican landscape," in J. Wiseman and F. El-Baz (eds) *Remote Sensing in Archaeology*, Interdisciplinary Contributions to Archaeology book series, New York: Springer.

Sheets, P., Hoopes, J., Melson, W., McKee, B., Sever, T., Mueller, M., Chenault, M. and Bradley, J. (1991) "Prehistory and volcanism in the Arenal Area, Costa Rica," *Journal of Field Archaeology*, 18: 445–65.

Shell, C. (2002) "Airborne high-resolution digital, visible, infra-red, and thermal sensing for archaeology," in R.H. Bewley and W. Raczkowski (eds) *Aerial Archaeology: Developing Future Practice*, NATO Science book series, vol. 1, Amsterdam: IOS Press.

Shell, C.A. and Roughley, C.F. (2004) "Exploring the Loughcrew landscape: a new approach with airborne LIDAR," *Archaeology Ireland*, 18 (2): 20–3.

Sherratt, A.G. (2004) "Spotting tells from space," *Antiquity*, 78: 301.

Showater, P. (1993) "A thematic mapper analysis of the prehistoric Hohokam canal system, Phoenix, Arizona," *Journal of Field Archaeology*, 20: 77–90.

Shupeng, C. (2004) "Environmental remote sensing monitoring and management information system using for protection of cultural heritage," invited paper in C. Wang (ed.) *International Conference on Remote Sensing Archaeology*, Beijing: Chinese Center for Remote Sensing Archaeology.

Shuren, L, Xianhua, L., Xinyuan, W., Meng, Y., Zhiming, Z. and Kelong, T. (2004) "Proposal on the task of remote sensing archaeology in China," in C. Wang (ed.) *Proceedings of the International Conference for Remote Sensing Archaeology*, Beijing: Center for Remote Sensing Archaeology.

Sintubin, M., Phillipe., M., Similox-Tohon, D., Verhaert, G., Paulissen, E. and Waelkens, M. (2003) "Seismic catastrophes at the ancient city of Sagalassos (SW Turkey) and their implications for seismotectonics in the Burdur-Isparta area," *Geological Journal*, 38 (3–4): 359–74.

Sittler, B. and Schellberg, S. (2006) "The potential of LIDAR in assesing elements of cultural heritage hidden under forest canopies or overgrown by vegetation: possiblities and limits in detecting microrelief structures for archaeological surveys," in S. Campana and M. Forte (eds) *From Space to Place: 2nd International Conference on Remote Sensing in Archaeology*, Oxford: British Archaeology Reports.

Snow, E. (1979) *Remote Sensing Experiments in Cultural Resource Studies: Non-Destructive Methods of Archaeological Exploration, Survey, and Analysis*, by Thomas R. Lyons; and *Aerial Remote Sensing Techniques in Archaeology*, by Thomas R. Lyons and Robert K. Hitchcock. Reviewed in: *Bulletin for the Association of Preservation Technology*, 11 (4): 128–9.

Soetens, S., Sarris, A. and Vansteenhuyse, K. (2002) "Defining the Minoan cultural landscape by the use of GIS," in B. Warmbein (ed.) *Proceedings of the Conference Space Applications for Heritage Conservation*, Strasbourg: European Space Agency.

Soghor, C. (1967) "The excavations at Tell el-Rub'a," *Journal of the American Research Center in Egypt*, 6: 5–16.

Som, N. (2002) "Remote sensing and GIS technology for identification of conservation and heritage sites in urban planning," in B. Warmbein (ed.) *Proceedings of the Conference Space Applications for Heritage Conservation*, Strasbourg: European Space Agency.

Sonneman, T., Sauerbier, M., Remondino, F. and Schrotter, G. (2006) "Reality-based 3D modeling of the Angkorian temples using aerial imagery," in S. Campana and M. Forte (eds) *From Space to Place: 2nd International Conference on Remote Sensing in Archaeology*, Oxford: British Archaeology Reports.

Soreide, F. (2000) "Cost effective deep water archaeology: preliminary investigations in Trondheim Harbour," *The International Journal of Nautical Archaeology*, 29 (2): 284–93.

Spencer, J. (1982) *Excavations at El-Ashmunein, I: The Topography of the Site*, London: British Museum Press.

Spencer, J. (1989) *Excavations at El-Ashmunein, II: The Temple Area*, London: British Museum Press.

Spencer, J. (1993) *Excavations at El-Ashmunein, III: The Town*, London: British Museum Press.

St. Joseph, J.K.S. (ed.) (1966) *The Uses of Air Photography*, London: John Baker.

Stafford, C., Leigh, D. and Asch, D. (1992) "Prehistoric settlement and landscape change on alluvial fans in the Upper Mississippi River Valley," *Geoarchaeology* 7 (4): 287–314.

Stanley, J.D. and Jorstad, T.F. (2006) "Short contribution: buried canopic channel identified near Egypt's Nile Delta coast with radar (SRTM) imagery," *Geoarchaeology* 21 (5): 503–14.

Stargardt, J. (2004) "Reconstructing the ancient landscape of peninsular Thailand," in C. Wang (ed.) *International Conference on Remote Sensing Archaeology*, Beijing: Chinese Center for Remote Sensing Archaeology.

Steadman, S. (2000) "Spatial patterning and social complexity on prehistoric Anatolian tell sites: models for mounds," *Journal for Anthropological Archaeology*, 19(2): 164–99.

Stein, A. (1919) "Air photography of ancient sites," *The Geographical Journal*, 54: 200.

Stein, A. (1940) "Surveys on the Roman frontier in Iraq and Transjordan," *The Geographical Journal*, 95 (6): 428–38.

Stein, C. and Cullen, B. (1994) "Satellite imagery and archaeology: a case study from Nikopolis," *American Journal of Archaeology*, 98 (2): 316.

Steiner, C.B. (1987) Review of M. Banta and C. Hinsley, "From Site to Sight: Anthropology", *Photography, and the Power of Imagery*, Harvard University Press: Boston. In African Arts, 20 (3): 81–2.

Stern, R. and Salam, M.A. (1996) "The origin of the great Nile bend from Sir-C/X-Sar imagery," *Science*, 274(5293): 1696–8.

Stewart, D. (2001) "New tricks with old maps: urban landscape change, GIS, and historic preservation in the less developed world," *The Professional Geographer*, 53 (3): 361–73.

Stichelbaut, B. (2006) "The application of First World War aerial photography to archaeology: the Belgian images," *Antiquity*, 80 (307): 161–72.

Stine, R. and Decker, T. (1990) "Archaeology, data integration and GIS," in K. Allen, S. Green and E. Zubrow, *Interpreting Space: GIS and Archaeology*, Bristol, PA: Taylor and Francis.

Stone, E. (2008) "Patterns of looting in southern Iraq," *Antiquity*, 82 (315): 125–38.

Stubbs, J. and McKees, K. (2007) "Applications of remote sensing to the understanding and management of cultural heritage sites," in J. Wiseman and F. El-Baz (eds) *Remote Sensing in Archaeology*, Interdisciplinary Contributions to Archaeology book series, New York: Springer.

Sultan, M., Fiske, M., Stein, T., Gamal, M., Abdel-Hady, Y., El-Araby, H., Madani, A., Mehanee, S. and Becker, R. (1999) "Satellite based monitoring of urbanization in the Nile Delta, Egypt," *Ambio*, 28: 628–31.

Summers, G. (1992) "An aerial survey of Cevre Kale, Yarasli," *Anatolian Studies*, 42: 179–206.

Supajanya, T. (1989) "Remote sensing application in archaeological study in Tuny Kula Roghai, Northeast Thailand," *Proceedings of Franco-Thai Workshop on Remote Sensing Nov. 2–4, 1989*, Khon Kaen.

Sykes, L. (1997) "Cities on the Silk Road," *Geographical Magazine*, 69: 23–6.

Symanzik, J., Cook, D., Lewin, N., Majure, J.J. and Megretskaia, I. (2000) "Linking ArcView and XGobi: insight behind the front end," *Journal of Computational and Graphical Statistics*, 9 (3): 470–90.

Tan, K., Wan, Y., Zhou, X., Song, D. and Quan, D. (2006) "The application of remote sensing technology in the archaeological study of the Mausoleum of Emperor Qinshihuang," *International Journal of Remote Sensing*, 27 (16): 3347–63.

Tartaglia, L.J. (1973) "Infrared photography: an application of remote sensing to archaeology," *Anthropology U.C.L.A*, 5 (2): 1–95.

Tartaron, T.F. (2003) "The archaeological survey: sampling strategies and field methods," *Hesperia Supplements*, 32: 23–46.

Taylor, P. (2007) "High tech archaeology supports quest for Noah's Ark: can high resolution satellite imagery certify one of ancient history's most coveted prizes?" Online. Available HTTP: <http://www.eijournal.com/Noah's_Ark.asp> (accessed 8 September 2008).

Thakker, P.S. (2002) "Archaeology through space: experience in Indian subcontinent," in B. Warmbein (ed.) *Proceedings of the Conference Space Applications for Heritage Conservation*, Strasbourg: European Space Agency.

Thakran, R.C. (2000) "Implications of partition on protohistoric investigations in the Ghaggar-Ganga Basins," *Social Scientist*, 28 (1–2): 42–67.

Thompson, H. (1967) "A new development in archaeological air photography," *Antiquity*, 41: 225–7.

Tieszen, L.L., Reed, B.C., Bliss, N.B., Wylie, B.K. and DeJong, D.D. (1997) "NDVI, C3, and C4 production, and distributions in the Great Plains grassland land cover classes," *Ecological Applications*, 7 (1): 59–78.

Timor, G. (2004) "Space and GIS technology in paleoenvironmental analysis (old maps, satellite images, and digital elevation models in archaeology)," *Antaeus*, 27: 135–44.

Toprak, V. (2002) "Surface processes: obstacles in aerial archaeology, examples from Turkey," in R.H. Brewley and W. Raczkowski (eds) *Aerial Archaeology: Developing Future Practice*, NATO Science book series, vol. 1, Amsterdam: IOS Press.

Traviglia, A. (2006) "Archaeological usability of hyperspectral images: sucesses and failures of image processing techniques," in S. Campana and M. Forte (eds) *From Space to Place: 2nd International Conference on Remote Sensing in Archaeology*, Oxford: British Archaeology Reports.

Trelogan, J., Crawford, M., Teng, L., Kwon, O. and Carter, J. (1999) "Mapping the features of the Chora of Chersonesos via remotely sensed data," *Proceedings of the IGARSS 1999 Geoscience and Remote Sensing Symposium*, 5: 2569–71.

Trelogan, J.M.C. and Carter, J. (2002) "Monitoring the ancient countryside: remote sensing and GIS at the Chora of Chersonesos (Crimea, Ukraine)," in B. Warmbein (ed.) *Proceedings of the Conference Space Applications for Heritage Conservation,* Strasbourg: European Space Agency.

Tykot, R.H. (1994) *New Developments in Archaeological Science. A Joint Symposium of the Royal Society and the British Academy, February 1991,* by A. M. Pollard (ed.). Reviewed in: *American Journal of Archaeology,* 98 (4): 774–6.

Ur, J. (2003) "Corona satellite photography ancient road networks: a northern Mesopotamian case study," *Antiquity,* 77: 102–15.

Ur, J. (2005) "Sennacherib's northern Assyrian canals: new insights from satellite imagery and aerial photography," *Iraq,* 67: 317–45.

Ur, J. (2006) "Google Earth and archaeology," *The SAA Archaeological Record,* 6 (3): 35–8.

Urwin, N. and Ireland, T. (1992) "Satellite imagery and landscape archaeology: interim report on the environmental component of the Vinhais Landscape Archaeology Project, North Portugal," *Mediterranean Archaeology,* 5: 121–31.

Van Andel, T.H. (1998) "Paleosols, red sediments, and the Old Stone Age in Greece," *Geoarchaeology,* 13 (4): 361–90.

Van den Brink, E. (1987) "A geo-archaeological survey in the East Delta, Egypt: the first two seasons, a preliminary report," *Mitteilungen des Deutschen Archaologischen Instituts Abteilung Kairo,* 43: 4–31.

Vercoutter, J. (1976) *Mirgissa I,* Paris: Centre National de la Recherche Scientifique.

Verhoven, G. and Loenders, J. (2006) "Looking through black-tinted glasses—a remotely controlled infrared eye in the sky," in S. Campana and M. Forte (eds) *From Space to Place: 2nd International Conference on Remote Sensing in Archaeology,* Oxford: British Archaeology Reports.

Vermeulen, F. (1998) "A Computer-aided Geo-archaeological Survey of the Classical Landscape of Central Anatolia," in J.A Barcelo, J.A. et al (eds), *New Techniques for Old Times CAA 98, Computer Applications and Quantitative Methods in Archaeology, Proceedings of the 26th Conference, Barcelona,* March 1998, BAR-International Series: Oxford.

Vicent, J., Ormeno, S., Martinez-Navarete, M. and Delgado, J. (2006) "The Kargaly Project: modelling Bronze Age landscapes in the Steppe," in S. Campana and M. Forte (eds) *From Space to Place: 2nd International Conference on Remote Sensing in Archaeology,* Oxford: British Archaeology Reports.

Vining, B.R. and Wiseman, J. (2006) "Multispectral and synthetic aperture radar remote-sensing-based models for Holocene coastline development in the Ambracian Gulf, Epirus, Greece," *Archaeological Prospection,* 13 (4): 258–68.

Wang, C. and Huadong, G. (2004) *Proceedings of the International Conference for Remote Sensing Archaeology,* Beijing: Chinese Center for Remote Sensing Archaeology.

Watson, R.A. (1976) "Inference in archaeology," *American Antiquity,* 41 (1): 58–66.

Weiss, H. (1991) "Archaeology in Syria," *American Journal of Archaeology,* 95 (4): 683–740.

Weller, E.T. (2006) "Satellites, survey, and settlement: the late classic Maya utilization of bajos (seasonal swamps) at Tikal and Yaxha, Guatemala," in S. Campana and M. Forte (eds) *From Space to Place: 2nd International Conference on Remote Sensing in Archaeology,* Oxford: British Archaeology Reports.

Welzenbach, M. (1995) "Search for the lost city," *Reader's Digest,* October: 84–89.

Wendorf, F., Close, A. and Schild, R. (1987) "A survey of the Egyptian radar channels: an example of applied field archaeology," *Journal of Field Archaeology,* 14: 43–63.

Wenlie, Z (1998) *The Qin Terracotta Army,* London: Scala Books.

Wiegend, T. (1920) *Wissenschaftliche Veröffentlichungen des deutsch-türkischen Denkmalschutz-Kommandos 1,* Berlin: de Gruyter.

Wilkinson, K., Beck, A.R. and Philip, G. (2006) "Satellite imagery as a resource in the prospection for archaeological sites in central Syria," *Geoarchaeology,* 21 (7): 735–50.

Wilkinson, T.J. (1989) "Extensive sherd scatters and land-use intensity: some recent results," *Journal of Field Archaeology*, 16 (1): 31–46.

Wilkinson, T.J. (2001) "Surface collection, field walking, theory and practice, sampling theories," in A. Pollard and D. Brothwell (eds) *Handbook of Archaeological Sciences*, New York: John Wiley.

Wilkinson, T.J. (2002) "Archaeological survey of Tell Beydar region, Syria 1997," in K. Van Lerberghe and G. Voet (eds) *Tell Beydar Environmental and Technical Studies*, Begijnhof: Brepols.

Wilkinson, T.J. (2003) *Archaeological Landscapes of the Near East*, Tuscon: University of Arizona Press.

Wilkinson, T.J., Bintliff, J., Curvers, H.H., Halstead, P., Kohl, P.L., Liverani, M., McCorriston, J., Oates, J., Scwartz, G.M., Thuesen, I., Weiss, H. and Courty, M. (1994) "The structure and dynamics of dry-farming states in Upper Mesopotamia [and comments and reply]," *Current Anthropology*, 35 (5): 483–520.

Wilkinson, T.J., Ur, J. and Casana, J. (2004) "Nucleation to dispersal: trends in settlement patterns in the northern Fertile Crescent," in S. Alcock and J. Cherry (eds) *Side-by-Side Survey: Comparative Regional Studies in the Mediterranean World*, Oxford: Oxbow.

Wilkinson, T.J., Wilkinson, E., Ur, J.A. and Altaweel, A. (2005) "Landscape and settlement in the Neo-Assyrian Empire," *Bulletin of the American Schools of Oriental Research*, 340: 23–56.

Williams-Hunt, P.D.R. (1950) "Irregular earthworks in eastern Siam: an air survey," *Antiquity*, 24: 30–36.

Willey, G.R. (1990) "Recent Advances in Maya Archaeology," *Bulletin of the American Academy of Arts and Sciences*, 43 (8): 24–35.

Williams, P., Couture N. and Blom, D. (2007) "Urban structure at Tiwanaku: geophysical investigations in the Andean Altiplano," in J. Wiseman and F. El-Baz (eds) *Remote Sensing in Archaeology*, Interdisciplinary Contributions to Archaeology book series, New York: Springer.

Williamson, T. (1998) "Questions of preservation and destruction," in P. Everson and T. Williamson (eds), *The Archaeology of Landscape: Studies Presented to Christopher Taylor*, Manchester and New York: Manchester University Press.

Williamson, R., Hurst, W. and Jeffe, M. (2002) "Satellite remote sensing for archaeology and historic preservation: mapping the ancient trails of Southeast Utah (ESA-SP515)," in B. Warmbein (ed.) *Proceedings of the Conference Space Applications for Heritage Conservation*, Strasbourg: European Space Agency.

Williamson, R.A. (1987) "Technology, preservation policy, and the National Park Service," *The Public Historian*, 9 (2): 118–24.

Williamson, R.A. and Warren-Findley, J. (1991) "Technology transfer, historic preservation, and public policy," *The Public Historian*, 13 (3): 15–32.

Wilson, C. (1976) *Sinai*, Jerusalem: Ariel Publishing House.

Wilson, D.R. (2000) *Air Photo Interpretation for Archaeologists*, Stroud: History Press.

Winterbottom, S. and Dawson, T. (2003) "Islands of Coll and Tiree, the Inner Hebrides," *Archaeologia Polona*, 41: 287–8.

Wiseman, J. (1998) "Insight: Eagle Eye at NASA," *Archaeology*, 51 (4). Online. Available HTTP: <http://www.archaeology.org/9807/abstracts/insight.html> (accessed 8 September 2008).

Wiseman, J. and El-Baz F. (eds) (2007) *Remote Sensing in Archaeology*, Interdisciplinary Contributions to Archaeology book series, New York: Springer.

Wiseman, J. and Zachos, K. (2003) "The Nikopolis Project: concept, aims, and organization," *Hesperia Supplements*, 32: 1–22.

Wiseman, J.R. (1989) "Archaeology today: from the classroom to the field and elsewhere," *American Journal of Archaeology*, 93 (3): 437–44.

Wiseman, J.R. (1996) "Wonders of radar imagery: glimpses of the ancient world from space," *Archaeology*, 49: 14–18.

Witten, A.J. (2005) *Handbook of Geophysics and Archaeology*, London: Equinox Publishing.

Wynn, J.C. (1986) "A review of geophysical methods used in archaeology," *Geoarchaeology*, 1 (3): 245–57.

Wynn, J.C. (1990) "Applications of high-resolution geophysical methods to archaeology," in N.P. Lasca and J. Donahue (eds) *Archaeological Geology of North America*, Boulder: Geological Society of America.

Xiaohu, Z. (2004) "The preprocessing of hyperspectral remote sensing on Mausoleum Qin Shihuang," in C. Wang (ed.) *International Conference on Remote Sensing Archaeology*, Beijing: Chinese Center for Remote Sensing Archaeology.

Xin-Yuan, W., Ying-Qiu, Z., Yingcheng, L. and Chao, G. (2004) "On remote sensing archaeology analysis for transformation of traffic function of Sui Dynasty Tongji Canal," in C. Wang (ed.) *International Conference on Remote Sensing Archaeology*, Beijing: Chinese Center for Remote Sensing Archaeology.

Yakam-Simen, F., Nezry, E. and Ewing, J. (1999) "A legendary lost city found in the Honduran Tropical Forest using ERS-2 and JERS-1 SAR imagery," *Proceedings of the IGARSS 1999 Geoscience and Remote Sensing Symposium*, 5: 2578–80.

Yoshimura, S., Kondo, J., Hasegawa, S., Sakata, T., Etaya, M., Nakagawa, T., Nishimoto, S., "A preliminary report of the general survey at Dahshur North, Egypt." *Annual Report of the Collegium Mediterranistarum. Mediterraneus* 20 , 3–24.

Yugsi, F., Eisenbeiss, H., Remondino, R. and Winkler, W. (2006) "Multi-temporal monitoring of landslides in archaeological mountainous environments using optical imagery: the case of El-Tambo, Ecuador," in S. Campana and M. Forte (eds) *From Space to Place: 2nd International Conference on Remote Sensing in Archaeology*, Oxford: British Archaeology Reports.

Yuqing, W., Kelong, T., Xiaohu, Z., Dewen, S., Qingbo, D. and Xinlong, N. (2004) "Discussion about the function of remotely sensed images in archaeology," in C. Wang (ed.) *International Conference on Remote Sensing Archaeology*, Beijing: Chinese Center for Remote Sensing Archaeology.

Zhang, L. and Wu, J. (2006) "Remote sensing archaeology for ancient cities structure of Pingyao and Liandzhu, Yuhang City, Zhejiang Province, China," in S. Campana and M. Forte (eds) *From Space to Place: 2nd International Conference on Remote Sensing in Archaeology*, Oxford: British Archaeology Reports.

Ziebart, M., Dare, P., Williams, T. and Herrmann, G. (2002) "Acquisition, registration, and application of Ikonos space imagery for the cultural world heritage site at Merv, Turkmenistan," in B. Warmbein (ed.) *Proceedings of the Conference Space Applications for Heritage Conservation*, Strasbourg: European Space Agency.

Zubrow, E. (2007) "Remote sensing, fractals, and cultural landscapes: an ethnographic prolegomenon using U2 imagery," in J. Wiseman and F. El-Baz (eds) *Remote Sensing in Archaeology*, Interdisciplinary Contributions to Archaeology book series, New York: Springer.

Zubrow, E., Allen, K. and Green, S. (1990) *Interpreting Space: The Use of GIS in Archaeology*, London: Taylor and Francis.

Zurawski, B. (1993) "Low altitude aerial photography in archaeological fieldwork: the case of Nubia," *Archaeologia Polona*, 31: 243–56.

INDEX

Page references followed by f indicate a figurative illustration, t indicates a table

An environmentally friendly book printed and bound in England by www.printondemand-worldwide.com

PEFC Certified

This product is
from sustainably
managed forests
and controlled
sources

www.pefc.org

PEFC/16-33-415

This book is made entirely of chain-of-custody materials; FSC materials for the cover and PEFC materials for the text pages.

#0279 - 130812 - C0 - 246/174/17 - PB